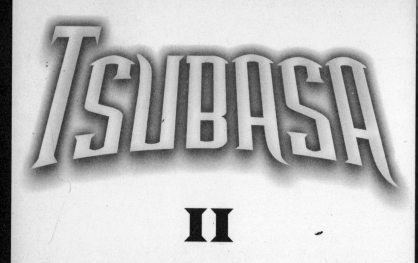

TSUBASA

II

CLAMP

TRANSLATED AND ADAPTED BY
William Flanagan

LETTERED BY
Dana Hayward

BALLANTINE BOOKS · NEW YORK

A Del Rey Trade Paperback Original

Tsubasa, vol. 11 copyright © 2005 by CLAMP
English translation copyright © 2006 by CLAMP

Published in the United States by Del Rey Books, an imprint of The Random House Publishing Group, a division of Random House, Inc., New York.

DEL REY is a registered trademark and the Del Rey colophon is a trademark of Random House, Inc.

Publication rights arranged through Kodansha, Ltd.

First published in Japan in 2005 by Kodansha, Ltd., Tokyo.

ISBN 0-345-48528-9

Printed in the United States of America

www.delreymanga.com

9 8 7 6 5 4 3 2

Translation and adaptation—William Flanagan

Lettering—Dana Hayward

Contents

Tsubasa crosses over with *xxxHOLiC*. Although it isn't necessary to read *xxxHOLiC* to understand the events in *Tsubasa*, you'll get to see the same events from different perspectives if you read both series!

Honorifics Explained

Throughout the Del Rey Manga books, you will find Japanese honorifics left intact in the translations. For those not familiar with how the Japanese use honorifics and, more important, how they differ from American honorifics, we present this brief overview.

Politeness has always been a critical facet of Japanese culture. Ever since the feudal era, when Japan was a highly stratified society, use of honorifics—which can be defined as polite speech that indicates relationship or status—has played an essential role in the Japanese language. When addressing someone in Japanese, an honorific usually takes the form of a suffix attached to one's name (example: "Asuna-san"), or as a title at the end of one's name or in place of the name itself (example: "Negi-sensei," or simply "Sensei!").

Honorifics can be expressions of respect or endearment. In the context of manga and anime, honorifics give insight into the nature of the relationship between characters. Many English translations leave out these important honorifics, and therefore distort the feel of the original Japanese. Because Japanese honorifics contain nuances that English honorifics lack, it is our policy at Del Rey not to translate them. Here, instead, is a guide to some of the honorifics you may encounter in Del Rey Manga.

-san: This is the most common honorific, and is equivalent to Mr., Miss, Ms., Mrs. It is the all-purpose honorific and can be used in any situation where politeness is required.

-sama: This is one level higher than "-san." It is used to confer great respect.

-dono: This comes from the word "tono," which means "lord." It is an even higher level than "-sama" and confers utmost respect.

-kun: This suffix is used at the end of boys' names to express familiarity or endearment. It is also sometimes used by men amongst friends, or when addressing someone younger or of a lower station.

-chan: This is used to express endearment, mostly toward girls. It is also used for little boys, pets, and even among lovers. It gives a sense of childish cuteness.

Bozu: This is an informal way to refer to a boy, similar to the English term "kid" or "squirt."

Sempai/Senpai: This title suggests that the addressee is one's senior in a group or organization. It is most often used in a school setting, where underclassmen refer to their upperclassmen as "sempai." It can also be used in the workplace, such as when a newer employee addresses an employee who has seniority in the company.

Kohai: This is the opposite of "sempai," and is used toward underclassmen in school or newcomers in the workplace. It connotes that the addressee is of a lower station.

Sensei: Literally meaning "one who has come before," this title is used for teachers, doctors, or masters of any profession or art.

-[blank]: This is usually forgotten in these lists, but it is perhaps the most significant difference between Japanese and English. The lack of honorific means that the speaker has permission to address the person in a very intimate way. Usually, only family, spouses, or very close friends have this kind of permission. Known as *yobisute*, it can be gratifying when someone who has earned the intimacy starts to call one by one's name without an honorific. But when that intimacy hasn't been earned, it can also be very insulting.

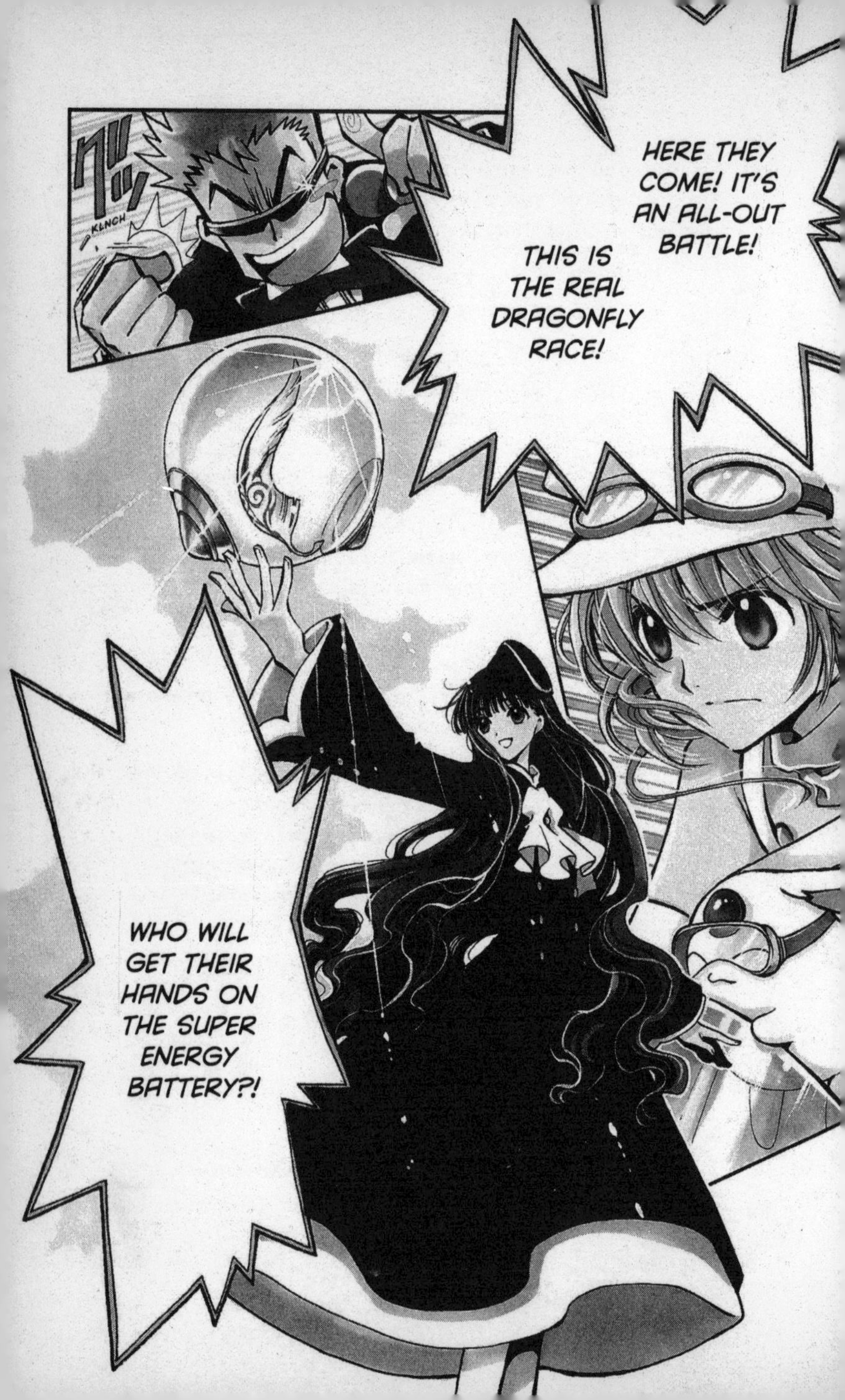
HERE THEY COME! IT'S AN ALL-OUT BATTLE!
THIS IS THE REAL DRAGONFLY RACE!
KLNCH
WHO WILL GET THEIR HANDS ON THE SUPER ENERGY BATTERY?!

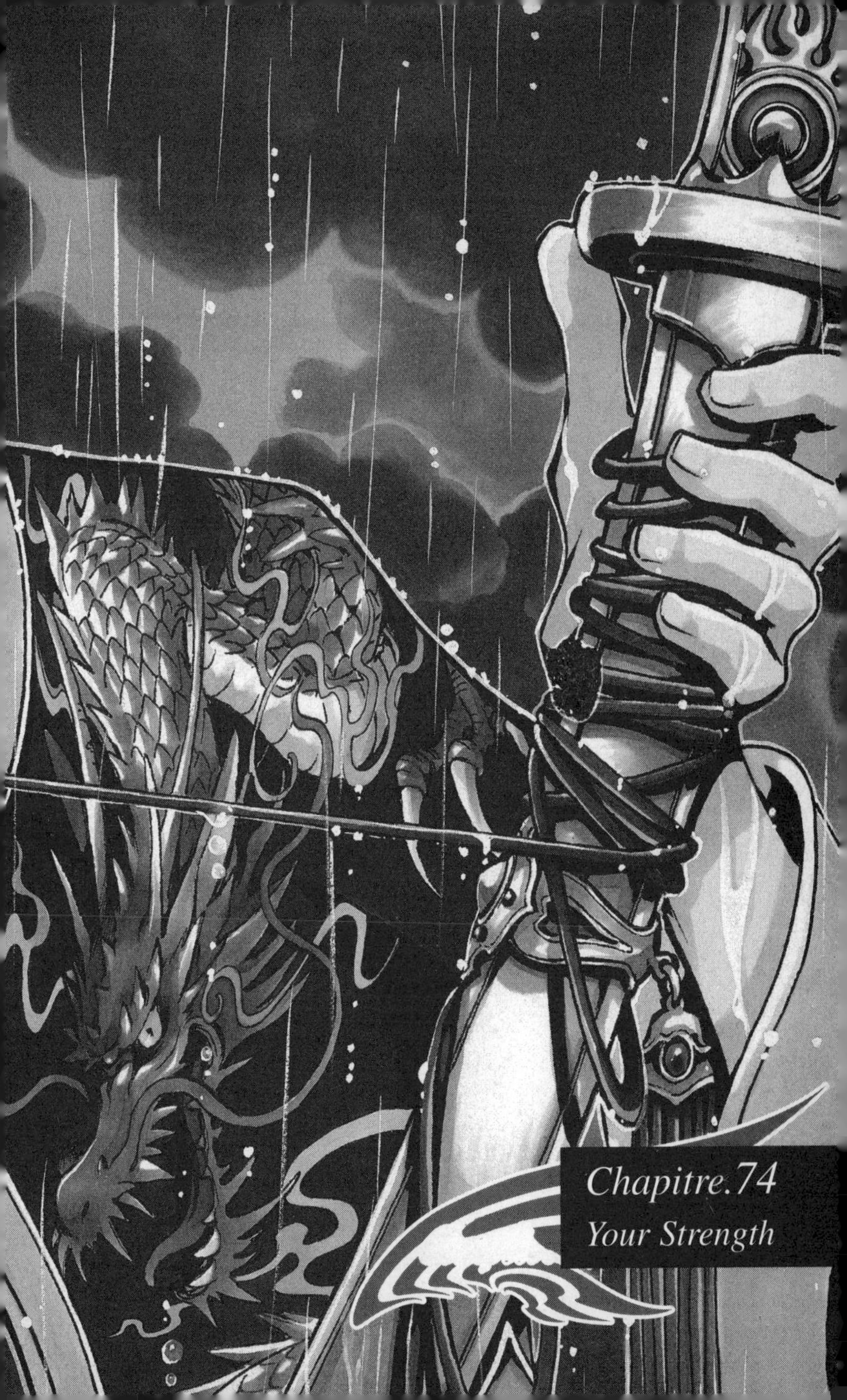

Chapitre.74
Your Strength

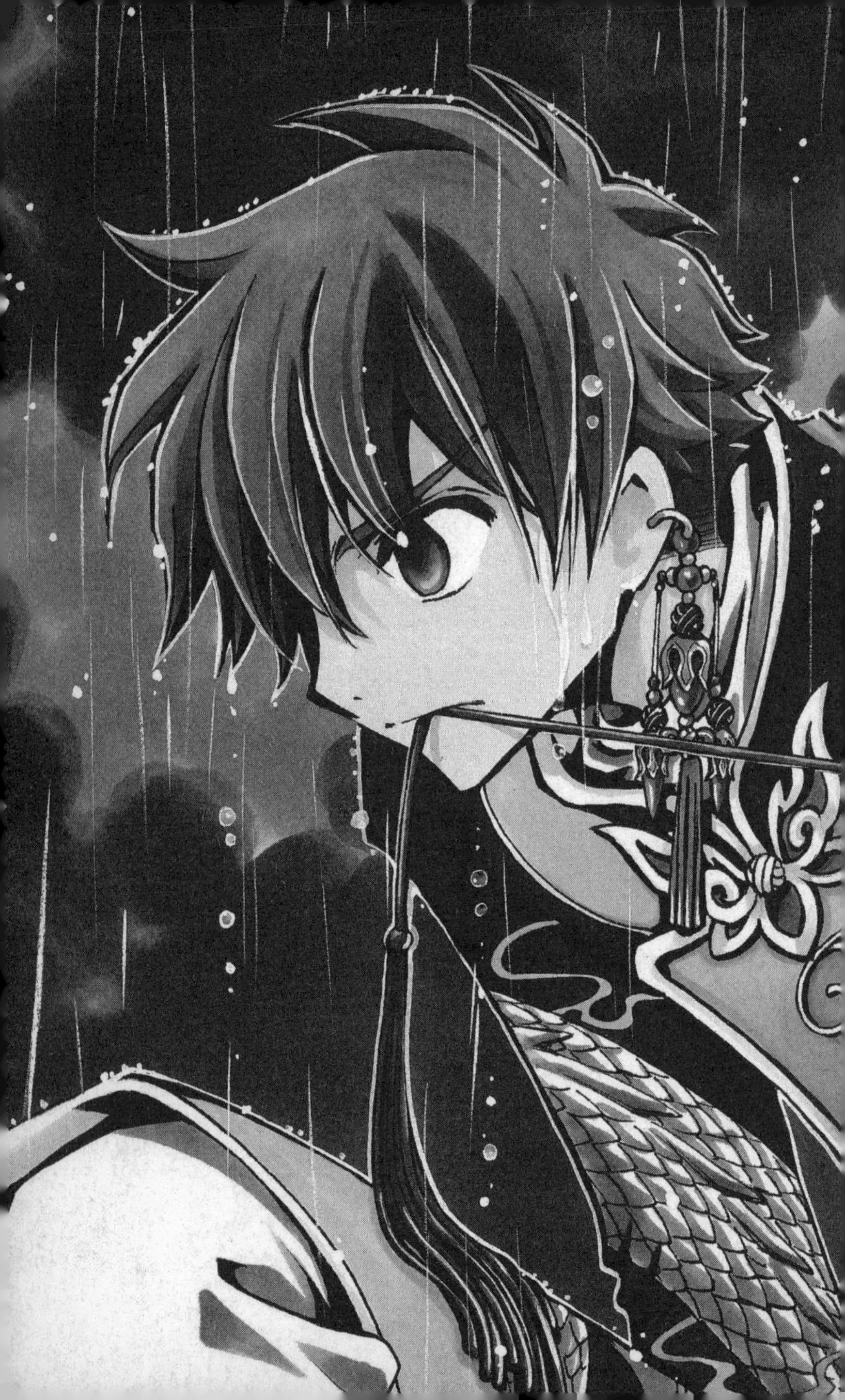

ツバサ

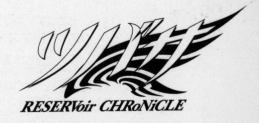

RESERVoir CHRoNiCLE

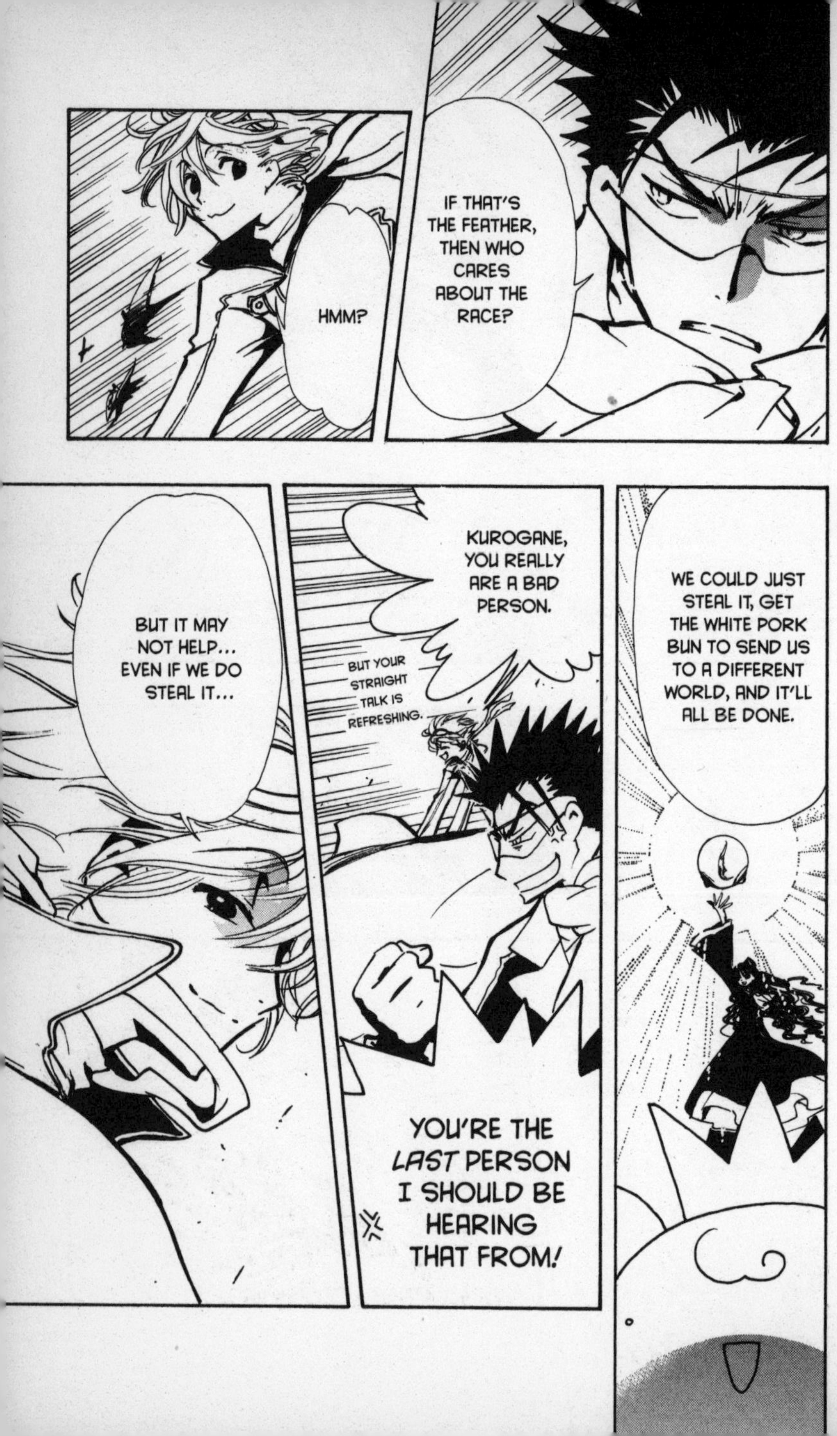
IF THAT'S THE FEATHER, THEN WHO CARES ABOUT THE RACE?
HMM?
WE COULD JUST STEAL IT, GET THE WHITE PORK BUN TO SEND US TO A DIFFERENT WORLD, AND IT'LL ALL BE DONE.
KUROGANE, YOU REALLY ARE A BAD PERSON.
BUT YOUR STRAIGHT TALK IS REFRESHING.
YOU'RE THE LAST PERSON I SHOULD BE HEARING THAT FROM!
BUT IT MAY NOT HELP... EVEN IF WE DO STEAL IT...

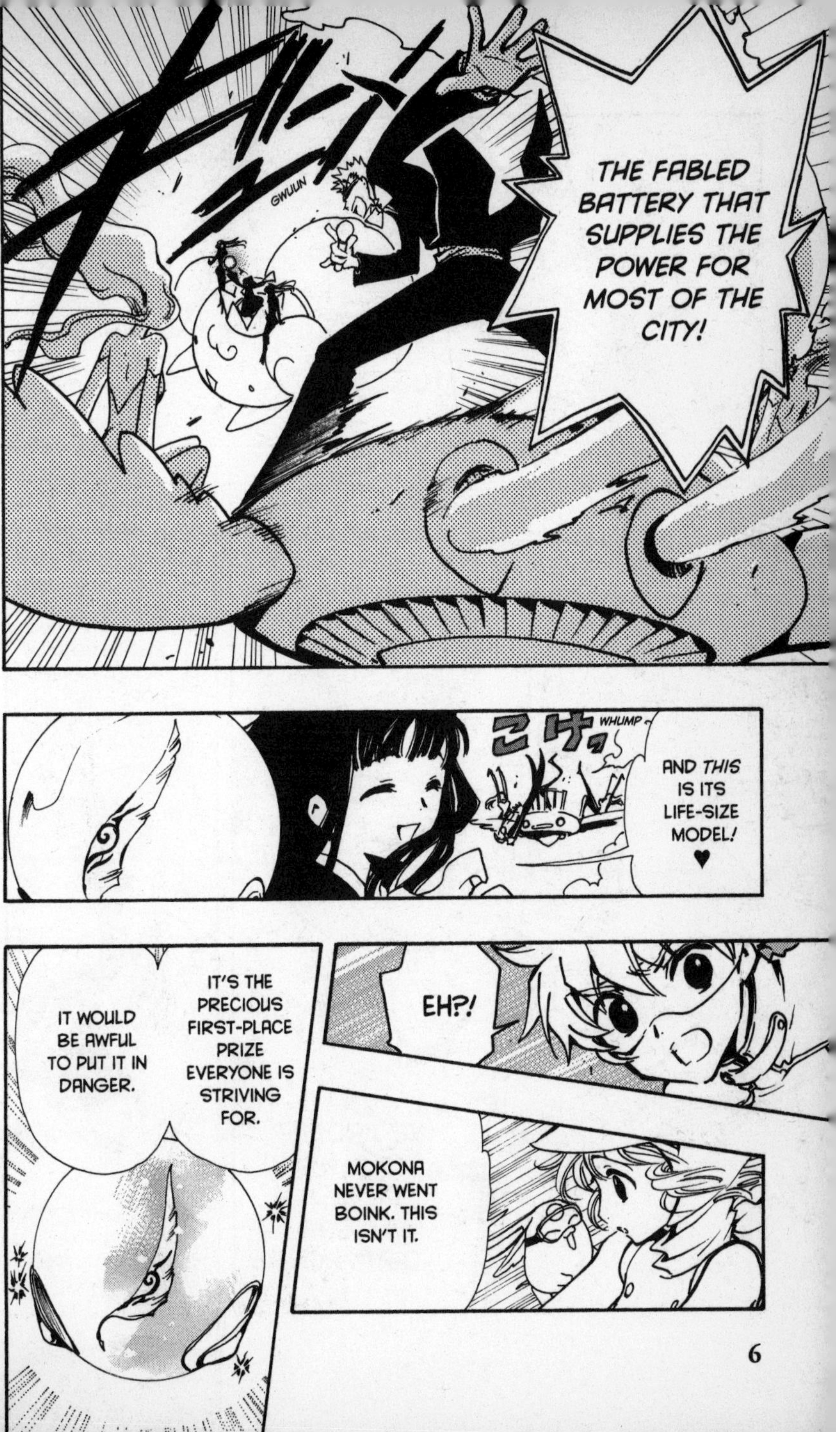
GWUUN
THE FABLED BATTERY THAT SUPPLIES THE POWER FOR MOST OF THE CITY!
WHUMP
AND *THIS* IS ITS LIFE-SIZE MODEL! ♥
EH?!
MOKONA NEVER WENT BOINK. THIS ISN'T IT.
IT'S THE PRECIOUS FIRST-PLACE PRIZE EVERYONE IS STRIVING FOR.
IT WOULD BE AWFUL TO PUT IT IN DANGER.

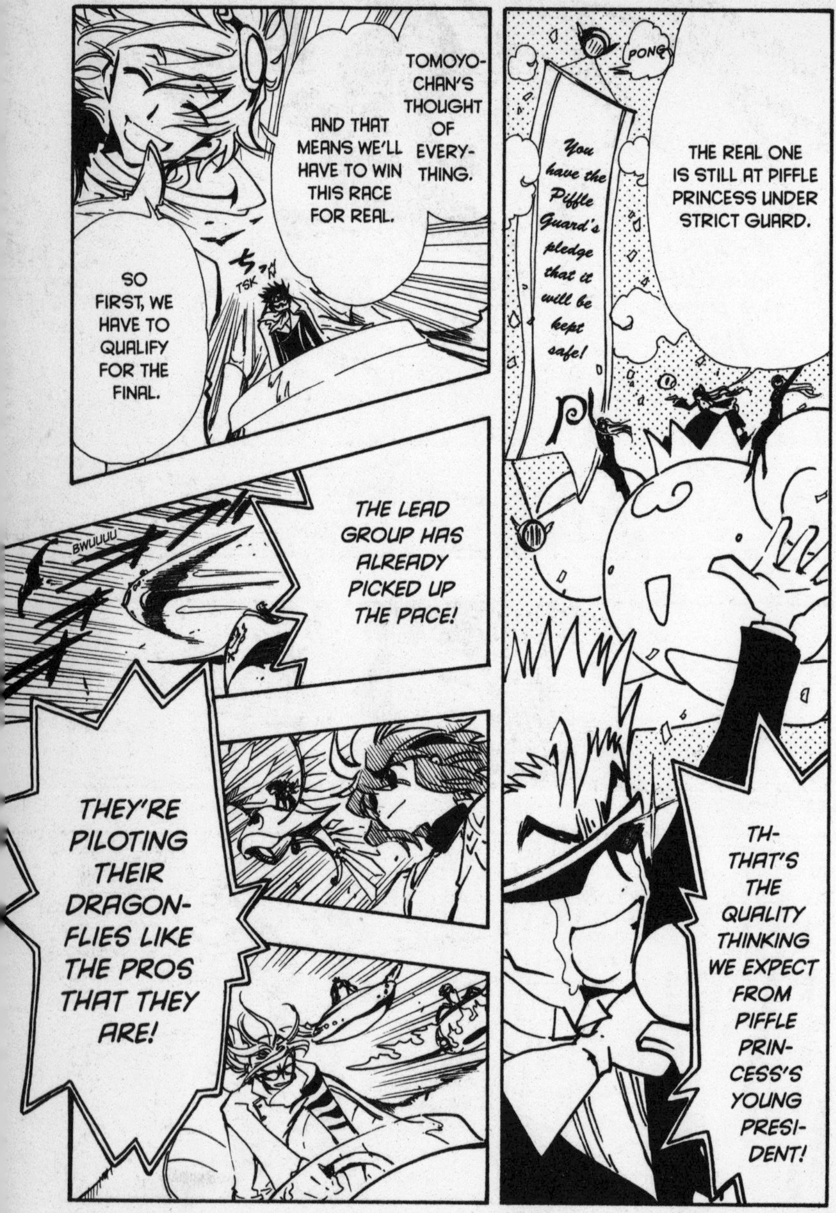
PONG
THE REAL ONE IS STILL AT PIFFLE PRINCESS UNDER STRICT GUARD.
You have the Piffle Guard's pledge that it will be kept safe!
TOMOYO-CHAN'S THOUGHT OF EVERYTHING.
AND THAT MEANS WE'LL HAVE TO WIN THIS RACE FOR REAL.
TSK
SO FIRST, WE HAVE TO QUALIFY FOR THE FINAL.
TH-THAT'S THE QUALITY THINKING WE EXPECT FROM PIFFLE PRINCESS'S YOUNG PRESIDENT!
BWUUUU
THE LEAD GROUP HAS ALREADY PICKED UP THE PACE!
THEY'RE PILOTING THEIR DRAGONFLIES LIKE THE PROS THAT THEY ARE!

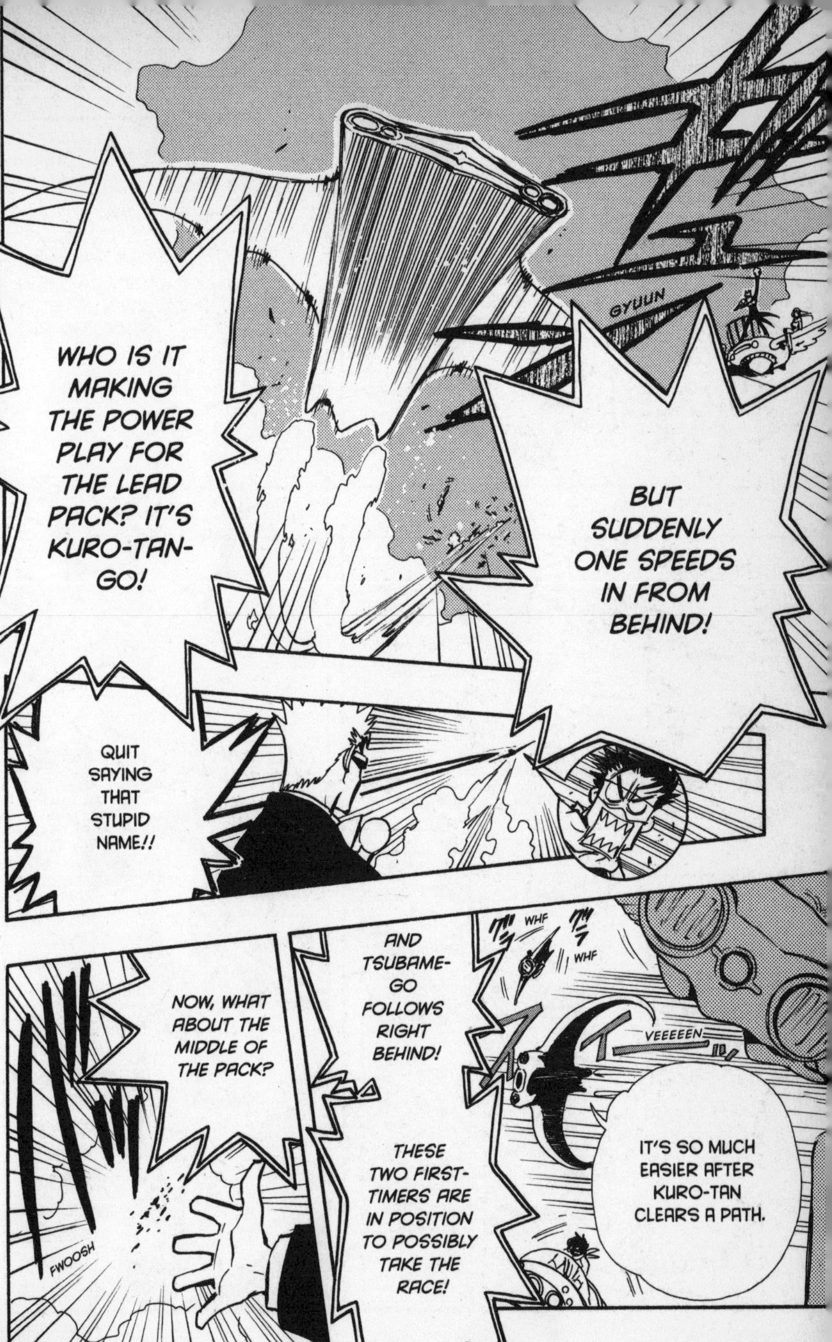
GYUUN
BUT SUDDENLY ONE SPEEDS IN FROM BEHIND!
WHO IS IT MAKING THE POWER PLAY FOR THE LEAD PACK? IT'S KURO-TAN-GO!
QUIT SAYING THAT STUPID NAME!!
WHF
WHF
AND TSUBAME-GO FOLLOWS RIGHT BEHIND!
VEEEEEN
IT'S SO MUCH EASIER AFTER KURO-TAN CLEARS A PATH.
THESE TWO FIRST-TIMERS ARE IN POSITION TO POSSIBLY TAKE THE RACE!
NOW, WHAT ABOUT THE MIDDLE OF THE PACK?
FWOOSH

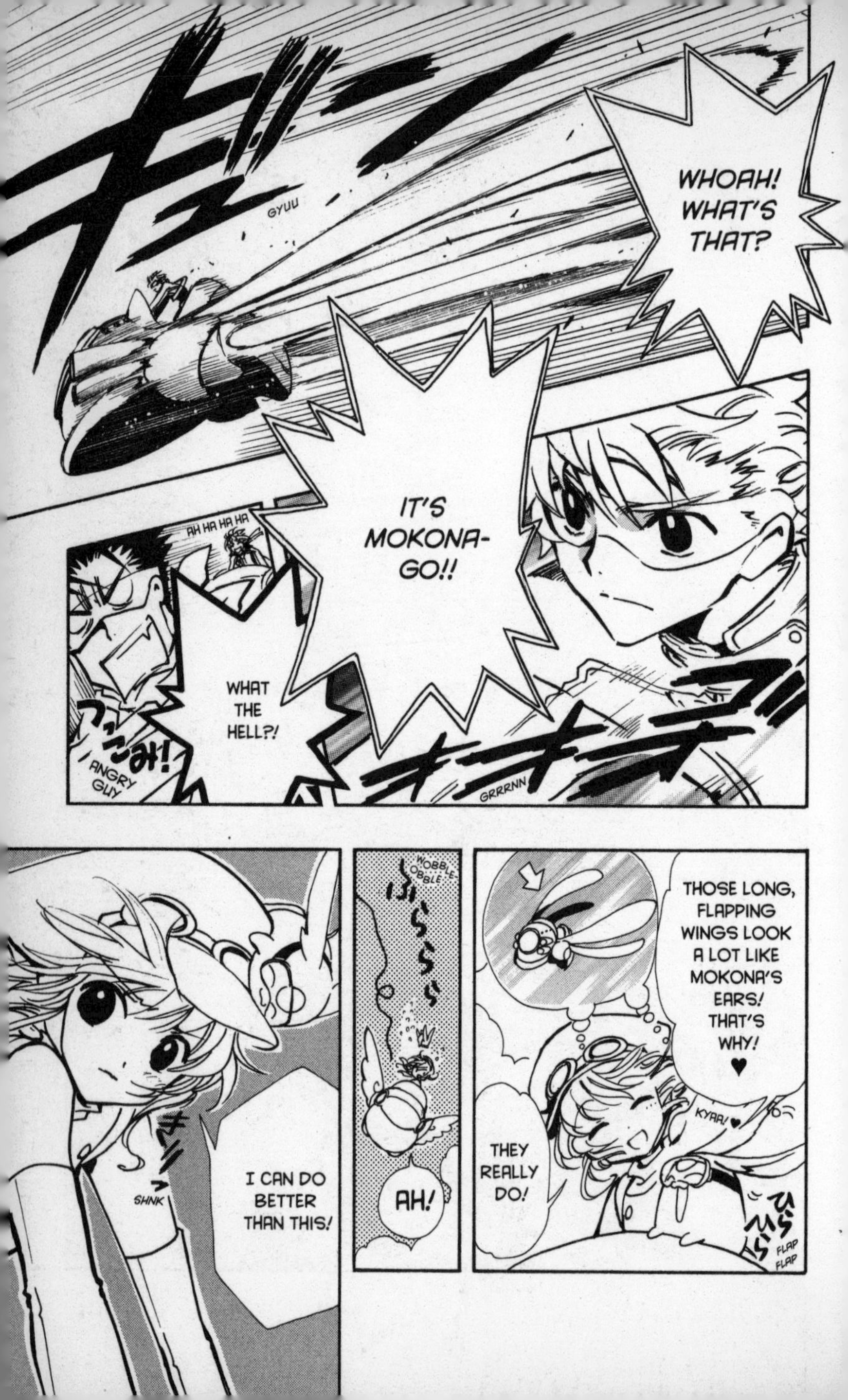
WHOAH! WHAT'S THAT?
GYUU
IT'S MOKONA-GO!!
AH HA HA HA
GRRRNN
WHAT THE HELL?!
ANGRY GUY
THOSE LONG, FLAPPING WINGS LOOK A LOT LIKE MOKONA'S EARS! THAT'S WHY! ♥
KYAA! ♥
FLAP FLAP
THEY REALLY DO!
WOBBLE OBBLE
AH!
I CAN DO BETTER THAN THIS!
SHNK

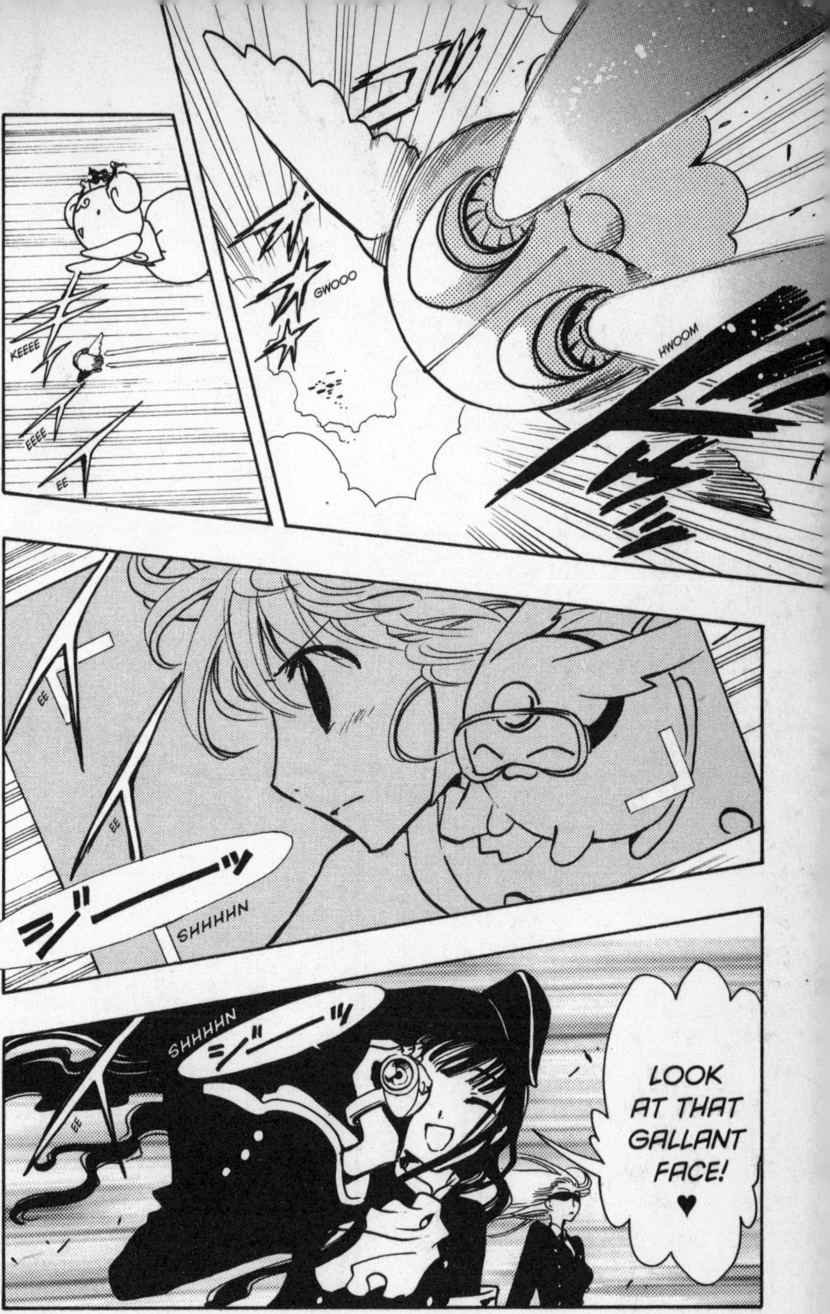
HWOOM
GWOOO
KEEEE
EEEE
EE
EE
EE
SHHHHN
LOOK AT THAT GALLANT FACE! ♥
SHHHHN
EE

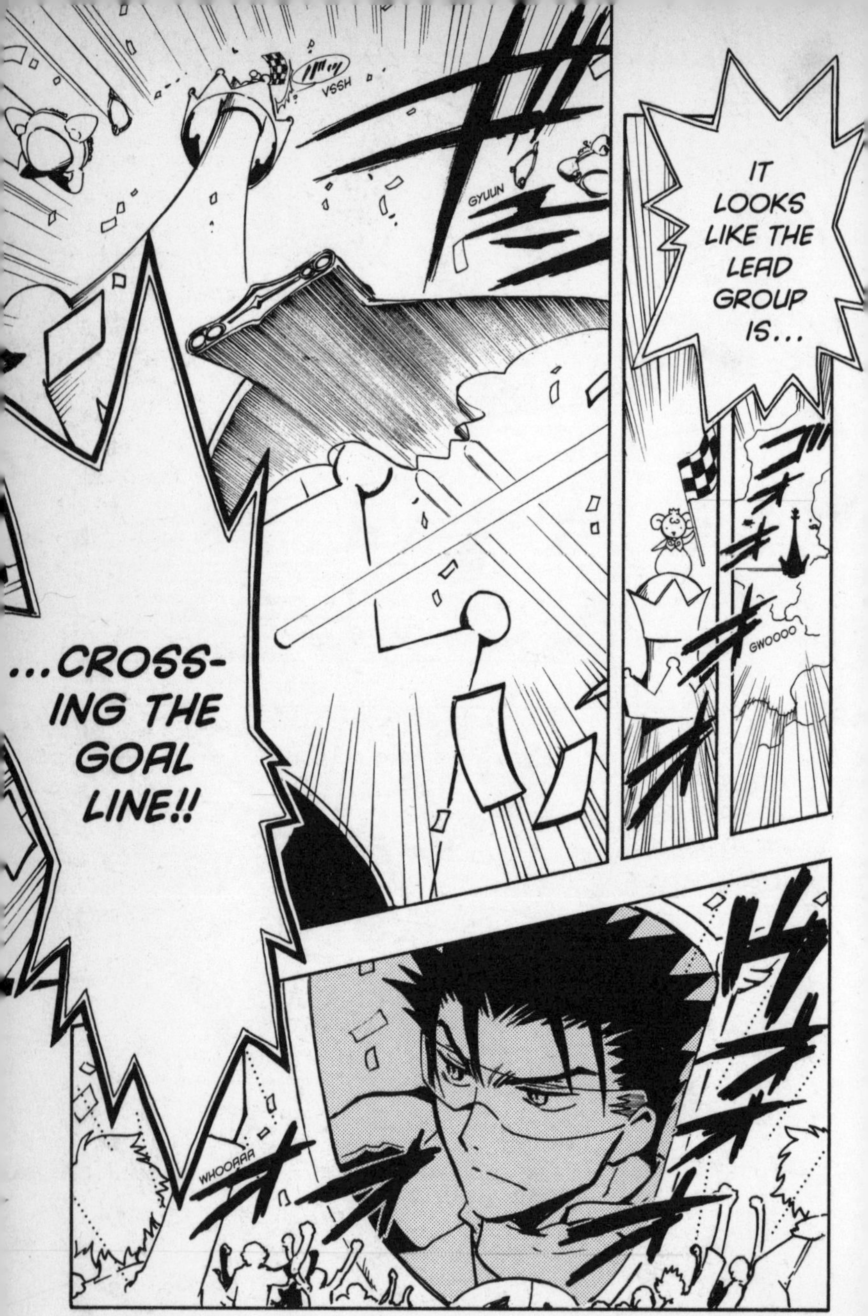
IT LOOKS LIKE THE LEAD GROUP IS...
GWOOOO
VSSH
GYUUN
...CROSSING THE GOAL LINE!!
WHOORRR

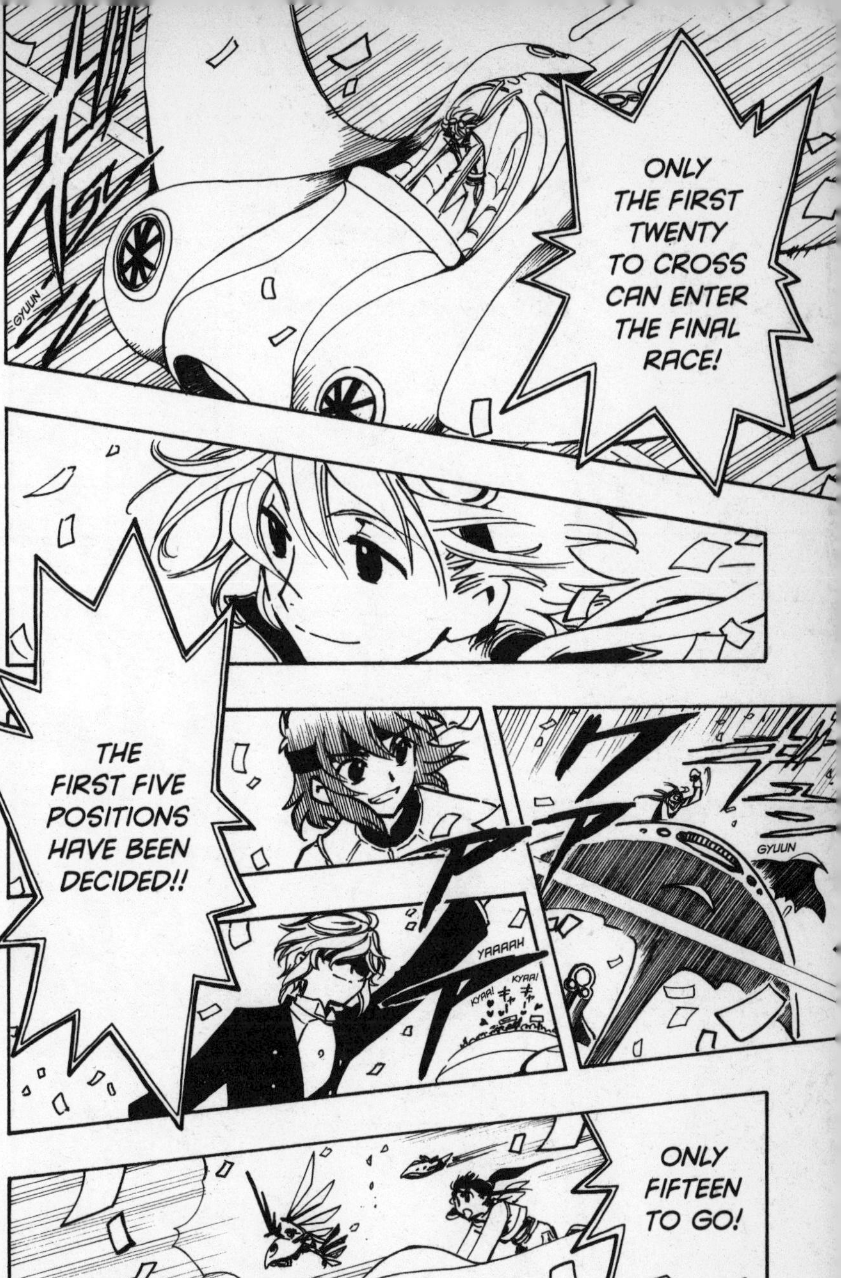

ONLY THE FIRST TWENTY TO CROSS CAN ENTER THE FINAL RACE!
GYUUN
GYUUN
THE FIRST FIVE POSITIONS HAVE BEEN DECIDED!!
YAAAAH
KYAA!
KYAA!
ONLY FIFTEEN TO GO!

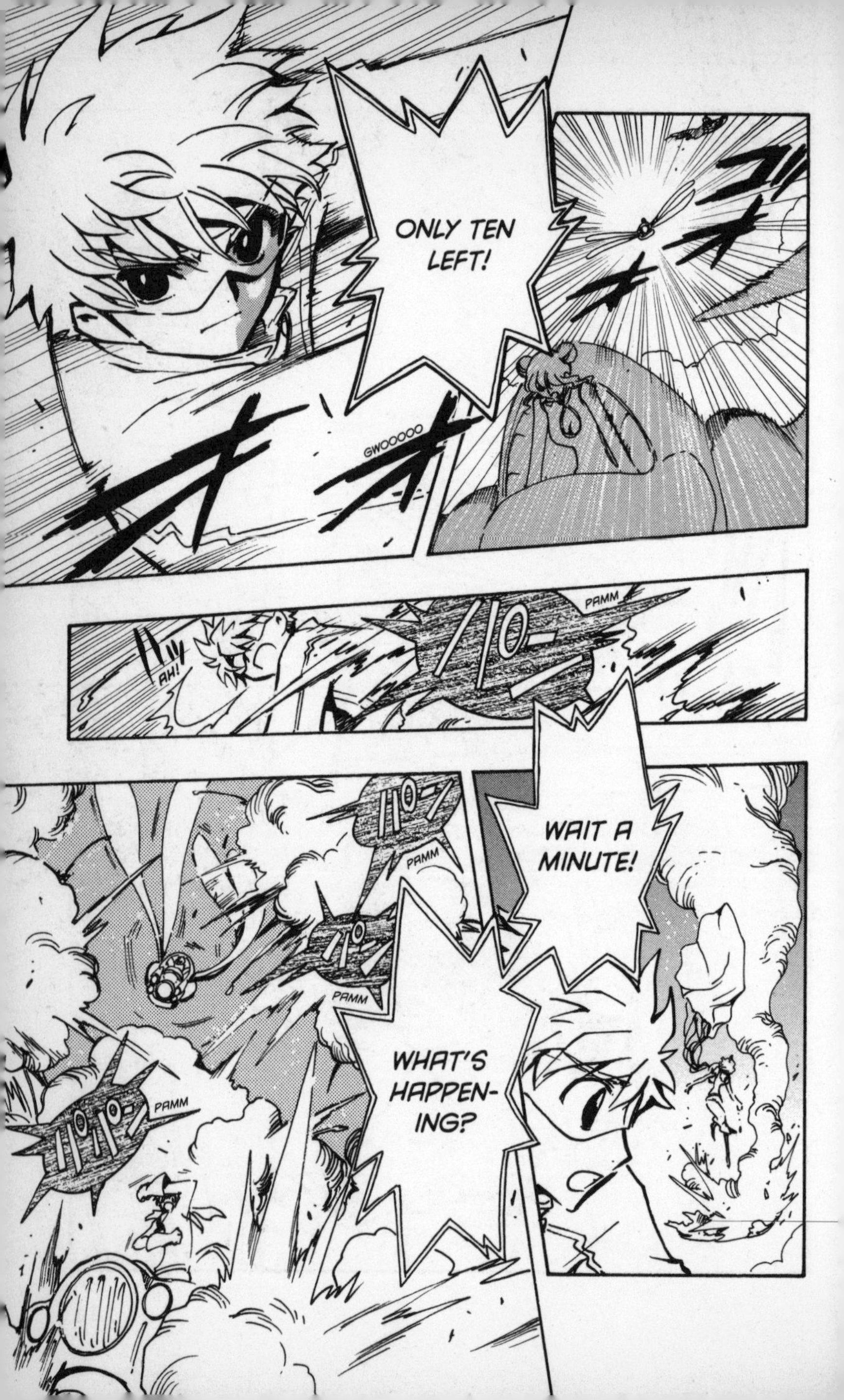
ONLY TEN LEFT!
GWOOOOO
PAMM
AH!
WAIT A MINUTE!
WHAT'S HAPPEN-ING?
PAMM
PAMM
PAMM

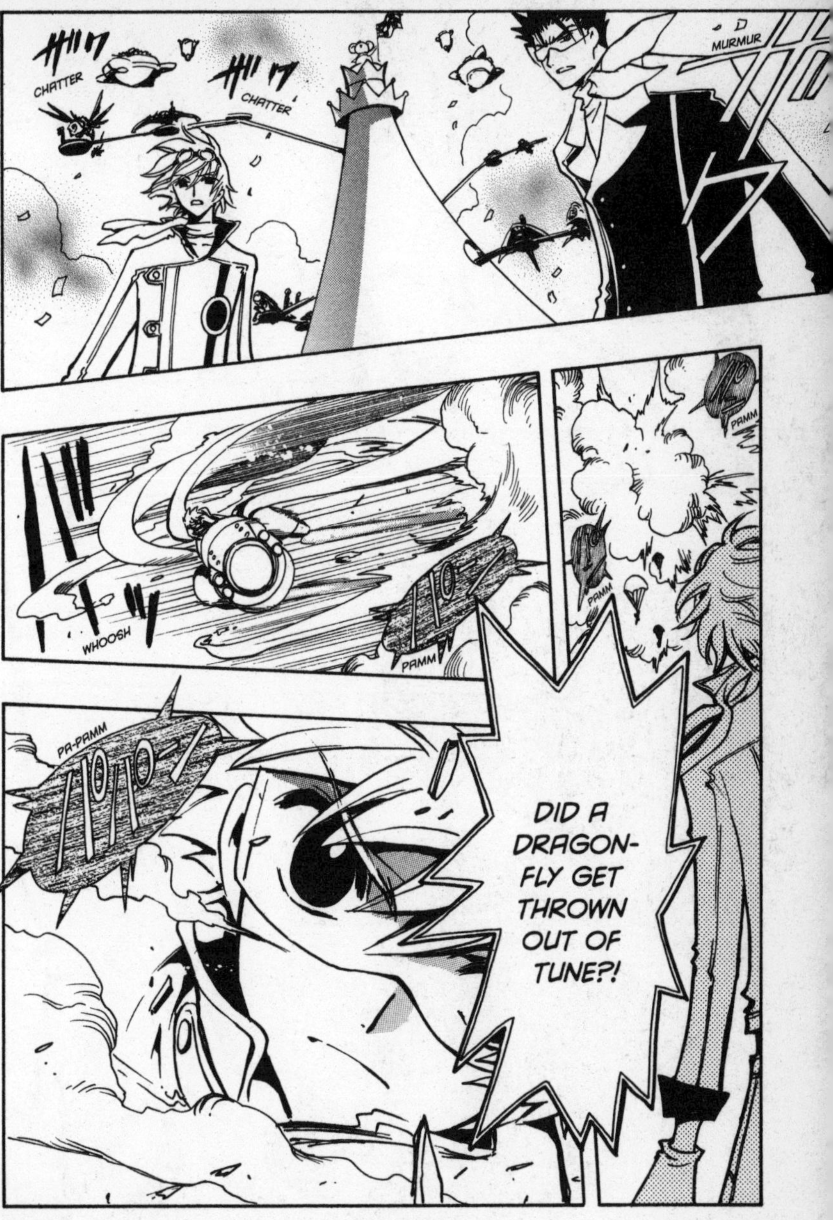
MURMUR
CHATTER
CHATTER
PAMM
PAMM
WHOOSH
PAMM
PA-PAMM
DID A DRAGON-FLY GET THROWN OUT OF TUNE?!

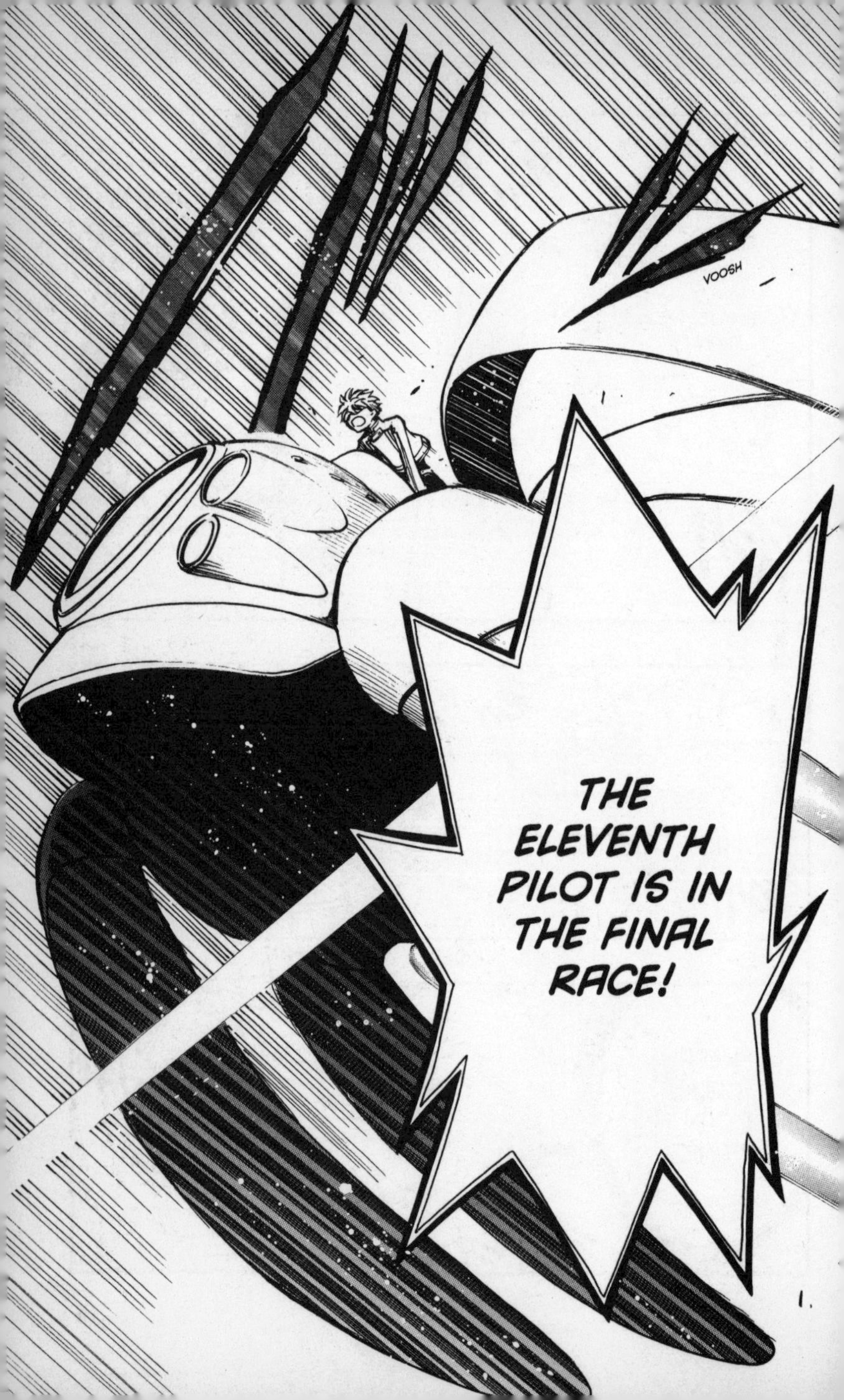
VOOSH
THE ELEVENTH PILOT IS IN THE FINAL RACE!

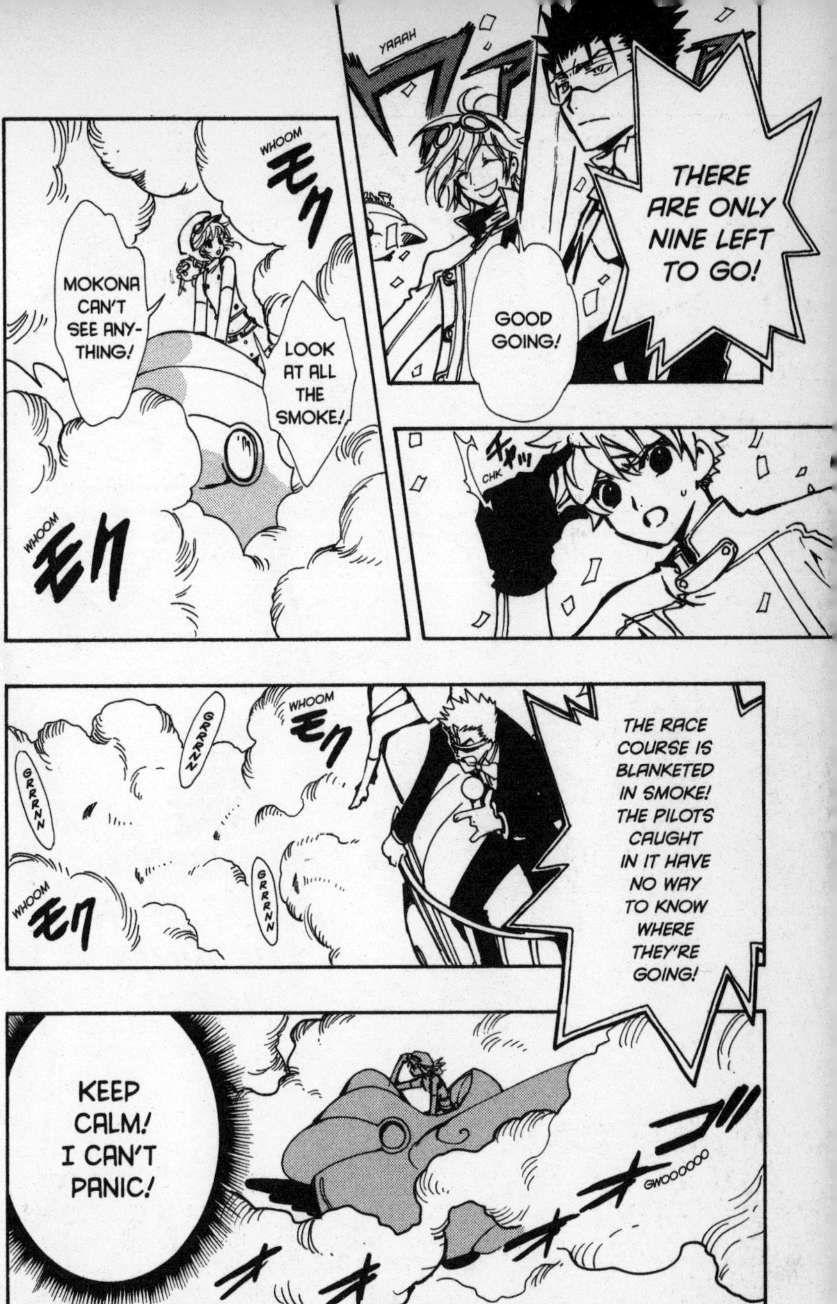

YAAAH
THERE ARE ONLY NINE LEFT TO GO!
GOOD GOING!
CHK
WHOOM
LOOK AT ALL THE SMOKE!
MOKONA CAN'T SEE ANY-THING!
WHOOM
THE RACE COURSE IS BLANKETED IN SMOKE! THE PILOTS CAUGHT IN IT HAVE NO WAY TO KNOW WHERE THEY'RE GOING!
WHOOM
GRRRNN
GRRRNN
GRRRNN
WHOOM
GWOOOOOO
KEEP CALM! I CAN'T PANIC!

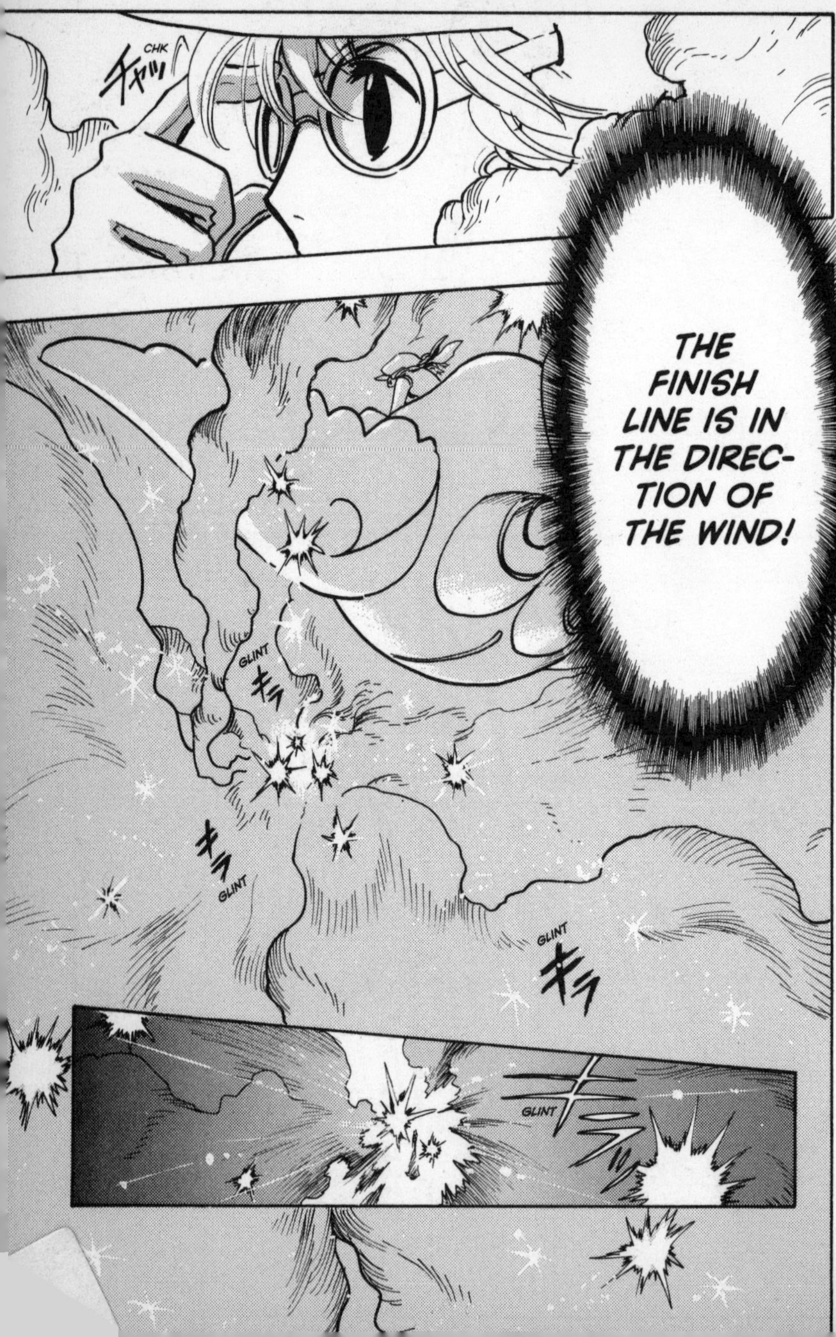

CHK
チャッ
THE FINISH LINE IS IN THE DIREC-TION OF THE WIND!
GLINT
キラ
キラ
GLINT
GLINT
キラ
キラ
GLINT

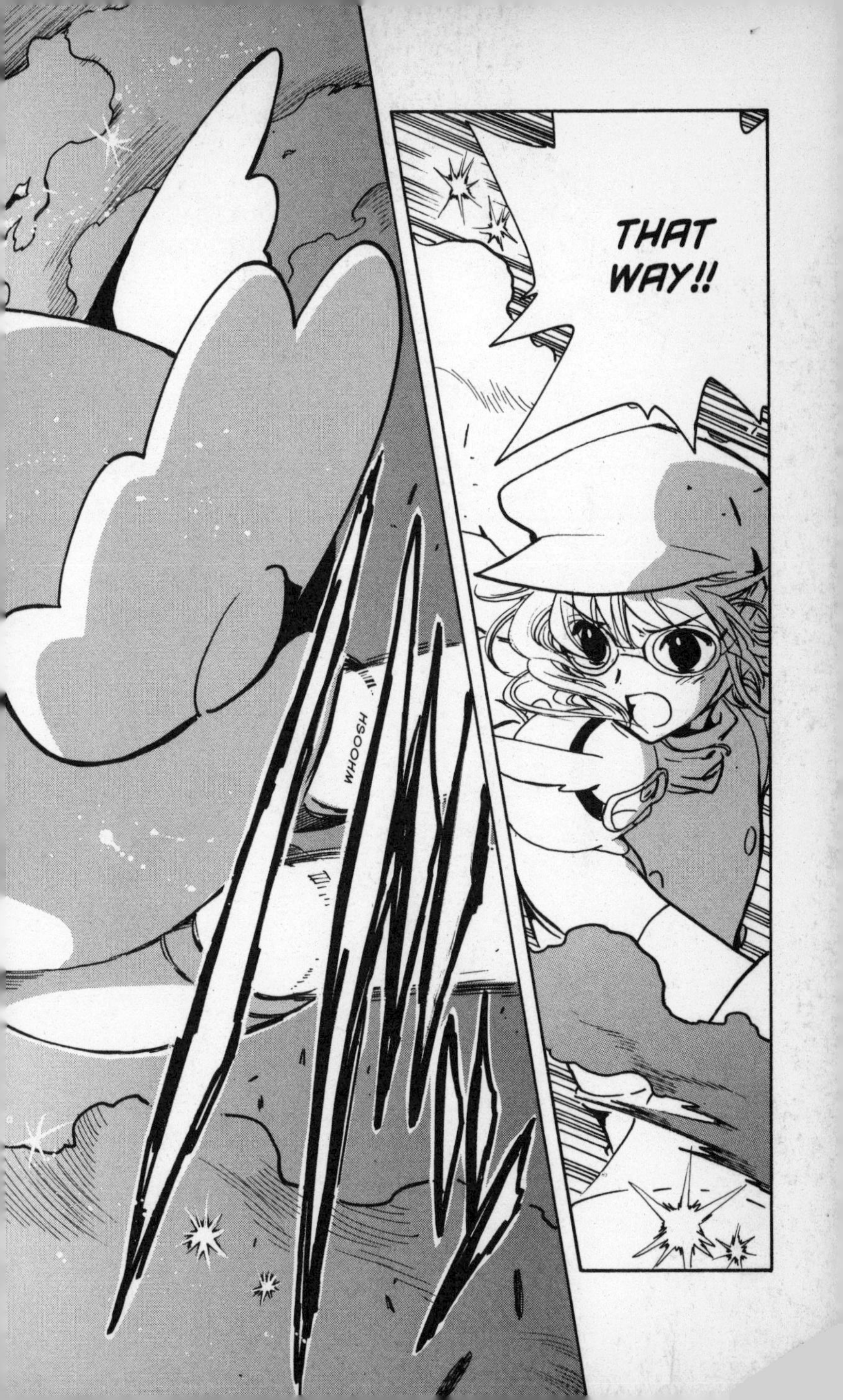
THAT WAY!!
WHOOSH

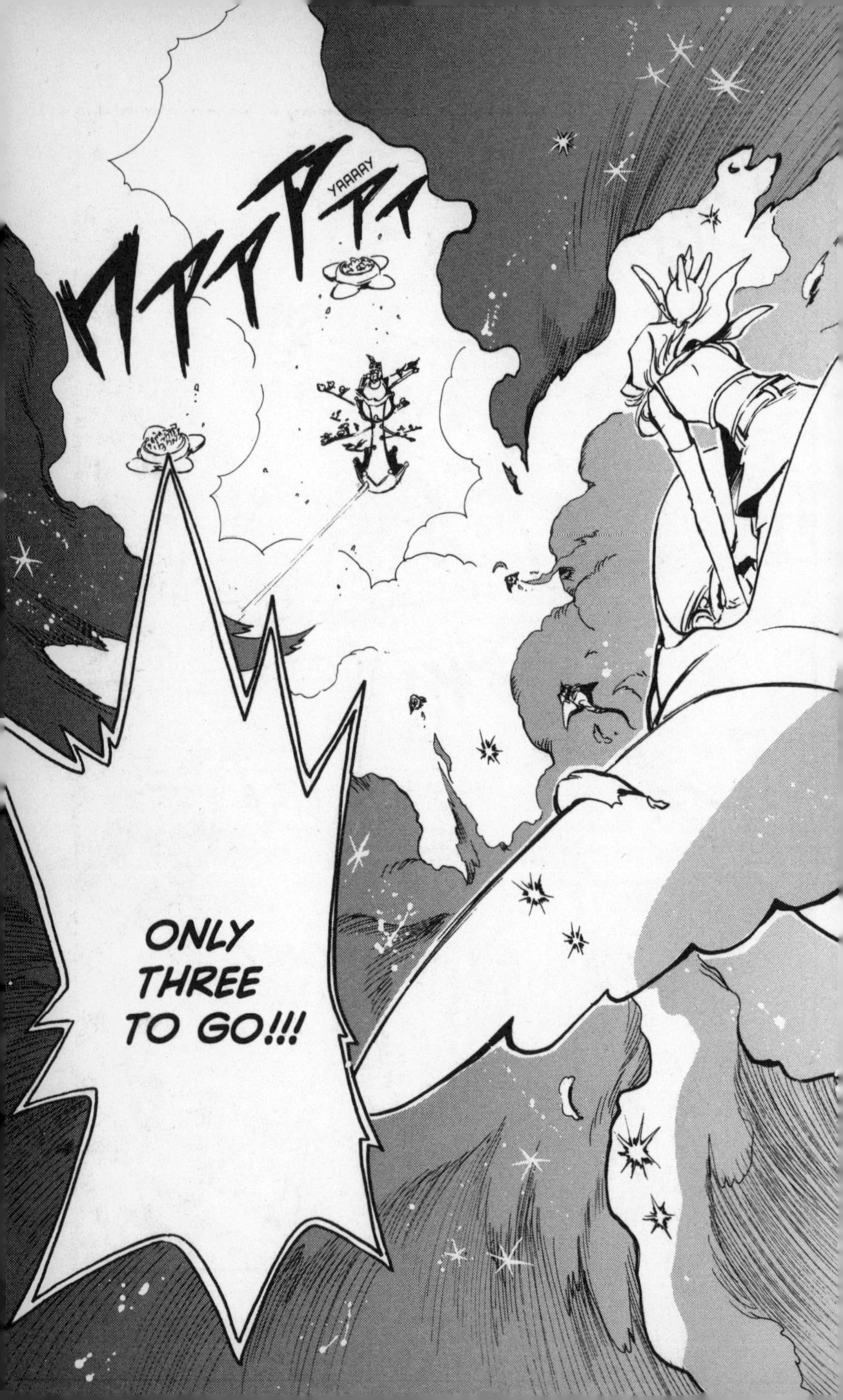
YAAAAY
ONLY THREE TO GO!!!

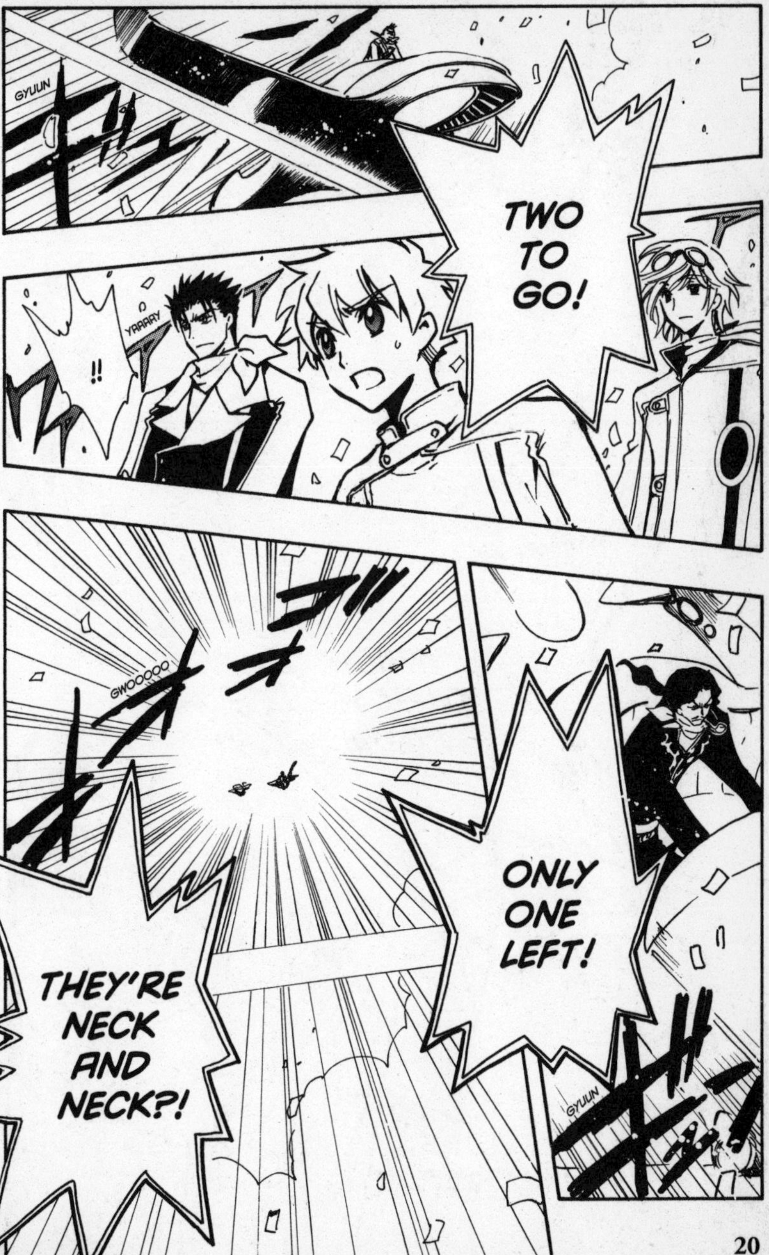
GYUUN
TWO TO GO!
YARRRY
!!
ONLY ONE LEFT!
GYUUN
GWOOOOO
THEY'RE NECK AND NECK?!

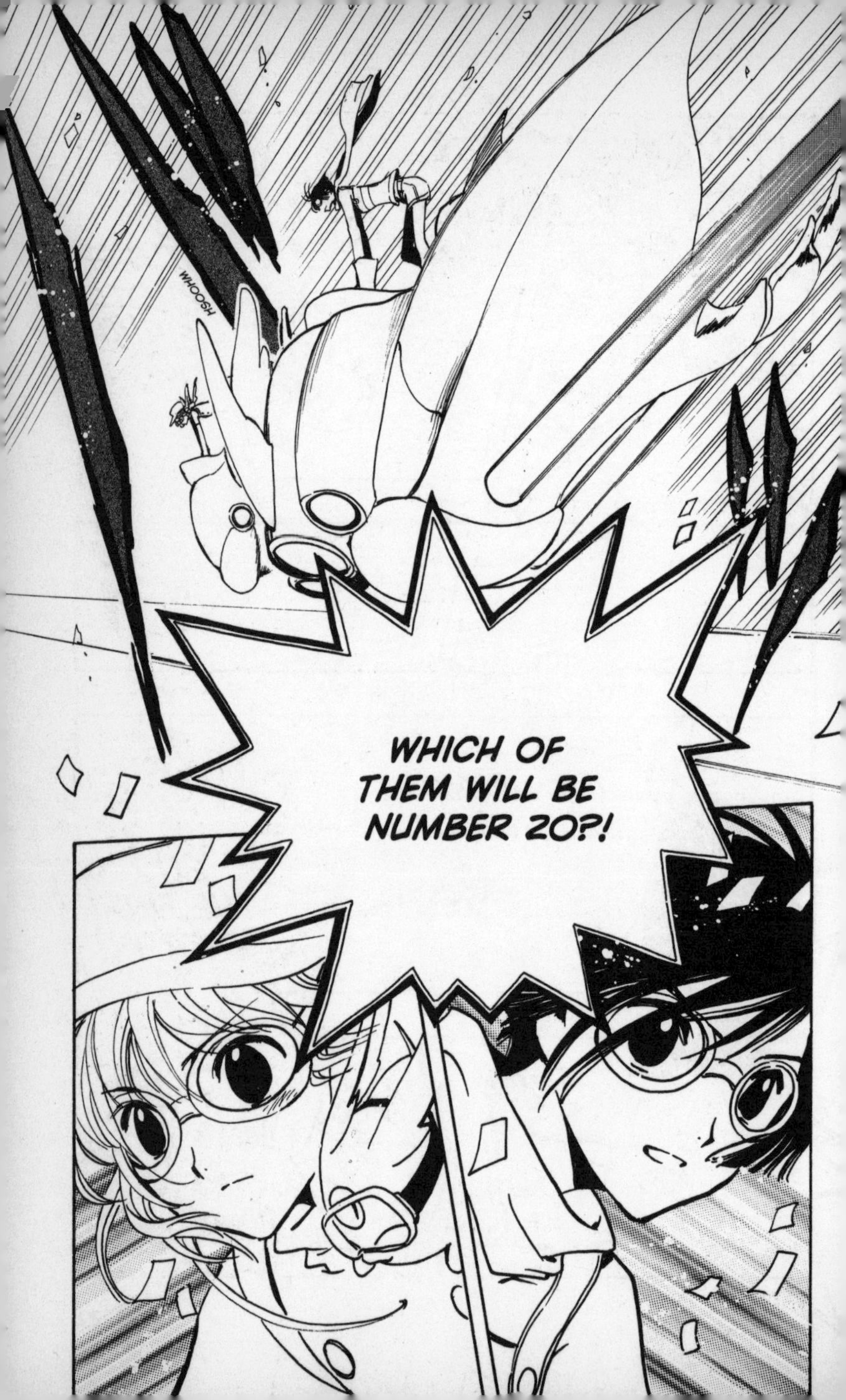
WHOOSH
WHICH OF THEM WILL BE NUMBER 20?!

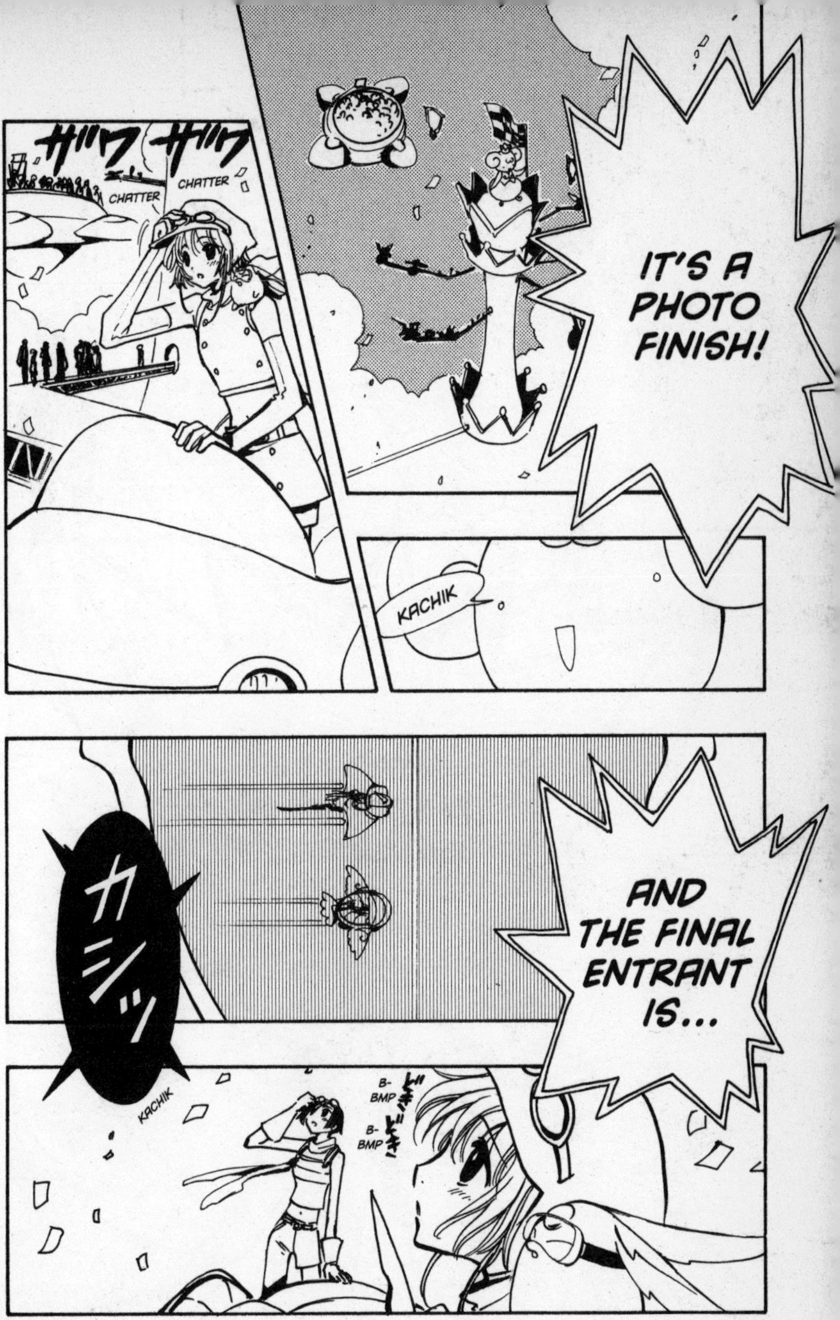
IT'S A PHOTO FINISH!
KACHIK
ザワ
ザワ
CHATTER
CHATTER
AND THE FINAL ENTRANT IS...
カシッ
B-BMP
B-BMP
KACHIK

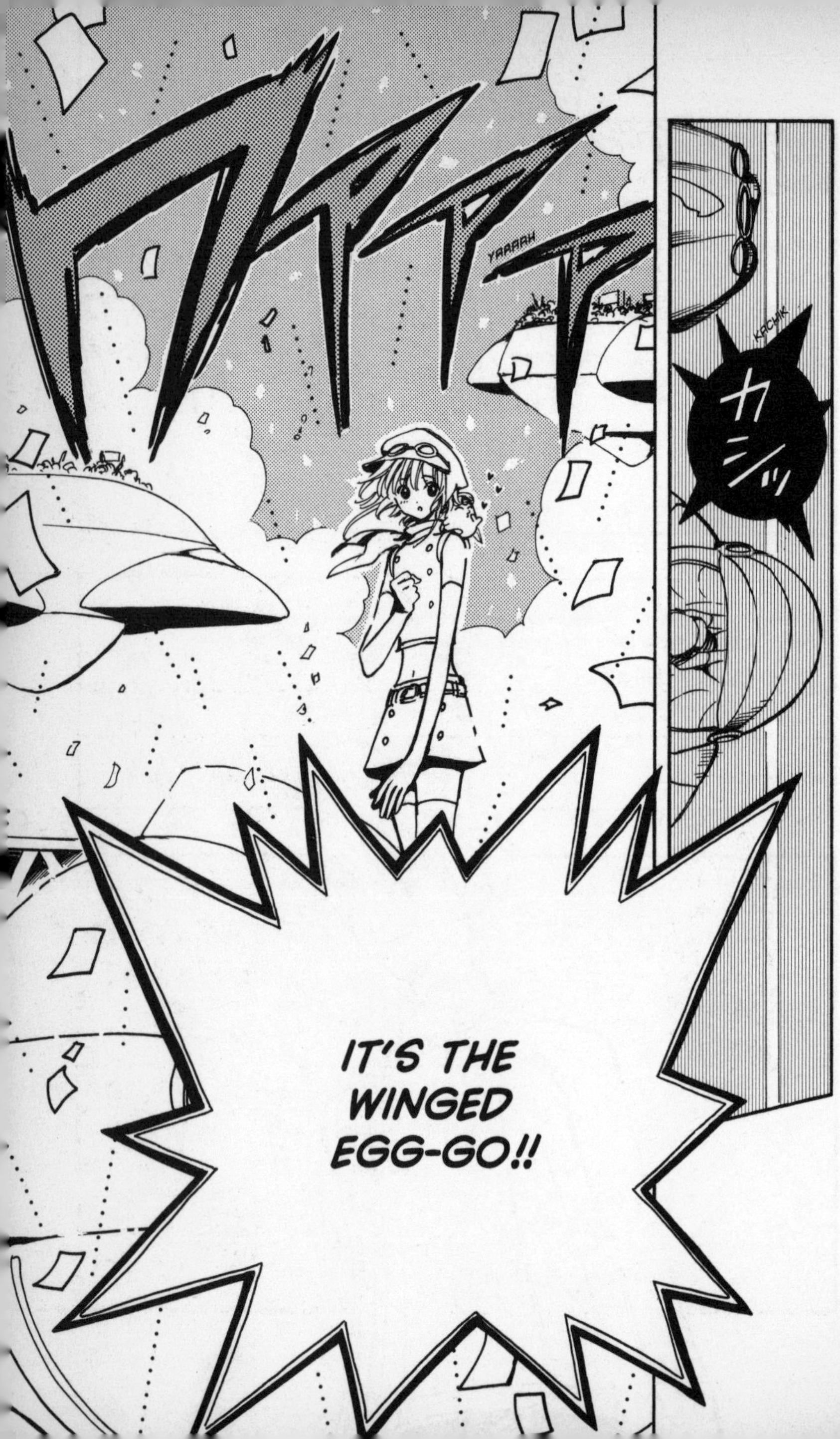
KACHIK
カシッ
YAAAAH
IT'S THE WINGED EGG-GO!!

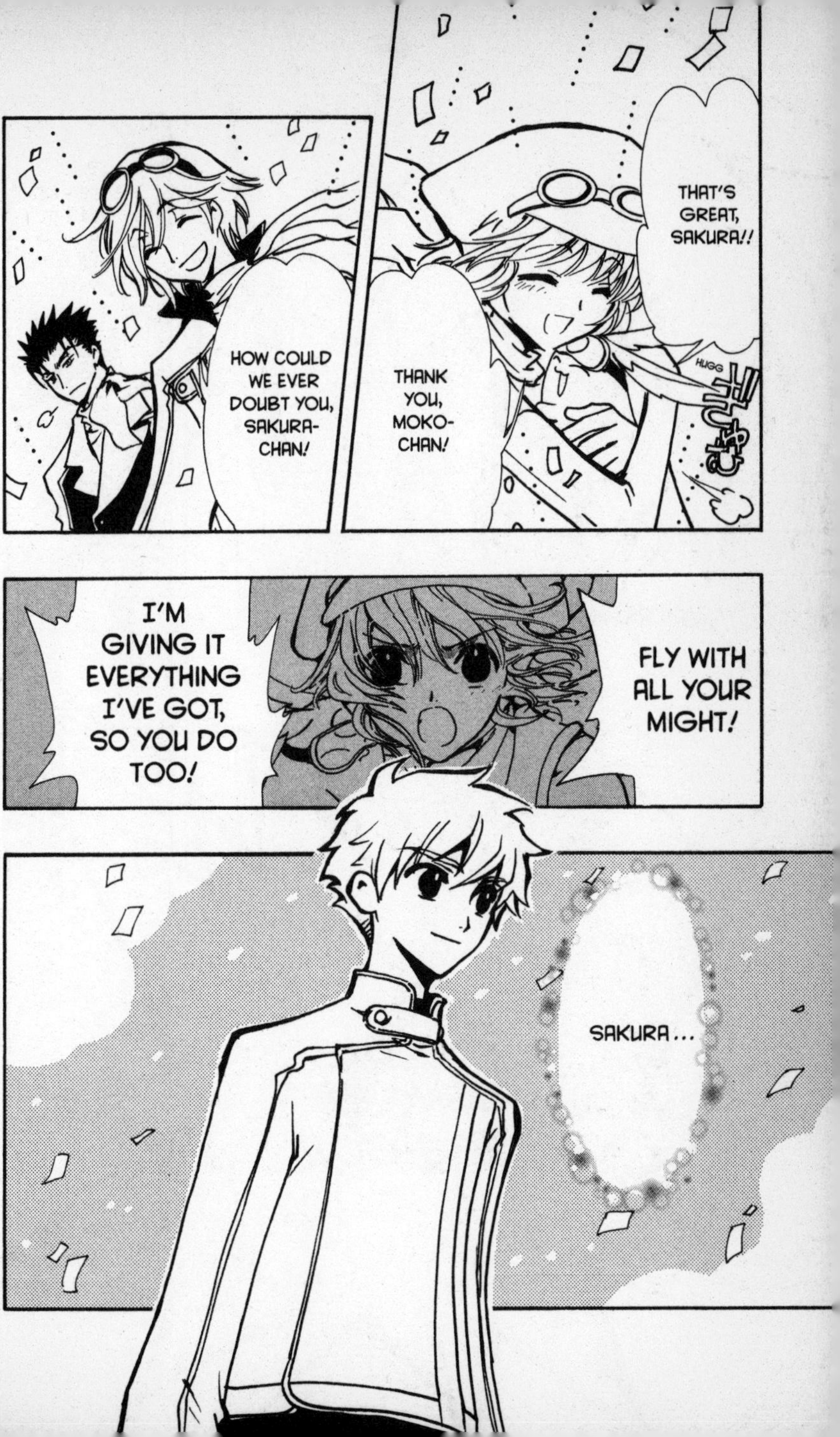
THAT'S GREAT, SAKURA!!
HUGG
THANK YOU, MOKO-CHAN!
HOW COULD WE EVER DOUBT YOU, SAKURA-CHAN!
FLY WITH ALL YOUR MIGHT!
I'M GIVING IT EVERYTHING I'VE GOT, SO YOU DO TOO!
SAKURA...

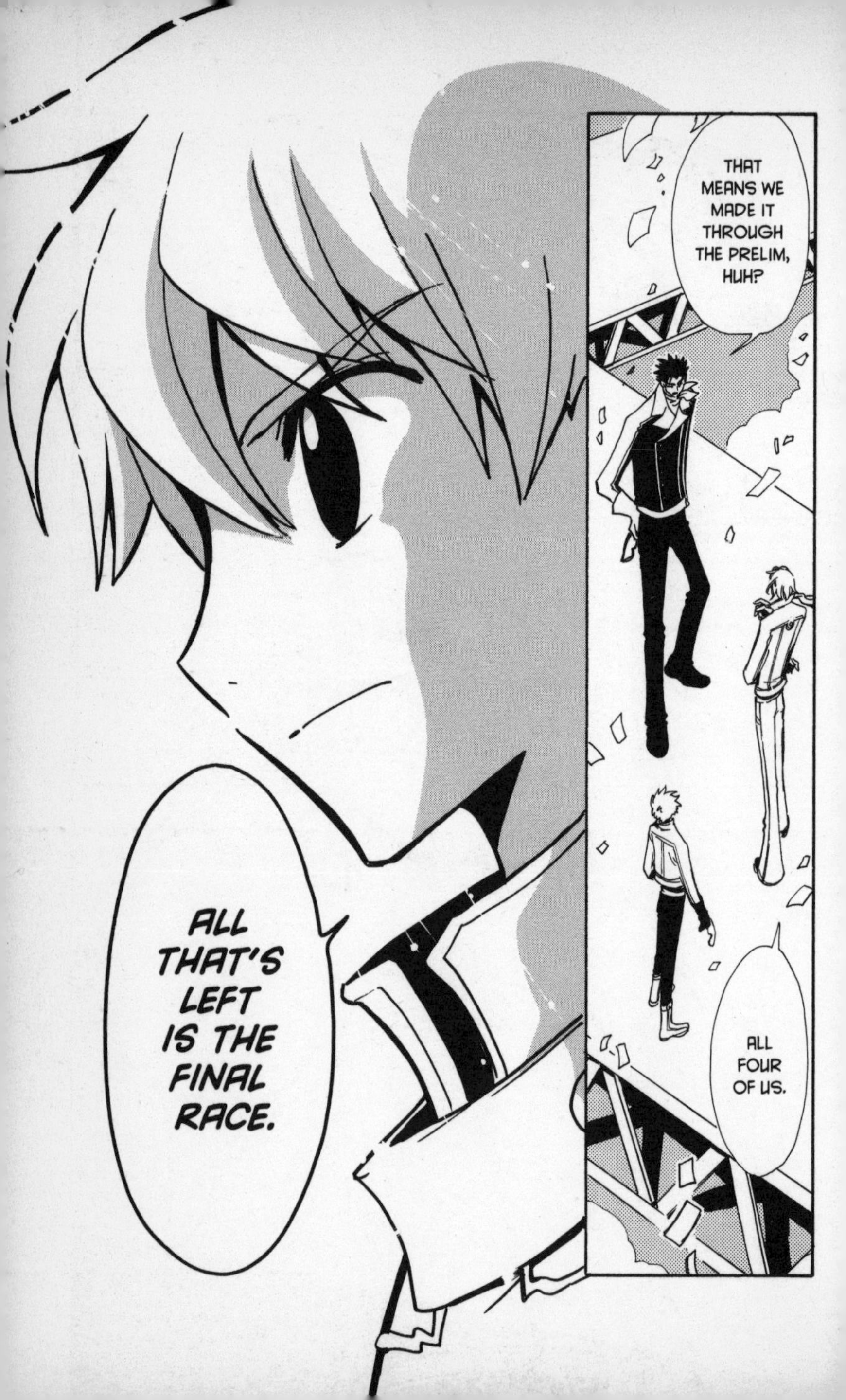
THAT MEANS WE MADE IT THROUGH THE PRELIM, HUH?
ALL FOUR OF US.
ALL THAT'S LEFT IS THE FINAL RACE.

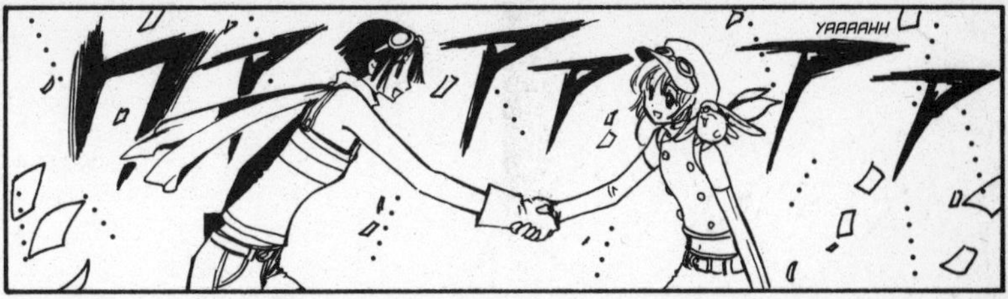
YAAAAHH

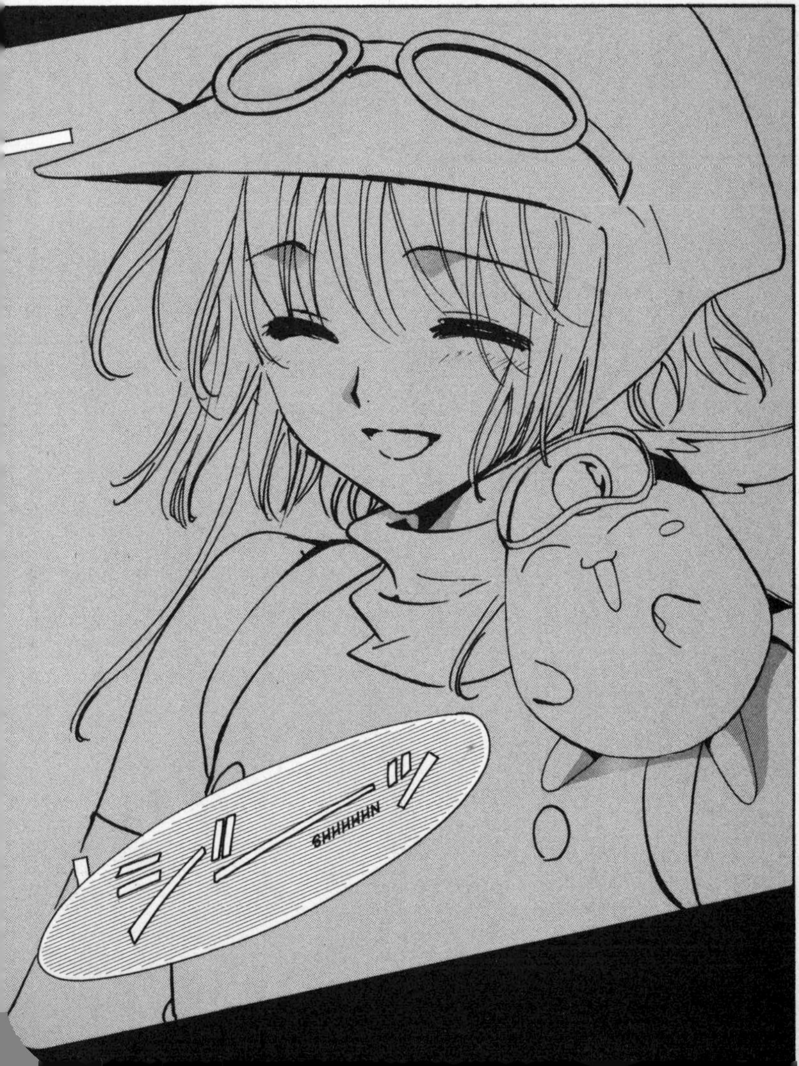
SHHHHHN

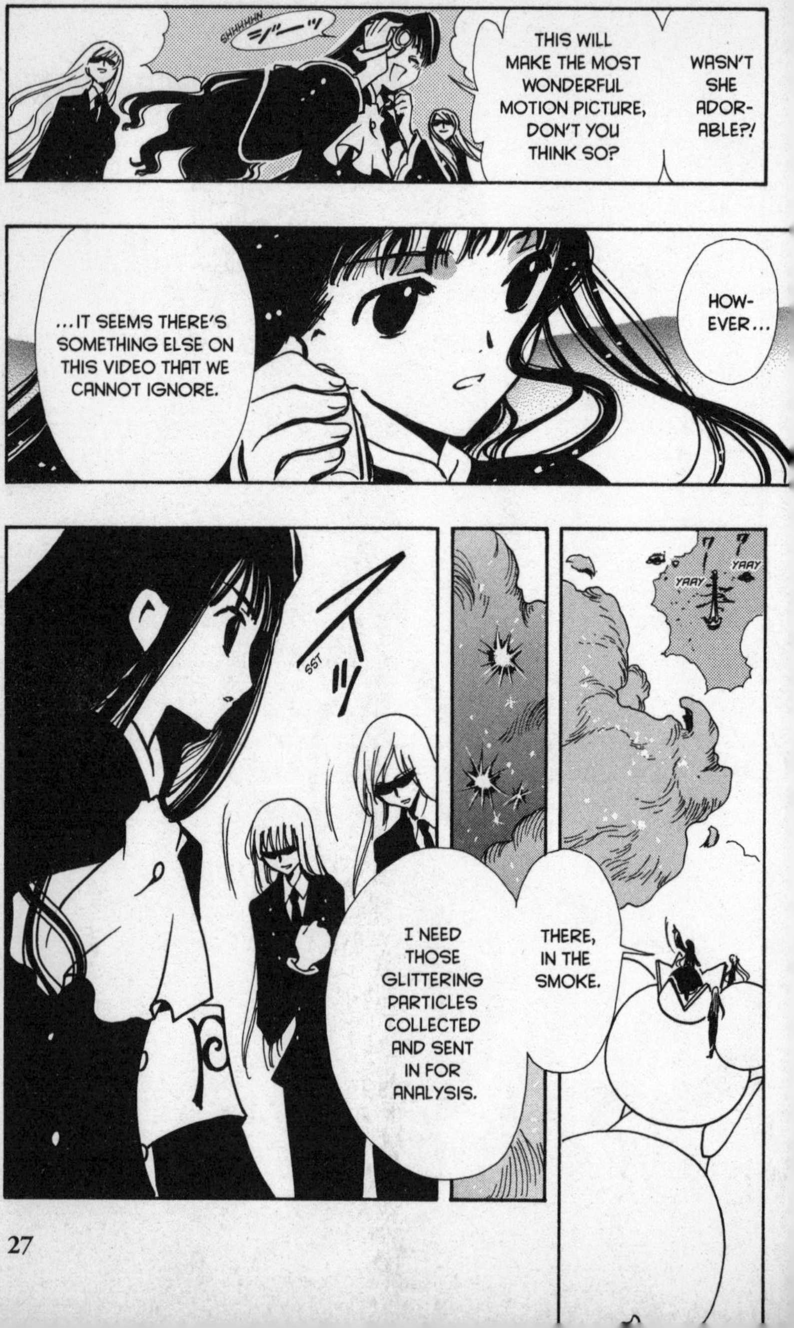
WASN'T SHE ADORABLE?!
THIS WILL MAKE THE MOST WONDERFUL MOTION PICTURE, DON'T YOU THINK SO?
SHHHHHN
HOW-EVER...
...IT SEEMS THERE'S SOMETHING ELSE ON THIS VIDEO THAT WE CANNOT IGNORE.
YAAY
YAAY
THERE, IN THE SMOKE.
I NEED THOSE GLITTERING PARTICLES COLLECTED AND SENT IN FOR ANALYSIS.
SST

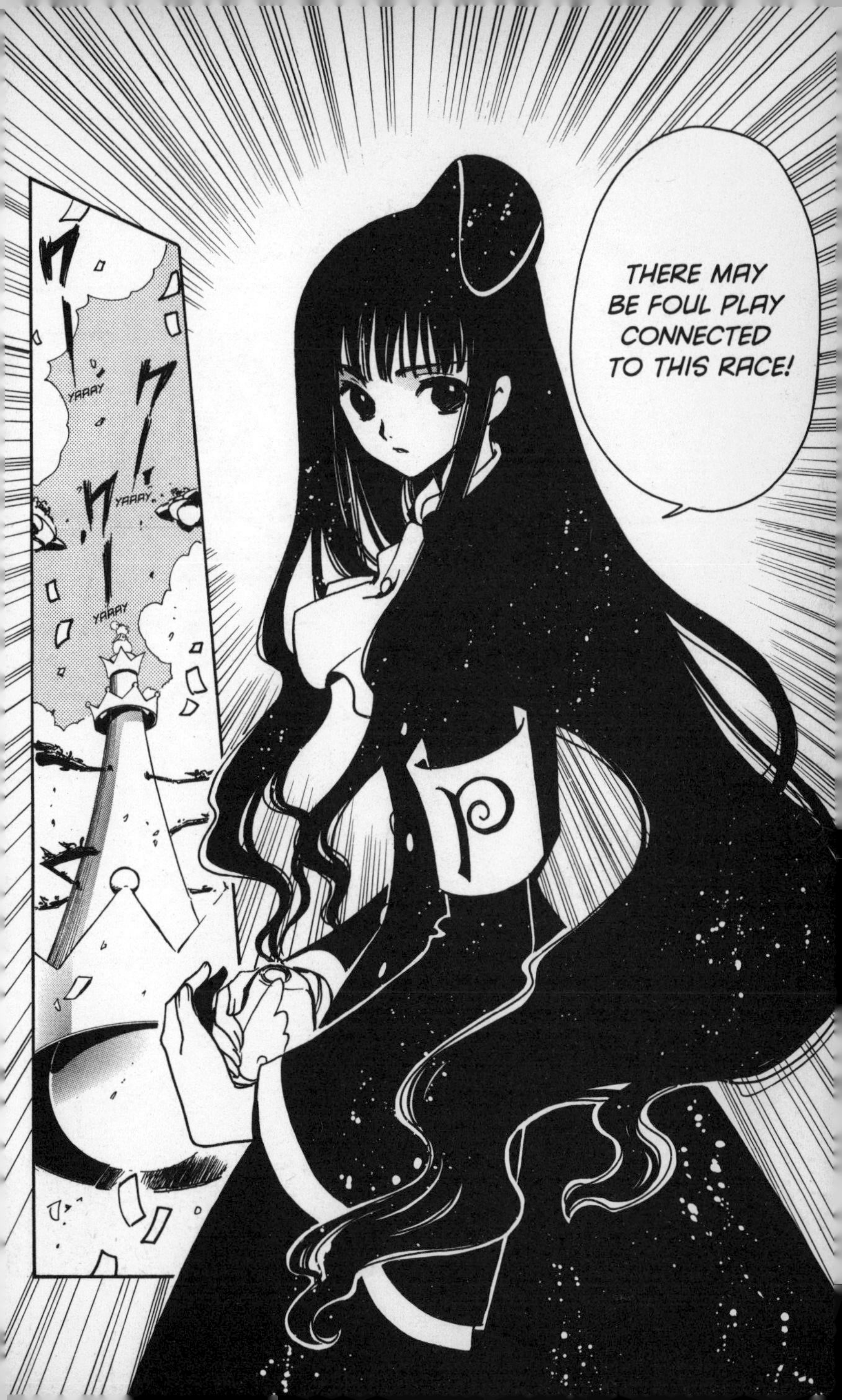
THERE MAY BE FOUL PLAY CONNECTED TO THIS RACE!
YAAAY
YAAAY
YAAAY

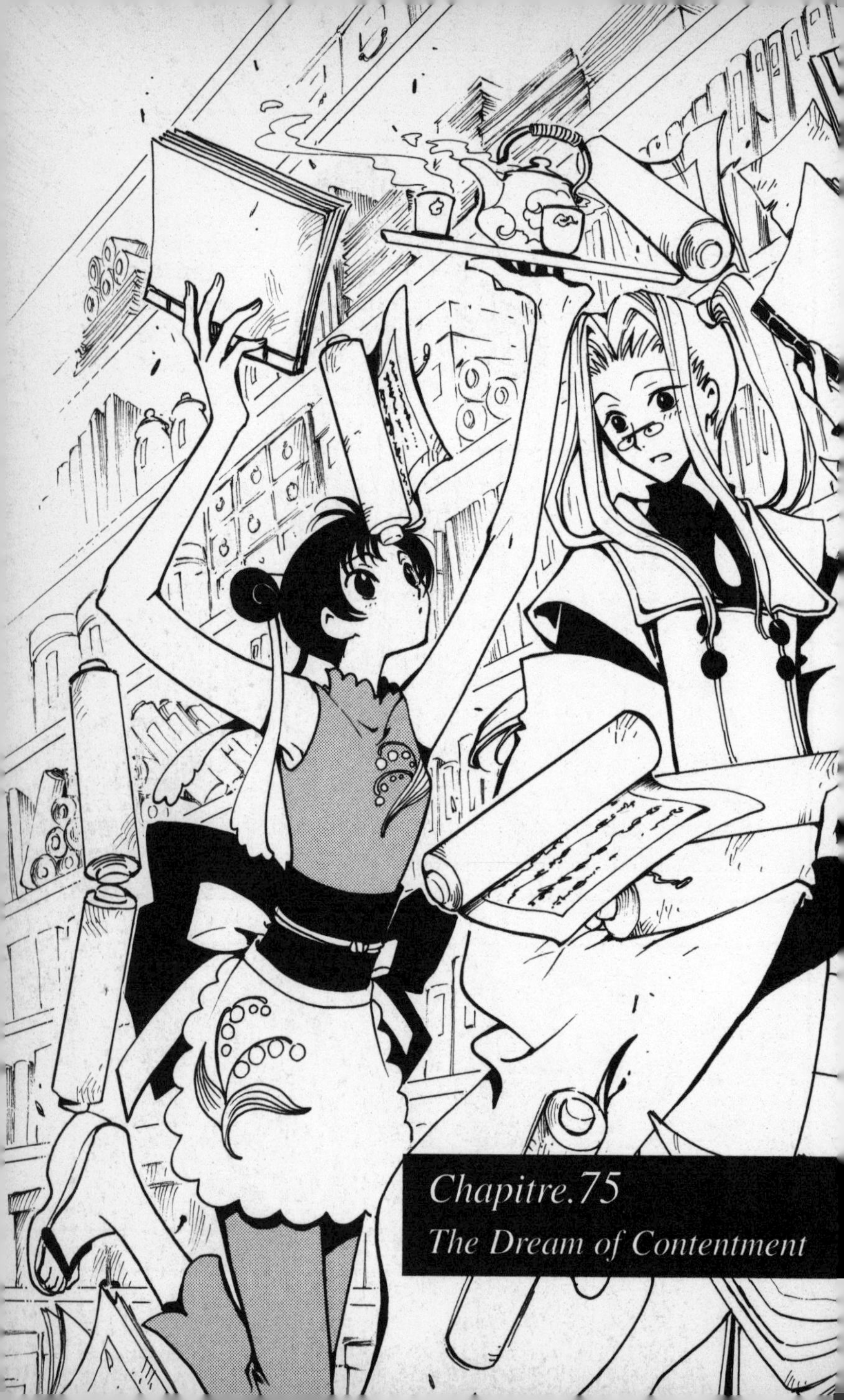
Chapitre.75
The Dream of Contentment

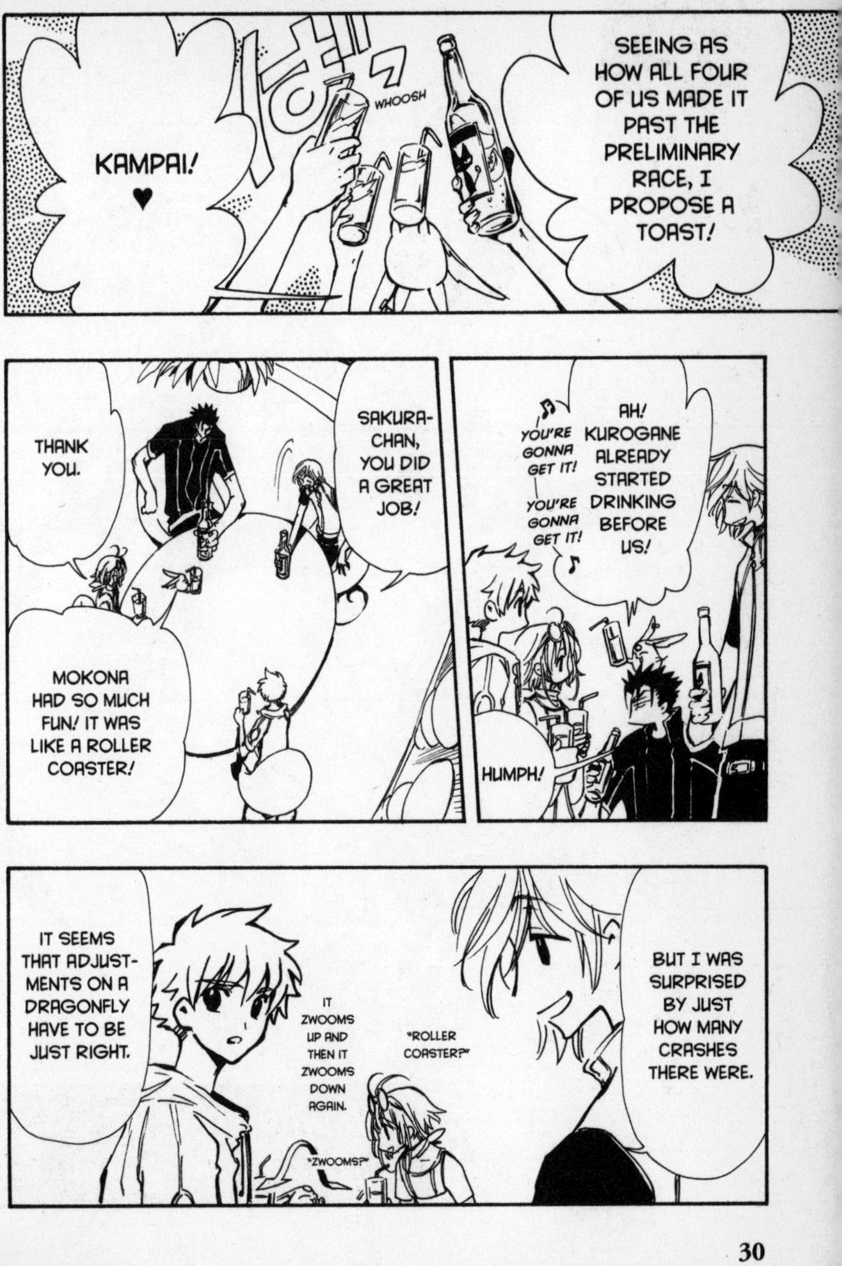
SEEING AS HOW ALL FOUR OF US MADE IT PAST THE PRELIMINARY RACE, I PROPOSE A TOAST!
WHOOSH
KAMPAI! ♥
AH! KUROGANE ALREADY STARTED DRINKING BEFORE US!
YOU'RE GONNA GET IT! YOU'RE GONNA GET IT!
HUMPH!
SAKURA-CHAN, YOU DID A GREAT JOB!
THANK YOU.
MOKONA HAD SO MUCH FUN! IT WAS LIKE A ROLLER COASTER!
BUT I WAS SURPRISED BY JUST HOW MANY CRASHES THERE WERE.
"ROLLER COASTER?"
IT ZWOOMS UP AND THEN IT ZWOOMS DOWN AGAIN.
"ZWOOMS?"
IT SEEMS THAT ADJUSTMENTS ON A DRAGONFLY HAVE TO BE JUST RIGHT.

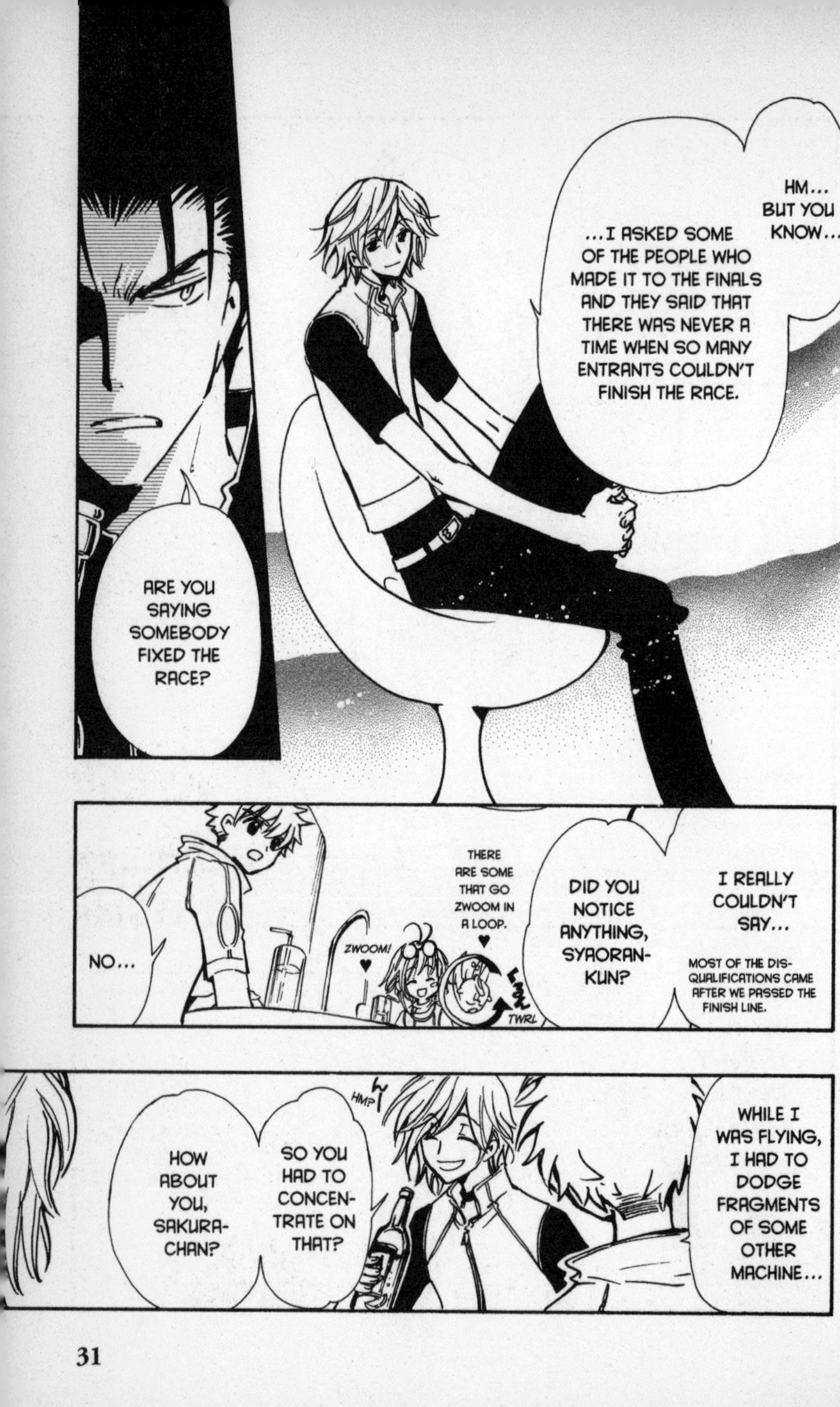
HM... BUT YOU KNOW...
...I ASKED SOME OF THE PEOPLE WHO MADE IT TO THE FINALS AND THEY SAID THAT THERE WAS NEVER A TIME WHEN SO MANY ENTRANTS COULDN'T FINISH THE RACE.
ARE YOU SAYING SOMEBODY FIXED THE RACE?
I REALLY COULDN'T SAY...
MOST OF THE DIS-QUALIFICATIONS CAME AFTER WE PASSED THE FINISH LINE.
DID YOU NOTICE ANYTHING, SYAORAN-KUN?
THERE ARE SOME THAT GO ZWOOM IN A LOOP. ♥
TWRL
ZWOOM! ♥
NO...
WHILE I WAS FLYING, I HAD TO DODGE FRAGMENTS OF SOME OTHER MACHINE...
HMP!
SO YOU HAD TO CONCENTRATE ON THAT?
HOW ABOUT YOU, SAKURA-CHAN?

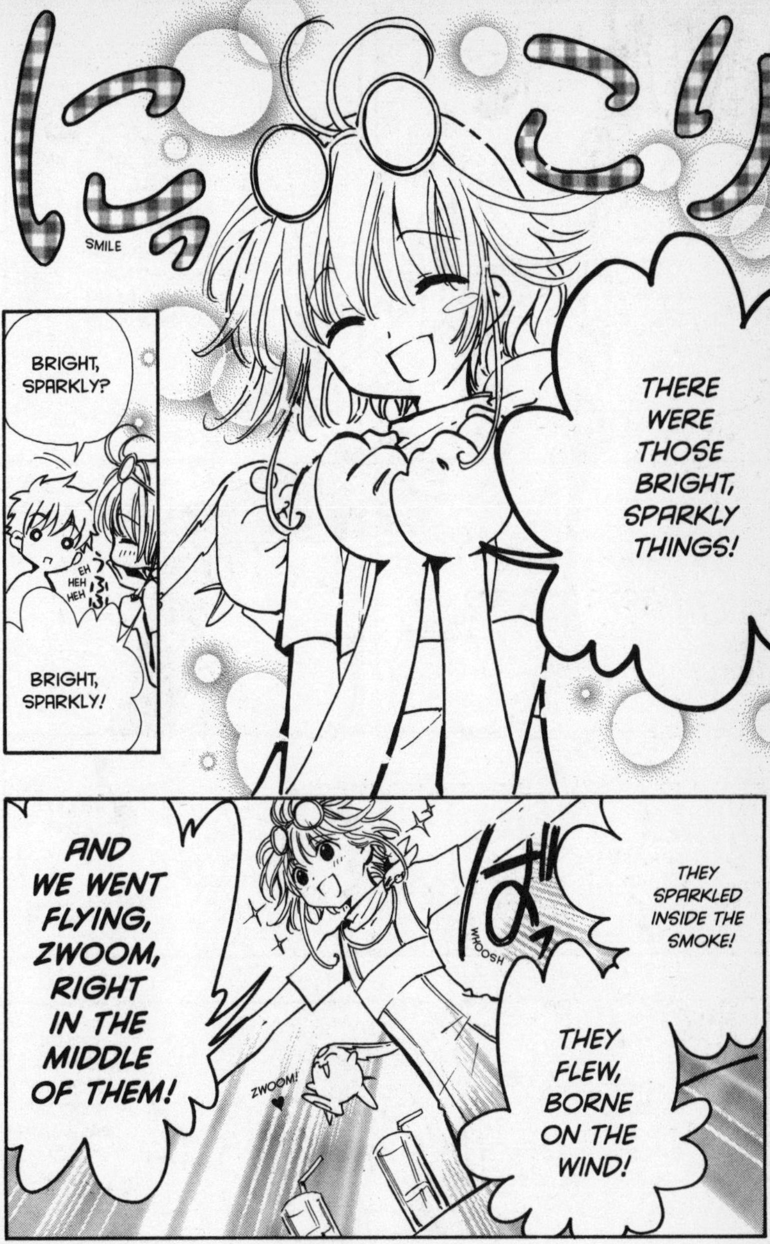
にっこり
SMILE
THERE WERE THOSE BRIGHT, SPARKLY THINGS!
BRIGHT, SPARKLY?
EH HEH HEH
BRIGHT, SPARKLY!
THEY SPARKLED INSIDE THE SMOKE!
THEY FLEW, BORNE ON THE WIND!
ばっ
WHOOSH
ZWOOM!
AND WE WENT FLYING, ZWOOM, RIGHT IN THE MIDDLE OF THEM!

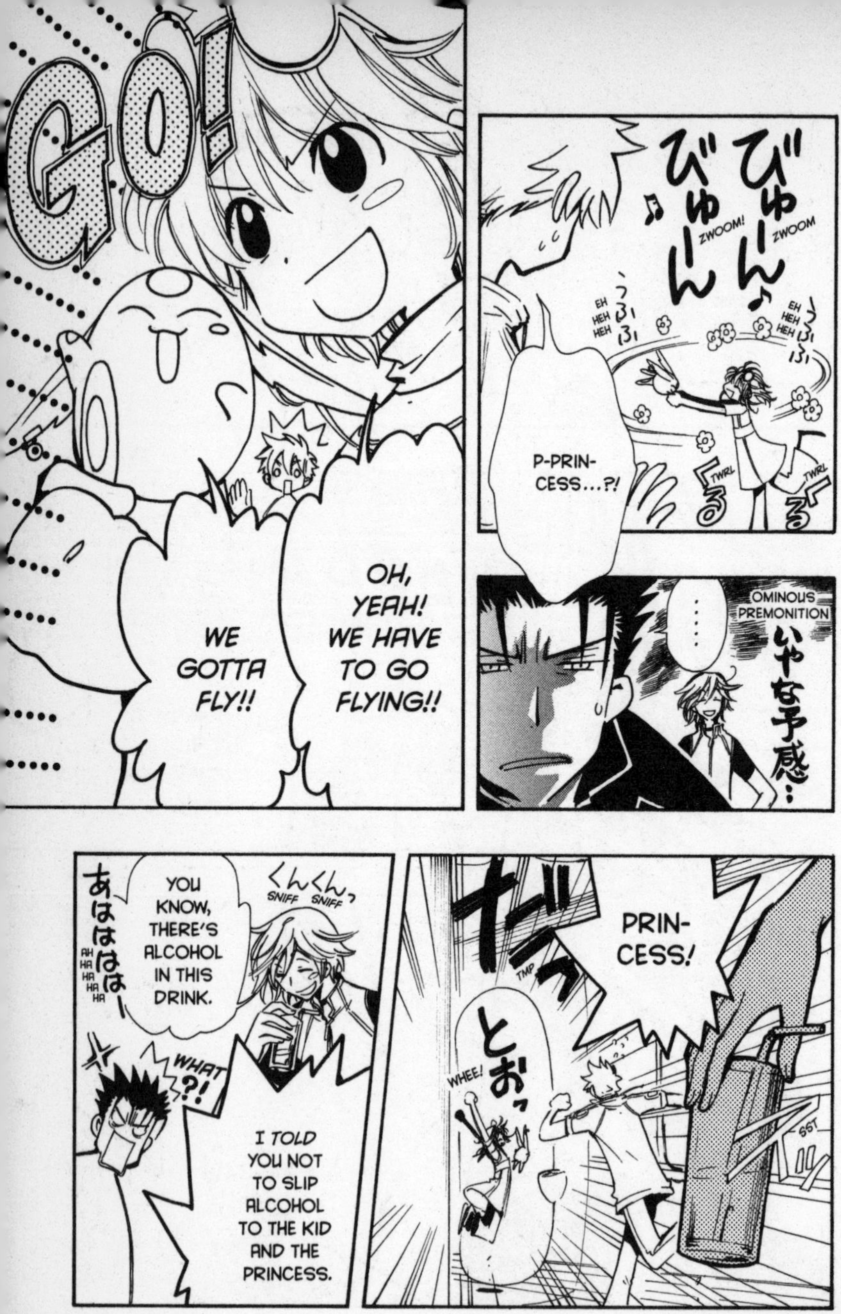
びゅーん♪
ZWOOM
びゅーん
ZWOOM!
うふふ
EH HEH HEH
うふふ
EH HEH HEH
P-PRIN-CESS...?!
くる
TWRL
くる
TWRL
.....
OMINOUS PREMONITION
いやな予感・・
GO!
OH, YEAH! WE HAVE TO GO FLYING!!
WE GOTTA FLY!!
PRIN-CESS!
ずっ
TMP
とぉっ
WHEE!
SST
くんくんっ
SNIFF SNIFF
YOU KNOW, THERE'S ALCOHOL IN THIS DRINK.
あははは
AH HA HA HA HA
WHAT?!
I TOLD YOU NOT TO SLIP ALCOHOL TO THE KID AND THE PRINCESS.

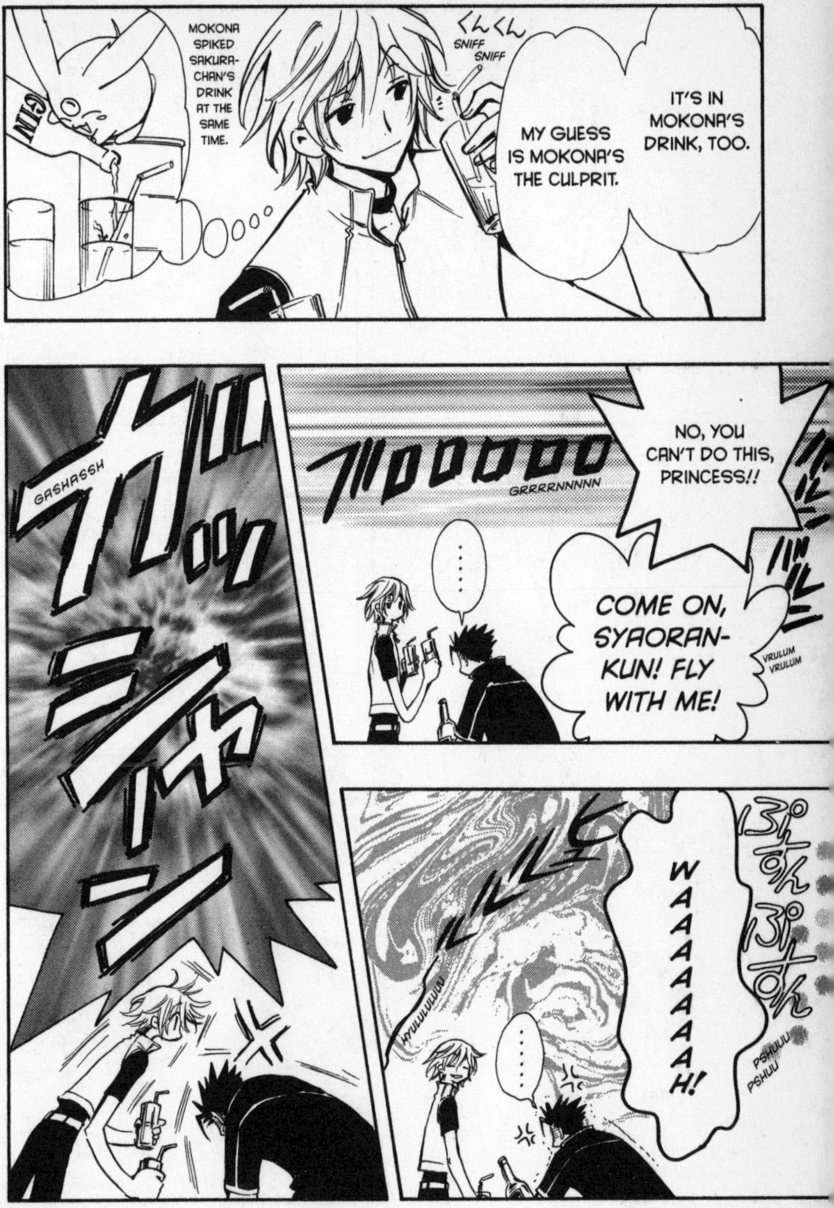
IT'S IN MOKONA'S DRINK, TOO.
MY GUESS IS MOKONA'S THE CULPRIT.
くんくん
SNIFF SNIFF
MOKONA SPIKED SAKURA-CHAN'S DRINK AT THE SAME TIME.
GIN
NO, YOU CAN'T DO THIS, PRINCESS!!
VRULUM VRULUM
COME ON, SYAORAN-KUN! FLY WITH ME!
GRRRRNNNNN
.....
ぷすん ぷすん
PSHUU PSHUU
WAAAAAAAAAH!
HYULULULULU
.....
GASHASSH

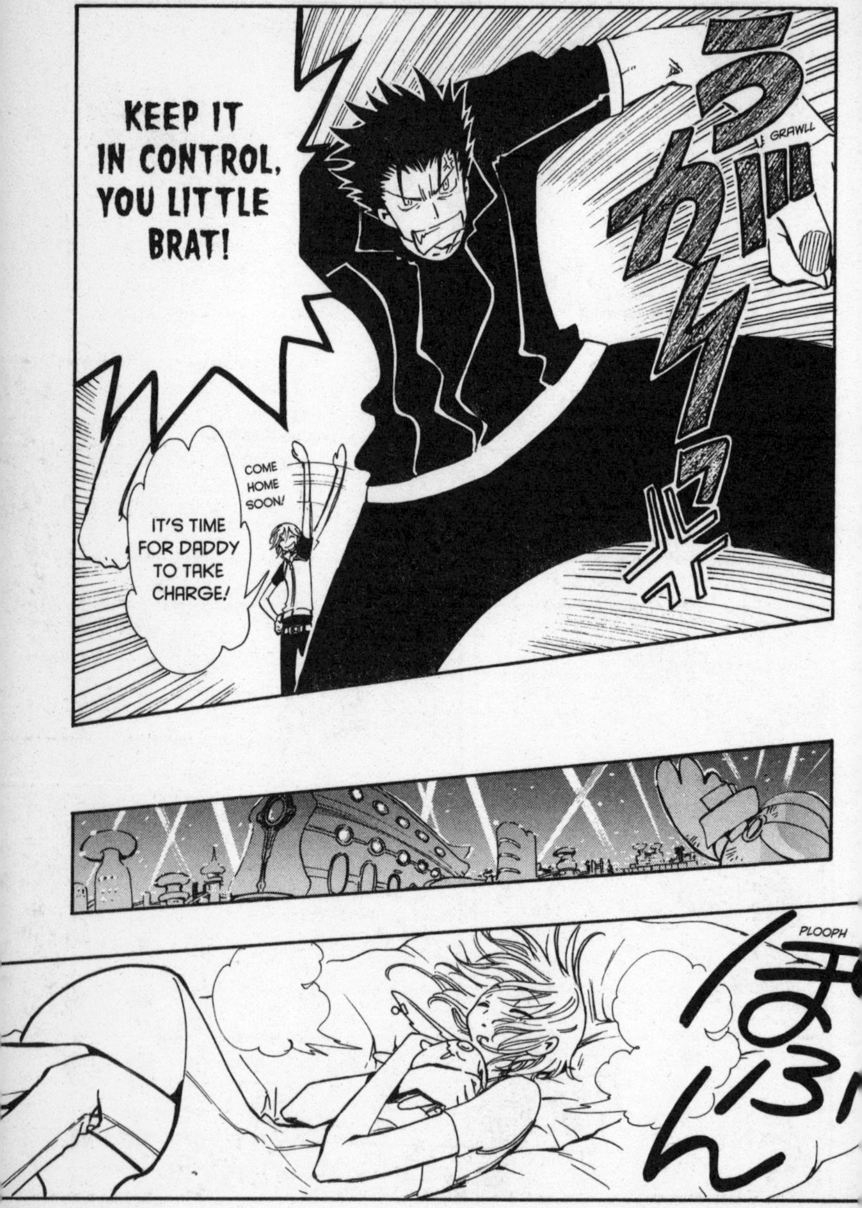
GRAWLL
KEEP IT IN CONTROL, YOU LITTLE BRAT!
COME HOME SOON!
IT'S TIME FOR DADDY TO TAKE CHARGE!
PLOOPH

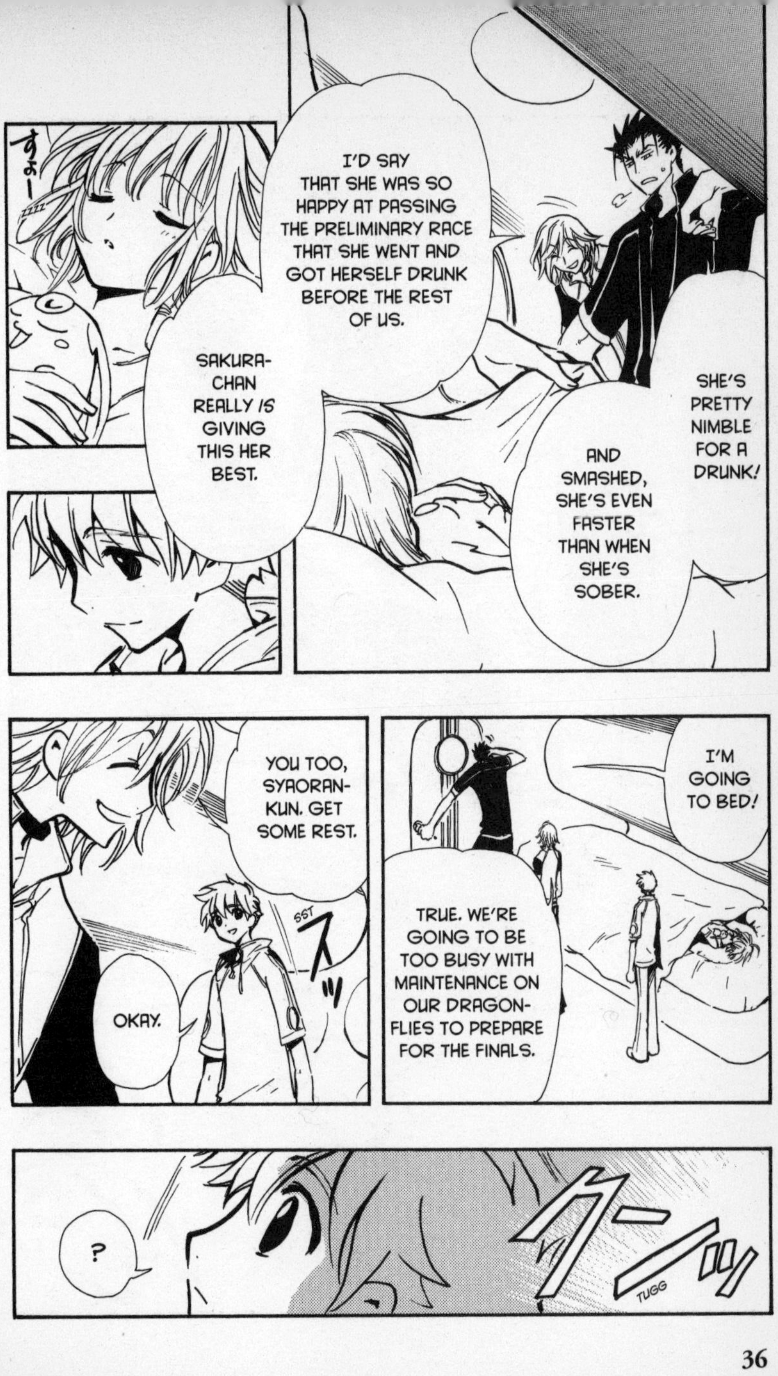
I'D SAY THAT SHE WAS SO HAPPY AT PASSING THE PRELIMINARY RACE THAT SHE WENT AND GOT HERSELF DRUNK BEFORE THE REST OF US.
SHE'S PRETTY NIMBLE FOR A DRUNK!
AND SMASHED, SHE'S EVEN FASTER THAN WHEN SHE'S SOBER.
すよー
SAKURA-CHAN REALLY *IS* GIVING THIS HER BEST.
I'M GOING TO BED!
TRUE. WE'RE GOING TO BE TOO BUSY WITH MAINTENANCE ON OUR DRAGON-FLIES TO PREPARE FOR THE FINALS.
YOU TOO, SYAORAN-KUN. GET SOME REST.
SST
OKAY.
TUGG
?

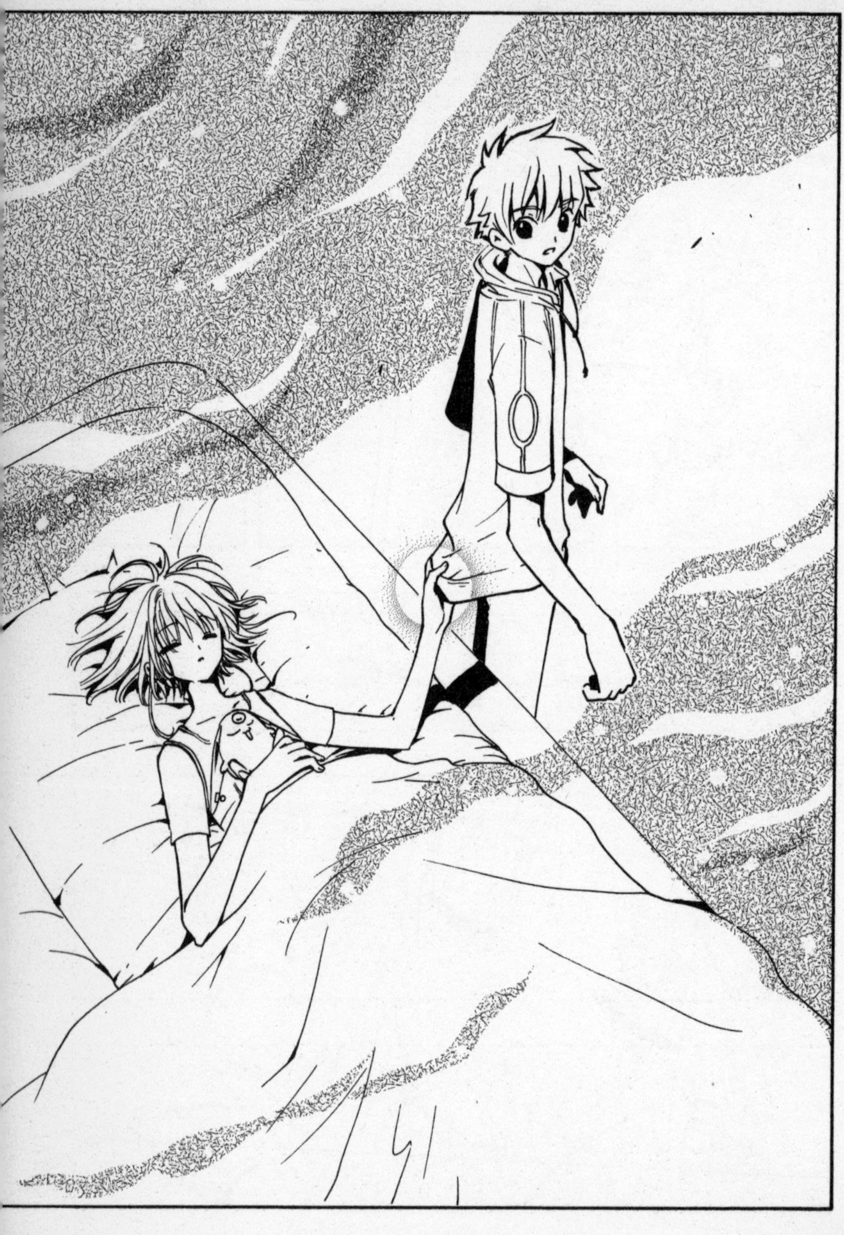

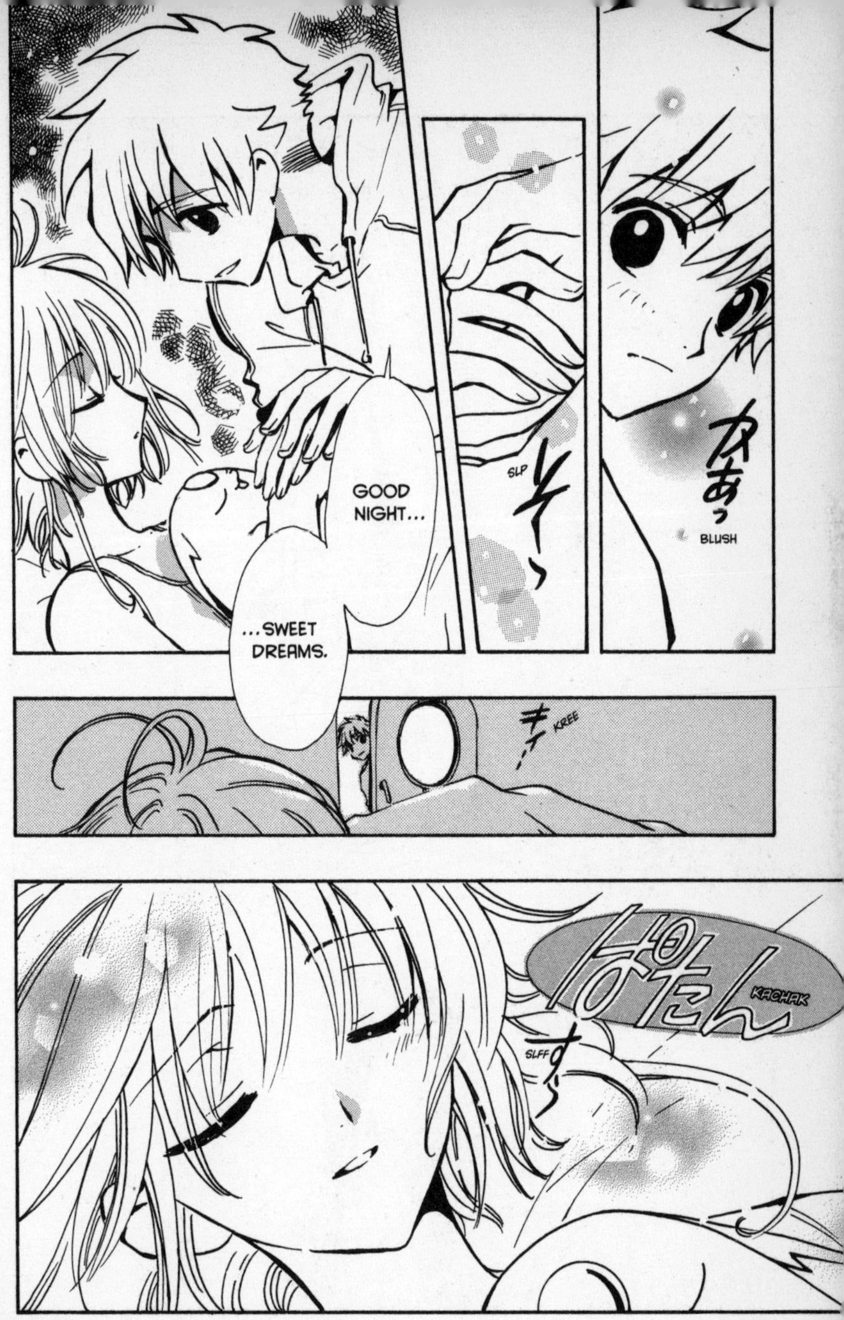
かあっ
BLUSH
SLP
GOOD NIGHT...
...SWEET DREAMS.
KREE
ぱたん
KACHAK
SLFF

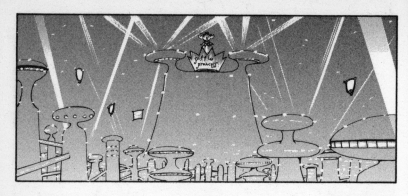

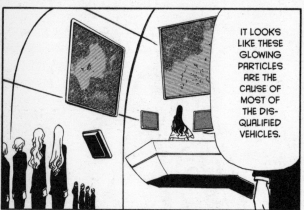

IT LOOKS LIKE THESE GLOWING PARTICLES ARE THE CAUSE OF MOST OF THE DISQUALIFIED VEHICLES.

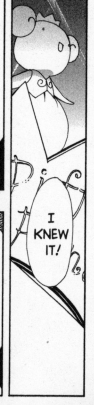

I KNEW IT!

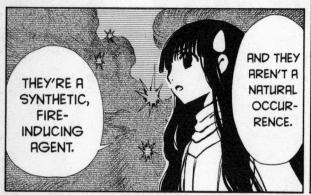

AND THEY AREN'T A NATURAL OCCURRENCE.

THEY'RE A SYNTHETIC, FIRE-INDUCING AGENT.

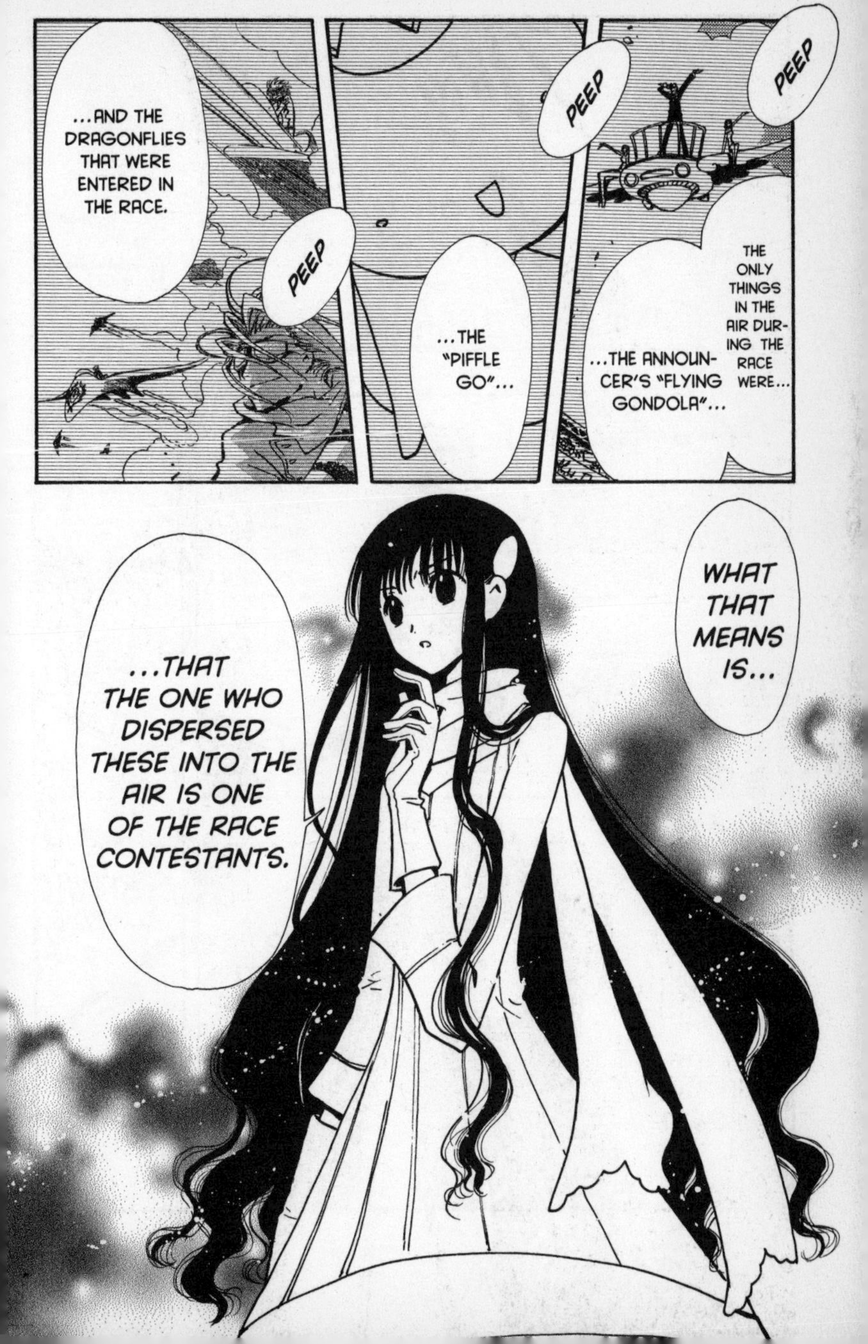

PEEP
PEEP
THE ONLY THINGS IN THE AIR DUR-ING THE RACE WERE...
...THE ANNOUN-CER'S "FLYING GONDOLA"...
...THE "PIFFLE GO"...
PEEP
...AND THE DRAGONFLIES THAT WERE ENTERED IN THE RACE.
WHAT THAT MEANS IS...
...THAT THE ONE WHO DISPERSED THESE INTO THE AIR IS ONE OF THE RACE CONTESTANTS.

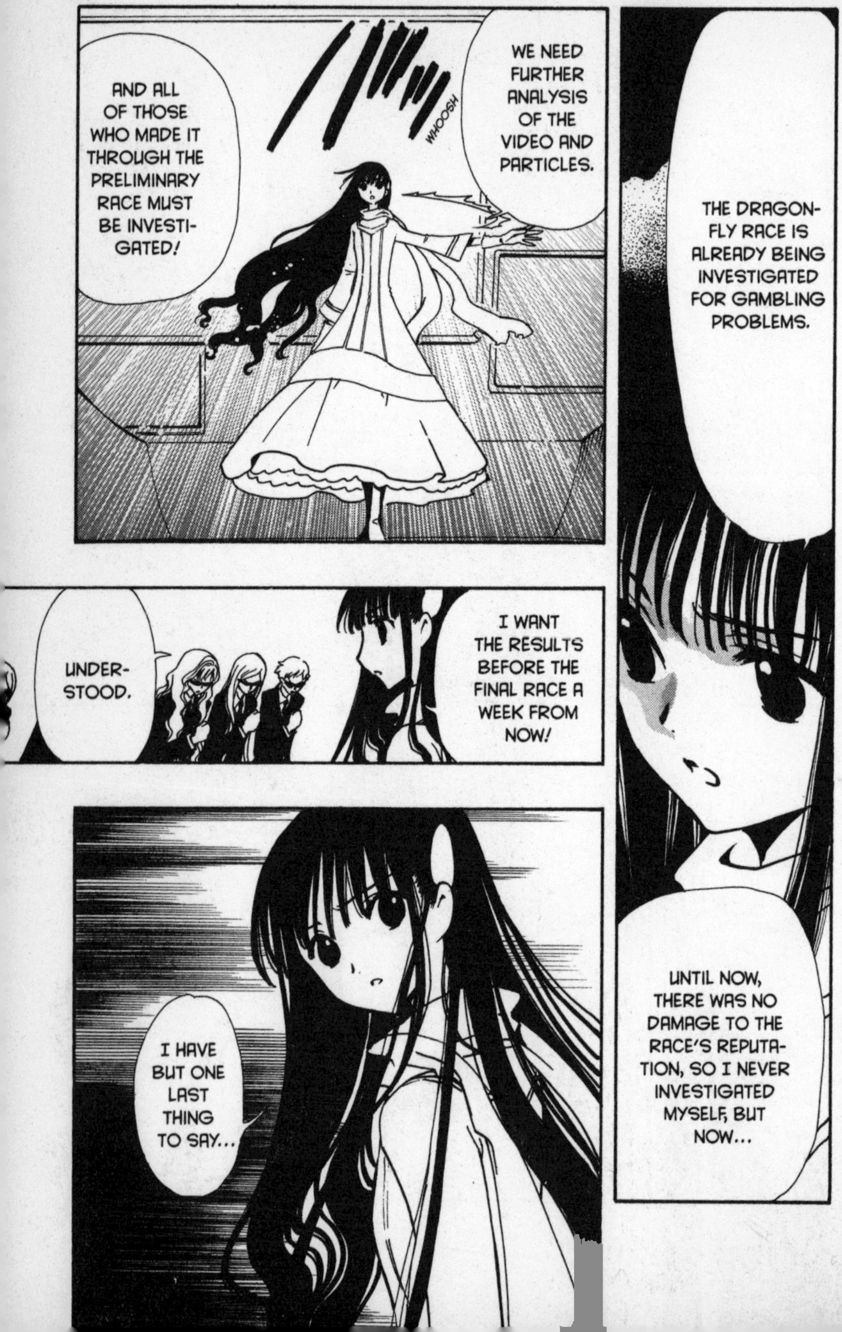
THE DRAGON-FLY RACE IS ALREADY BEING INVESTIGATED FOR GAMBLING PROBLEMS.
UNTIL NOW, THERE WAS NO DAMAGE TO THE RACE'S REPUTA-TION, SO I NEVER INVESTIGATED MYSELF, BUT NOW...
WE NEED FURTHER ANALYSIS OF THE VIDEO AND PARTICLES.
WHOOSH
AND ALL OF THOSE WHO MADE IT THROUGH THE PRELIMINARY RACE MUST BE INVESTI-GATED!
I WANT THE RESULTS BEFORE THE FINAL RACE A WEEK FROM NOW!
UNDER-STOOD.
I HAVE BUT ONE LAST THING TO SAY...

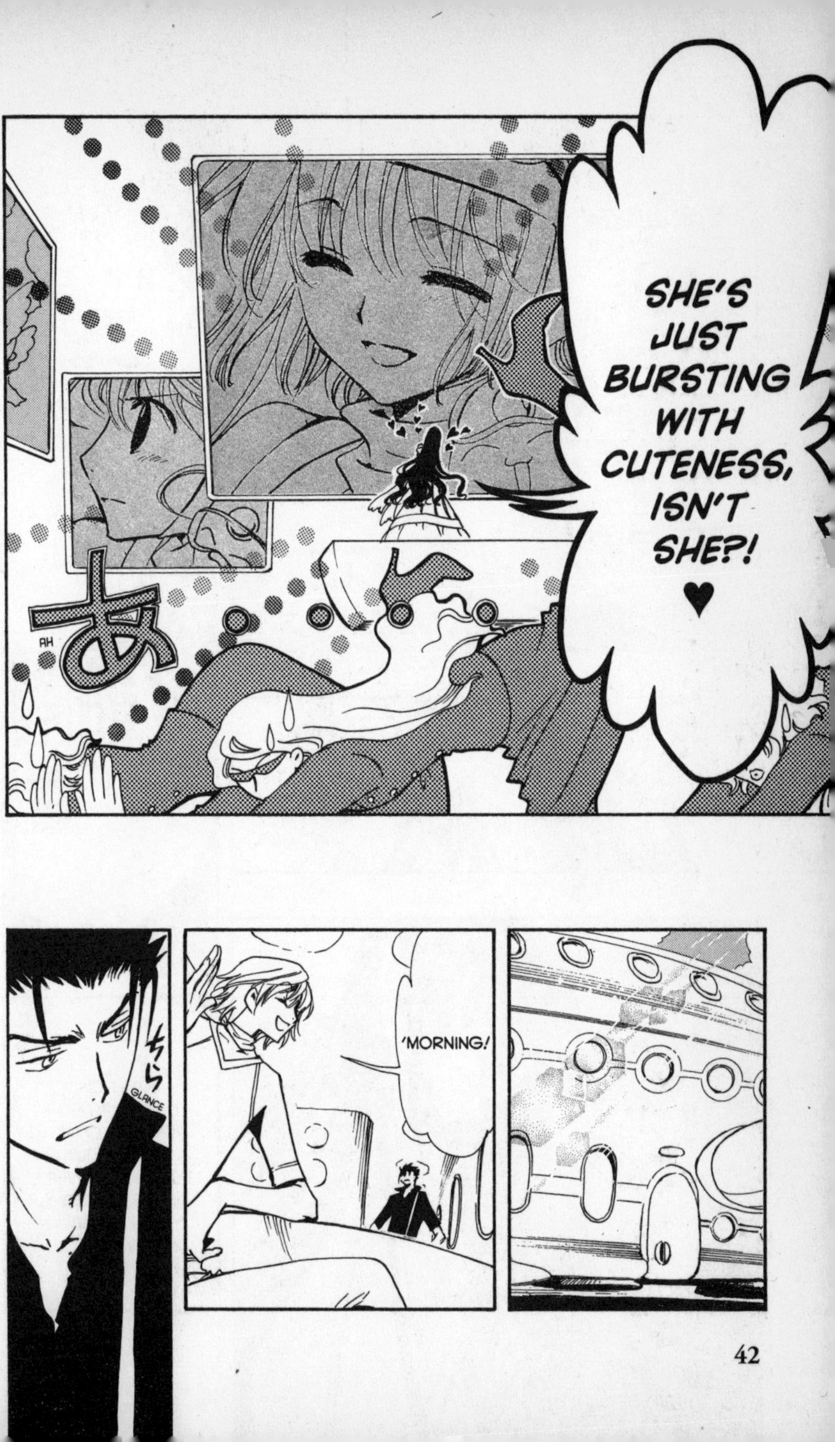
SHE'S JUST BURSTING WITH CUTENESS, ISN'T SHE?! ♥
あ
AH
'MORNING!
ちら
GLANCE

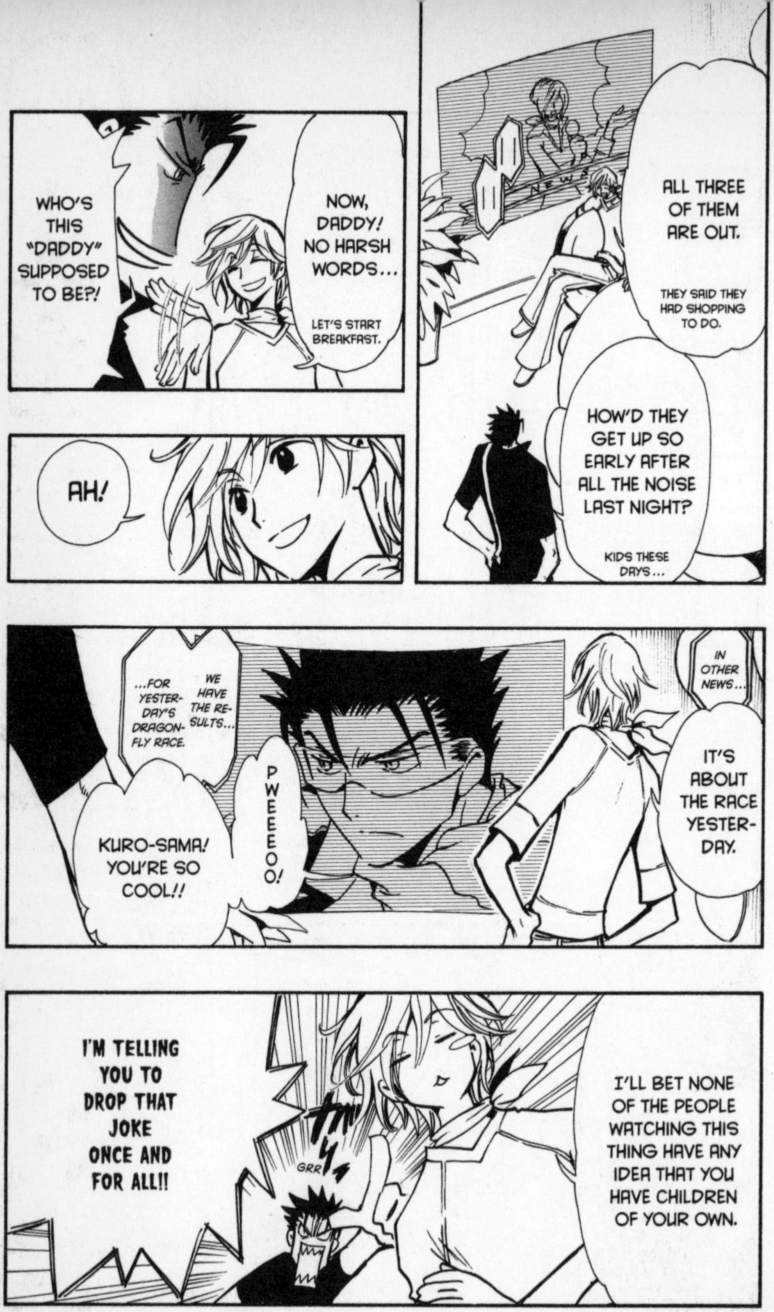
NEWS
ALL THREE OF THEM ARE OUT.
THEY SAID THEY HAD SHOPPING TO DO.
HOW'D THEY GET UP SO EARLY AFTER ALL THE NOISE LAST NIGHT?
KIDS THESE DAYS...
NOW, DADDY! NO HARSH WORDS...
LET'S START BREAKFAST.
WHO'S THIS "DADDY" SUPPOSED TO BE?!
AH!
IN OTHER NEWS...
IT'S ABOUT THE RACE YESTERDAY.
WE HAVE THE RESULTS...
...FOR YESTERDAY'S DRAGONFLY RACE.
PWEEEEOO!
KURO-SAMA! YOU'RE SO COOL!!
I'LL BET NONE OF THE PEOPLE WATCHING THIS THING HAVE ANY IDEA THAT YOU HAVE CHILDREN OF YOUR OWN.
GRR
I'M TELLING YOU TO DROP THAT JOKE ONCE AND FOR ALL!!

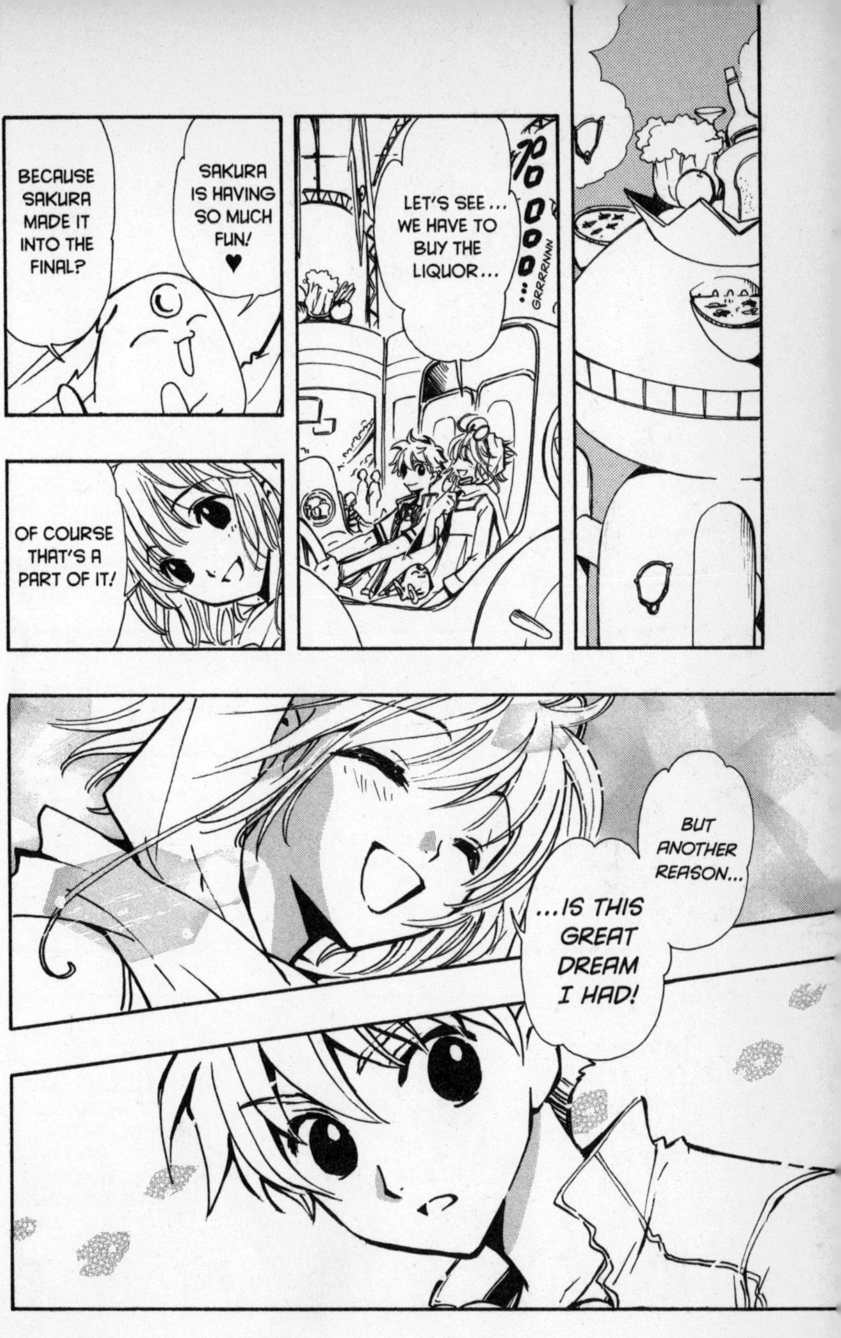
GRRRRNNN
LET'S SEE... WE HAVE TO BUY THE LIQUOR...
SAKURA IS HAVING SO MUCH FUN! ♥
BECAUSE SAKURA MADE IT INTO THE FINAL?
OF COURSE THAT'S A PART OF IT!
BUT ANOTHER REASON...
...IS THIS GREAT DREAM I HAD!

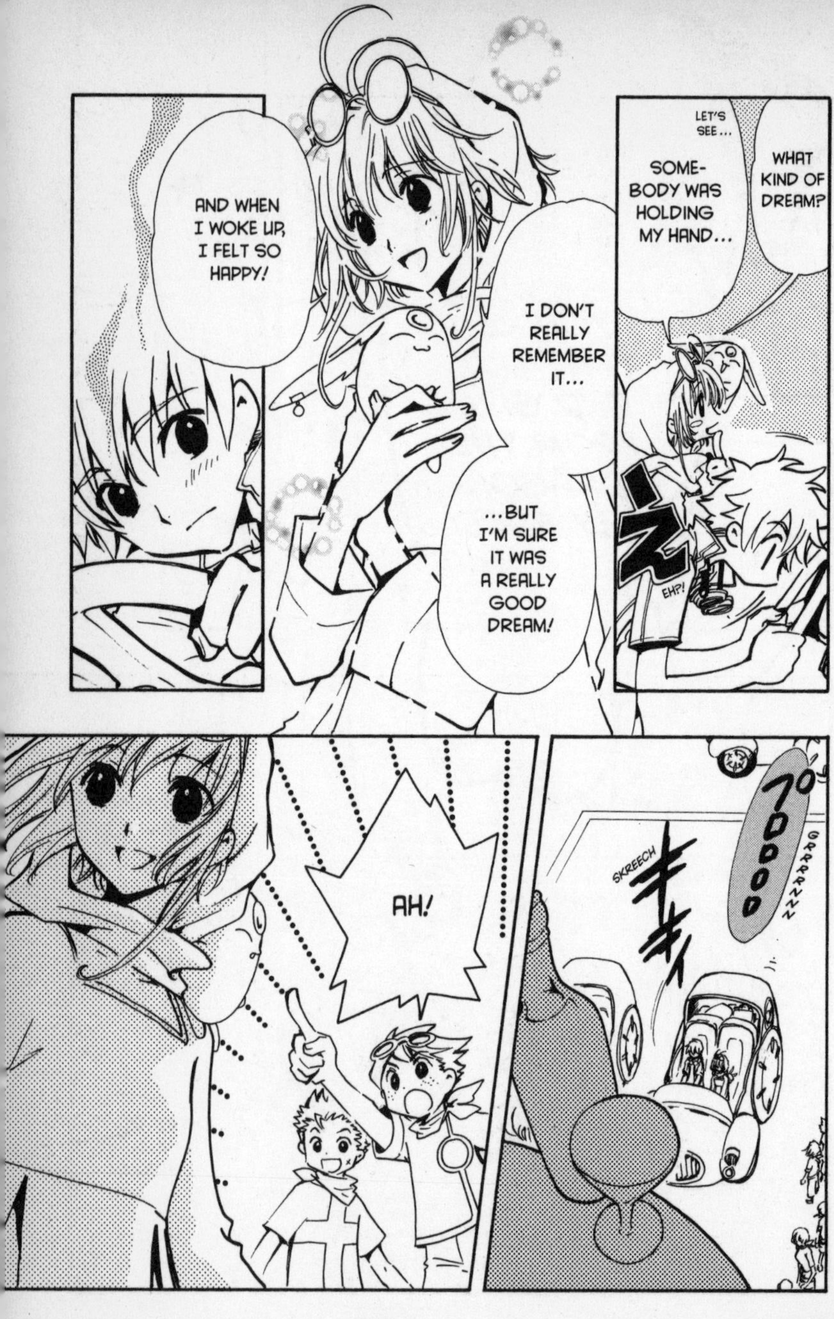
WHAT KIND OF DREAM?
LET'S SEE...
SOME-BODY WAS HOLDING MY HAND...
EHP!
I DON'T REALLY REMEMBER IT...
...BUT I'M SURE IT WAS A REALLY GOOD DREAM!
AND WHEN I WOKE UP, I FELT SO HAPPY!
GRRRRNNN
SKREECH
AH!

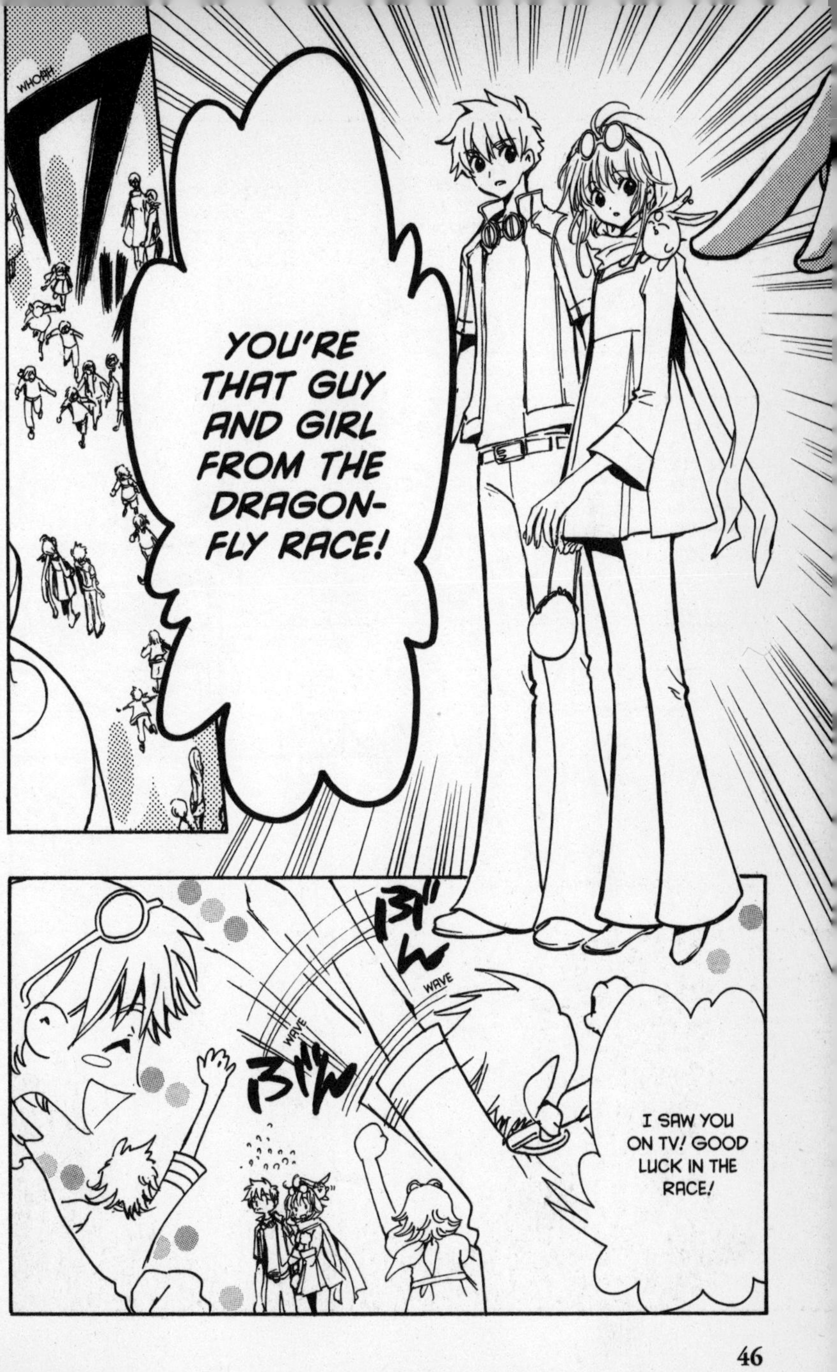
WHOAH
YOU'RE THAT GUY AND GIRL FROM THE DRAGON-FLY RACE!
I SAW YOU ON TV! GOOD LUCK IN THE RACE!
WAVE
WAVE

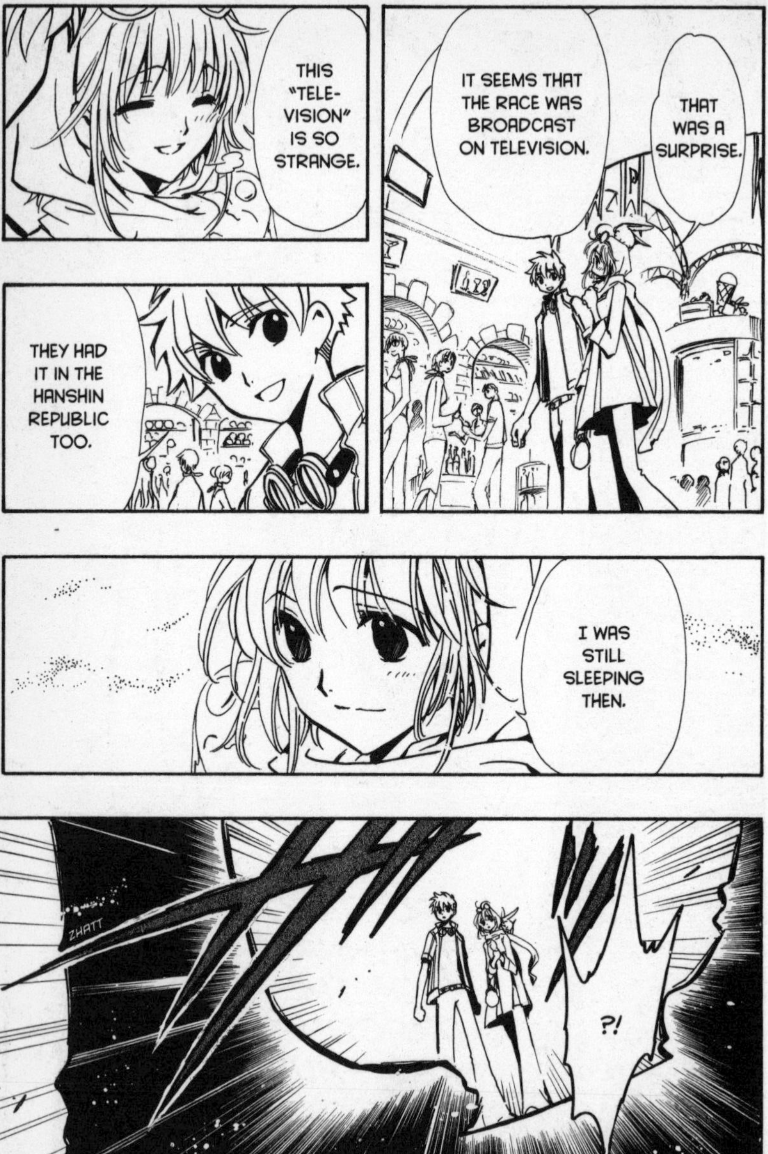
THAT WAS A SURPRISE.
IT SEEMS THAT THE RACE WAS BROADCAST ON TELEVISION.
THIS "TELE-VISION" IS SO STRANGE.
THEY HAD IT IN THE HANSHIN REPUBLIC TOO.
I WAS STILL SLEEPING THEN.
ZHATT
?!

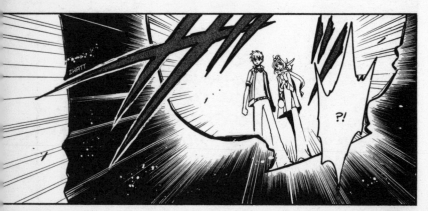

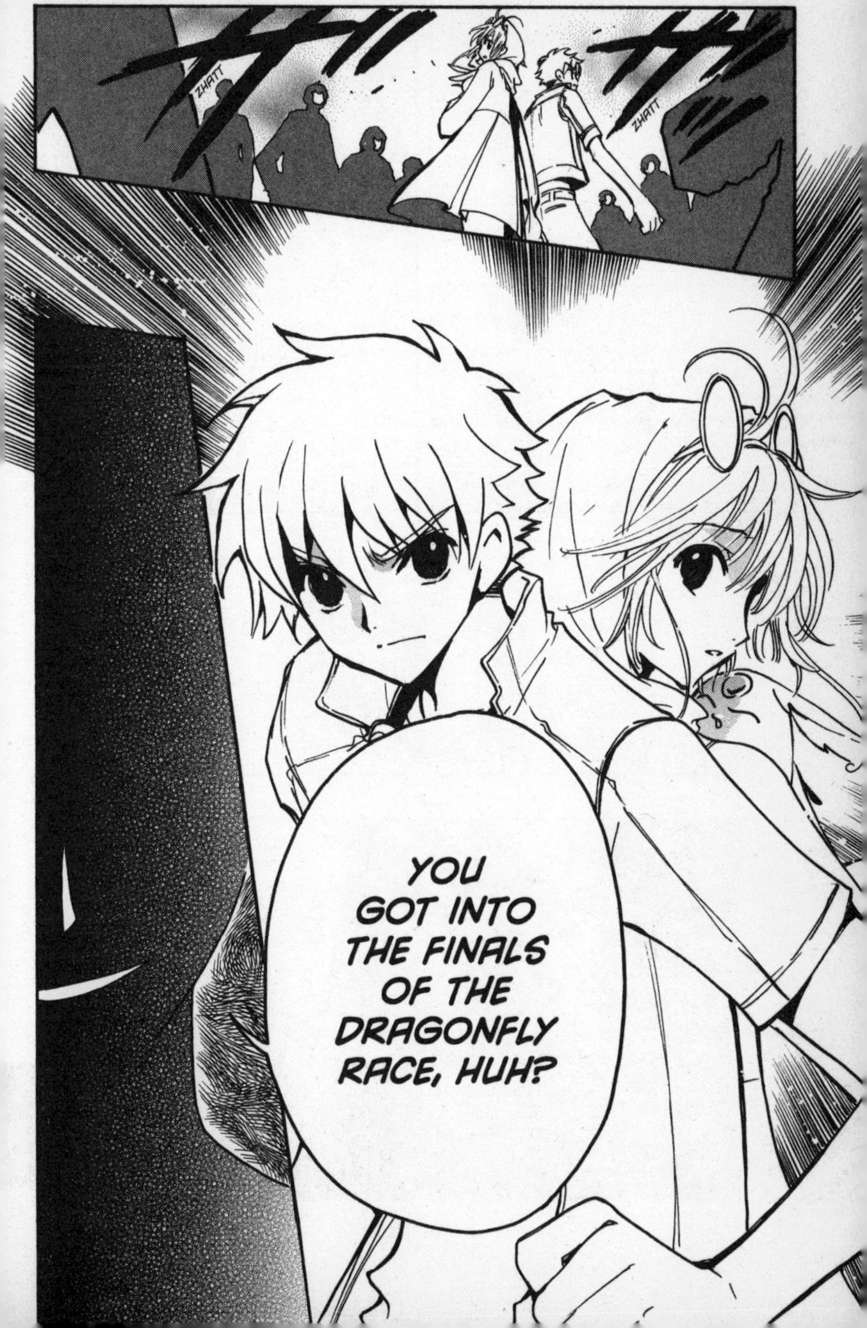
ZHATT
ZHATT
YOU GOT INTO THE FINALS OF THE DRAGONFLY RACE, HUH?

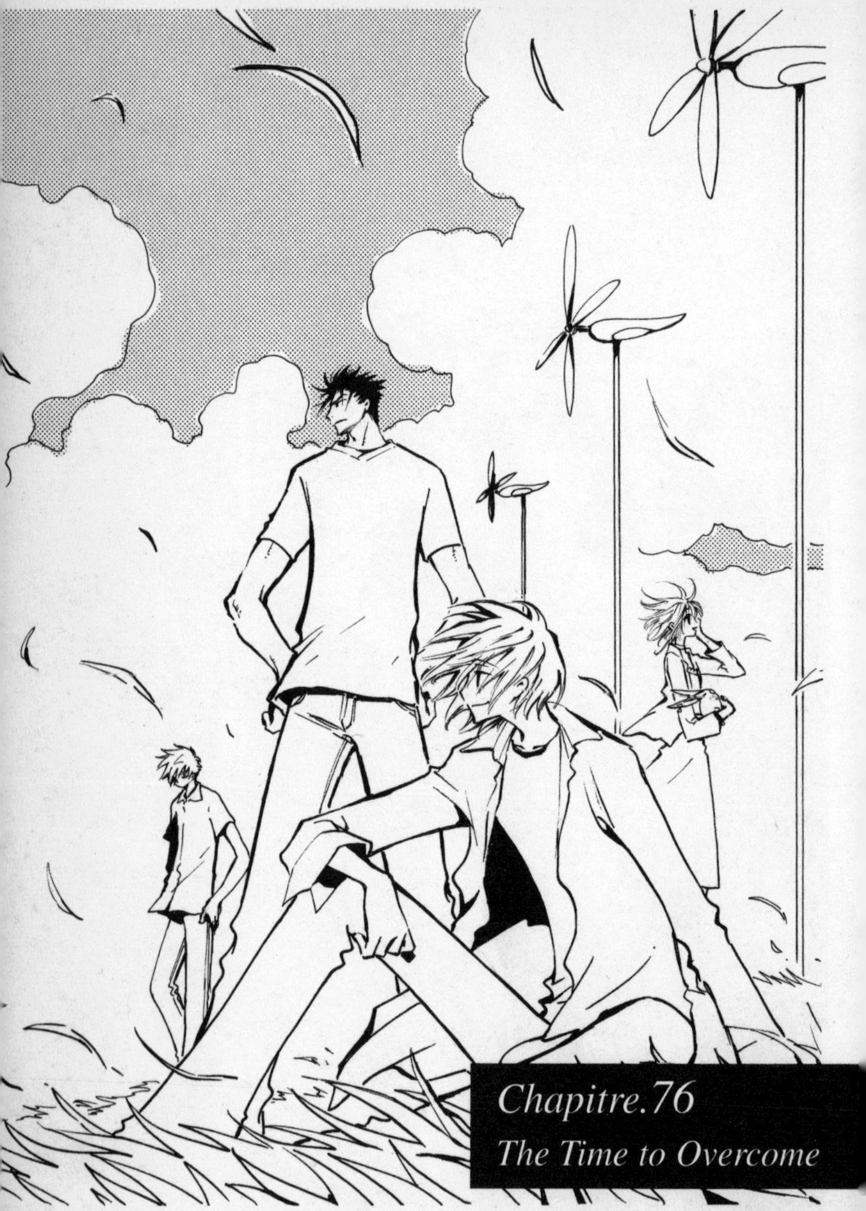

Chapitre.76
The Time to Overcome

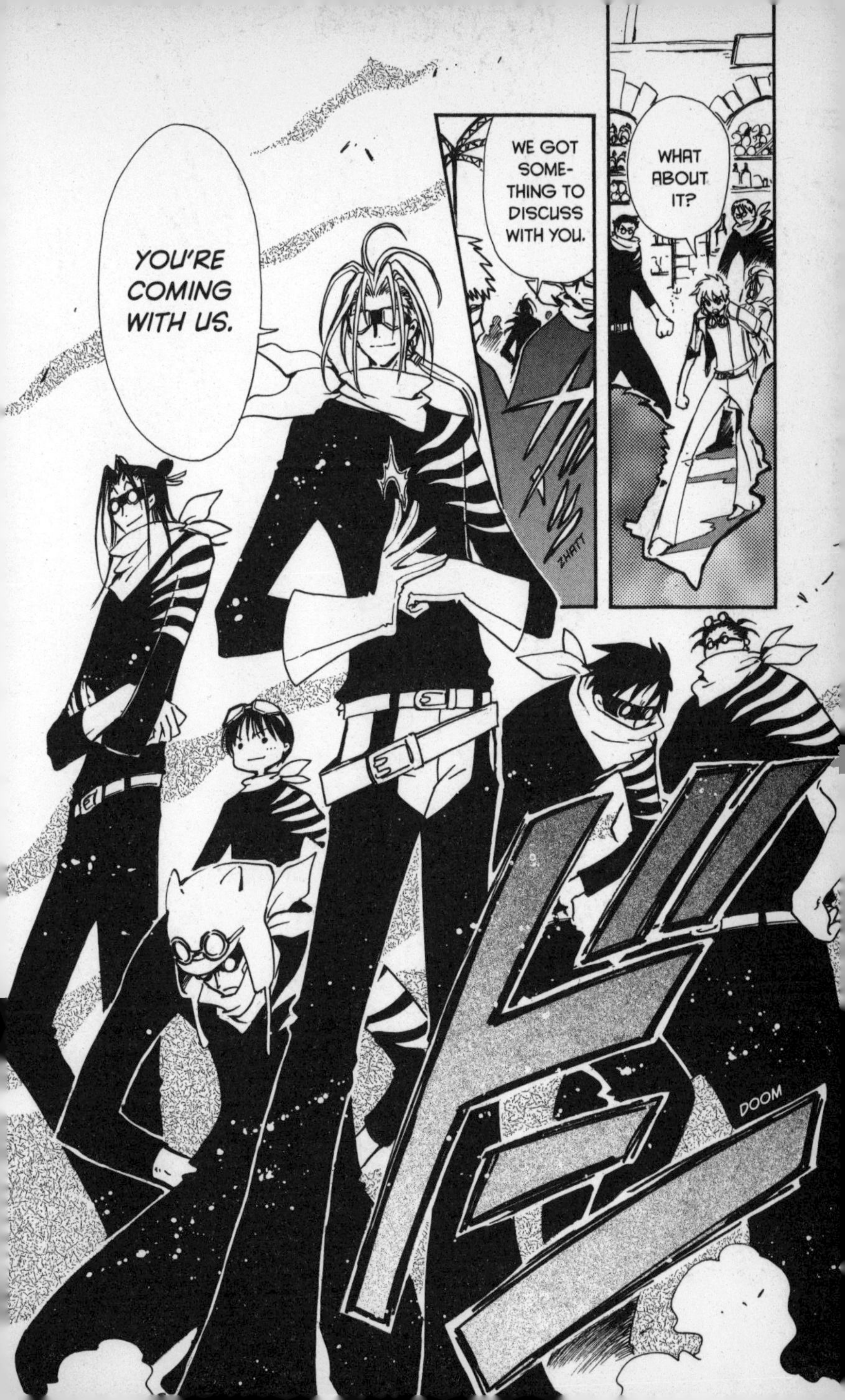
WHAT ABOUT IT?
WE GOT SOME-THING TO DISCUSS WITH YOU.
ZHATT
YOU'RE COMING WITH US.
DOOM

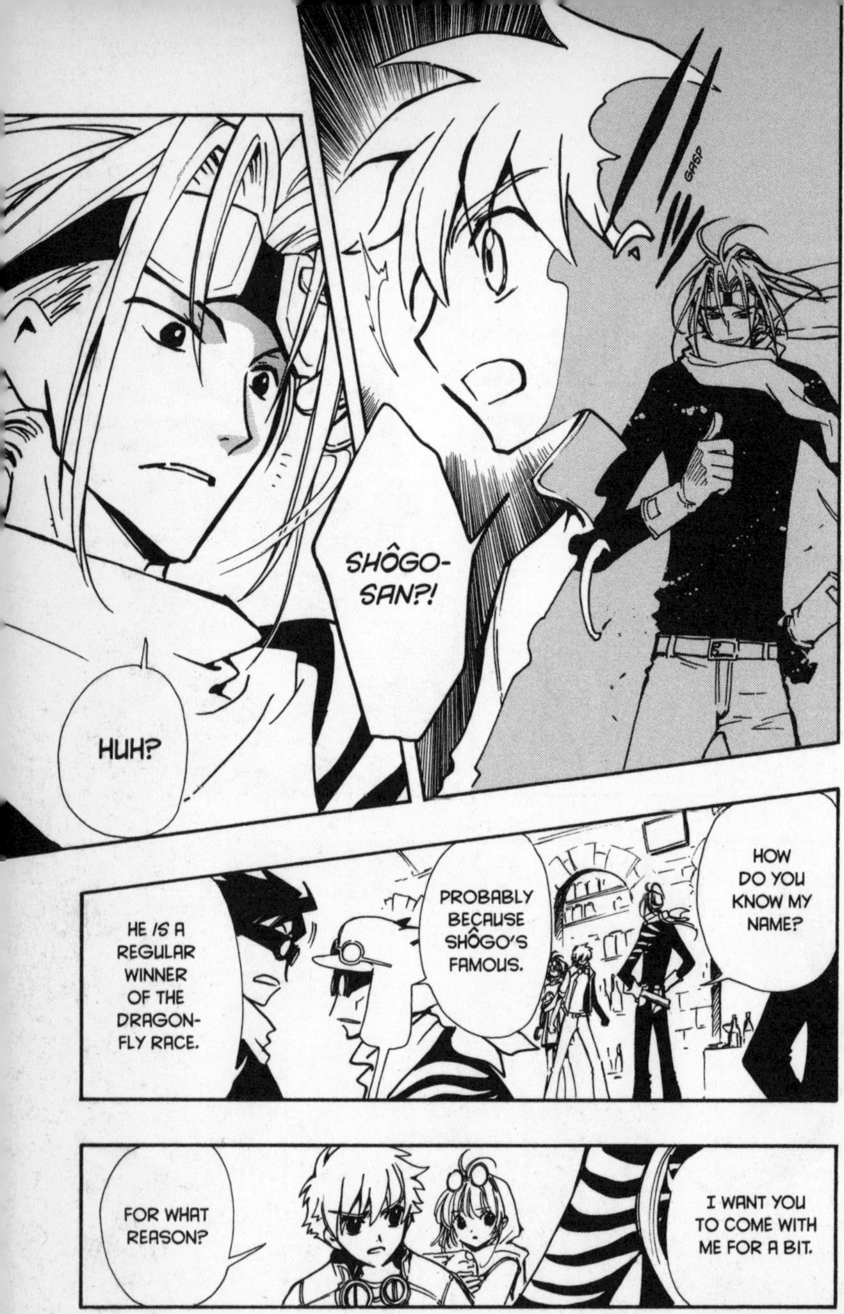
GASP
SHÔGO-SAN?!
HUH?
HOW DO YOU KNOW MY NAME?
PROBABLY BECAUSE SHÔGO'S FAMOUS.
HE IS A REGULAR WINNER OF THE DRAGON-FLY RACE.
I WANT YOU TO COME WITH ME FOR A BIT.
FOR WHAT REASON?

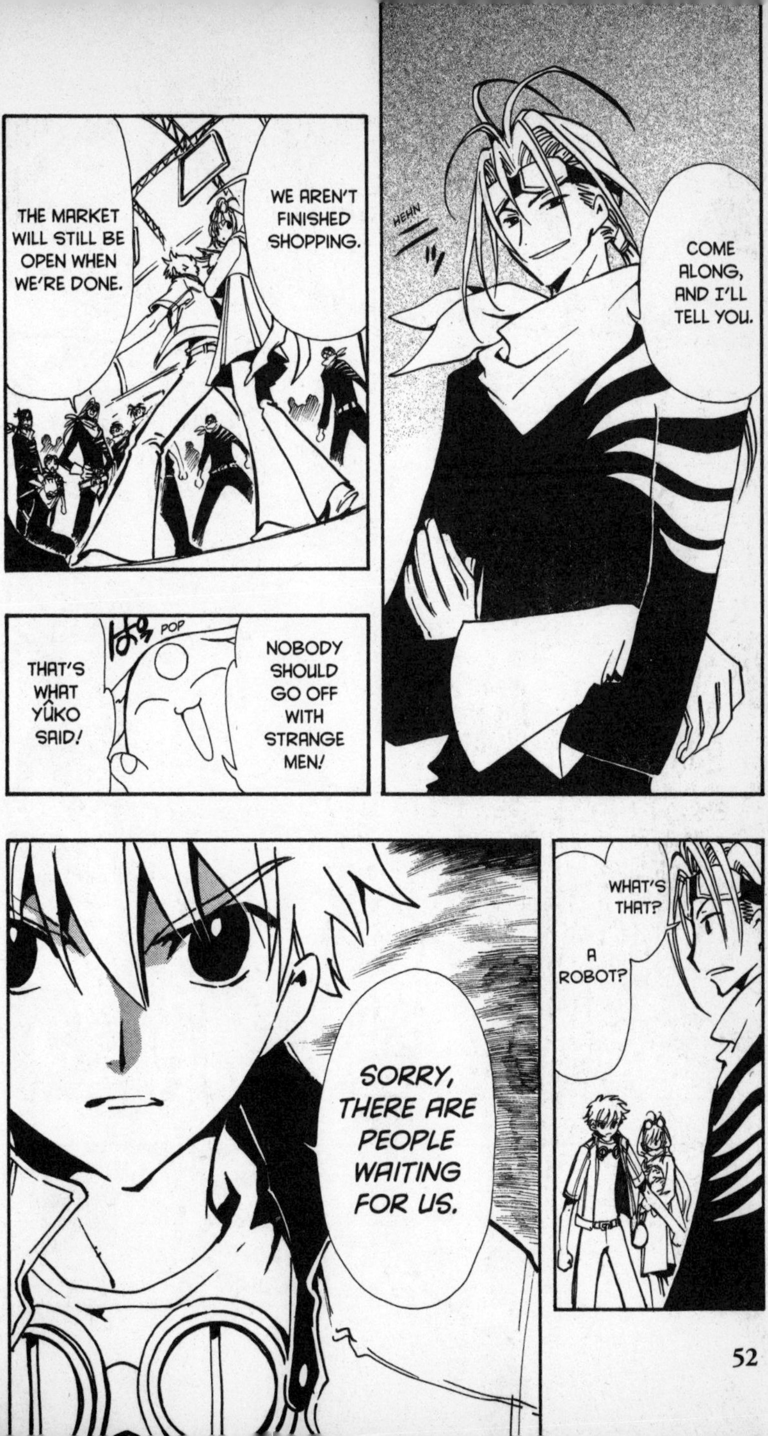
HEHN
COME ALONG, AND I'LL TELL YOU.
WE AREN'T FINISHED SHOPPING.
THE MARKET WILL STILL BE OPEN WHEN WE'RE DONE.
POP
NOBODY SHOULD GO OFF WITH STRANGE MEN!
THAT'S WHAT YÛKO SAID!
WHAT'S THAT?
A ROBOT?
SORRY, THERE ARE PEOPLE WAITING FOR US.

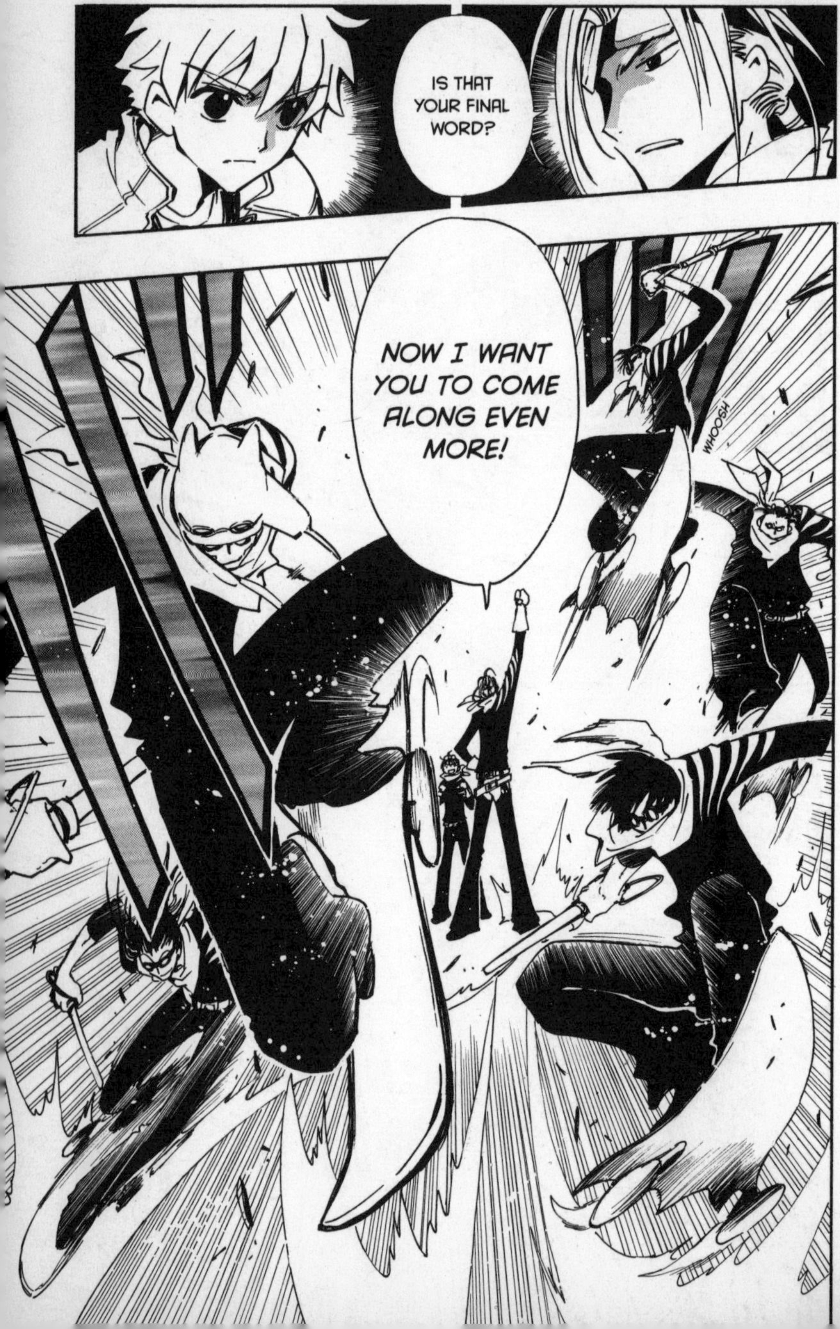
IS THAT YOUR FINAL WORD?
NOW I WANT YOU TO COME ALONG EVEN MORE!
WHOOSH

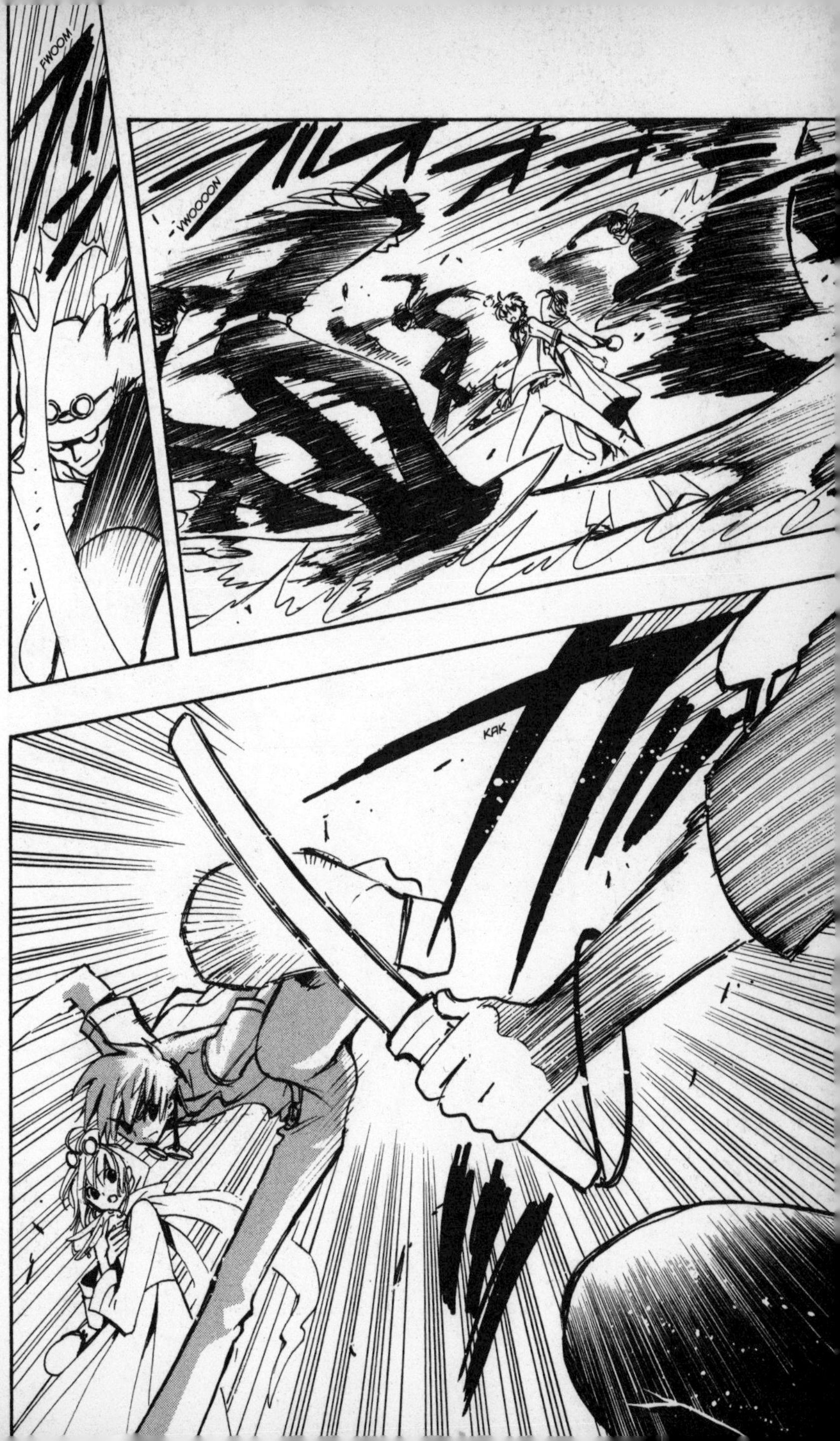
VWOOOON
FWOOM
KAK

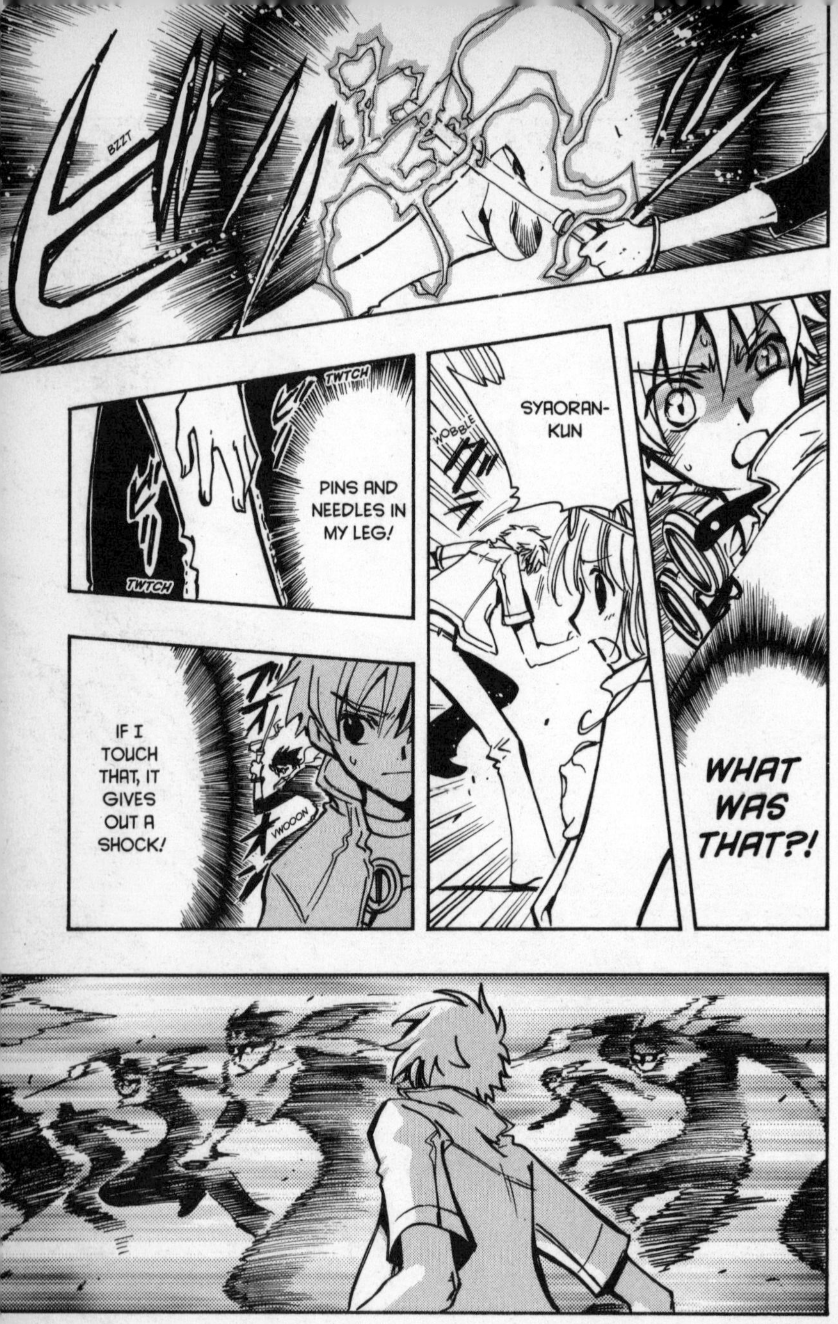
BZZT
WHAT WAS THAT?!
SYAORAN-KUN
WOBBLE
TWTCH
PINS AND NEEDLES IN MY LEG!
TWTCH
IF I TOUCH THAT, IT GIVES OUT A SHOCK!
VWOOON

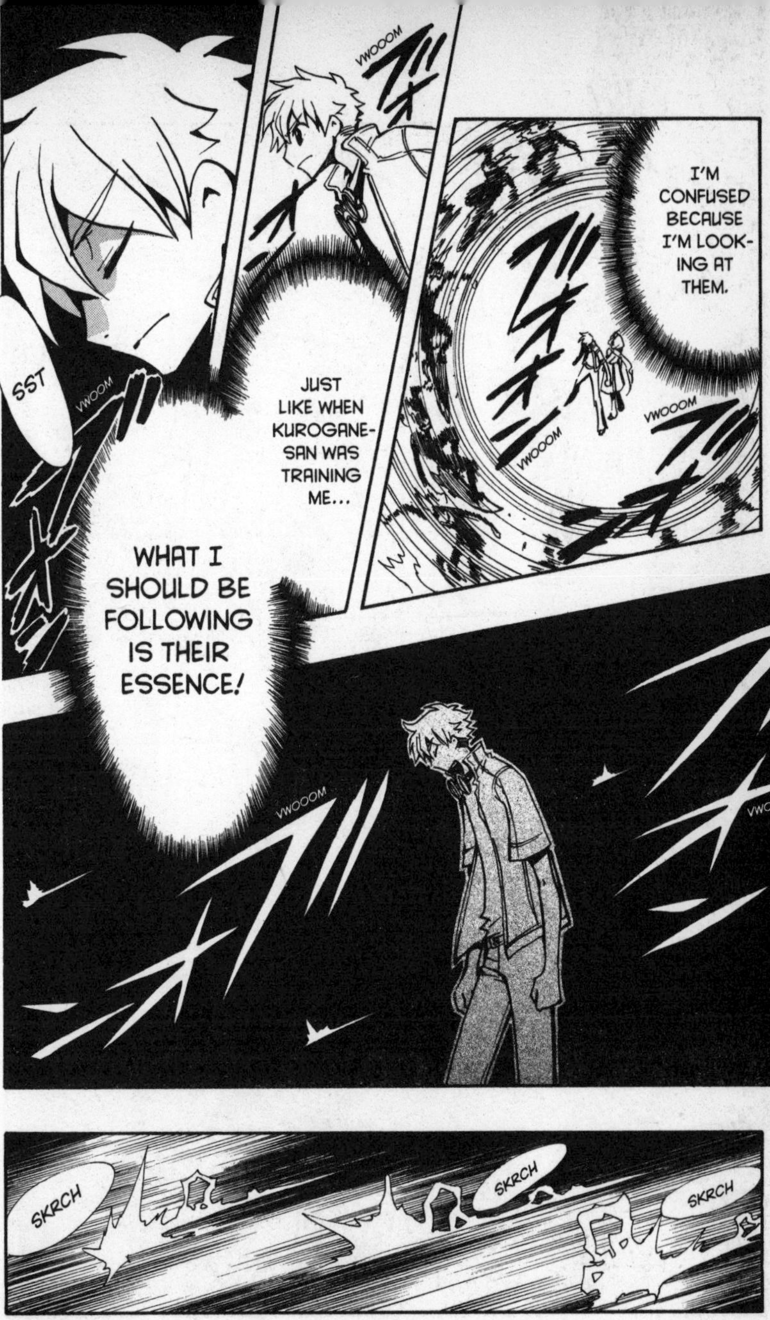
I'M CONFUSED BECAUSE I'M LOOKING AT THEM.
VWOOOM
VWOOOM
VWOOOM
JUST LIKE WHEN KUROGANE-SAN WAS TRAINING ME...
SST
VWOOM
WHAT I SHOULD BE FOLLOWING IS THEIR ESSENCE!
VWOOOM
VWOOOM
SKRCH
SKRCH
SKRCH

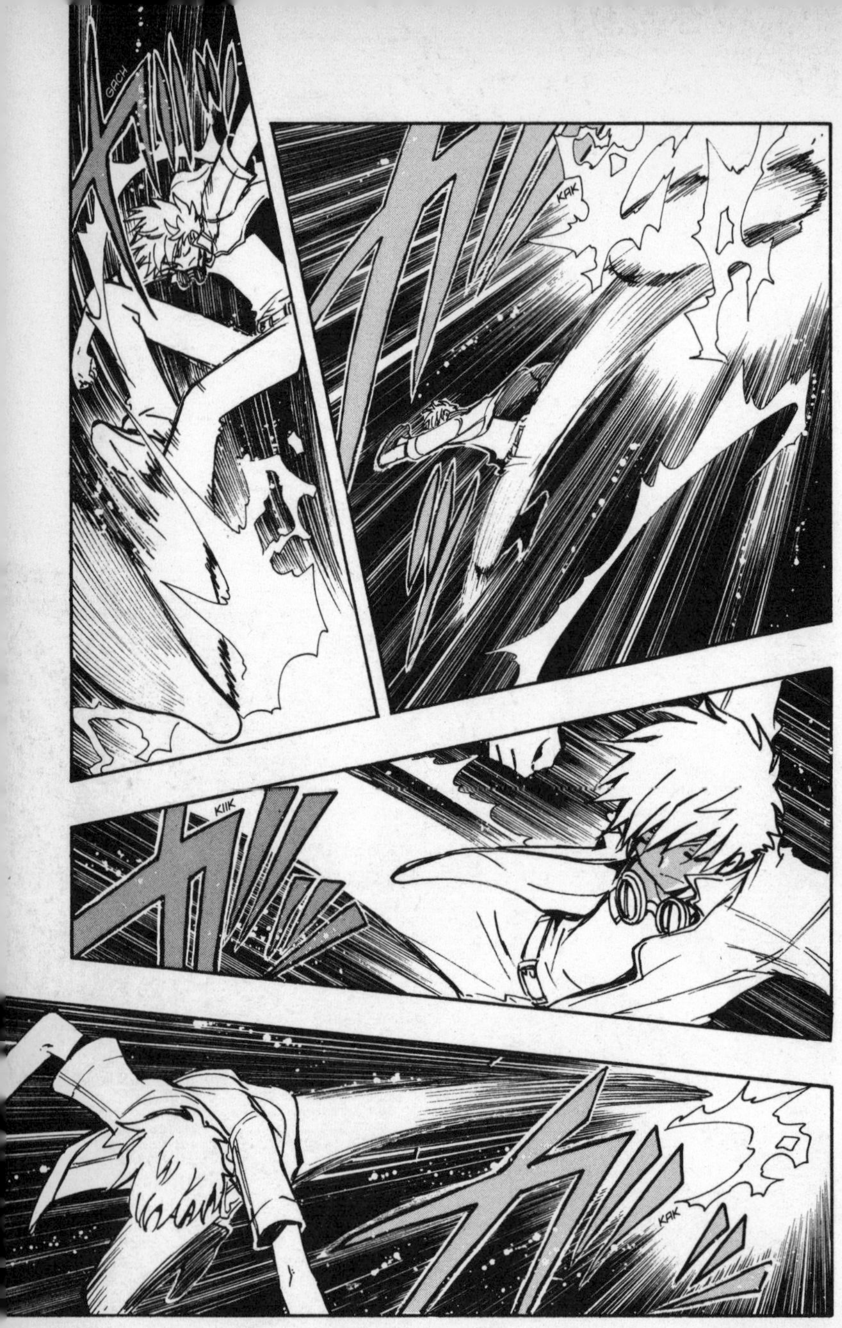
KAK
GACH
KIIK
KAK

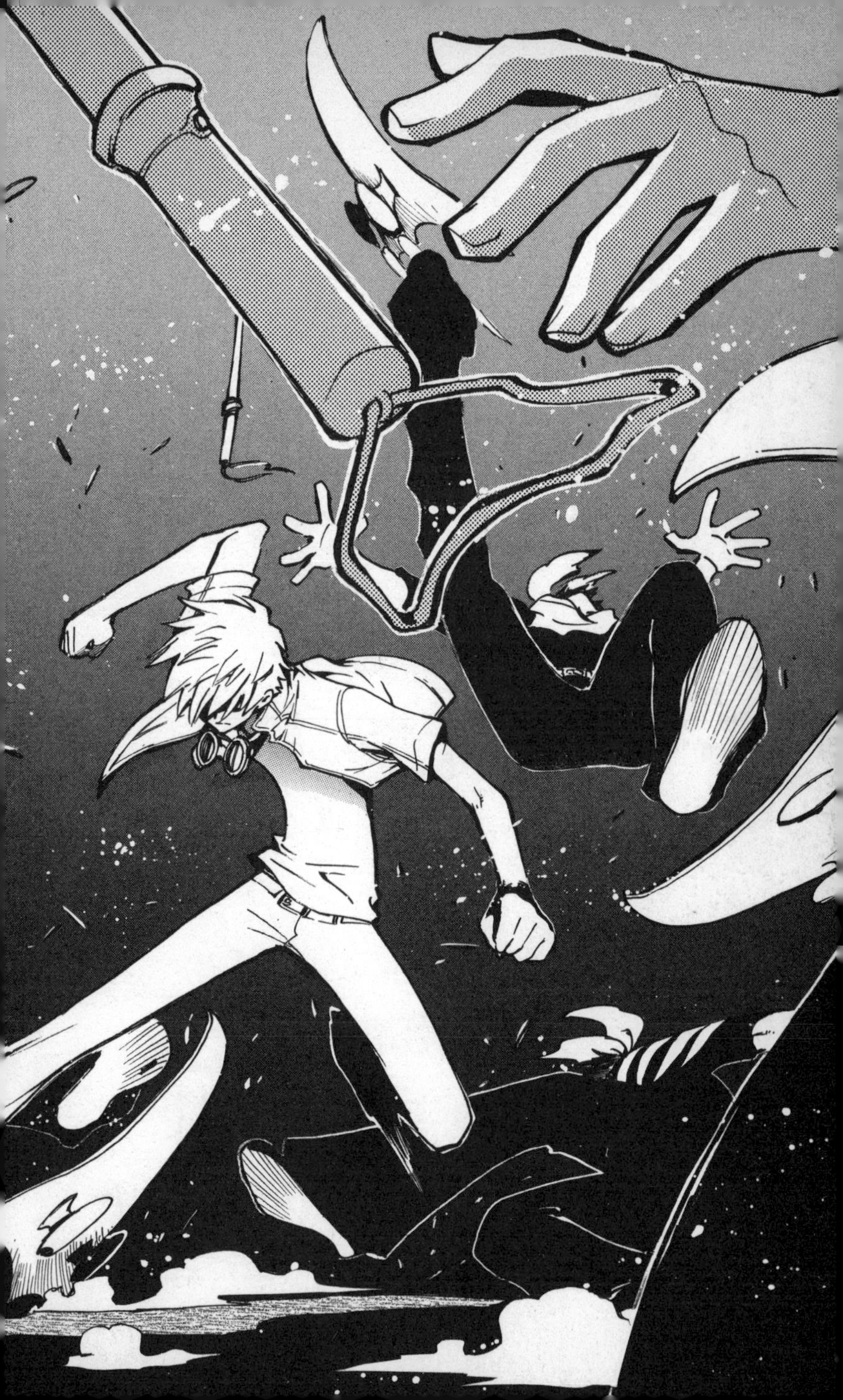

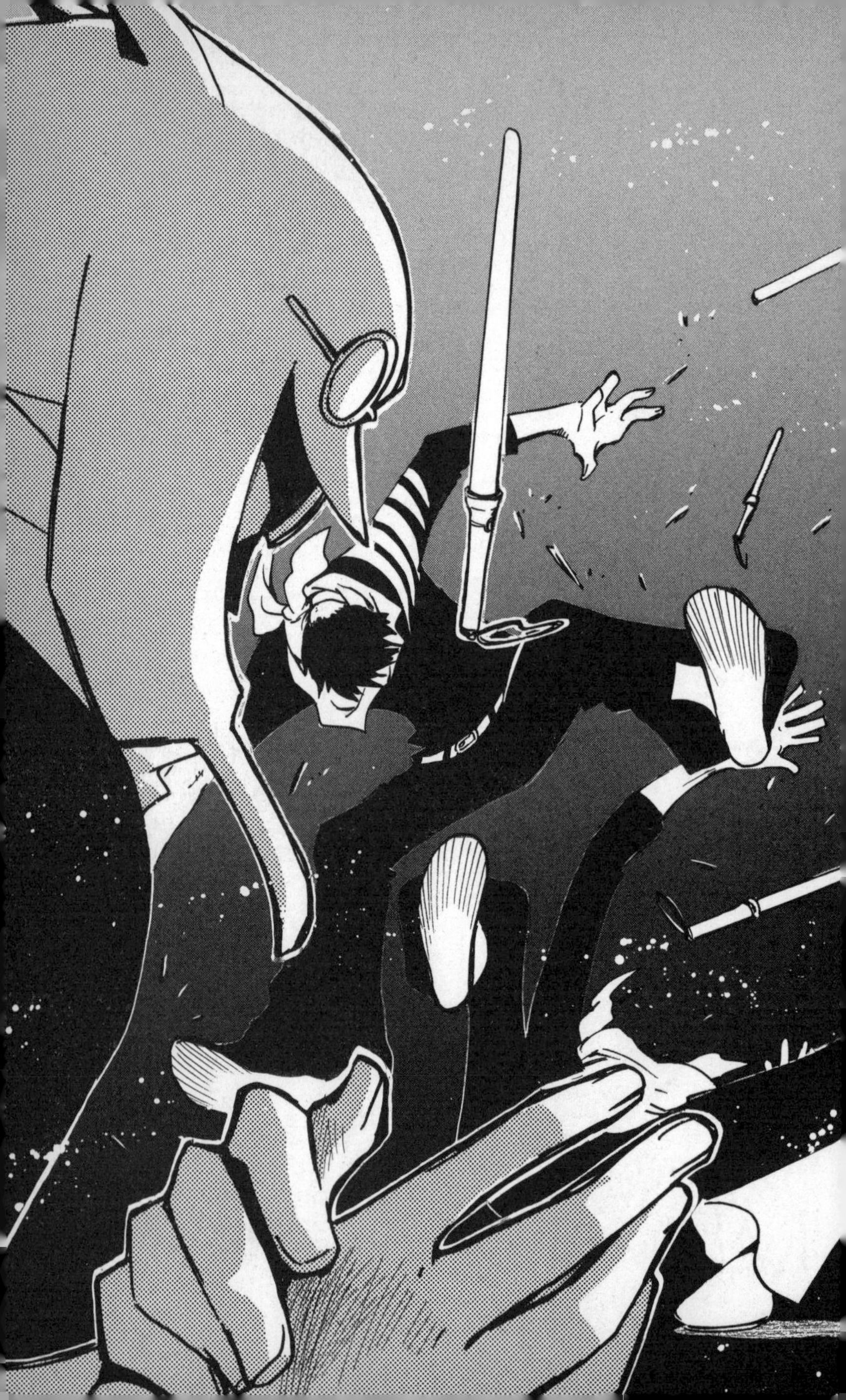

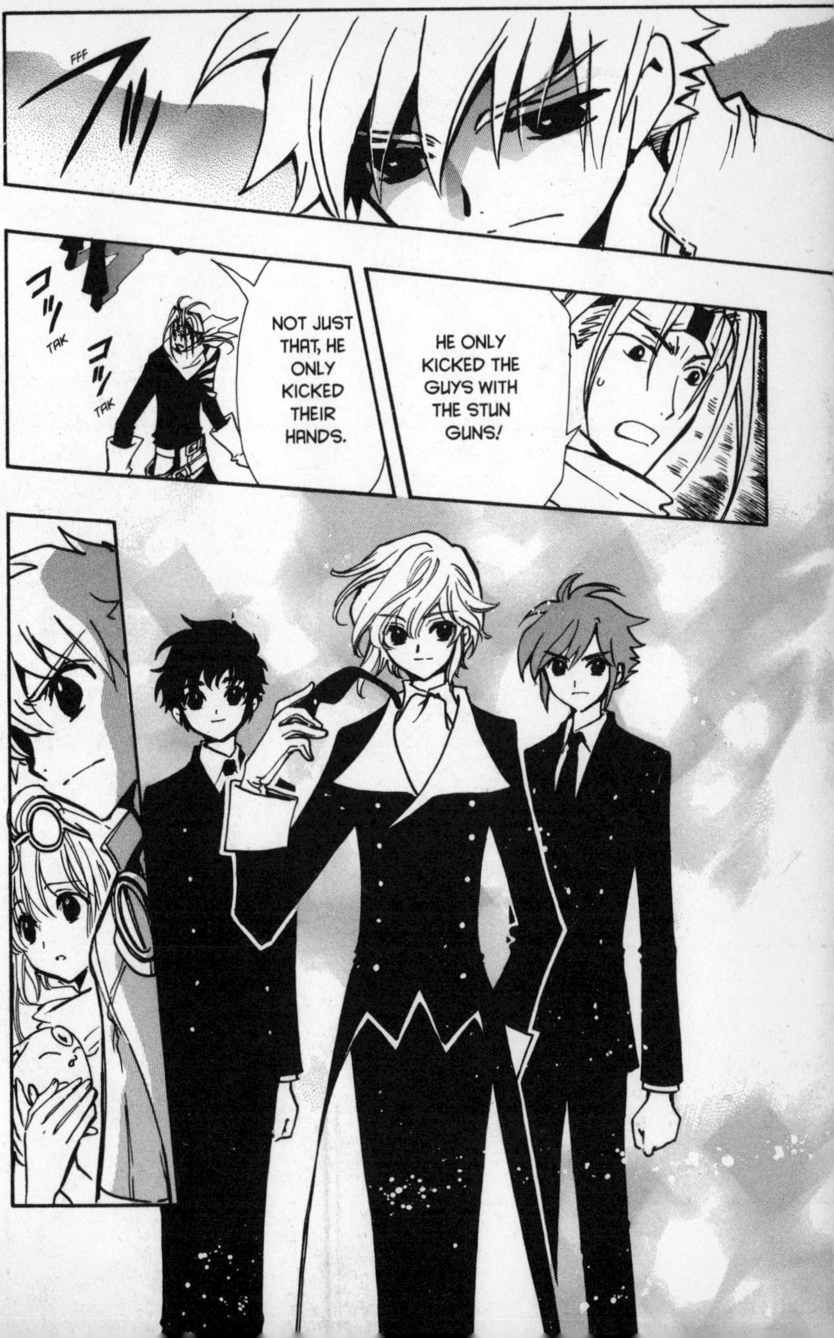

FFF
HE ONLY KICKED THE GUYS WITH THE STUN GUNS!
NOT JUST THAT, HE ONLY KICKED THEIR HANDS.
TAK
TAK

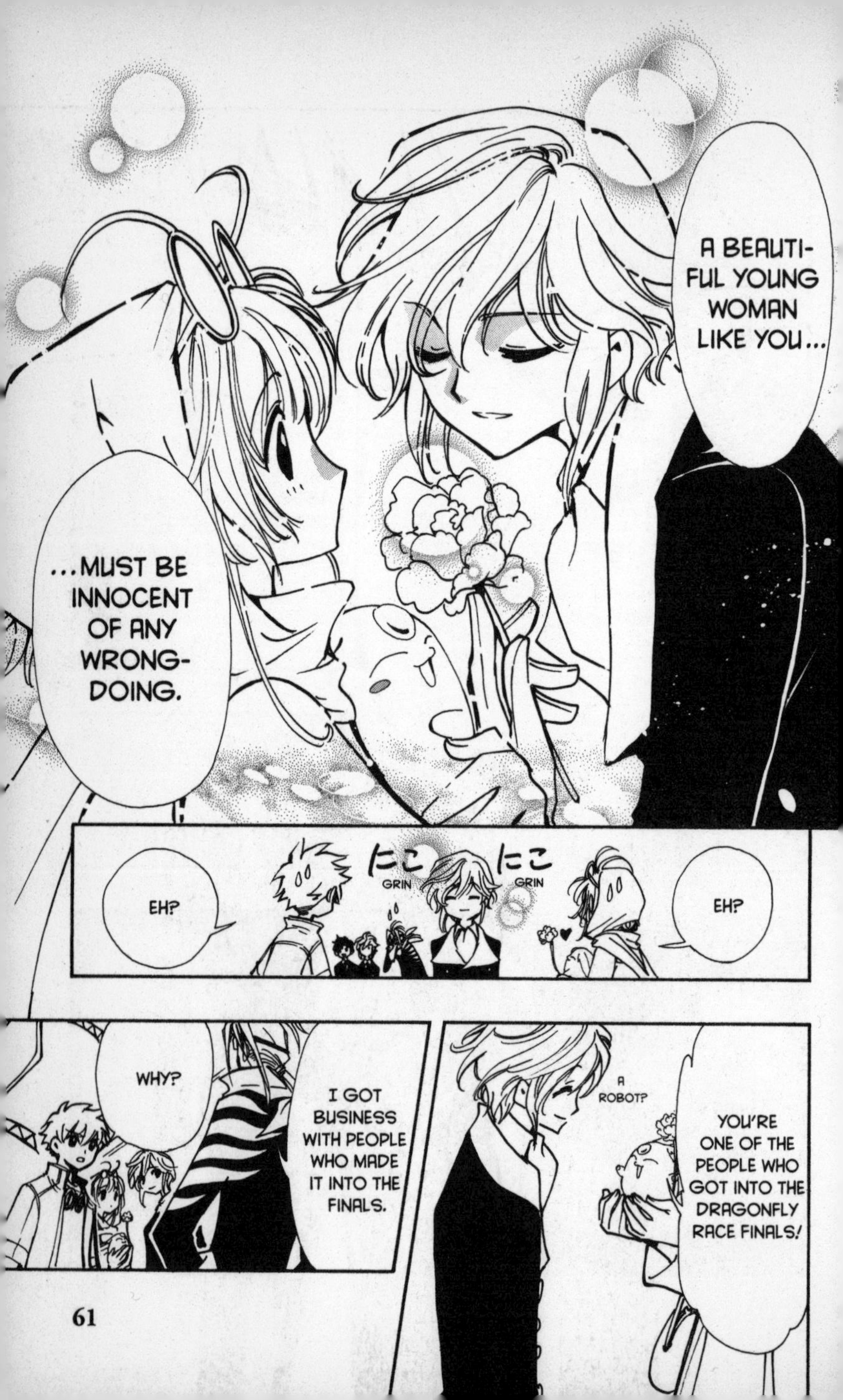
A BEAUTI-FUL YOUNG WOMAN LIKE YOU...
...MUST BE INNOCENT OF ANY WRONG-DOING.
EH?
にこ
GRIN
にこ
GRIN
EH?
YOU'RE ONE OF THE PEOPLE WHO GOT INTO THE DRAGONFLY RACE FINALS!
A ROBOT?
I GOT BUSINESS WITH PEOPLE WHO MADE IT INTO THE FINALS.
WHY?

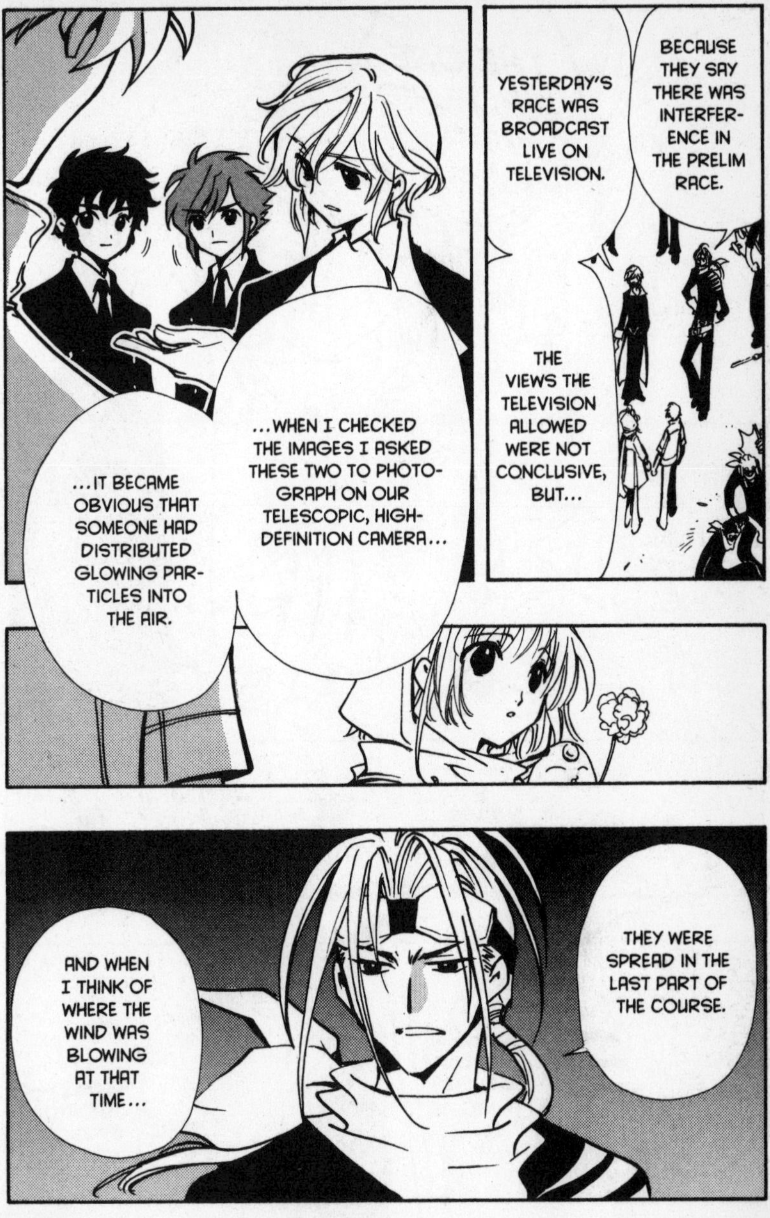
BECAUSE THEY SAY THERE WAS INTERFER-ENCE IN THE PRELIM RACE.
YESTERDAY'S RACE WAS BROADCAST LIVE ON TELEVISION.
THE VIEWS THE TELEVISION ALLOWED WERE NOT CONCLUSIVE, BUT...
...WHEN I CHECKED THE IMAGES I ASKED THESE TWO TO PHOTO-GRAPH ON OUR TELESCOPIC, HIGH-DEFINITION CAMERA...
...IT BECAME OBVIOUS THAT SOMEONE HAD DISTRIBUTED GLOWING PAR-TICLES INTO THE AIR.
THEY WERE SPREAD IN THE LAST PART OF THE COURSE.
AND WHEN I THINK OF WHERE THE WIND WAS BLOWING AT THAT TIME...

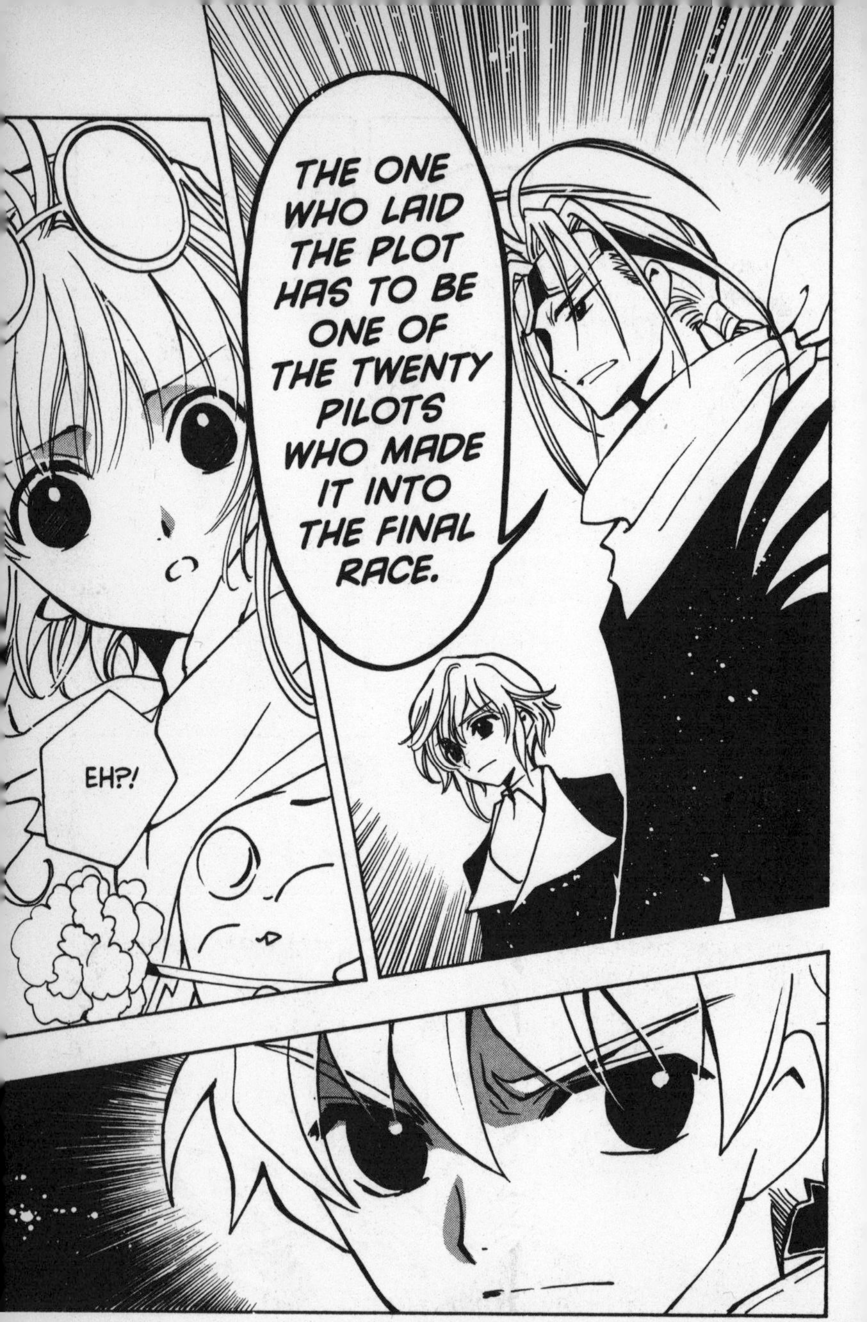
THE ONE WHO LAID THE PLOT HAS TO BE ONE OF THE TWENTY PILOTS WHO MADE IT INTO THE FINAL RACE.
EH?!

ツバサ

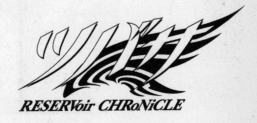

RESERVoir CHRoNiCLE

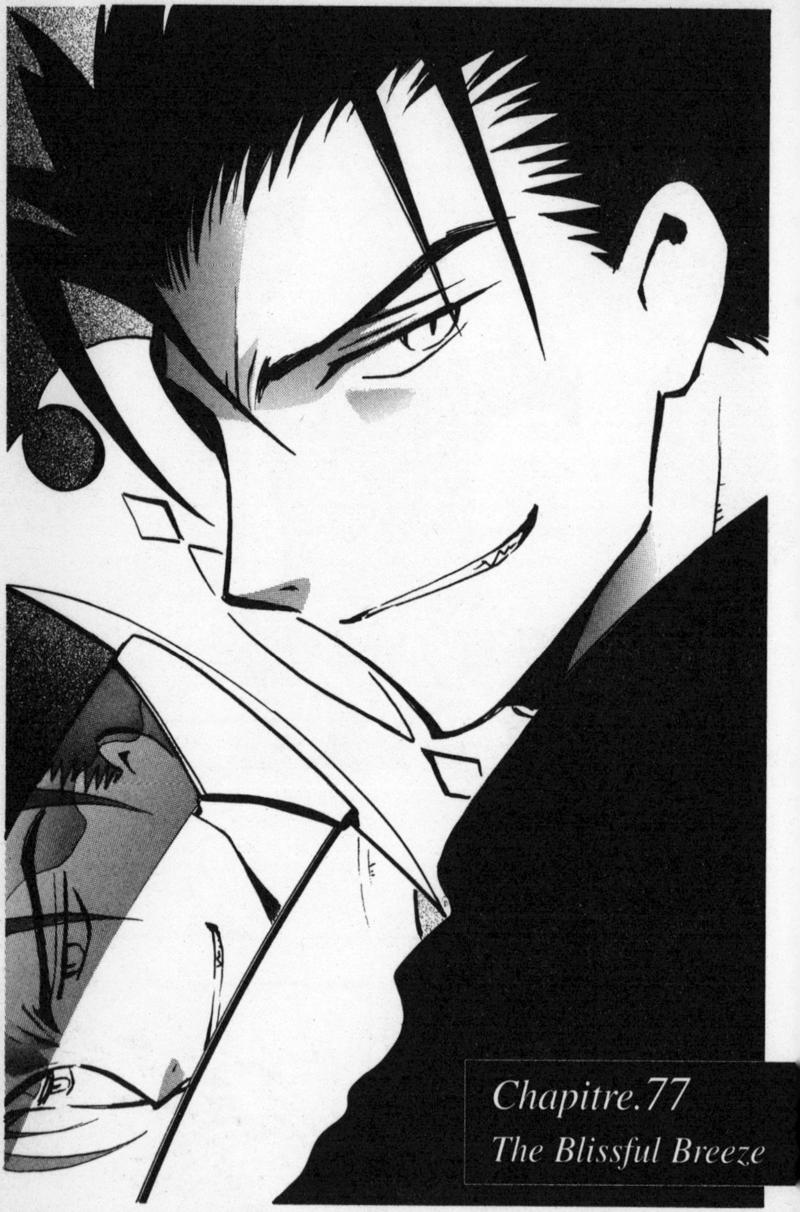
Chapitre.77
The Blissful Breeze

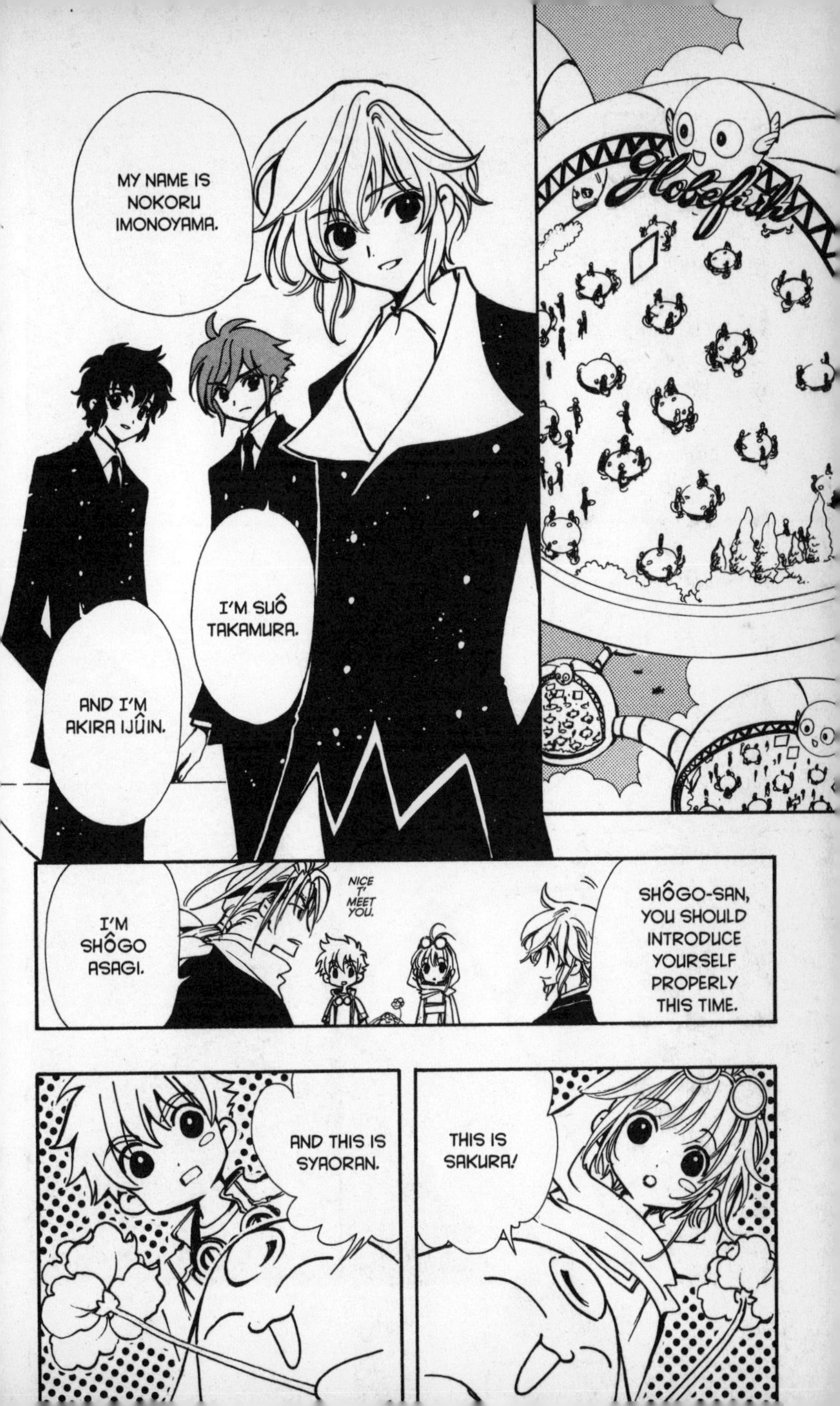
Globefish
MY NAME IS NOKORU IMONOYAMA.
I'M SUÔ TAKAMURA.
AND I'M AKIRA IJÛIN.
SHÔGO-SAN, YOU SHOULD INTRODUCE YOURSELF PROPERLY THIS TIME.
NICE T' MEET YOU.
I'M SHÔGO ASAGI.
THIS IS SAKURA!
AND THIS IS SYAORAN.

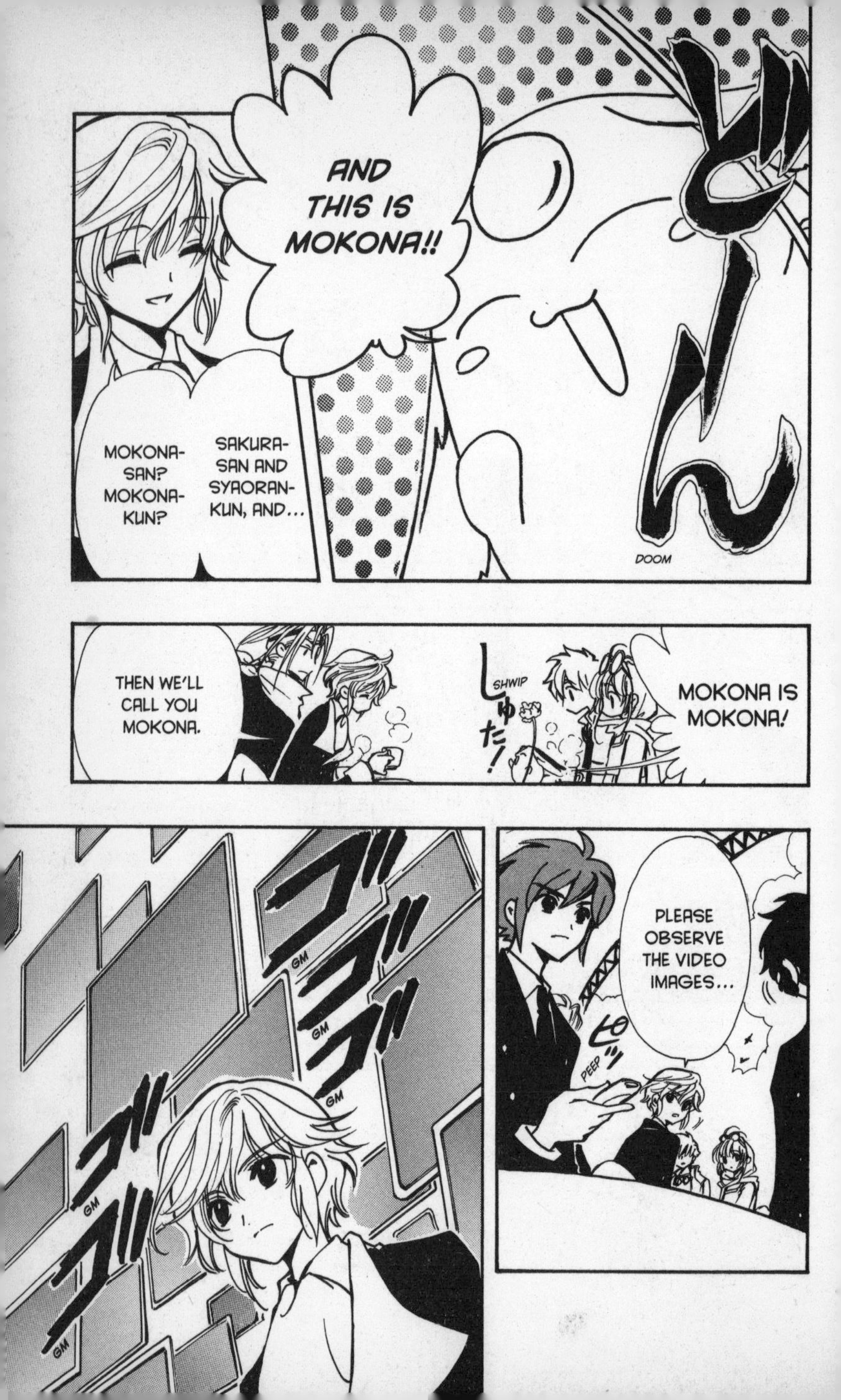
SAKURA-SAN AND SYAORAN-KUN, AND...
AND THIS IS MOKONA!!
DOOM
MOKONA-SAN? MOKONA-KUN?
MOKONA IS MOKONA!
SHWIP
THEN WE'LL CALL YOU MOKONA.
PEEP
PLEASE OBSERVE THE VIDEO IMAGES...
GM
GM
GM
GM
GM

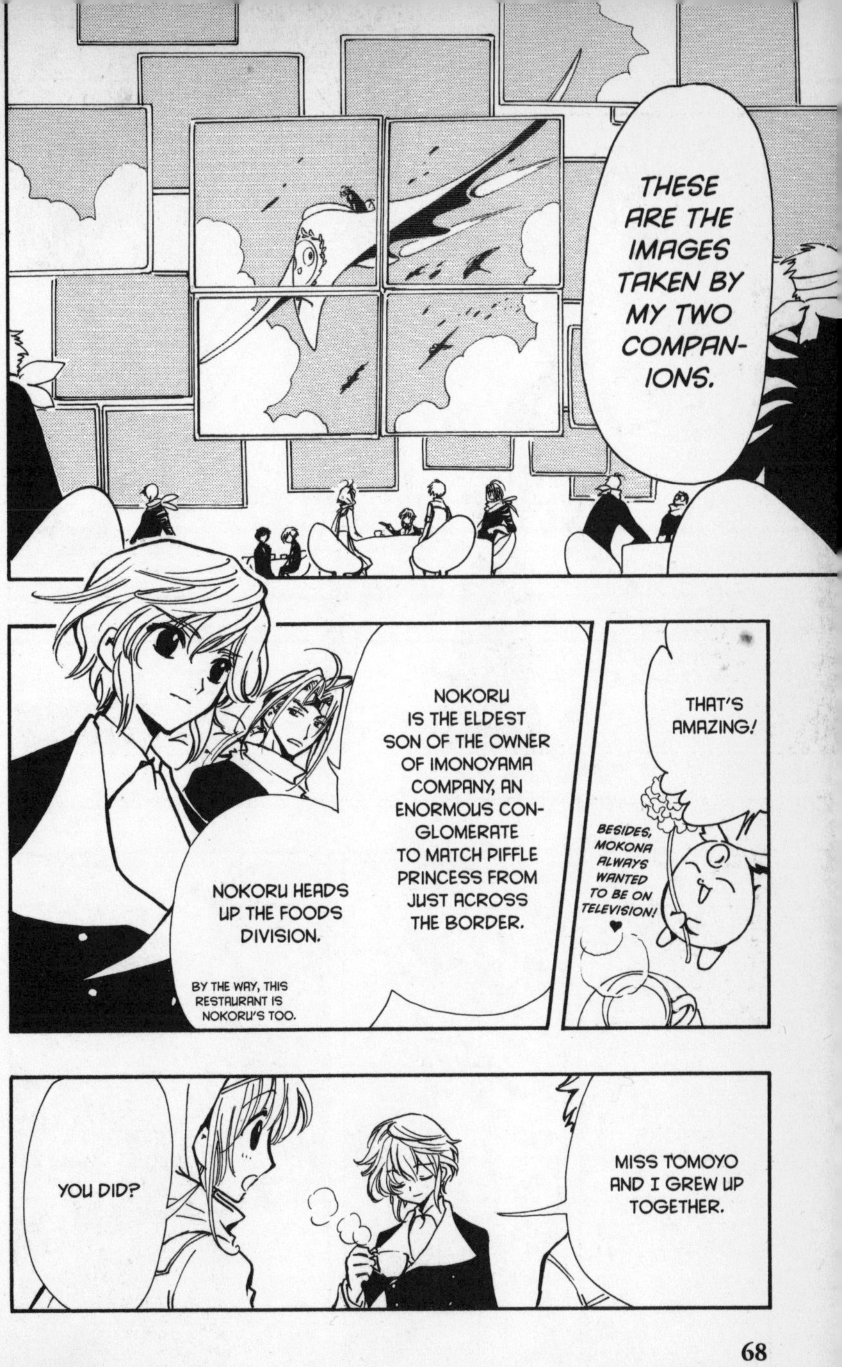
THESE ARE THE IMAGES TAKEN BY MY TWO COMPANIONS.
THAT'S AMAZING!
BESIDES, MOKONA ALWAYS WANTED TO BE ON TELEVISION! ♥
NOKORU IS THE ELDEST SON OF THE OWNER OF IMONOYAMA COMPANY, AN ENORMOUS CONGLOMERATE TO MATCH PIFFLE PRINCESS FROM JUST ACROSS THE BORDER.
NOKORU HEADS UP THE FOODS DIVISION.
BY THE WAY, THIS RESTAURANT IS NOKORU'S TOO.
MISS TOMOYO AND I GREW UP TOGETHER.
YOU DID?

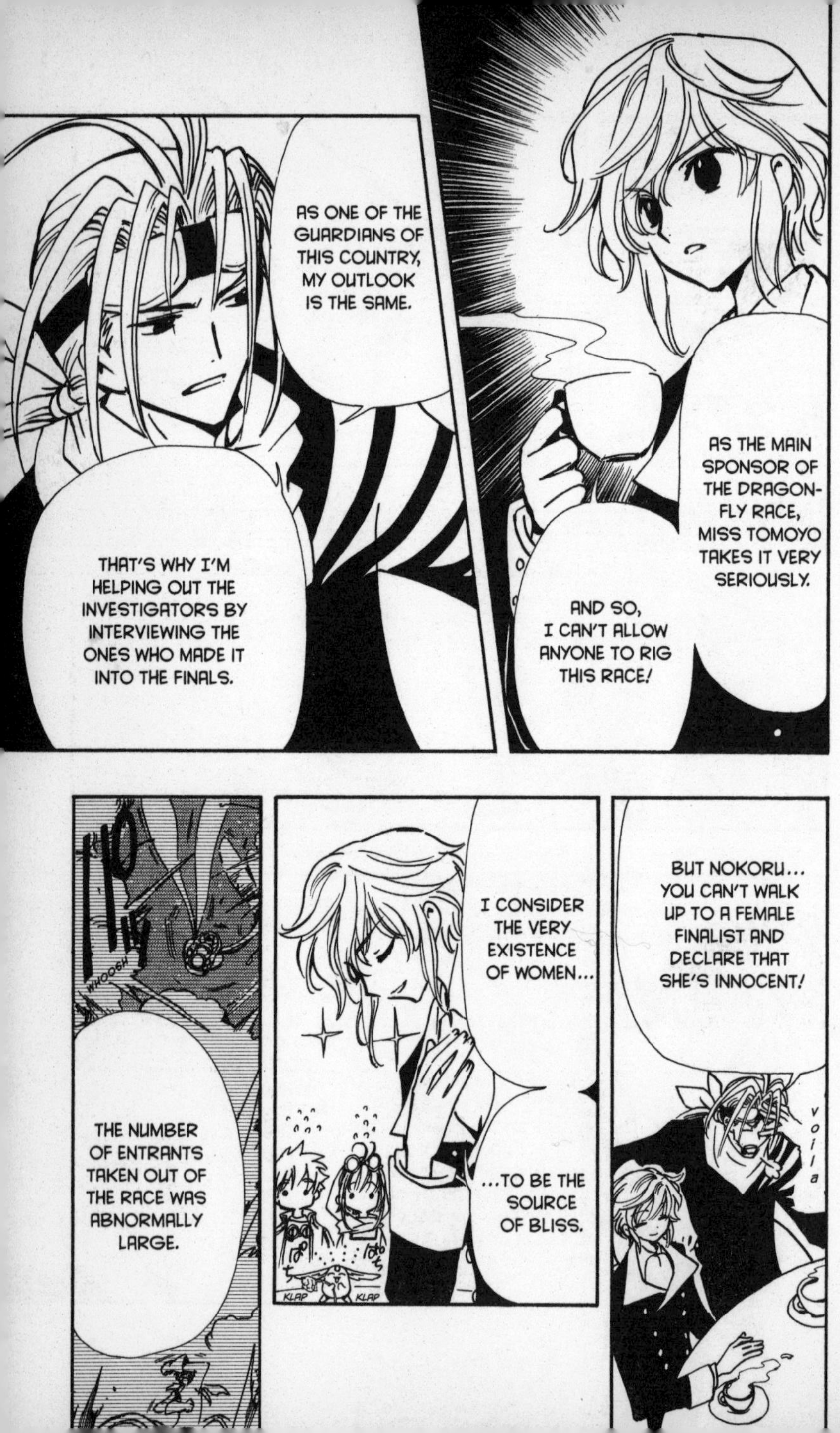
AS THE MAIN SPONSOR OF THE DRAGON-FLY RACE, MISS TOMOYO TAKES IT VERY SERIOUSLY.
AND SO, I CAN'T ALLOW ANYONE TO RIG THIS RACE!
AS ONE OF THE GUARDIANS OF THIS COUNTRY, MY OUTLOOK IS THE SAME.
THAT'S WHY I'M HELPING OUT THE INVESTIGATORS BY INTERVIEWING THE ONES WHO MADE IT INTO THE FINALS.
BUT NOKORU... YOU CAN'T WALK UP TO A FEMALE FINALIST AND DECLARE THAT SHE'S INNOCENT!
voila
I CONSIDER THE VERY EXISTENCE OF WOMEN...
...TO BE THE SOURCE OF BLISS.
KLAP
KLAP
WHOOSH
THE NUMBER OF ENTRANTS TAKEN OUT OF THE RACE WAS ABNORMALLY LARGE.

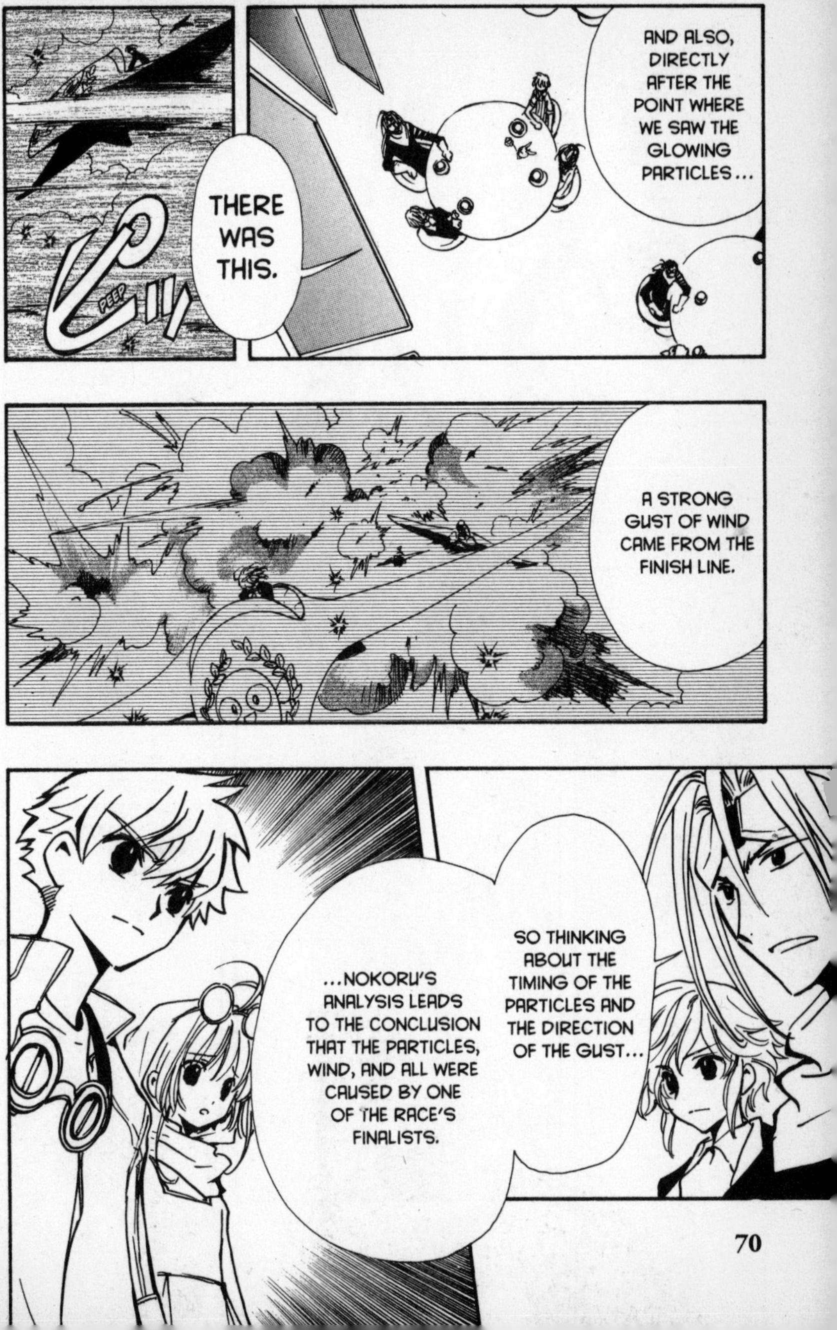
AND ALSO, DIRECTLY AFTER THE POINT WHERE WE SAW THE GLOWING PARTICLES...
THERE WAS THIS.
PEEP
A STRONG GUST OF WIND CAME FROM THE FINISH LINE.
SO THINKING ABOUT THE TIMING OF THE PARTICLES AND THE DIRECTION OF THE GUST...
...NOKORU'S ANALYSIS LEADS TO THE CONCLUSION THAT THE PARTICLES, WIND, AND ALL WERE CAUSED BY ONE OF THE RACE'S FINALISTS.

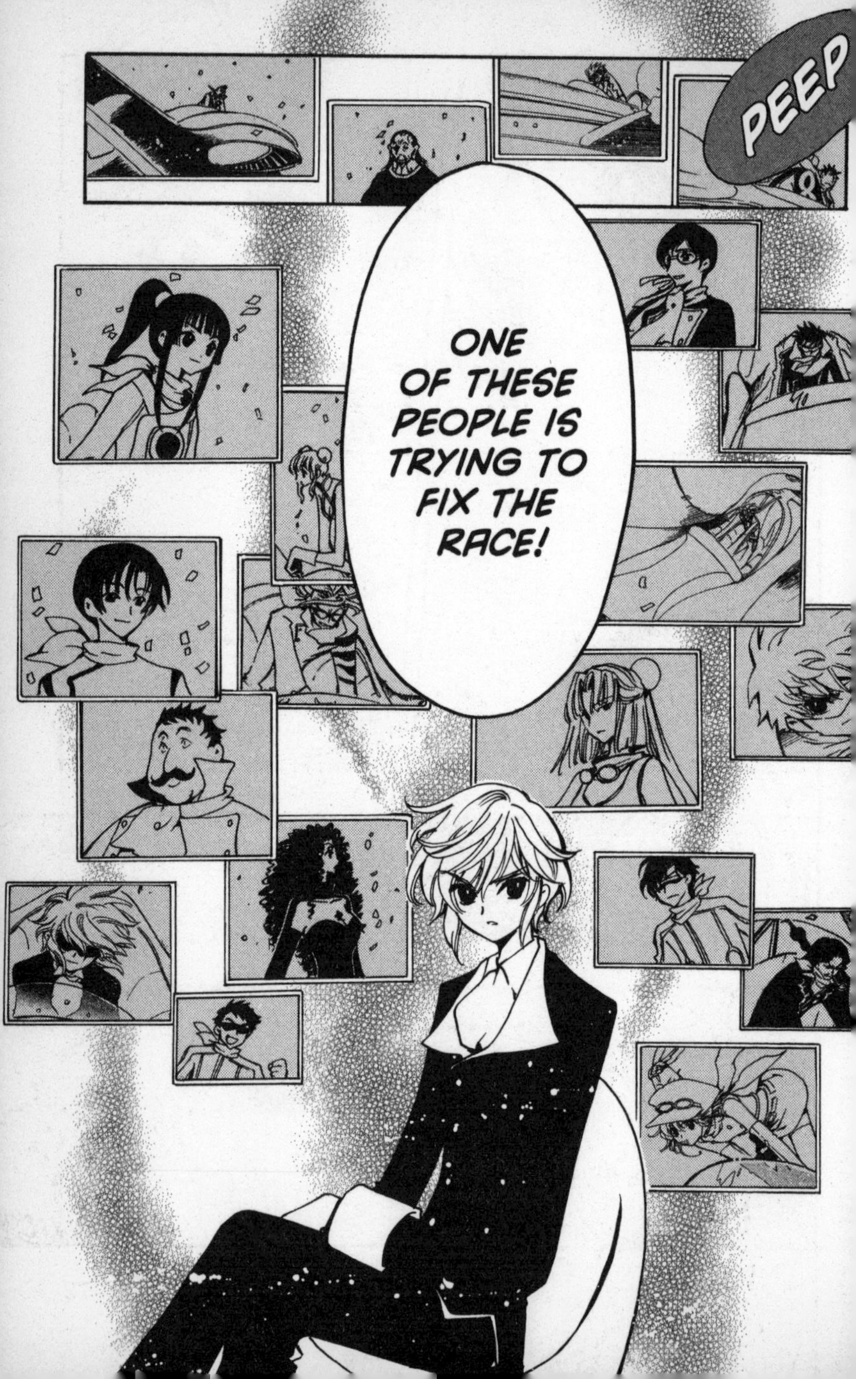
PEEP
ONE OF THESE PEOPLE IS TRYING TO FIX THE RACE!

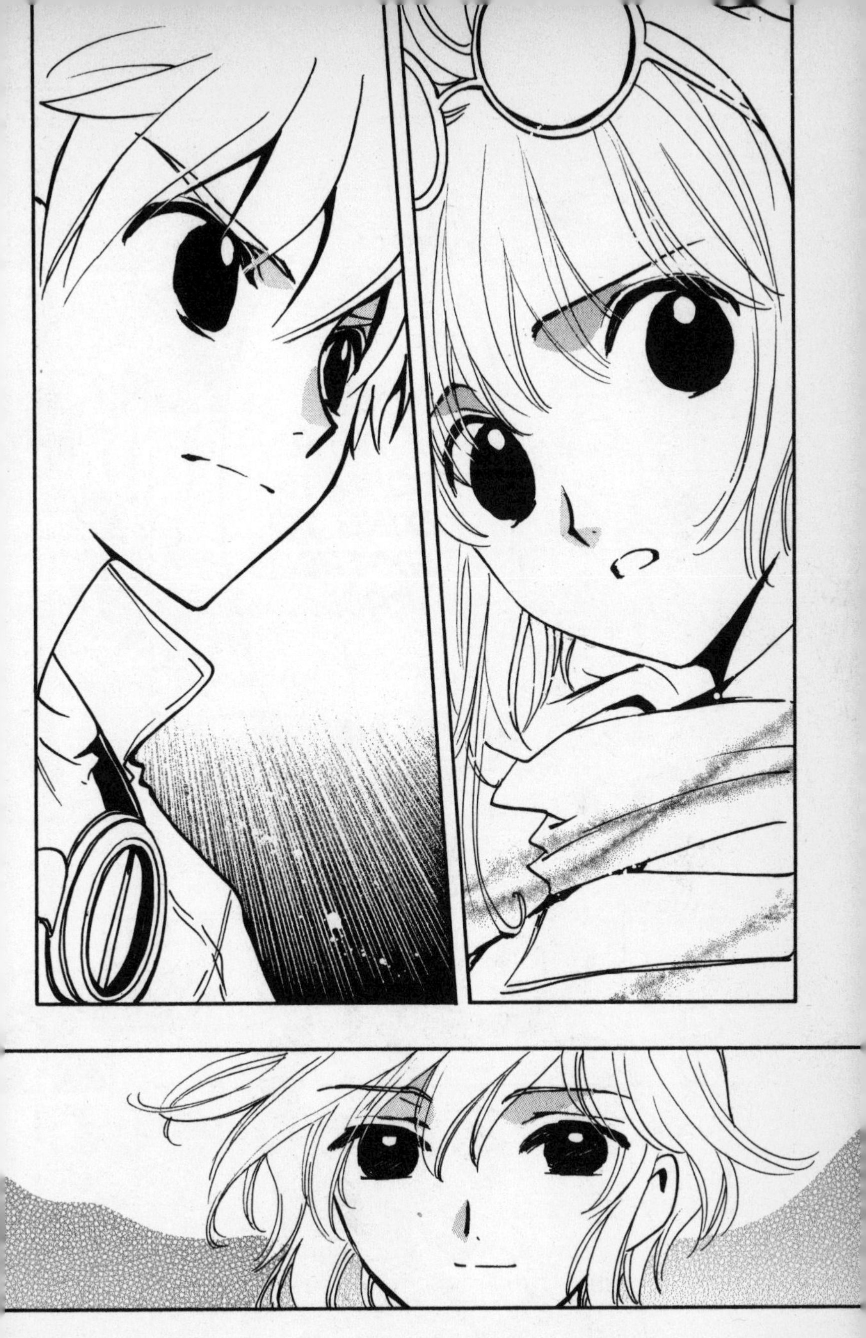

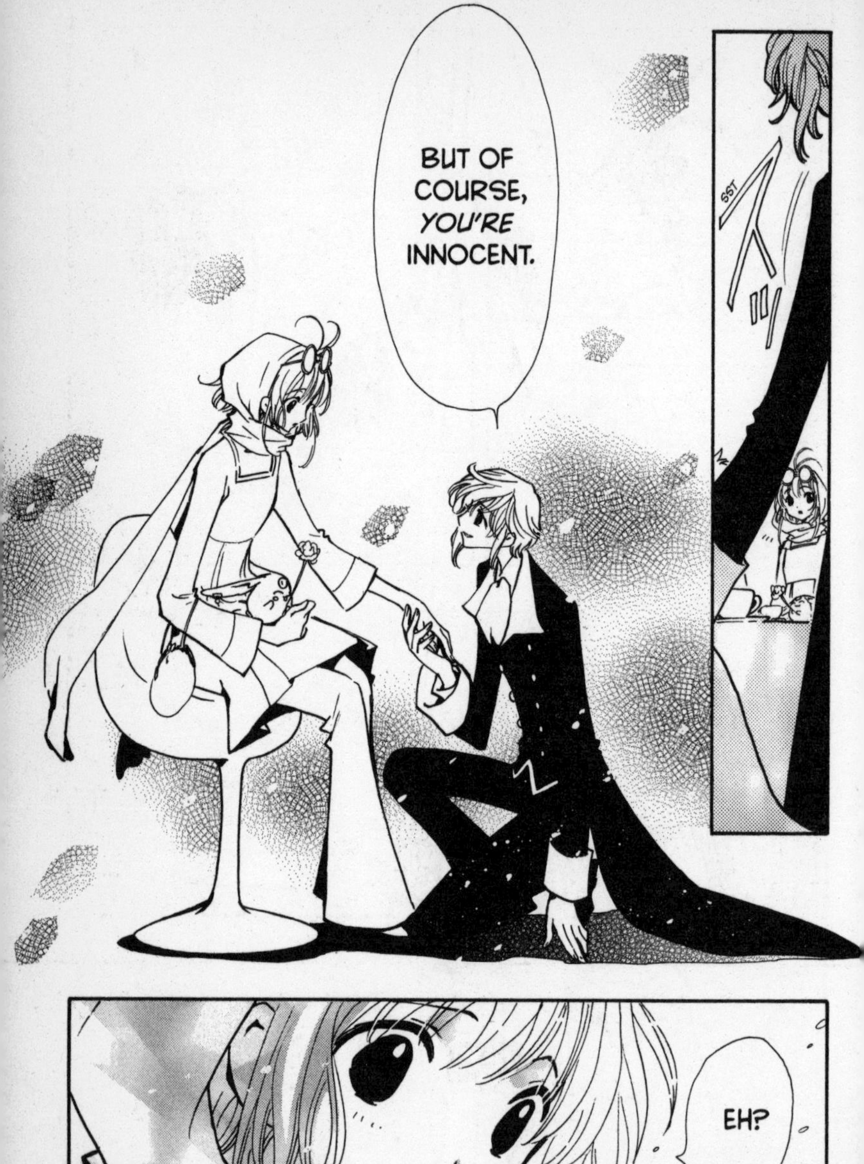
SST
BUT OF COURSE, *YOU'RE* INNOCENT.
EH?

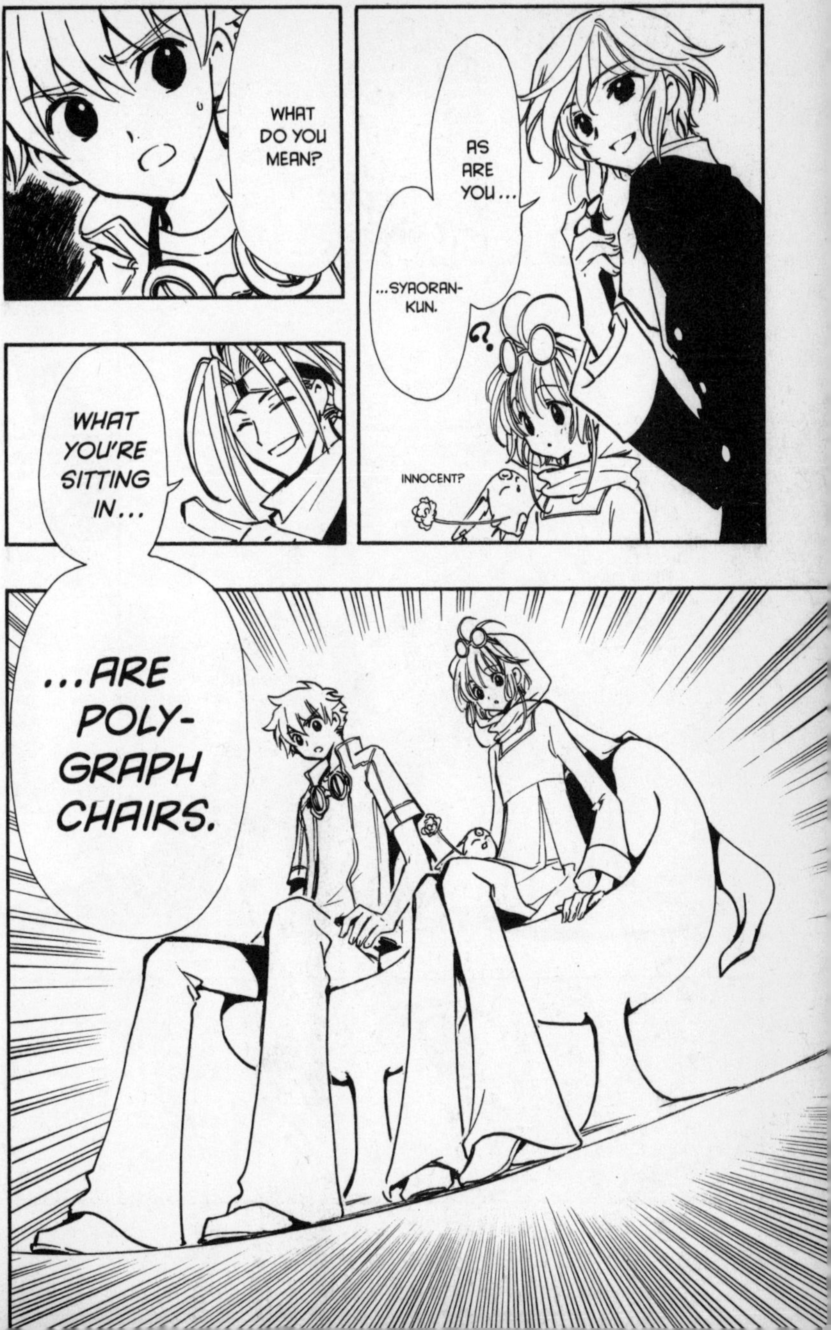
AS ARE YOU...
...SYAORAN-KUN.
INNOCENT?
WHAT DO YOU MEAN?
WHAT YOU'RE SITTING IN...
...ARE POLY-GRAPH CHAIRS.

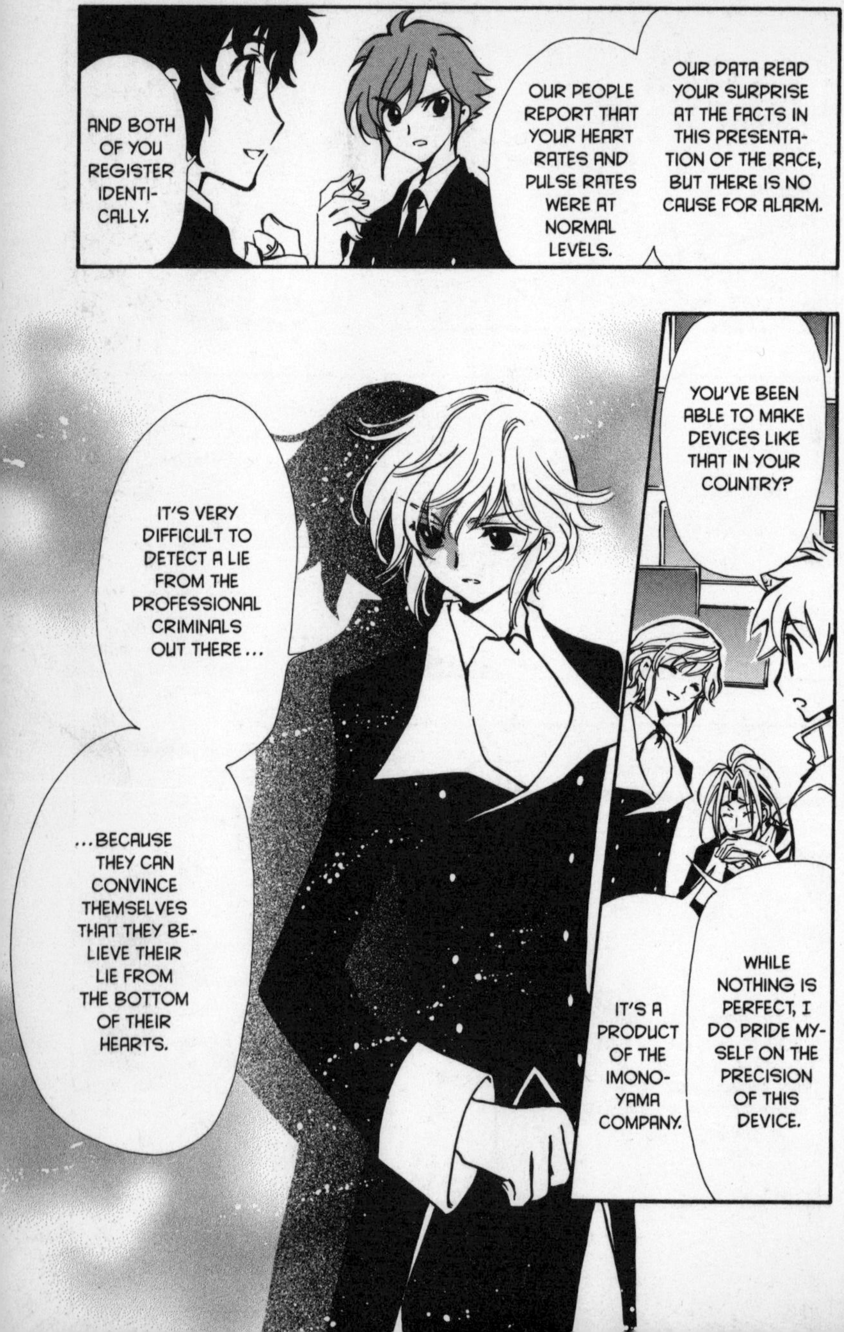
OUR DATA READ YOUR SURPRISE AT THE FACTS IN THIS PRESENTA-TION OF THE RACE, BUT THERE IS NO CAUSE FOR ALARM.
OUR PEOPLE REPORT THAT YOUR HEART RATES AND PULSE RATES WERE AT NORMAL LEVELS.
AND BOTH OF YOU REGISTER IDENTI-CALLY.
YOU'VE BEEN ABLE TO MAKE DEVICES LIKE THAT IN YOUR COUNTRY?
WHILE NOTHING IS PERFECT, I DO PRIDE MY-SELF ON THE PRECISION OF THIS DEVICE.
IT'S A PRODUCT OF THE IMONO-YAMA COMPANY.
IT'S VERY DIFFICULT TO DETECT A LIE FROM THE PROFESSIONAL CRIMINALS OUT THERE...
...BECAUSE THEY CAN CONVINCE THEMSELVES THAT THEY BE-LIEVE THEIR LIE FROM THE BOTTOM OF THEIR HEARTS.

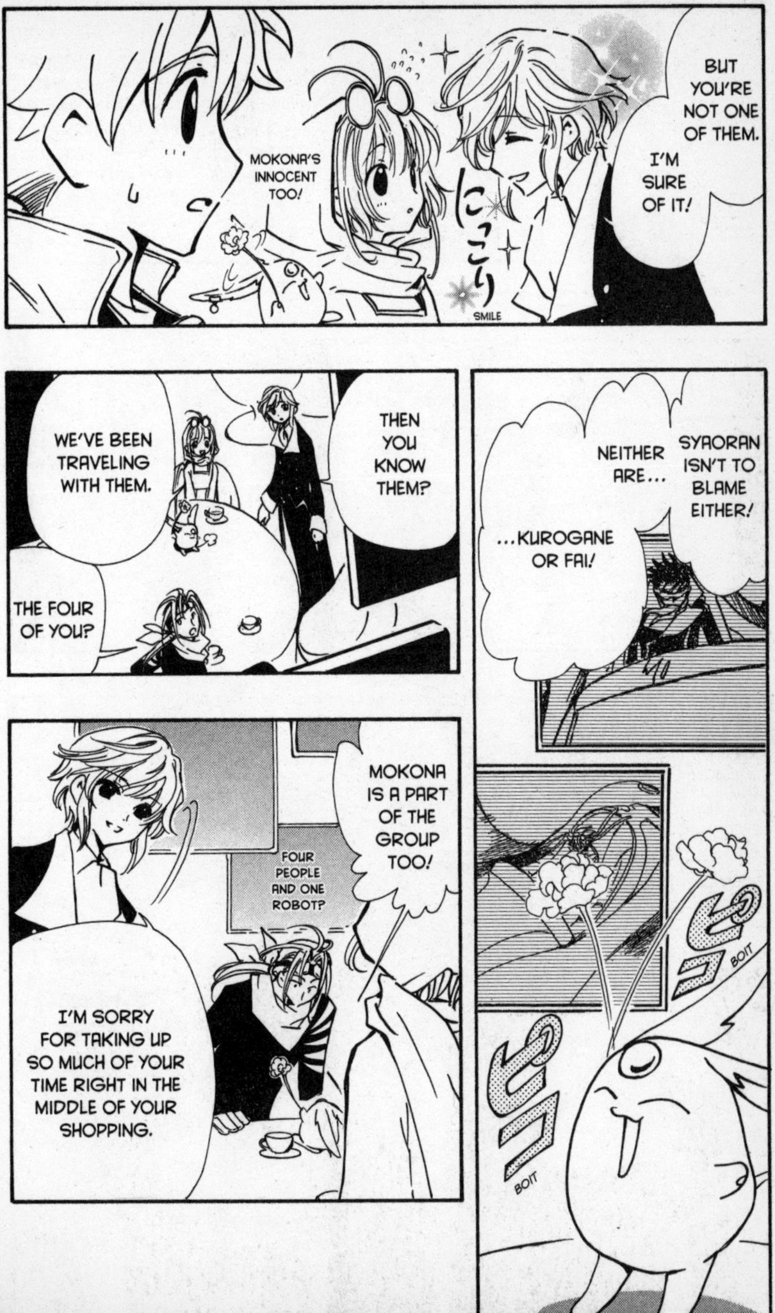
BUT YOU'RE NOT ONE OF THEM.
I'M SURE OF IT!
にっこり
SMILE
MOKONA'S INNOCENT TOO!
SYAORAN ISN'T TO BLAME EITHER!
NEITHER ARE...
...KUROGANE OR FAI!
BOIT
BOIT
THEN YOU KNOW THEM?
WE'VE BEEN TRAVELING WITH THEM.
THE FOUR OF YOU?
MOKONA IS A PART OF THE GROUP TOO!
FOUR PEOPLE AND ONE ROBOT?
I'M SORRY FOR TAKING UP SO MUCH OF YOUR TIME RIGHT IN THE MIDDLE OF YOUR SHOPPING.

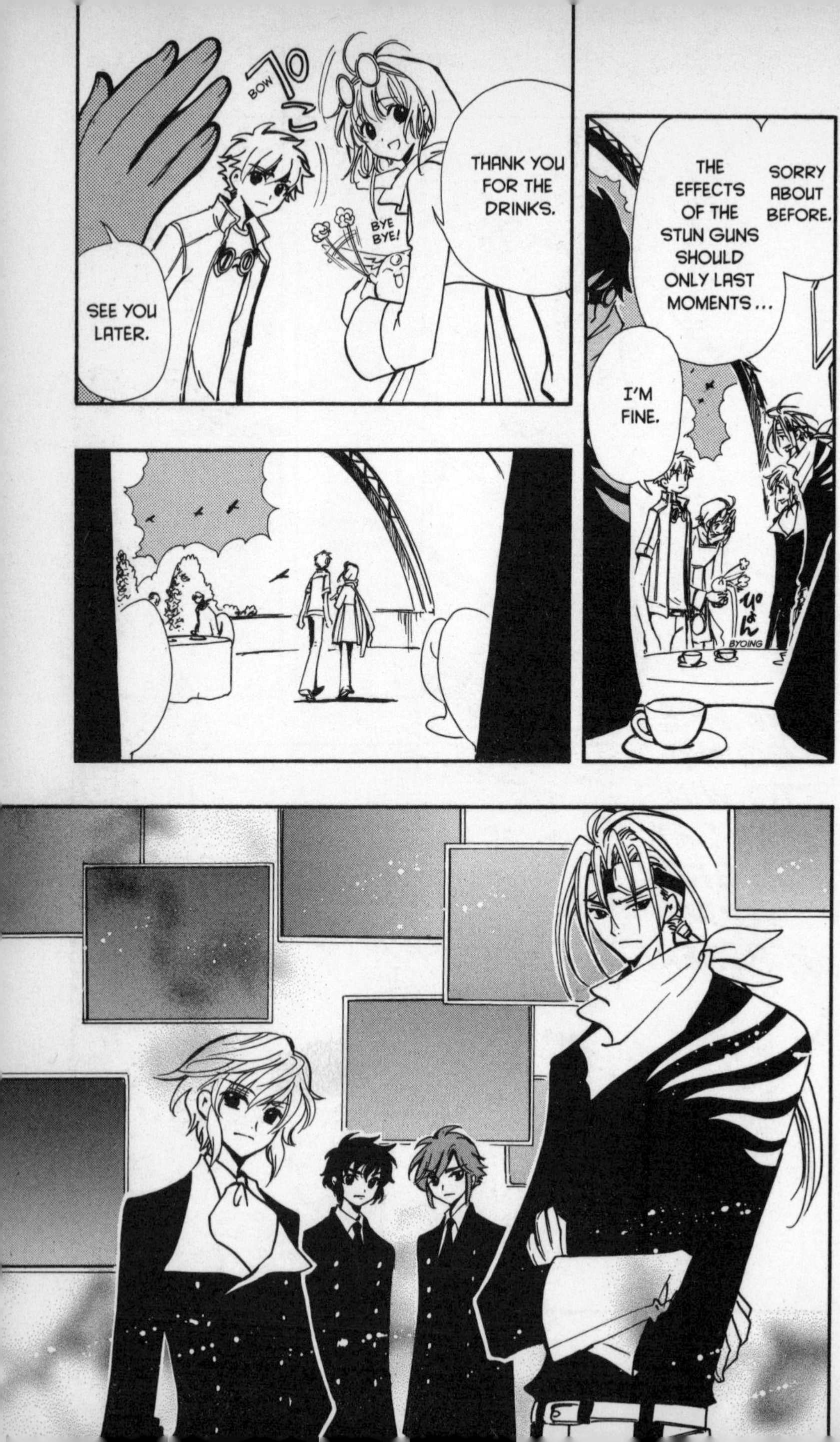
SORRY ABOUT BEFORE.
THE EFFECTS OF THE STUN GUNS SHOULD ONLY LAST MOMENTS...
I'M FINE.
ぴょん
BYOING
THANK YOU FOR THE DRINKS.
BOW
BYE BYE!
SEE YOU LATER.

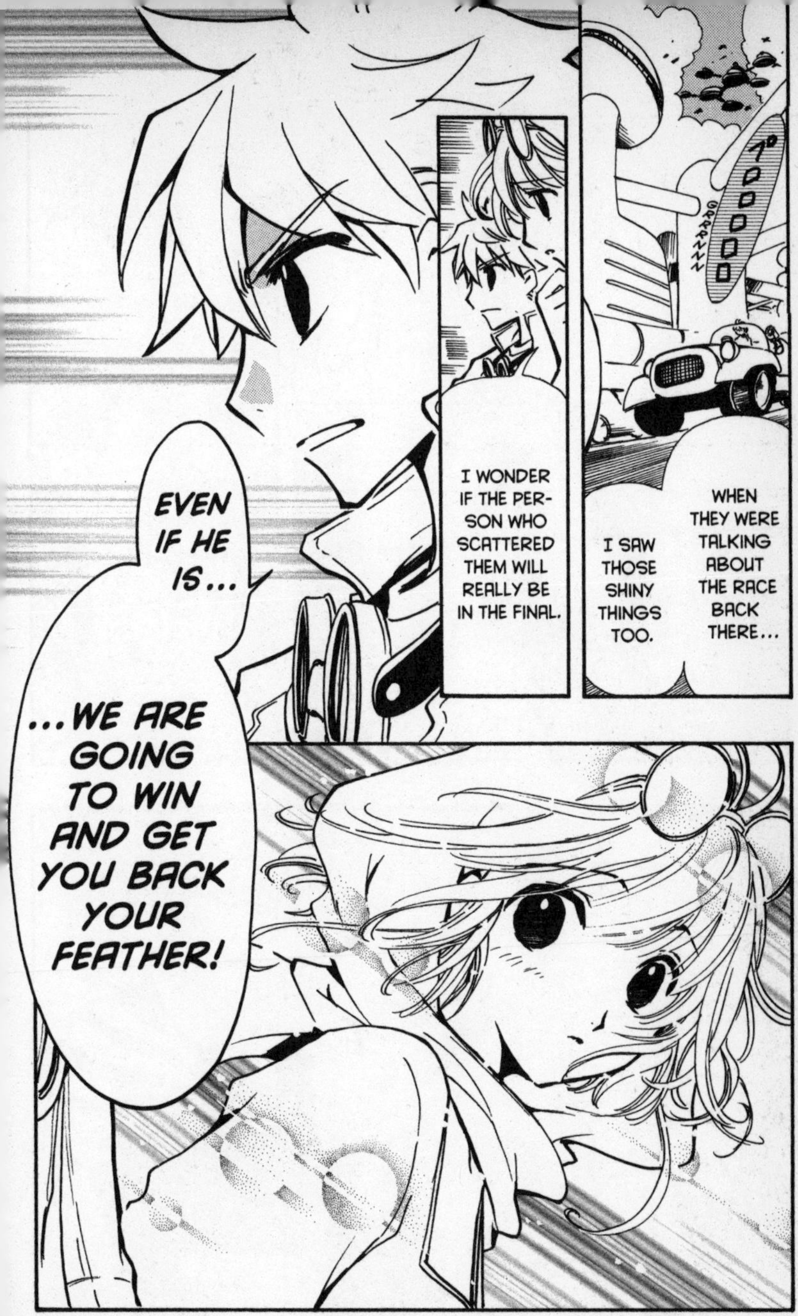
GRRRNNN
WHEN THEY WERE TALKING ABOUT THE RACE BACK THERE...
I SAW THOSE SHINY THINGS TOO.
I WONDER IF THE PER-SON WHO SCATTERED THEM WILL REALLY BE IN THE FINAL.
EVEN IF HE IS...
...WE ARE GOING TO WIN AND GET YOU BACK YOUR FEATHER!

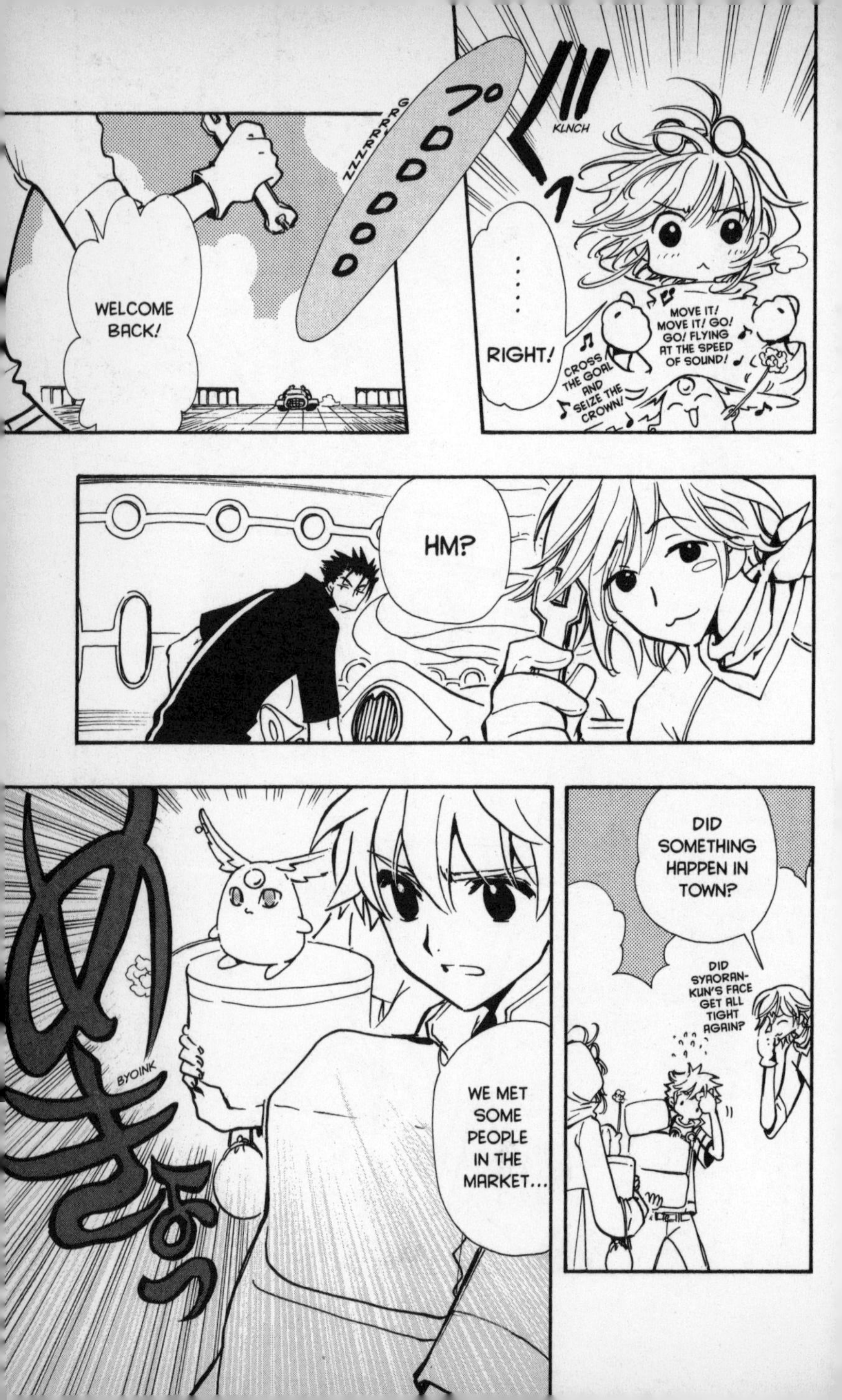
KLNCH
......
RIGHT!
MOVE IT! MOVE IT! GO! GO! FLYING AT THE SPEED OF SOUND!
CROSS THE GOAL AND SEIZE THE CROWN!
ZZZRRRRRG
WELCOME BACK!
HM?
DID SOMETHING HAPPEN IN TOWN?
DID SYAORAN-KUN'S FACE GET ALL TIGHT AGAIN?
BYOINK
WE MET SOME PEOPLE IN THE MARKET...

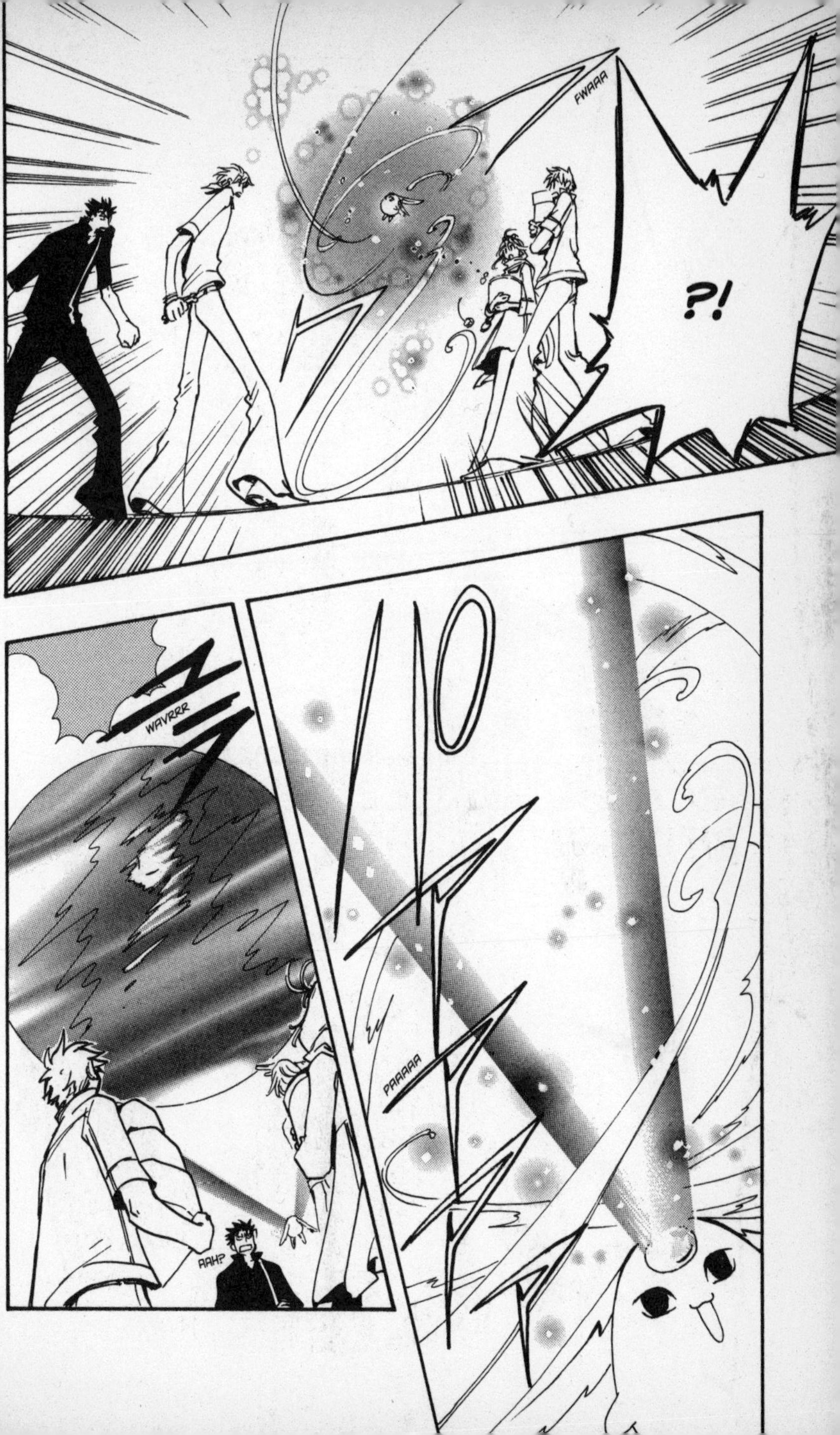
FWAAA
?!
PAAAAA
WAVRRR
AAH?

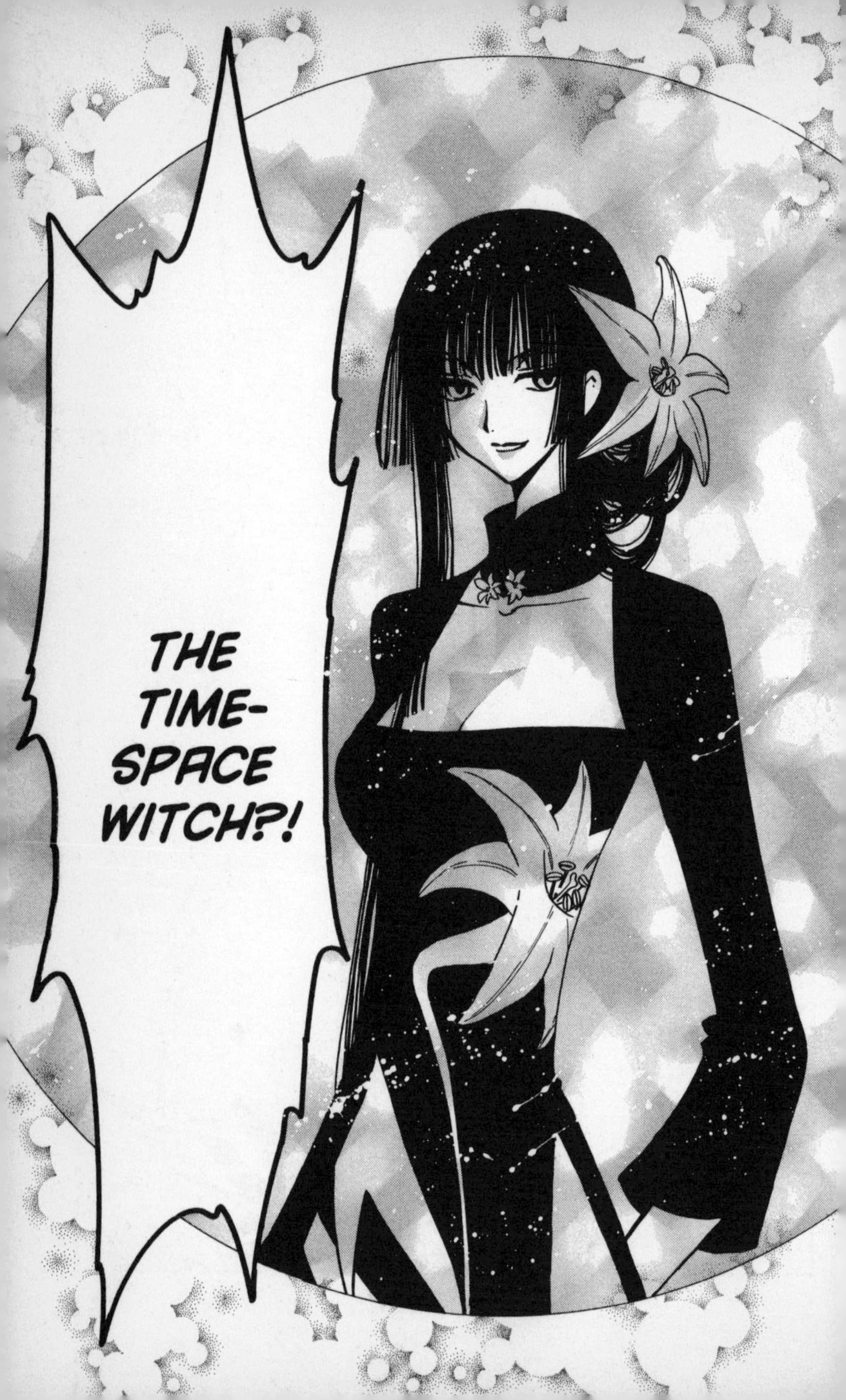
THE TIME-SPACE WITCH?!

ツバサ
RESERVoir CHRoNiCLE

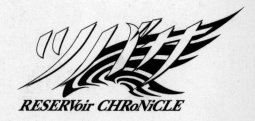

Chapitre.78
The Princess and the Witch

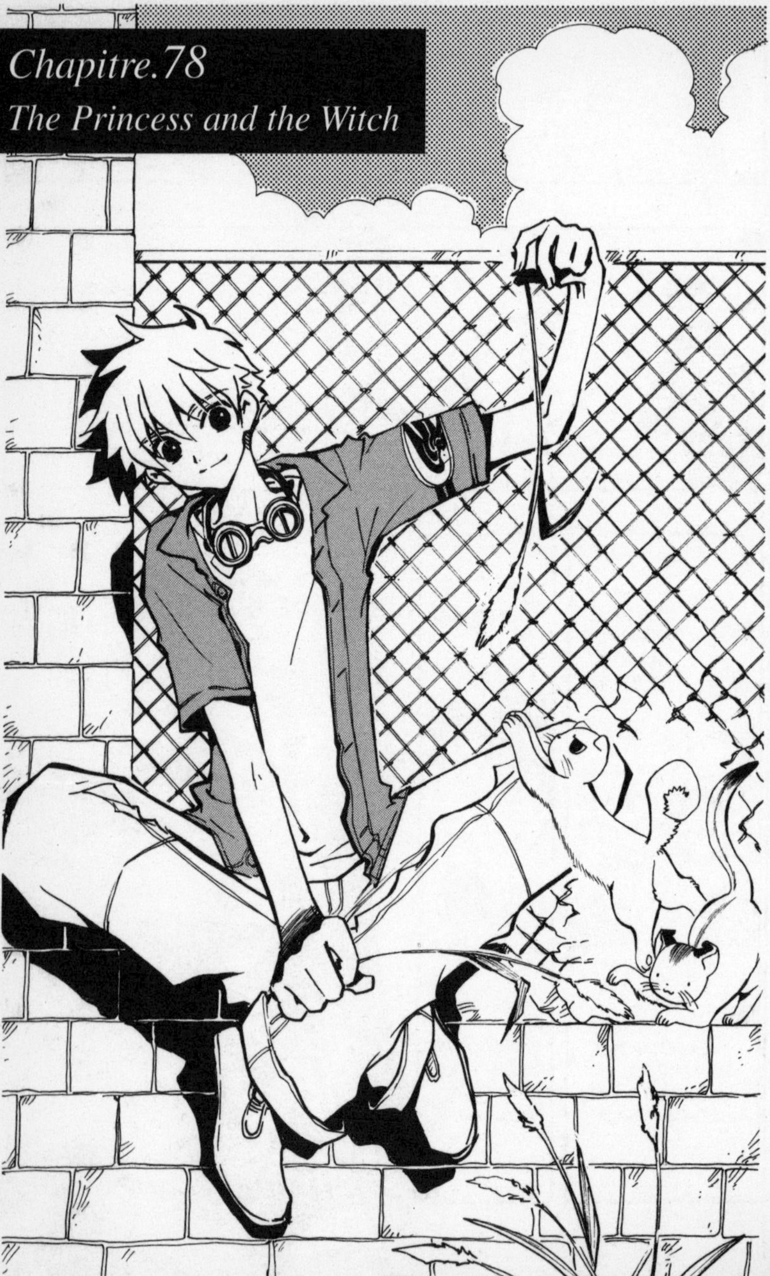

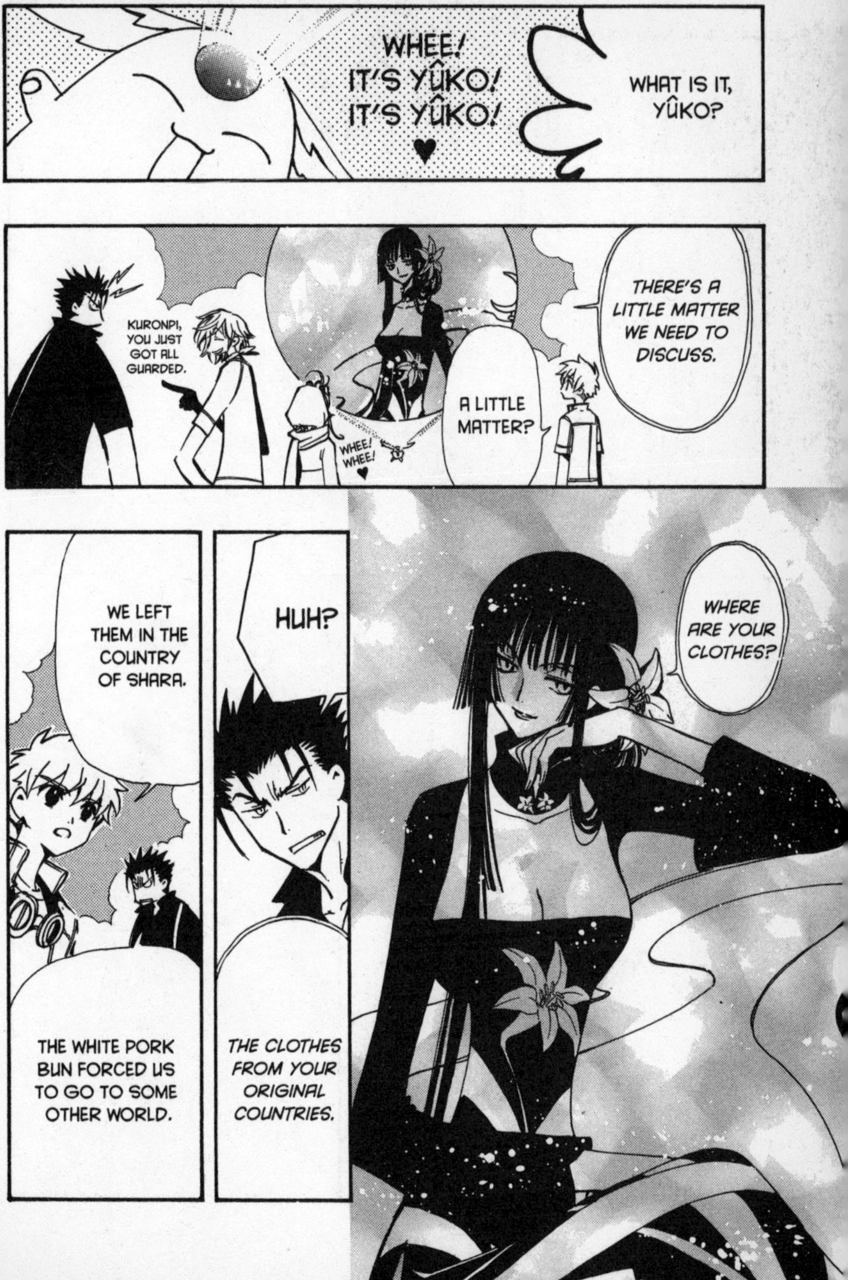

WHAT IS IT, YÛKO?
WHEE! IT'S YÛKO! IT'S YÛKO! ♥
THERE'S A LITTLE MATTER WE NEED TO DISCUSS.
A LITTLE MATTER?
WHEE! WHEE! ♥
KURONPI, YOU JUST GOT ALL GUARDED.
WHERE ARE YOUR CLOTHES?
HUH?
THE CLOTHES FROM YOUR ORIGINAL COUNTRIES.
WE LEFT THEM IN THE COUNTRY OF SHARA.
THE WHITE PORK BUN FORCED US TO GO TO SOME OTHER WORLD.

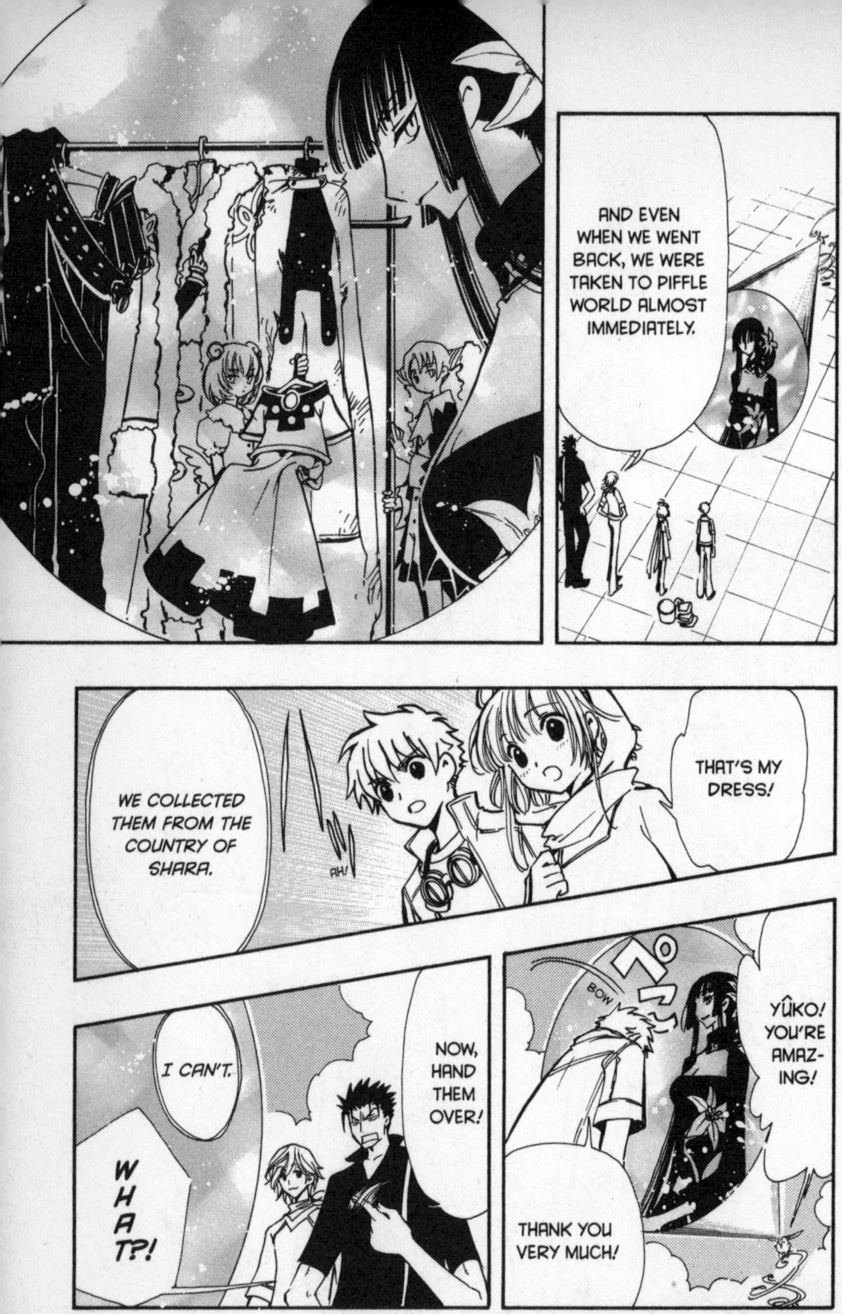
AND EVEN WHEN WE WENT BACK, WE WERE TAKEN TO PIFFLE WORLD ALMOST IMMEDIATELY.
THAT'S MY DRESS!
AH!
WE COLLECTED THEM FROM THE COUNTRY OF SHARA.
YÛKO! YOU'RE AMAZ-ING!
BOW
THANK YOU VERY MUCH!
NOW, HAND THEM OVER!
I CAN'T.
WHAT?!

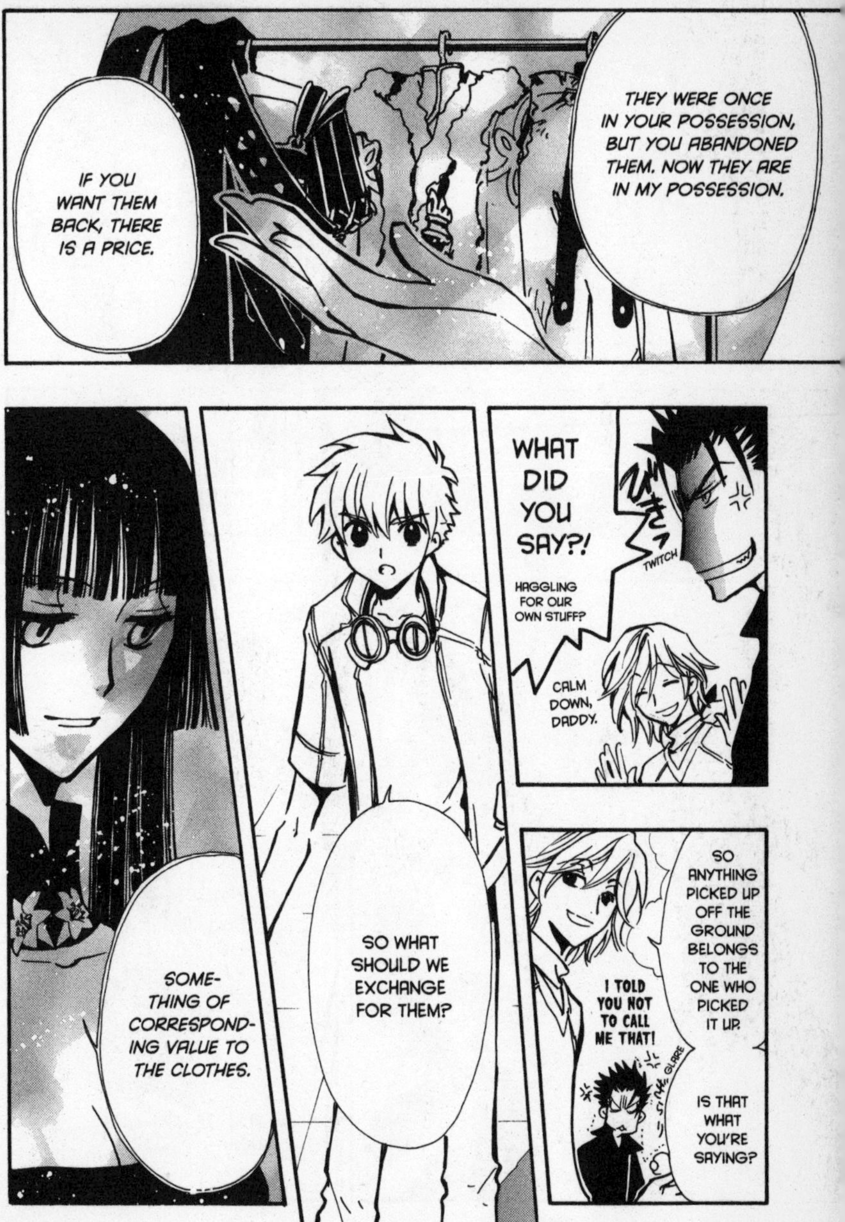
THEY WERE ONCE IN YOUR POSSESSION, BUT YOU ABANDONED THEM. NOW THEY ARE IN MY POSSESSION.
IF YOU WANT THEM BACK, THERE IS A PRICE.
WHAT DID YOU SAY?!
TWITCH
HAGGLING FOR OUR OWN STUFF?
CALM DOWN, DADDY.
SO ANYTHING PICKED UP OFF THE GROUND BELONGS TO THE ONE WHO PICKED IT UP.
IS THAT WHAT YOU'RE SAYING?
I TOLD YOU NOT TO CALL ME THAT!
GLARE
SO WHAT SHOULD WE EXCHANGE FOR THEM?
SOME-THING OF CORRESPOND-ING VALUE TO THE CLOTHES.

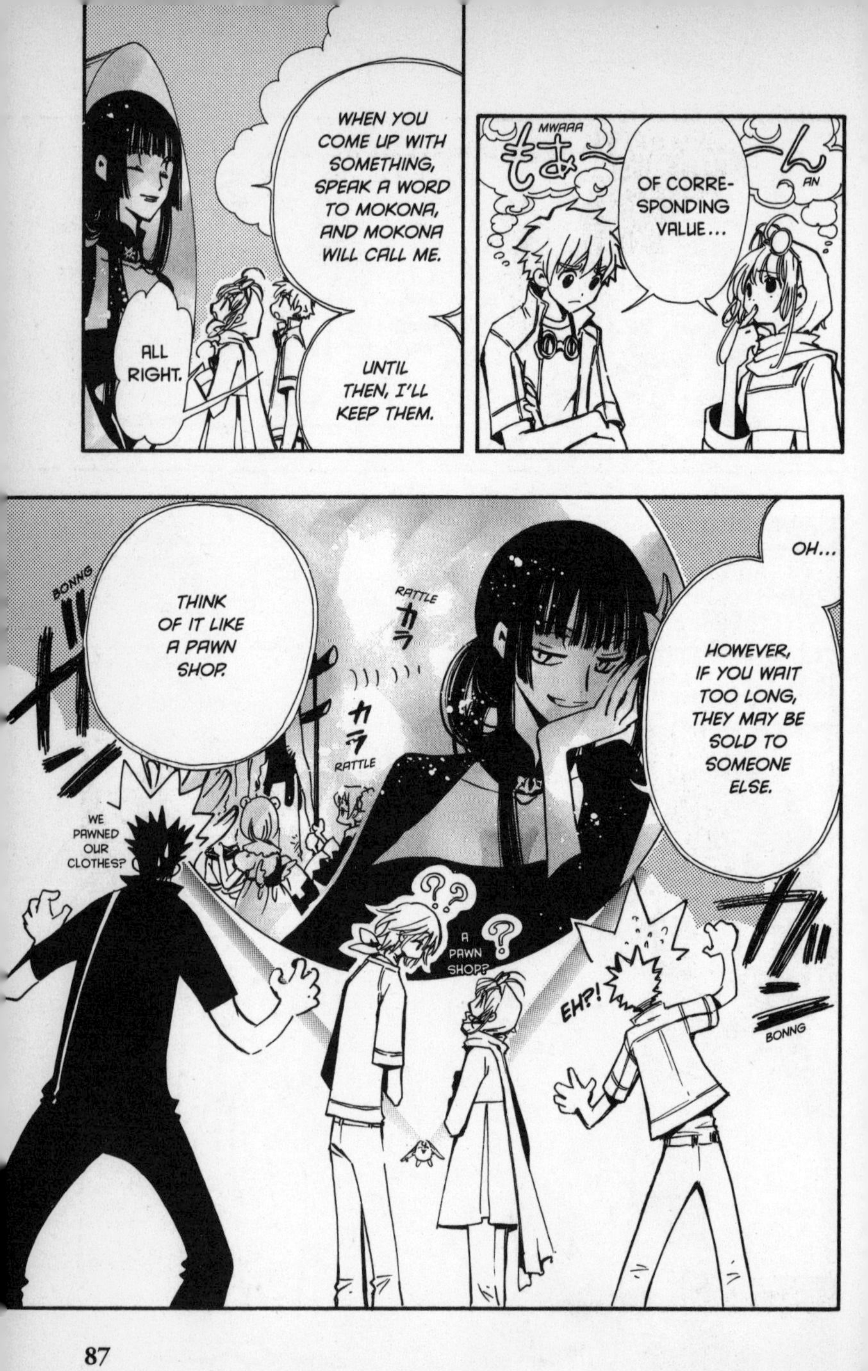
AN
OF CORRE-SPONDING VALUE...
MWAAA
WHEN YOU COME UP WITH SOMETHING, SPEAK A WORD TO MOKONA, AND MOKONA WILL CALL ME.
UNTIL THEN, I'LL KEEP THEM.
ALL RIGHT.
OH...
HOWEVER, IF YOU WAIT TOO LONG, THEY MAY BE SOLD TO SOMEONE ELSE.
RATTLE
RATTLE
THINK OF IT LIKE A PAWN SHOP.
BONNG
BONNG
EH?!
A PAWN SHOP?
WE PAWNED OUR CLOTHES?

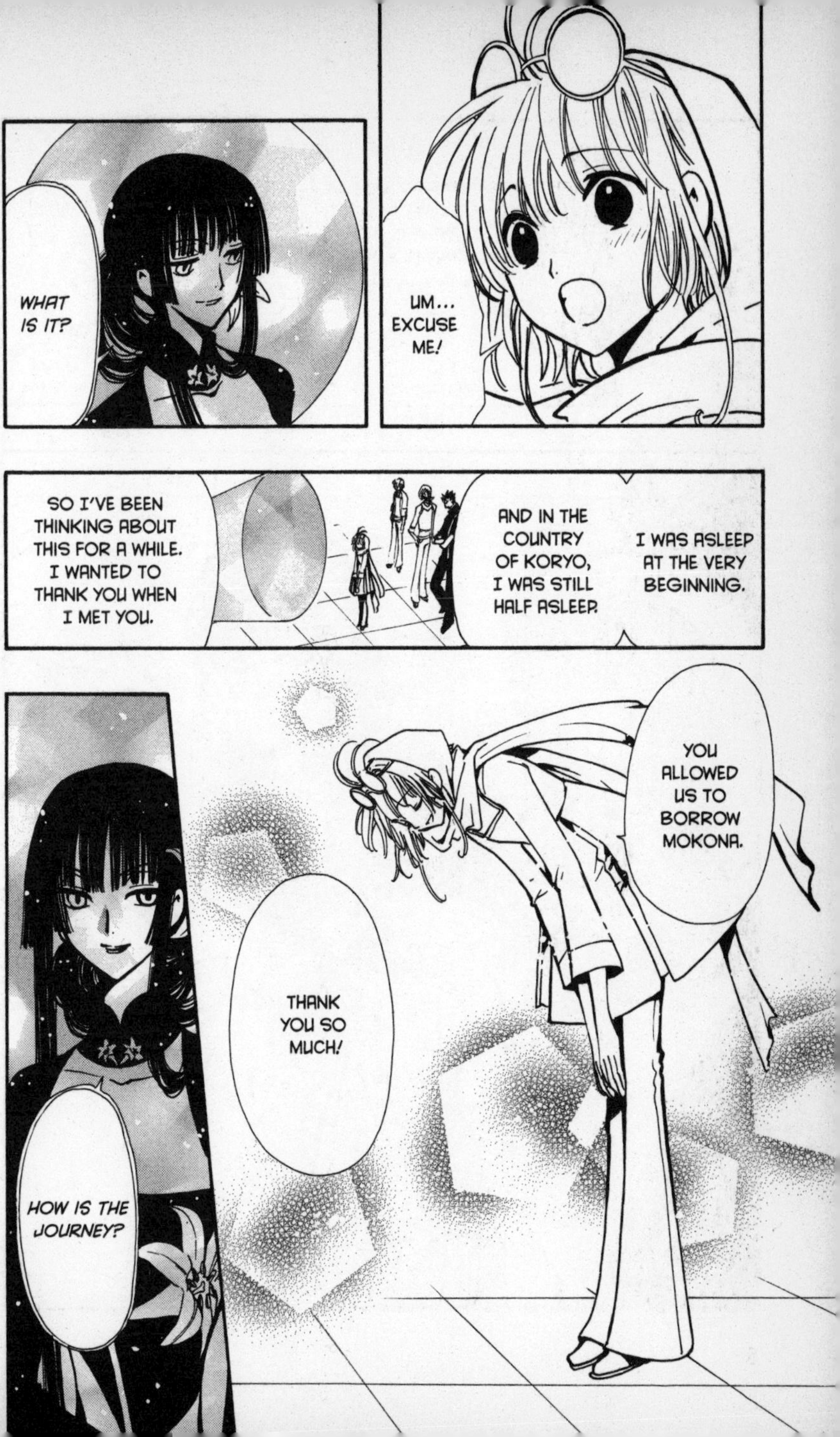
UM... EXCUSE ME!
WHAT IS IT?
I WAS ASLEEP AT THE VERY BEGINNING.
AND IN THE COUNTRY OF KORYO, I WAS STILL HALF ASLEEP.
SO I'VE BEEN THINKING ABOUT THIS FOR A WHILE. I WANTED TO THANK YOU WHEN I MET YOU.
YOU ALLOWED US TO BORROW MOKONA.
THANK YOU SO MUCH!
HOW IS THE JOURNEY?

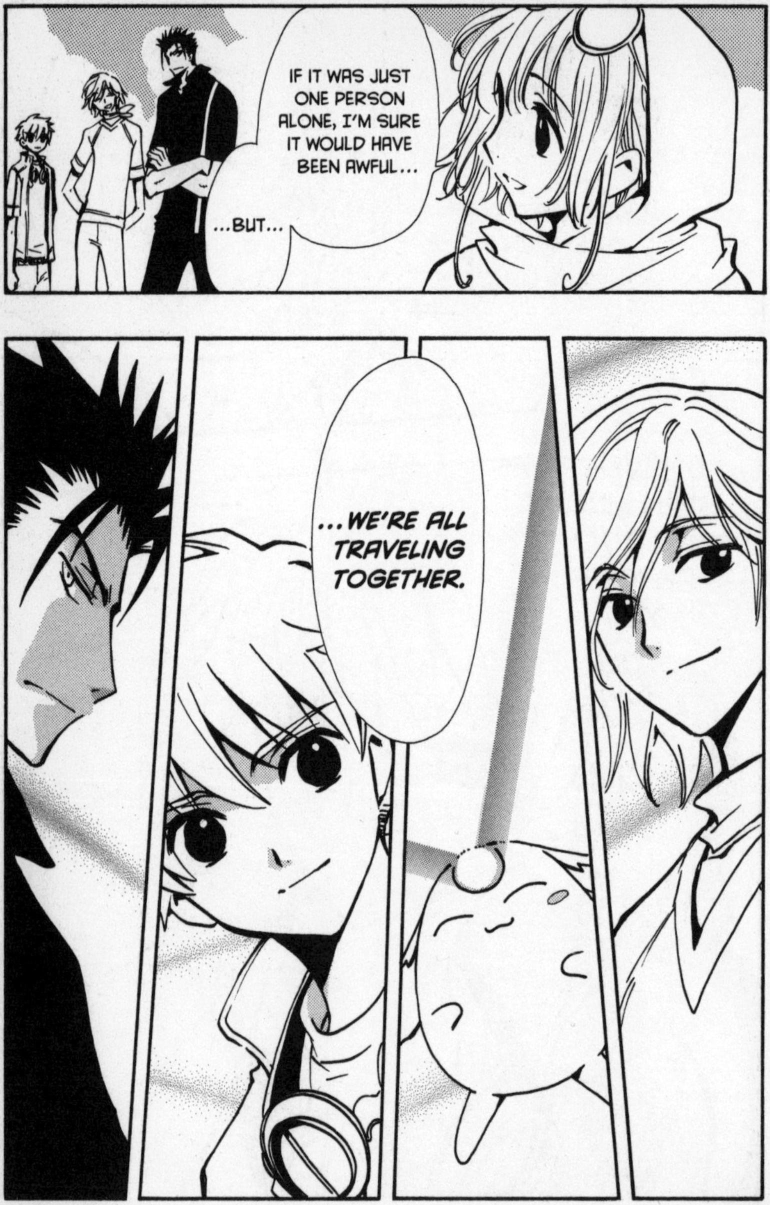
IF IT WAS JUST ONE PERSON ALONE, I'M SURE IT WOULD HAVE BEEN AWFUL...
...BUT...
...WE'RE ALL TRAVELING TOGETHER.

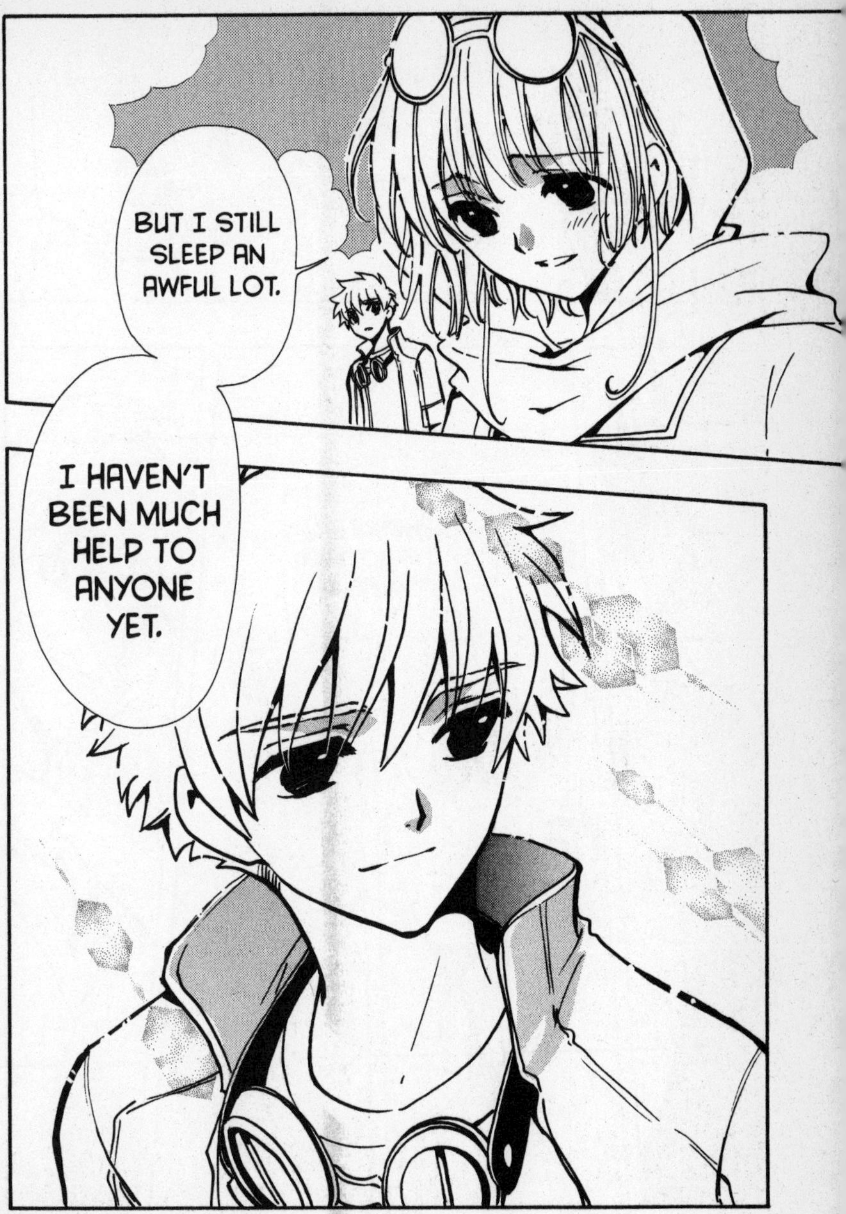
BUT I STILL SLEEP AN AWFUL LOT.
I HAVEN'T BEEN MUCH HELP TO ANYONE YET.

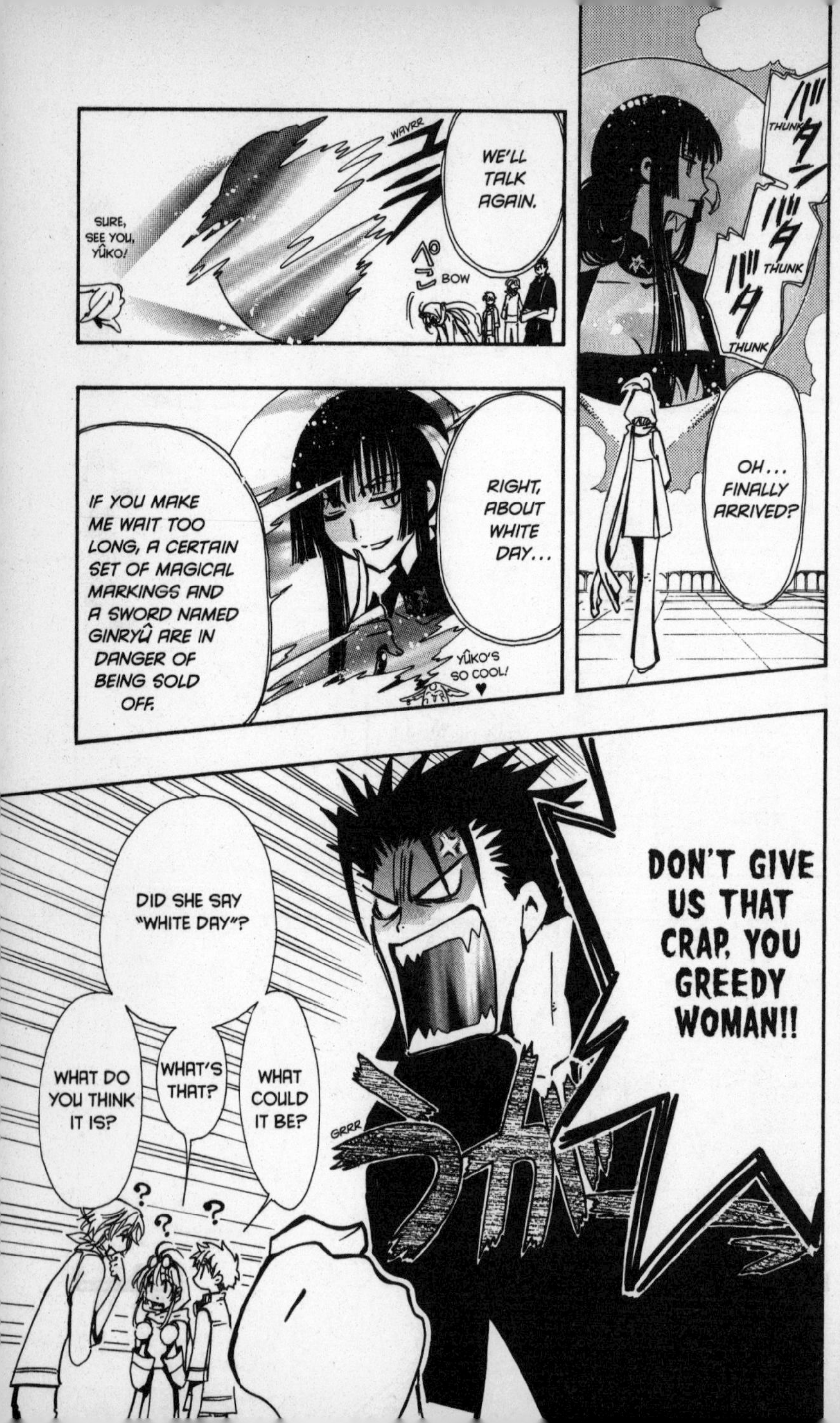
THUNK
THUNK
THUNK
OH... FINALLY ARRIVED?
WAVRR
WE'LL TALK AGAIN.
BOW
SURE, SEE YOU, YÛKO!
RIGHT, ABOUT WHITE DAY...
IF YOU MAKE ME WAIT TOO LONG, A CERTAIN SET OF MAGICAL MARKINGS AND A SWORD NAMED GINRYÛ ARE IN DANGER OF BEING SOLD OFF.
YÛKO'S SO COOL! ♥
DON'T GIVE US THAT CRAP, YOU GREEDY WOMAN!!
GRRR
DID SHE SAY "WHITE DAY"?
WHAT COULD IT BE?
WHAT'S THAT?
WHAT DO YOU THINK IT IS?

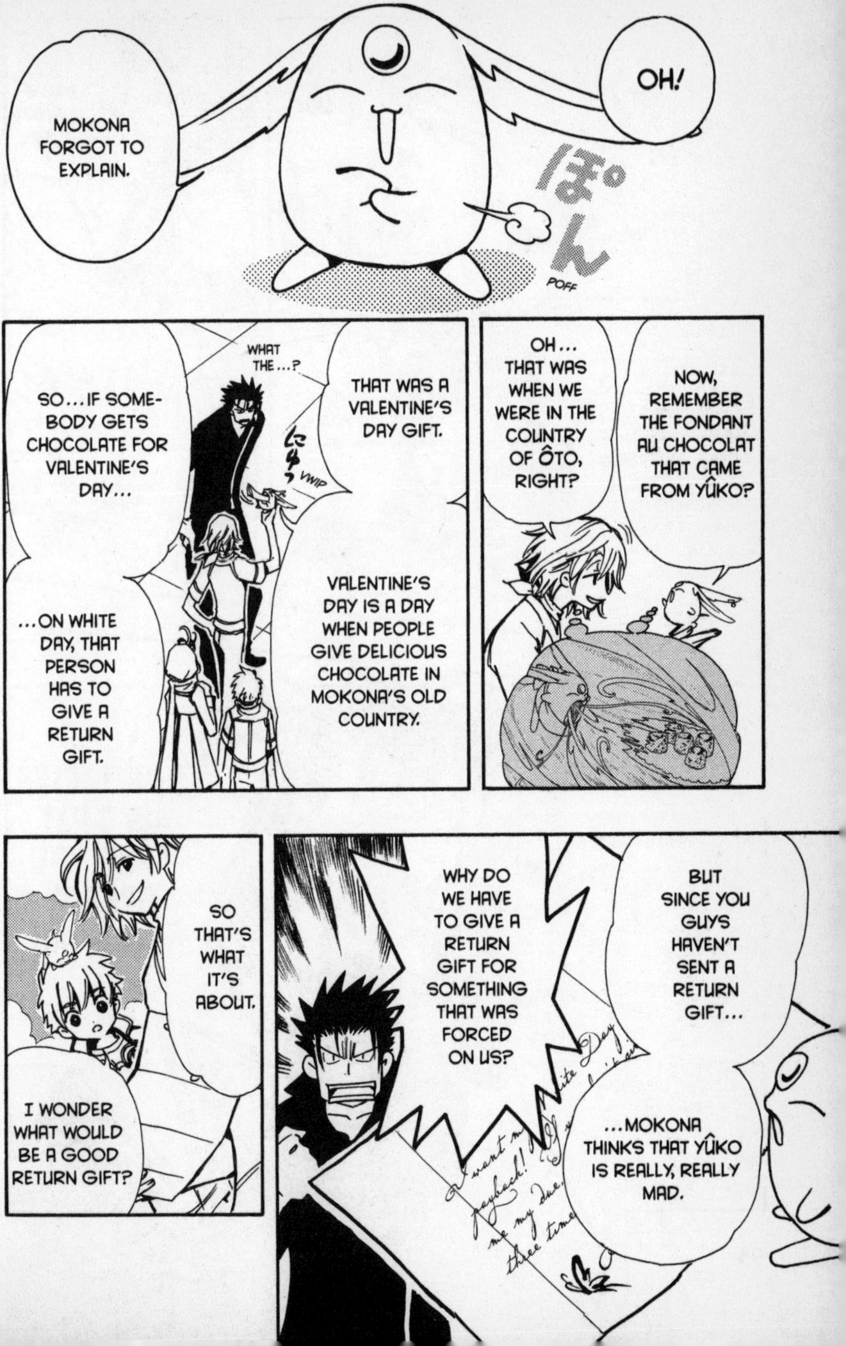
OH!
MOKONA FORGOT TO EXPLAIN.
ぽん
POFF
NOW, REMEMBER THE FONDANT AU CHOCOLAT THAT CAME FROM YÛKO?
OH… THAT WAS WHEN WE WERE IN THE COUNTRY OF ÔTO, RIGHT?
THAT WAS A VALENTINE'S DAY GIFT.
WHAT THE…?
にゅっ
VWIP
SO… IF SOMEBODY GETS CHOCOLATE FOR VALENTINE'S DAY…
VALENTINE'S DAY IS A DAY WHEN PEOPLE GIVE DELICIOUS CHOCOLATE IN MOKONA'S OLD COUNTRY.
…ON WHITE DAY, THAT PERSON HAS TO GIVE A RETURN GIFT.
BUT SINCE YOU GUYS HAVEN'T SENT A RETURN GIFT…
WHY DO WE HAVE TO GIVE A RETURN GIFT FOR SOMETHING THAT WAS FORCED ON US?
…MOKONA THINKS THAT YÛKO IS REALLY, REALLY MAD.
SO THAT'S WHAT IT'S ABOUT.
I WONDER WHAT WOULD BE A GOOD RETURN GIFT?

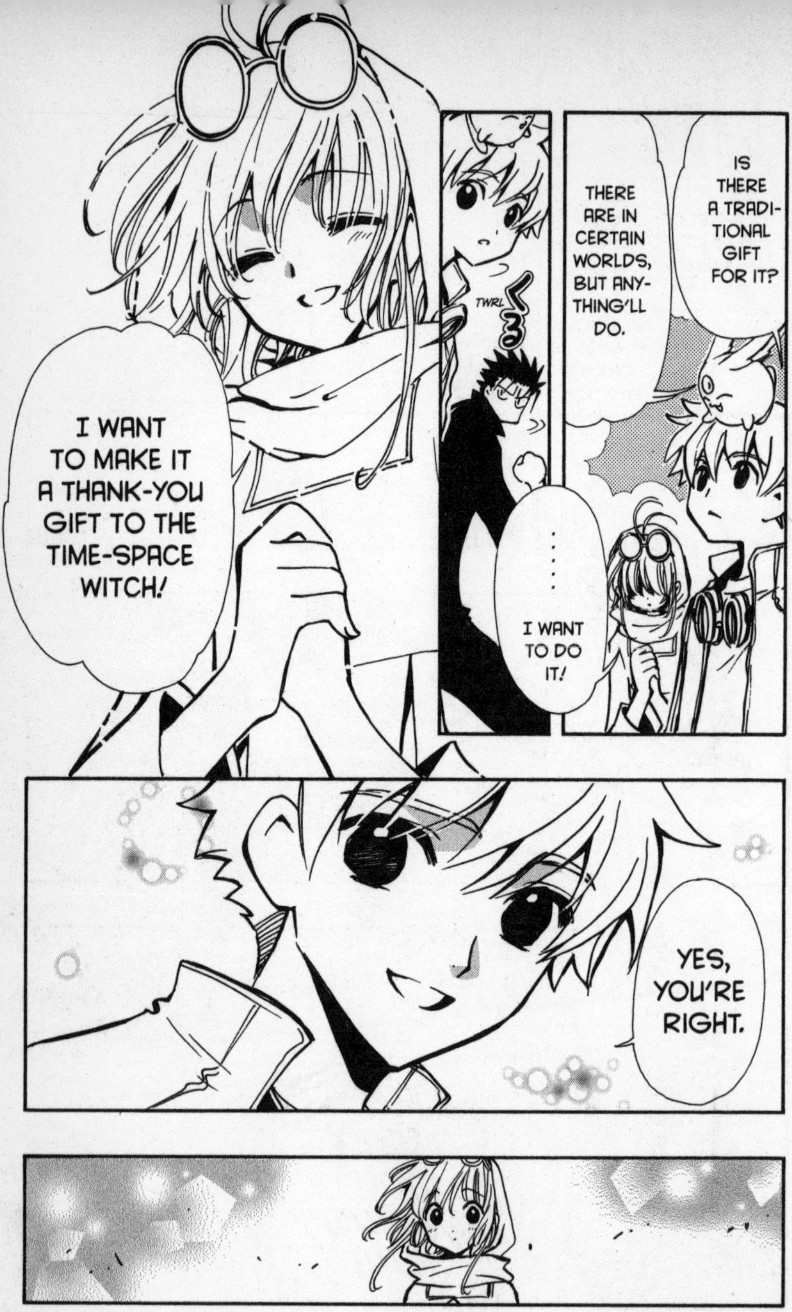
IS THERE A TRADITIONAL GIFT FOR IT?
THERE ARE IN CERTAIN WORLDS, BUT ANYTHING'LL DO.
くる
TWRL
.....
I WANT TO DO IT!
I WANT TO MAKE IT A THANK-YOU GIFT TO THE TIME-SPACE WITCH!
YES, YOU'RE RIGHT.

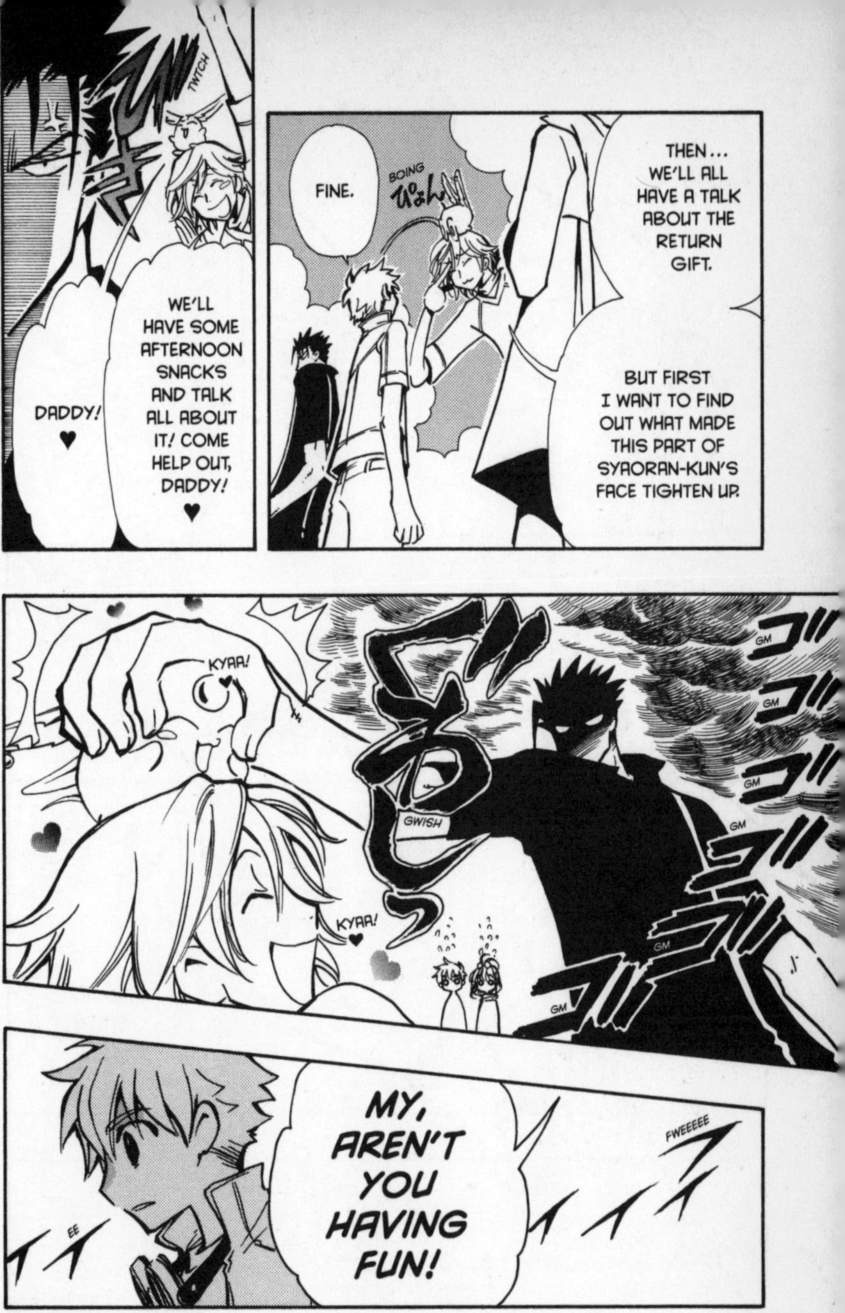
THEN... WE'LL ALL HAVE A TALK ABOUT THE RETURN GIFT.
BOING
FINE.
BUT FIRST I WANT TO FIND OUT WHAT MADE THIS PART OF SYAORAN-KUN'S FACE TIGHTEN UP.
TWITCH
WE'LL HAVE SOME AFTERNOON SNACKS AND TALK ALL ABOUT IT! COME HELP OUT, DADDY! ♥
DADDY! ♥
GM
GM
GM
GM
KYAA! ♥
GWISH
KYAA! ♥
GM
GM
FWEEEEE
MY, AREN'T YOU HAVING FUN!
EE

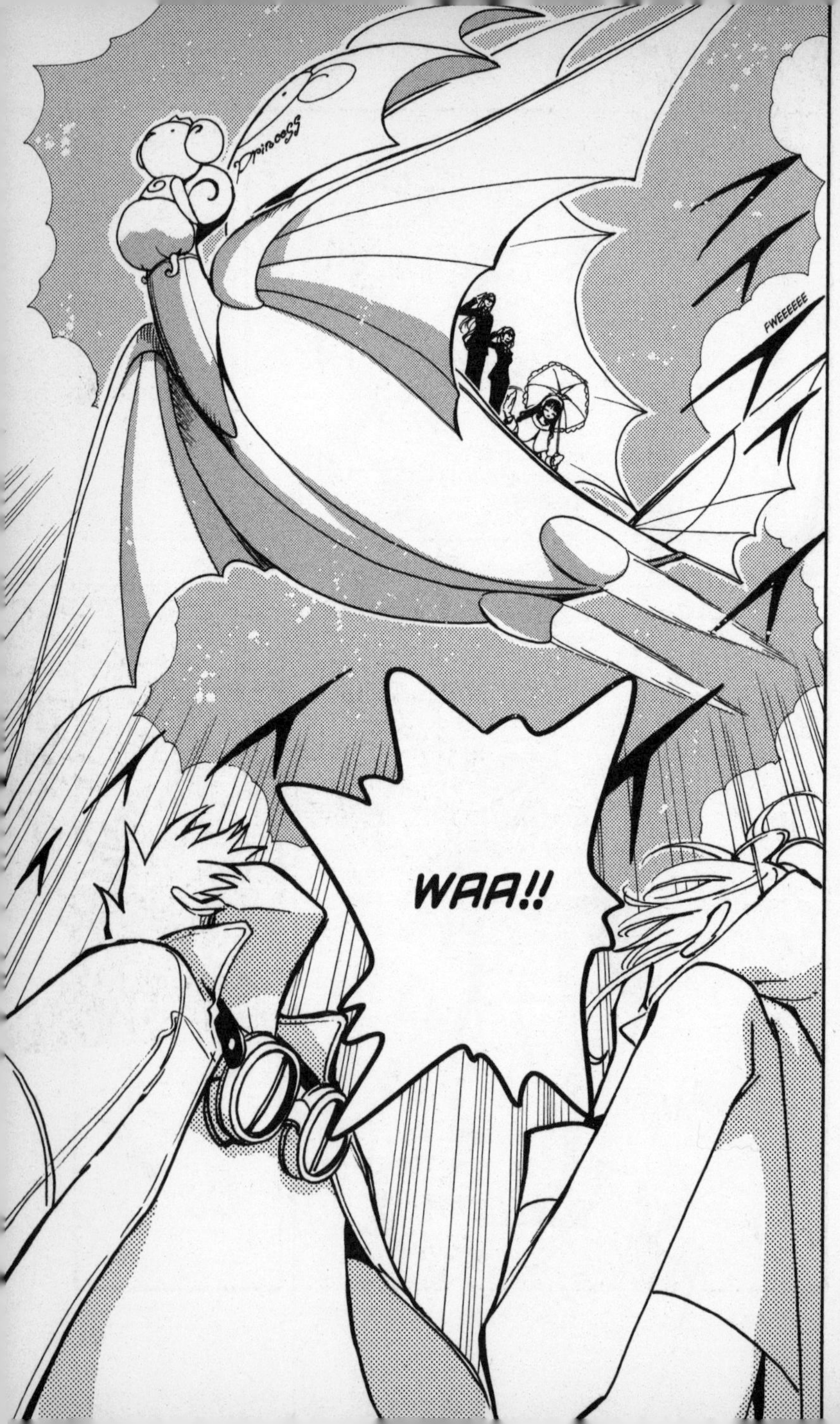
Princess
FWEEEEEE
WAA!!

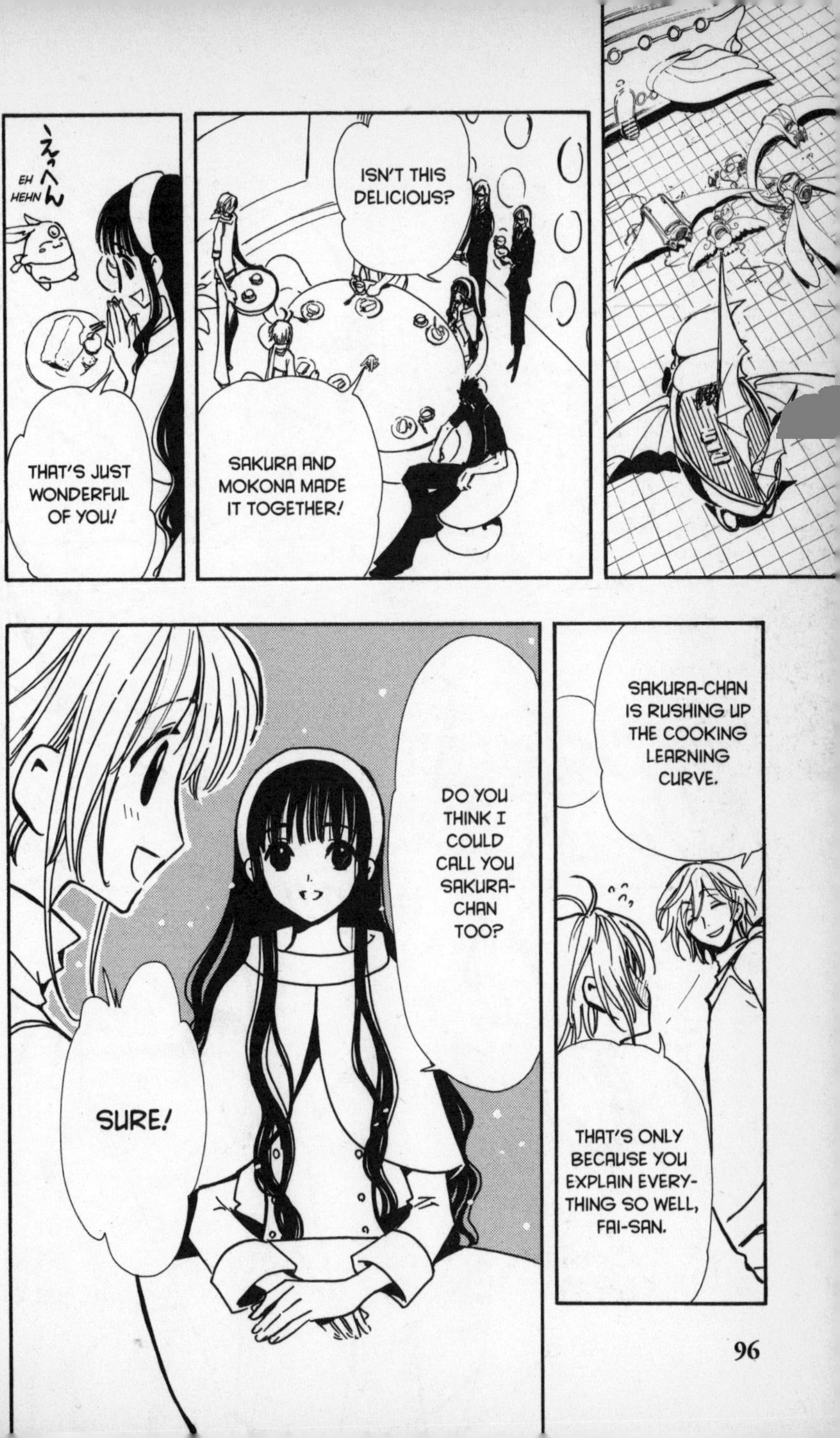
ISN'T THIS DELICIOUS?
SAKURA AND MOKONA MADE IT TOGETHER!
えへへん
EH HEHN
THAT'S JUST WONDERFUL OF YOU!
SAKURA-CHAN IS RUSHING UP THE COOKING LEARNING CURVE.
THAT'S ONLY BECAUSE YOU EXPLAIN EVERY-THING SO WELL, FAI-SAN.
DO YOU THINK I COULD CALL YOU SAKURA-CHAN TOO?
SURE!

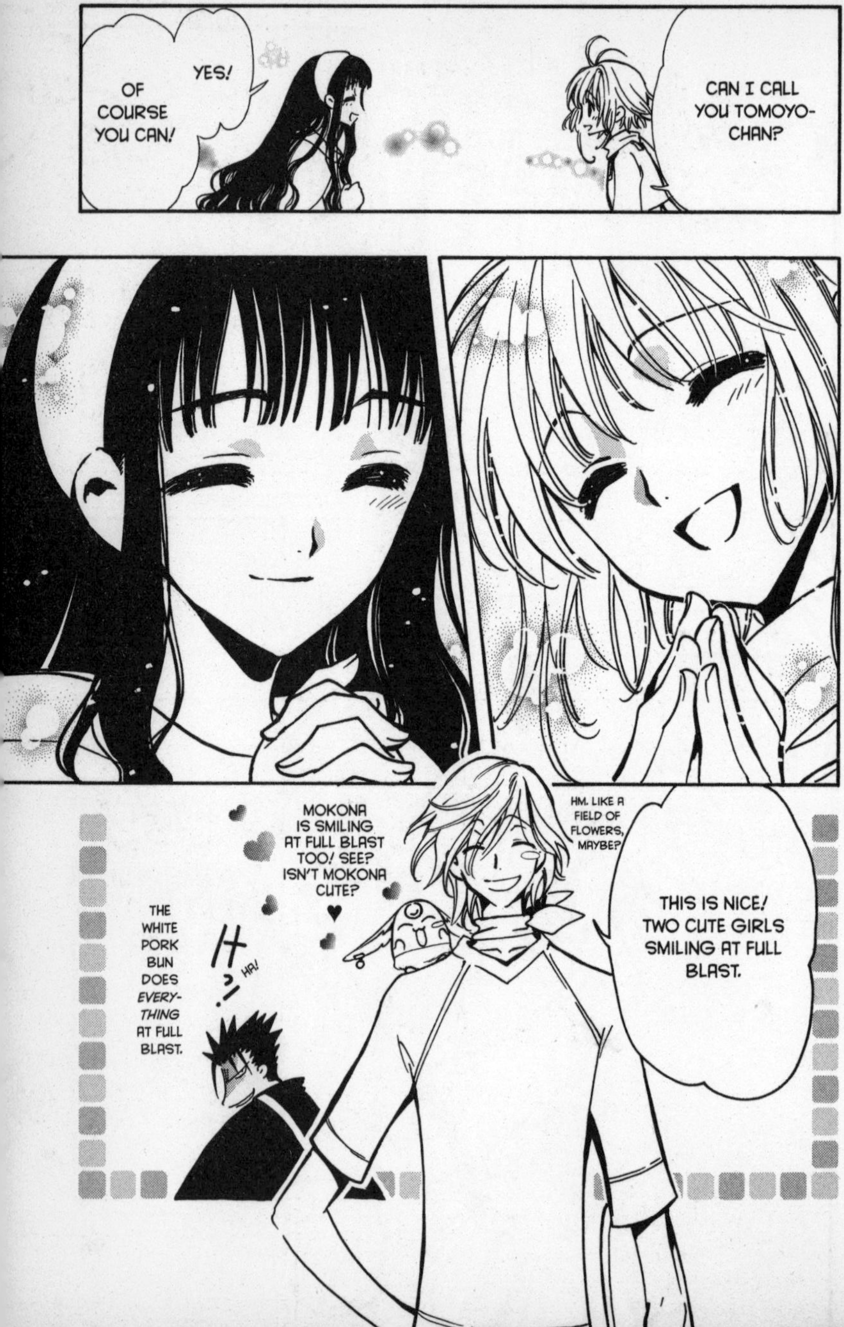

CAN I CALL YOU TOMOYO-CHAN?
YES!
OF COURSE YOU CAN!
THIS IS NICE! TWO CUTE GIRLS SMILING AT FULL BLAST.
HM. LIKE A FIELD OF FLOWERS, MAYBE?
MOKONA IS SMILING AT FULL BLAST TOO! SEE? ISN'T MOKONA CUTE?
HA!
THE WHITE PORK BUN DOES EVERYTHING AT FULL BLAST.

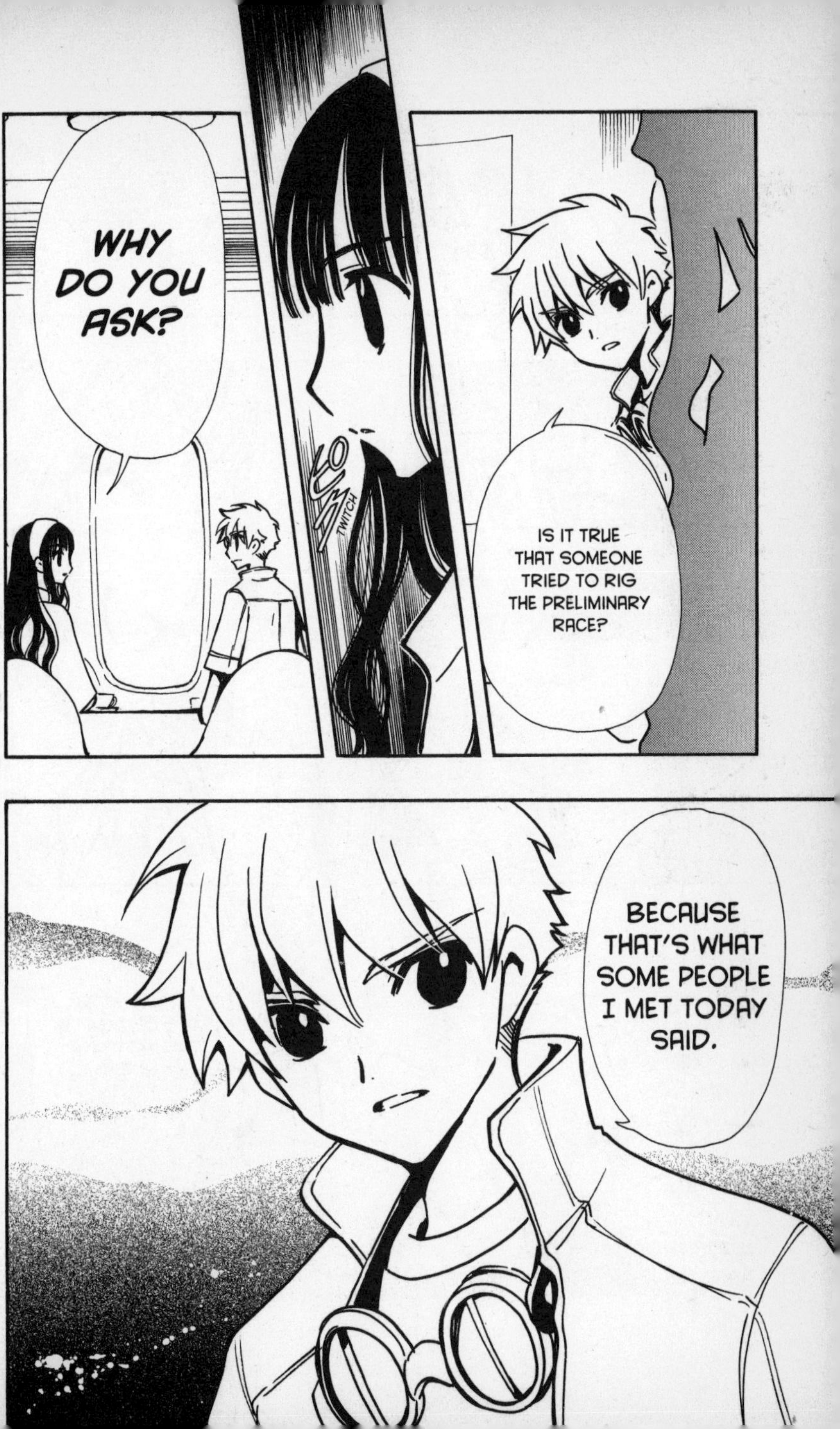
IS IT TRUE THAT SOMEONE TRIED TO RIG THE PRELIMINARY RACE?
TWITCH
WHY DO YOU ASK?
BECAUSE THAT'S WHAT SOME PEOPLE I MET TODAY SAID.

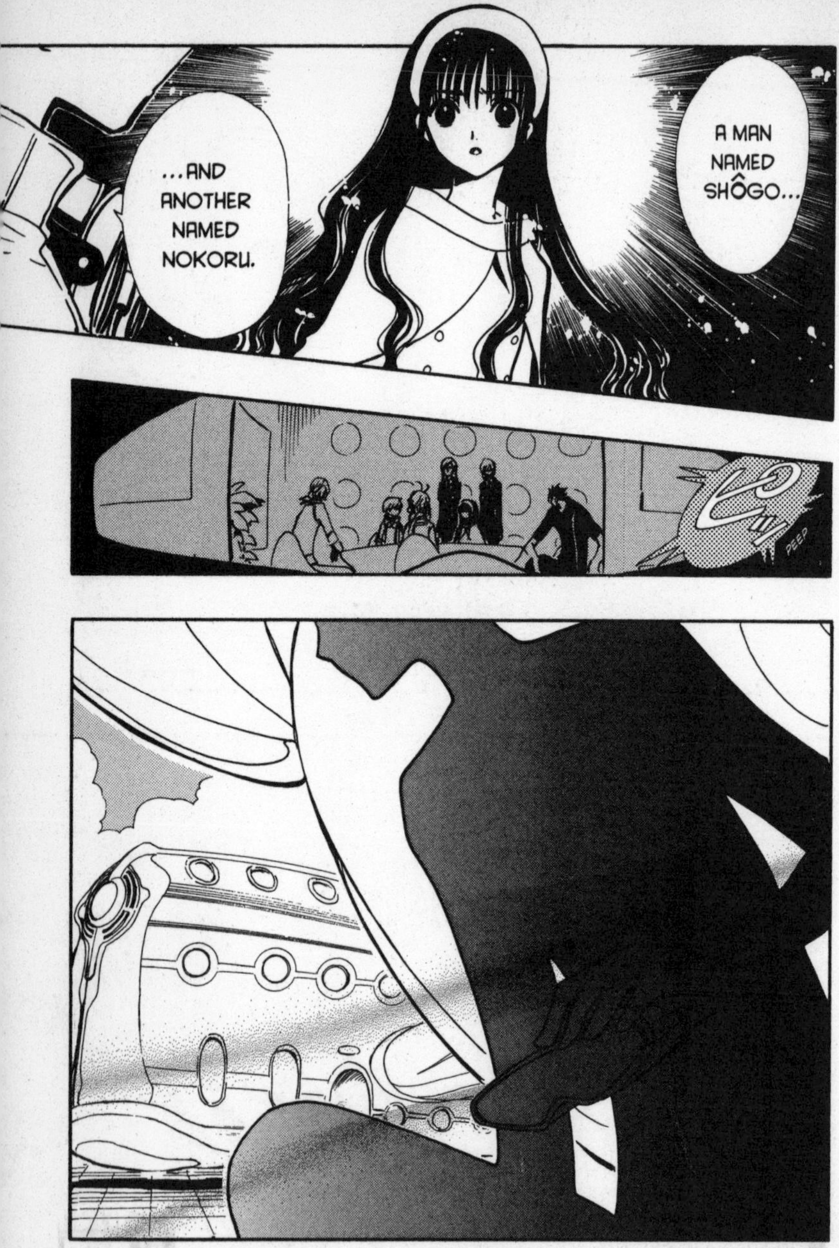
A MAN NAMED SHÔGO...
...AND ANOTHER NAMED NOKORU.
PEEP

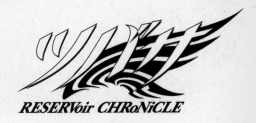

RESERVoir CHRoNiCLE

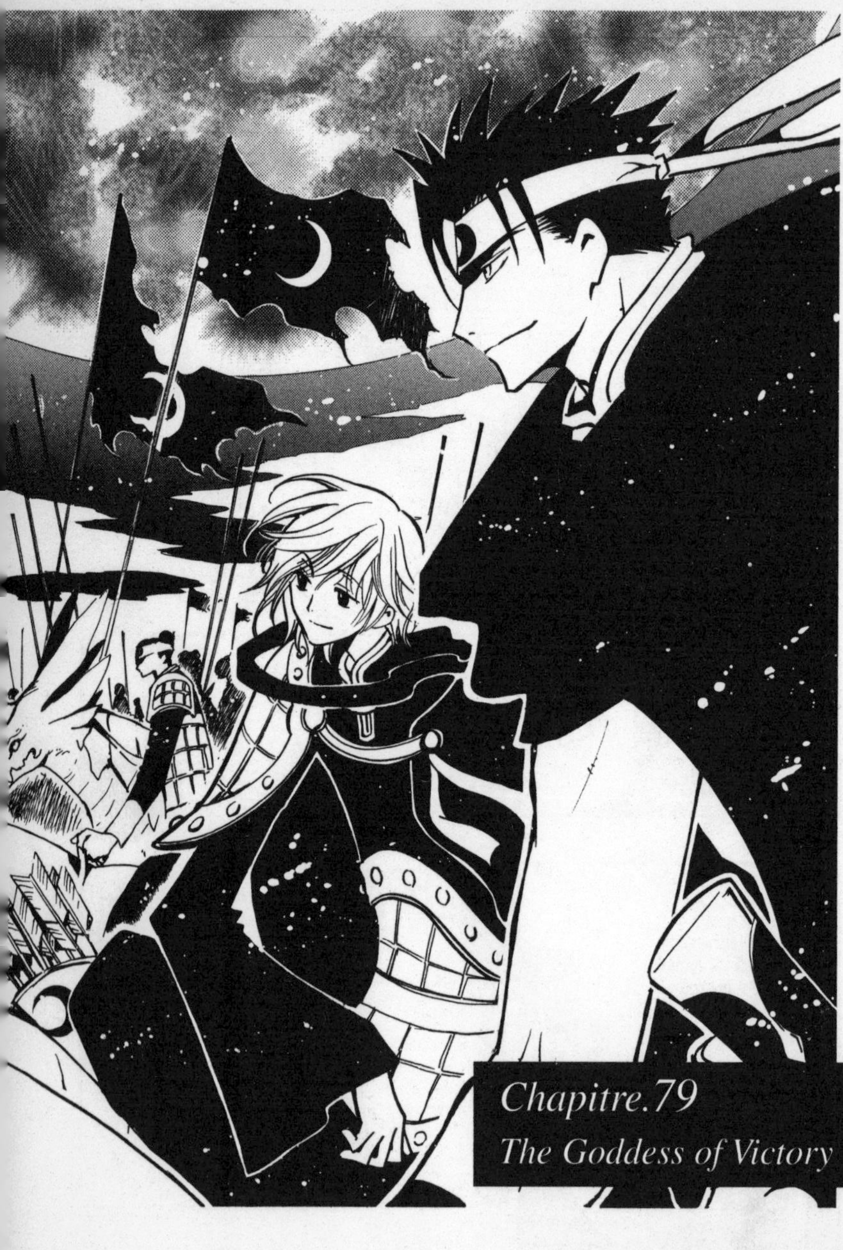
Chapitre.79
The Goddess of Victory

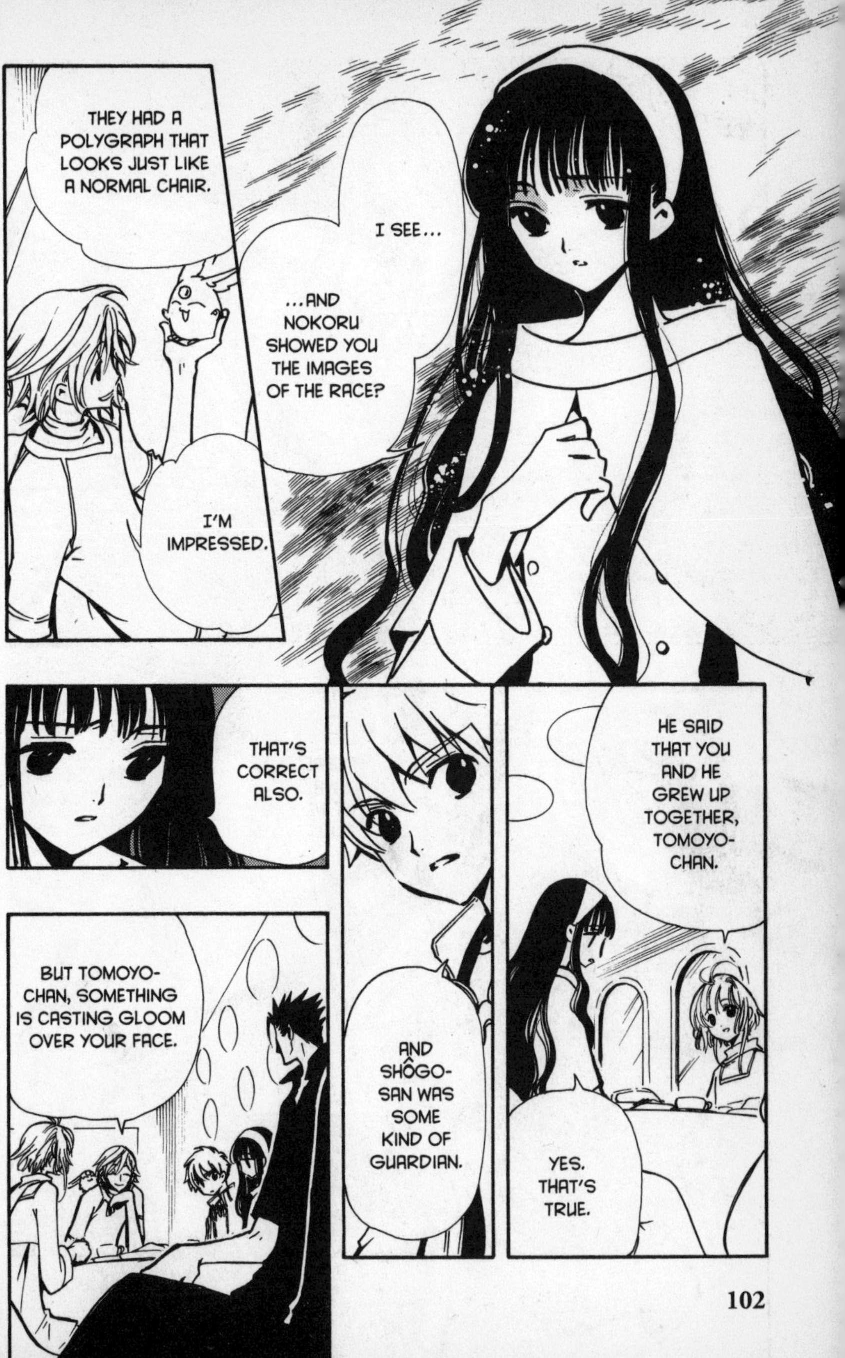
THEY HAD A POLYGRAPH THAT LOOKS JUST LIKE A NORMAL CHAIR.
I SEE...
...AND NOKORU SHOWED YOU THE IMAGES OF THE RACE?
I'M IMPRESSED.
HE SAID THAT YOU AND HE GREW UP TOGETHER, TOMOYO-CHAN.
AND SHÔGO-SAN WAS SOME KIND OF GUARDIAN.
YES. THAT'S TRUE.
THAT'S CORRECT ALSO.
BUT TOMOYO-CHAN, SOMETHING IS CASTING GLOOM OVER YOUR FACE.

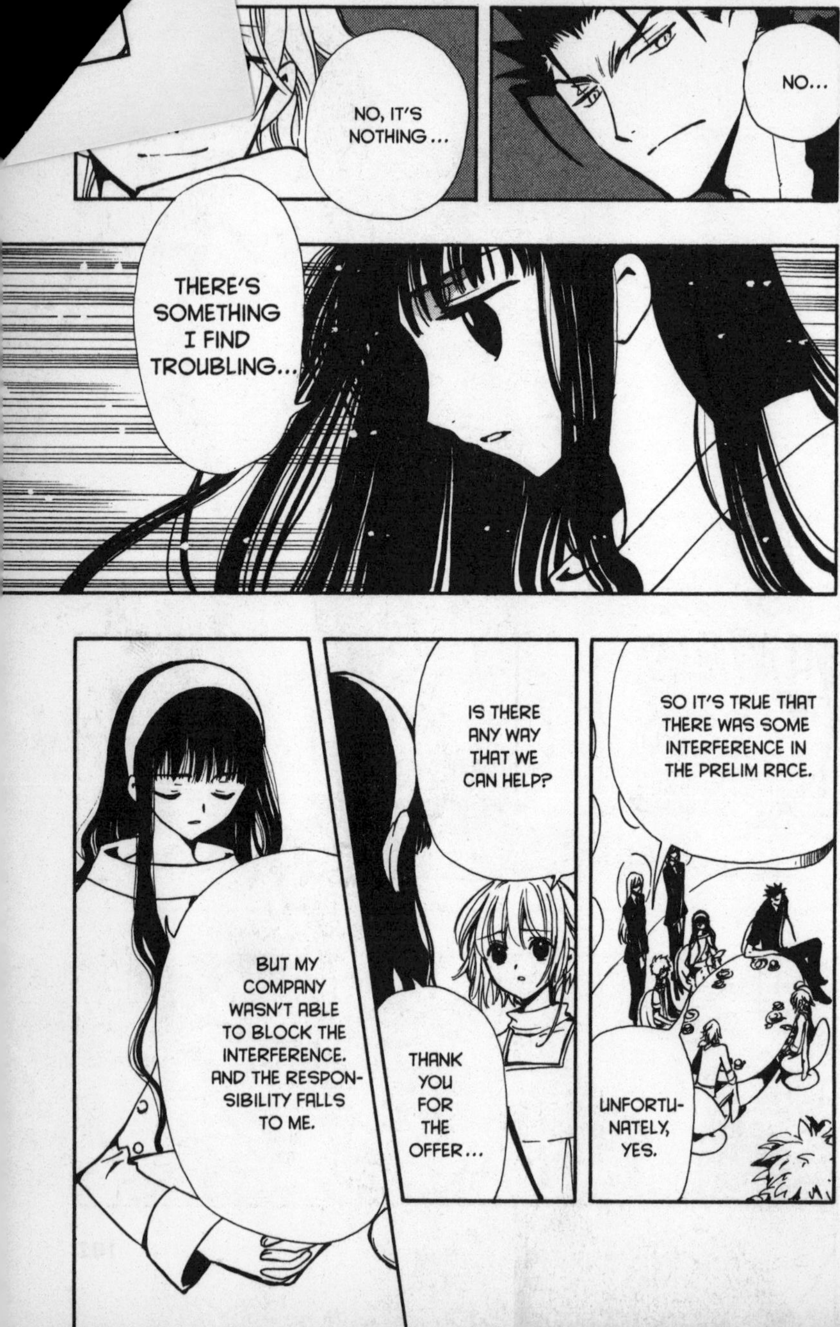
NO...
NO, IT'S NOTHING...
THERE'S SOMETHING I FIND TROUBLING...
SO IT'S TRUE THAT THERE WAS SOME INTERFERENCE IN THE PRELIM RACE.
UNFORTUNATELY, YES.
IS THERE ANY WAY THAT WE CAN HELP?
THANK YOU FOR THE OFFER...
BUT MY COMPANY WASN'T ABLE TO BLOCK THE INTERFERENCE. AND THE RESPONSIBILITY FALLS TO ME.

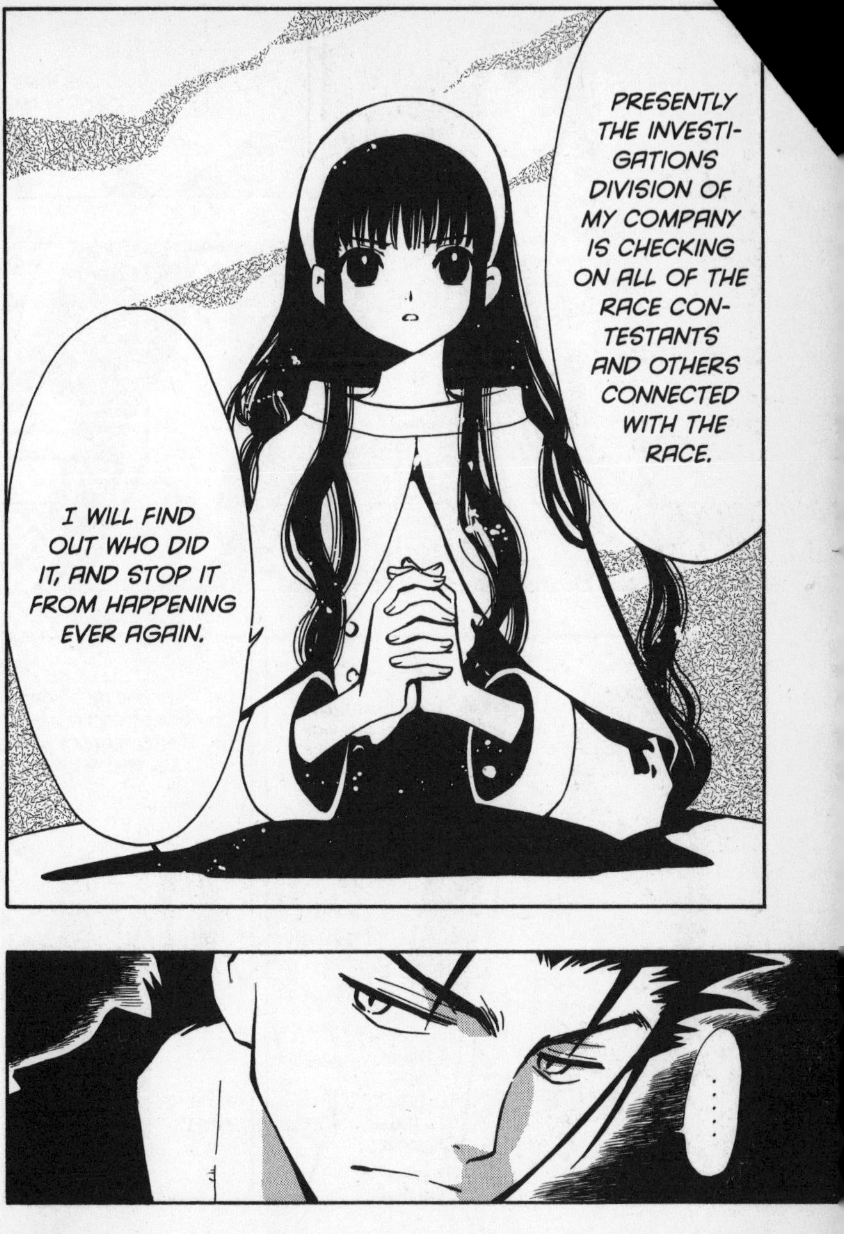
PRESENTLY THE INVESTI-GATIONS DIVISION OF MY COMPANY IS CHECKING ON ALL OF THE RACE CON-TESTANTS AND OTHERS CONNECTED WITH THE RACE.
I WILL FIND OUT WHO DID IT, AND STOP IT FROM HAPPENING EVER AGAIN.
.....

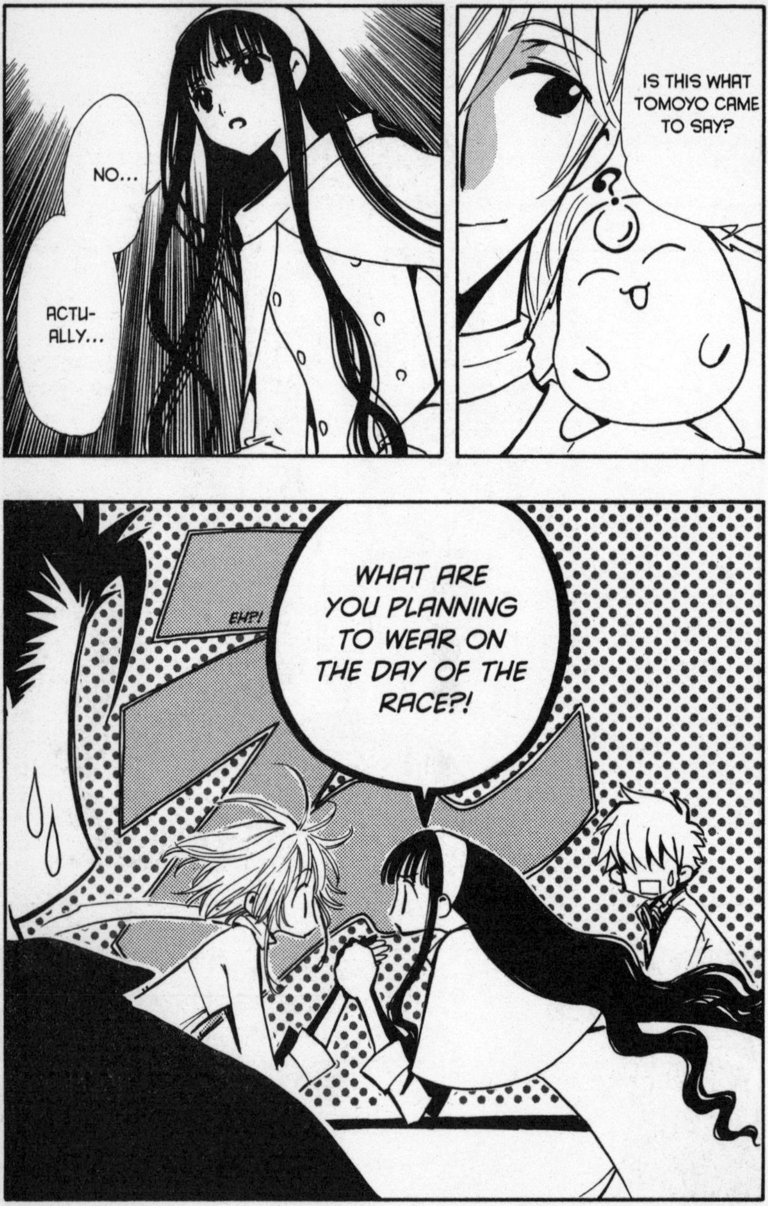
IS THIS WHAT TOMOYO CAME TO SAY?
NO...
ACTU-ALLY...
WHAT ARE YOU PLANNING TO WEAR ON THE DAY OF THE RACE?!
EH?!

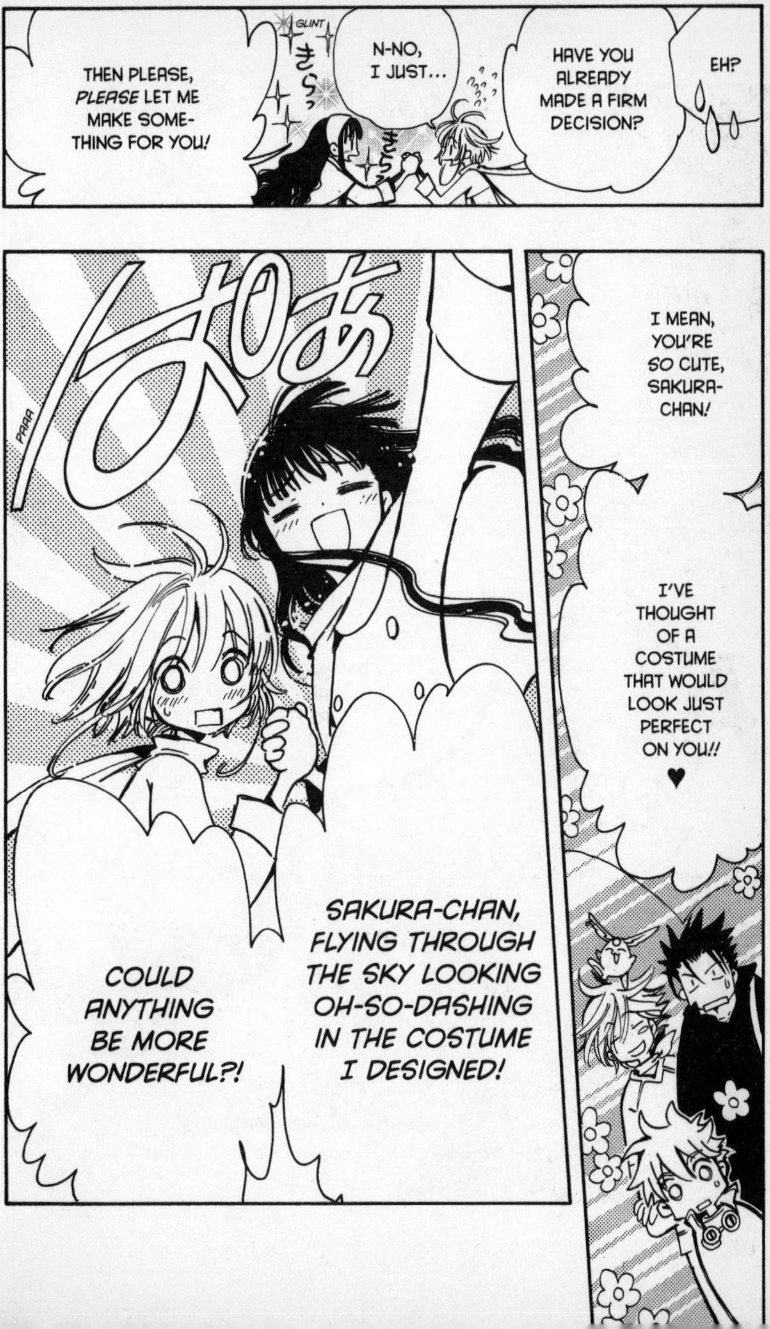
EH?
HAVE YOU ALREADY MADE A FIRM DECISION?
N-NO, I JUST...
GLINT
きらっ
THEN PLEASE, *PLEASE* LET ME MAKE SOME-THING FOR YOU!
I MEAN, YOU'RE *SO* CUTE, SAKURA-CHAN!
I'VE THOUGHT OF A COSTUME THAT WOULD LOOK JUST PERFECT ON YOU!! ♥
ぱあ
PAAA
SAKURA-CHAN, FLYING THROUGH THE SKY LOOKING OH-SO-DASHING IN THE COSTUME I DESIGNED!
COULD ANYTHING BE MORE WONDERFUL?!

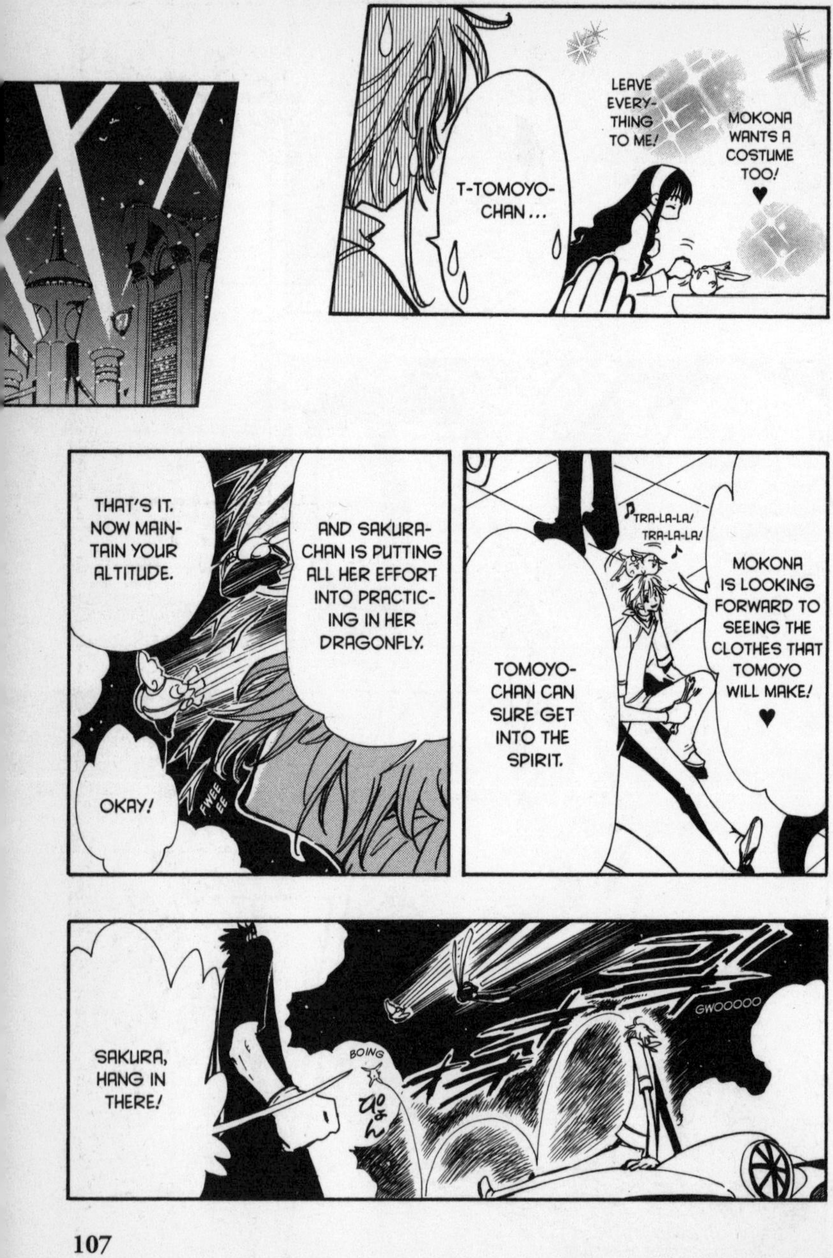
MOKONA WANTS A COSTUME TOO! ♥
LEAVE EVERY-THING TO ME!
T-TOMOYO-CHAN...
♪TRA-LA-LA! TRA-LA-LA!♪
MOKONA IS LOOKING FORWARD TO SEEING THE CLOTHES THAT TOMOYO WILL MAKE! ♥
TOMOYO-CHAN CAN SURE GET INTO THE SPIRIT.
AND SAKURA-CHAN IS PUTTING ALL HER EFFORT INTO PRACTIC-ING IN HER DRAGONFLY.
THAT'S IT. NOW MAIN-TAIN YOUR ALTITUDE.
FWEEEE
OKAY!
GWOOOOO
BOING
ぴょん
SAKURA, HANG IN THERE!

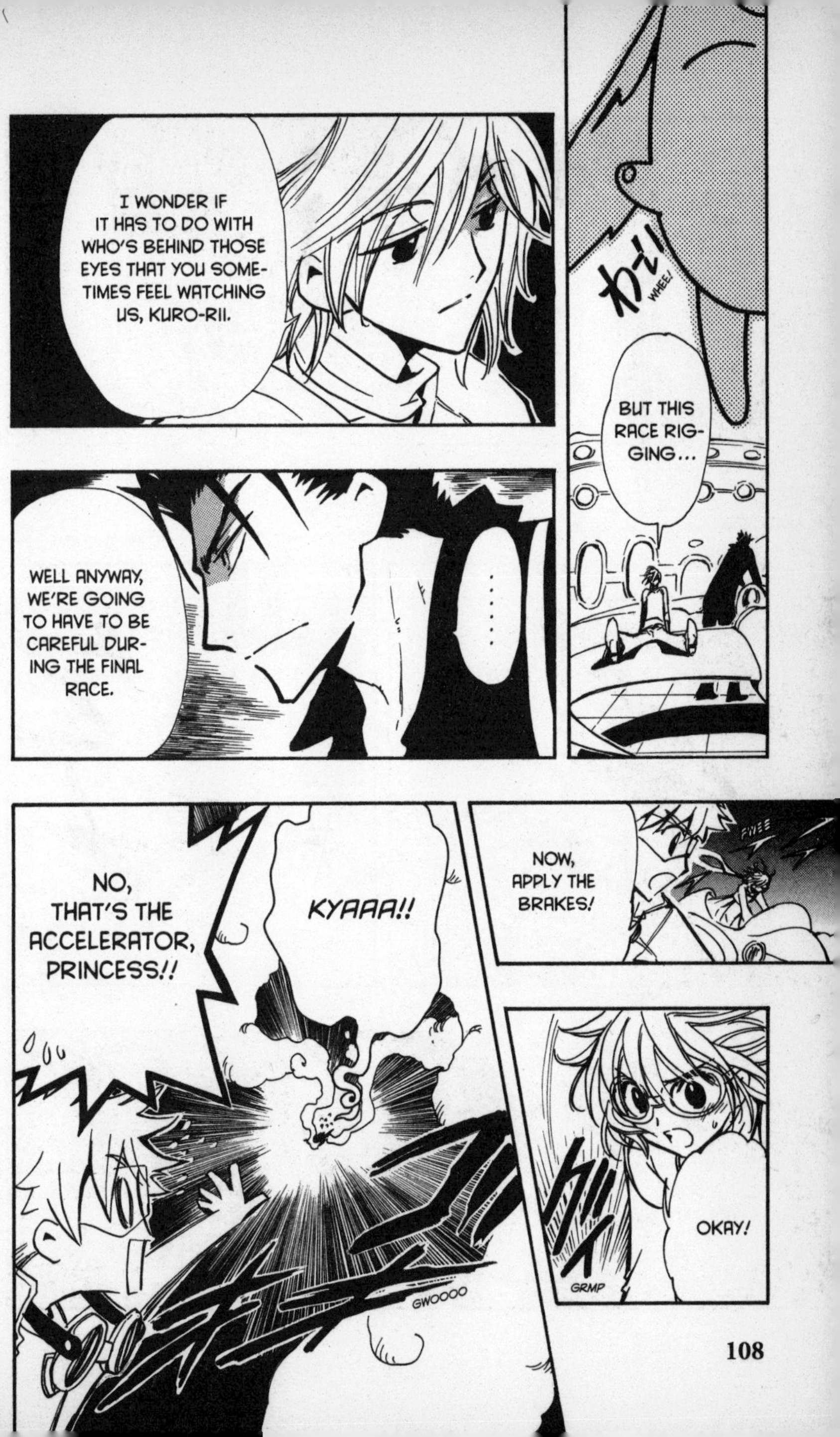
WHEE!
BUT THIS RACE RIGGING...
I WONDER IF IT HAS TO DO WITH WHO'S BEHIND THOSE EYES THAT YOU SOMETIMES FEEL WATCHING US, KURO-RII.
WELL ANYWAY, WE'RE GOING TO HAVE TO BE CAREFUL DURING THE FINAL RACE.
......
FWEE
NOW, APPLY THE BRAKES!
OKAY!
GRMP
KYAAA!!
NO, THAT'S THE ACCELERATOR, PRINCESS!!
GWOOOO

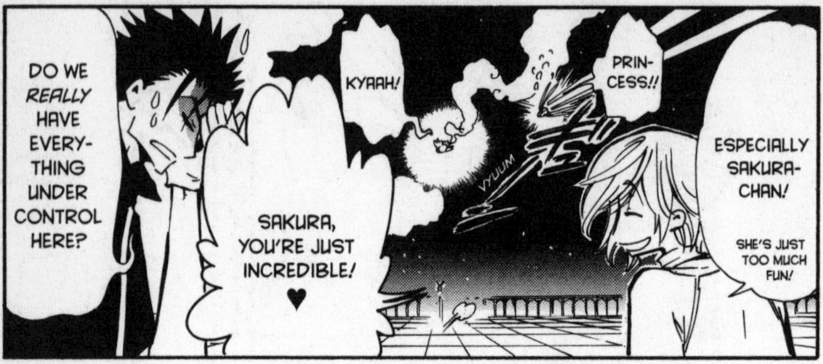
ESPECIALLY SAKURA-CHAN!
SHE'S JUST TOO MUCH FUN!
PRIN-CESS!!
VYUUM
KYAAH!
SAKURA, YOU'RE JUST INCREDIBLE! ♥
DO WE *REALLY* HAVE EVERY-THING UNDER CONTROL HERE?

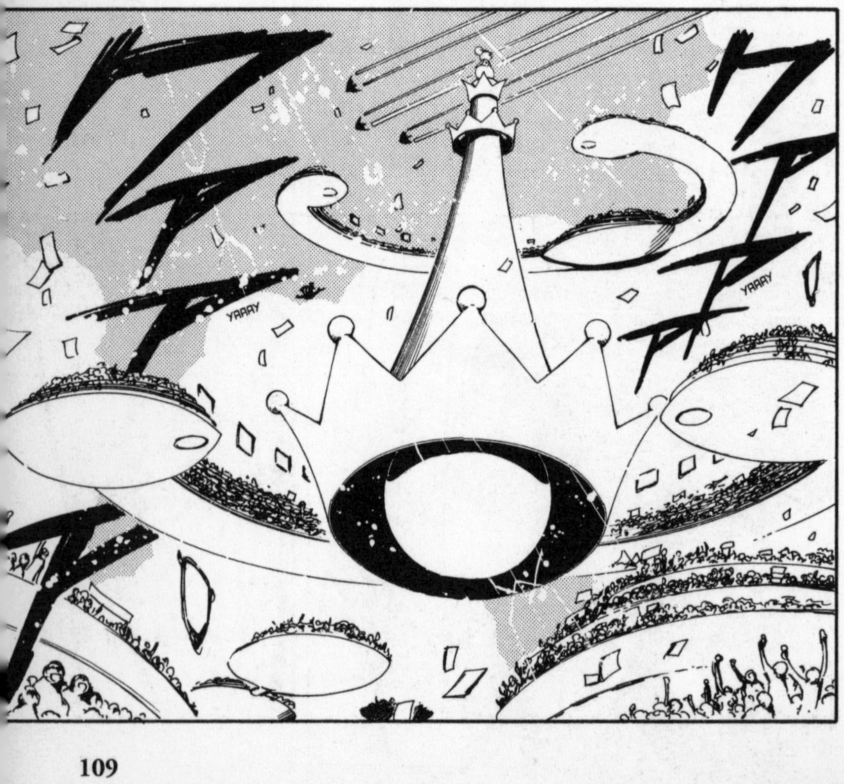
YAAAY
YAAAY

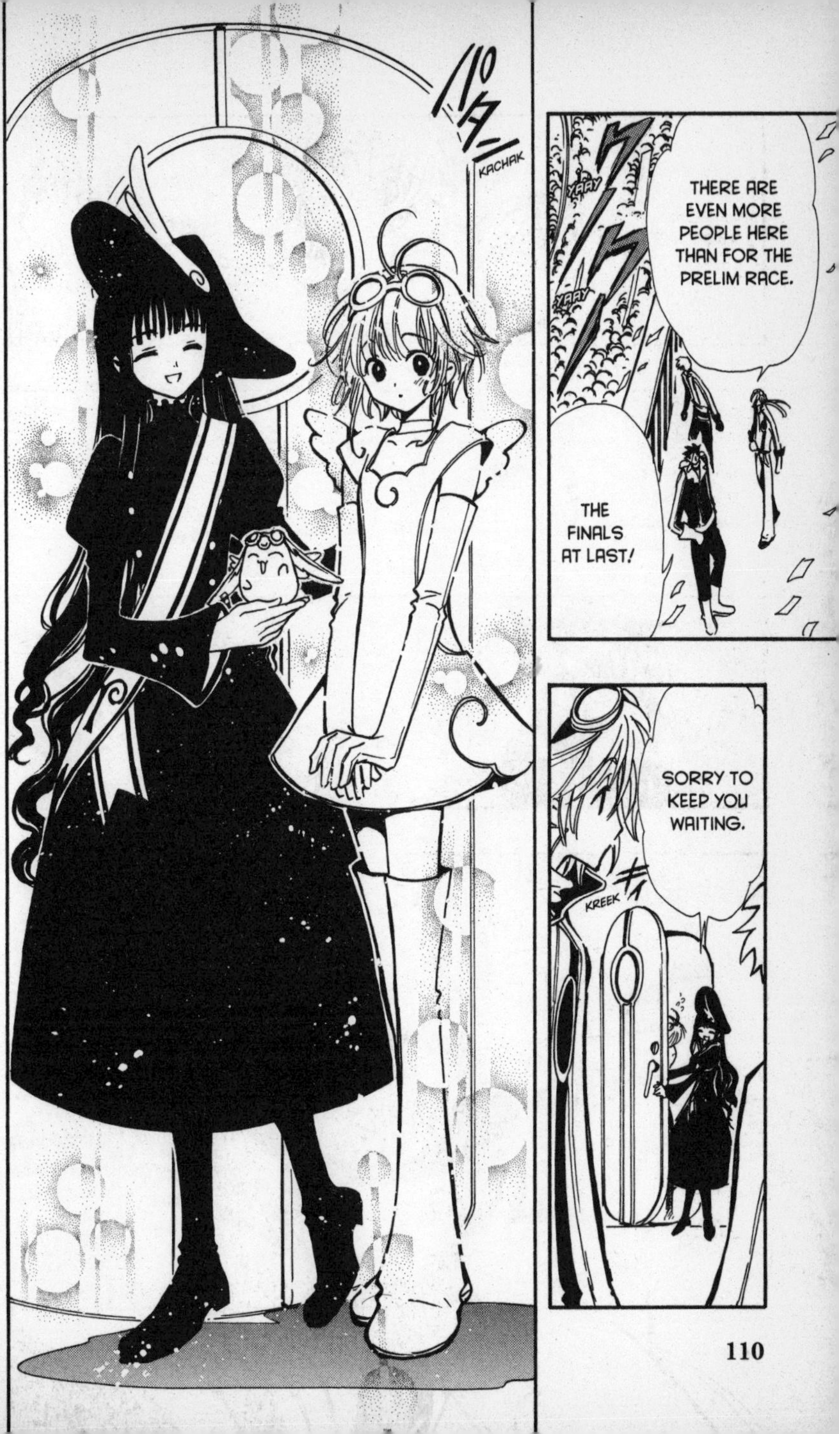
THERE ARE EVEN MORE PEOPLE HERE THAN FOR THE PRELIM RACE.
YAAY
YAAY
THE FINALS AT LAST!
SORRY TO KEEP YOU WAITING.
KREEK
KACHAK

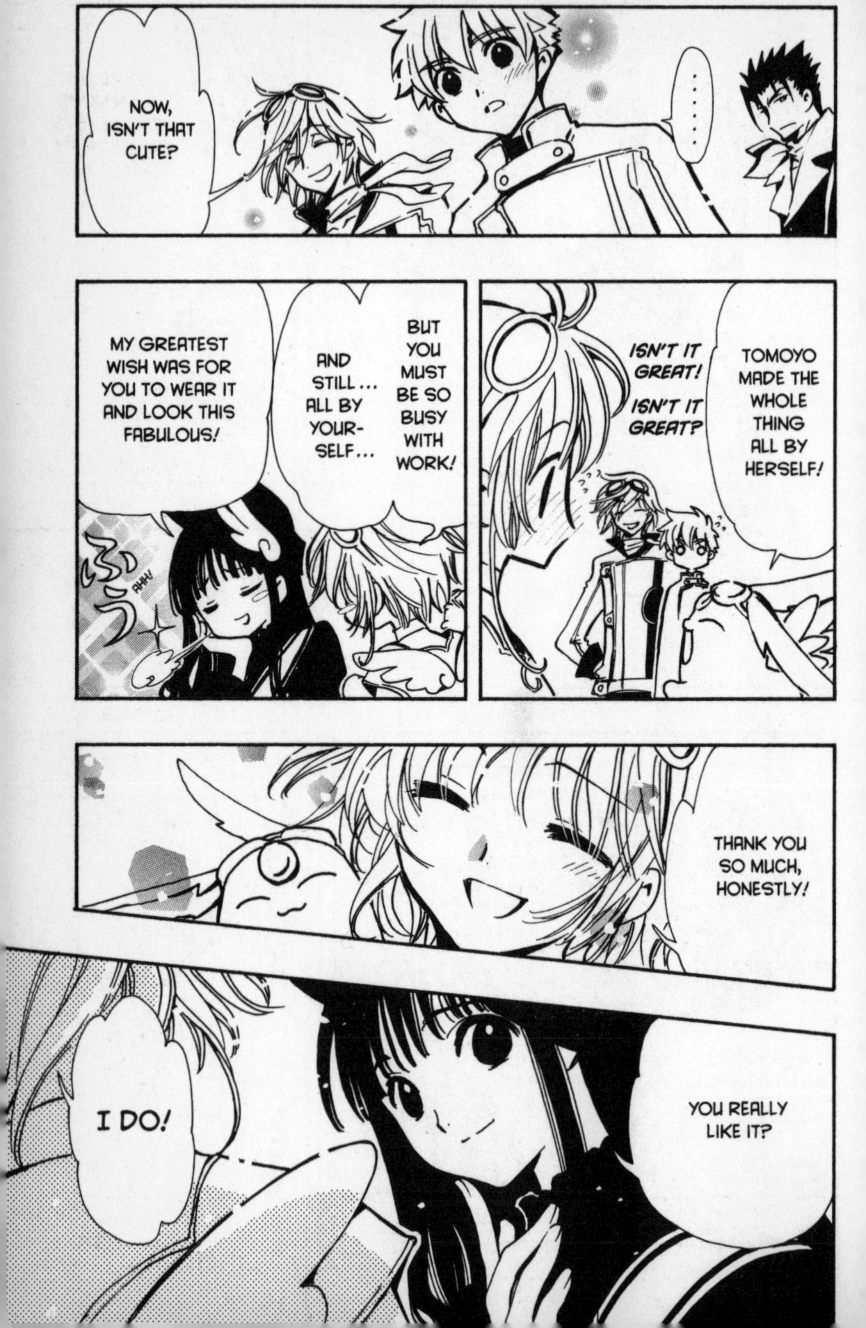
......
NOW, ISN'T THAT CUTE?
TOMOYO MADE THE WHOLE THING ALL BY HERSELF!
ISN'T IT GREAT! ISN'T IT GREAT?
BUT YOU MUST BE SO BUSY WITH WORK!
AND STILL... ALL BY YOUR-SELF...
MY GREATEST WISH WAS FOR YOU TO WEAR IT AND LOOK THIS FABULOUS!
ふう
AHH!
THANK YOU SO MUCH, HONESTLY!
YOU REALLY LIKE IT?
I DO!

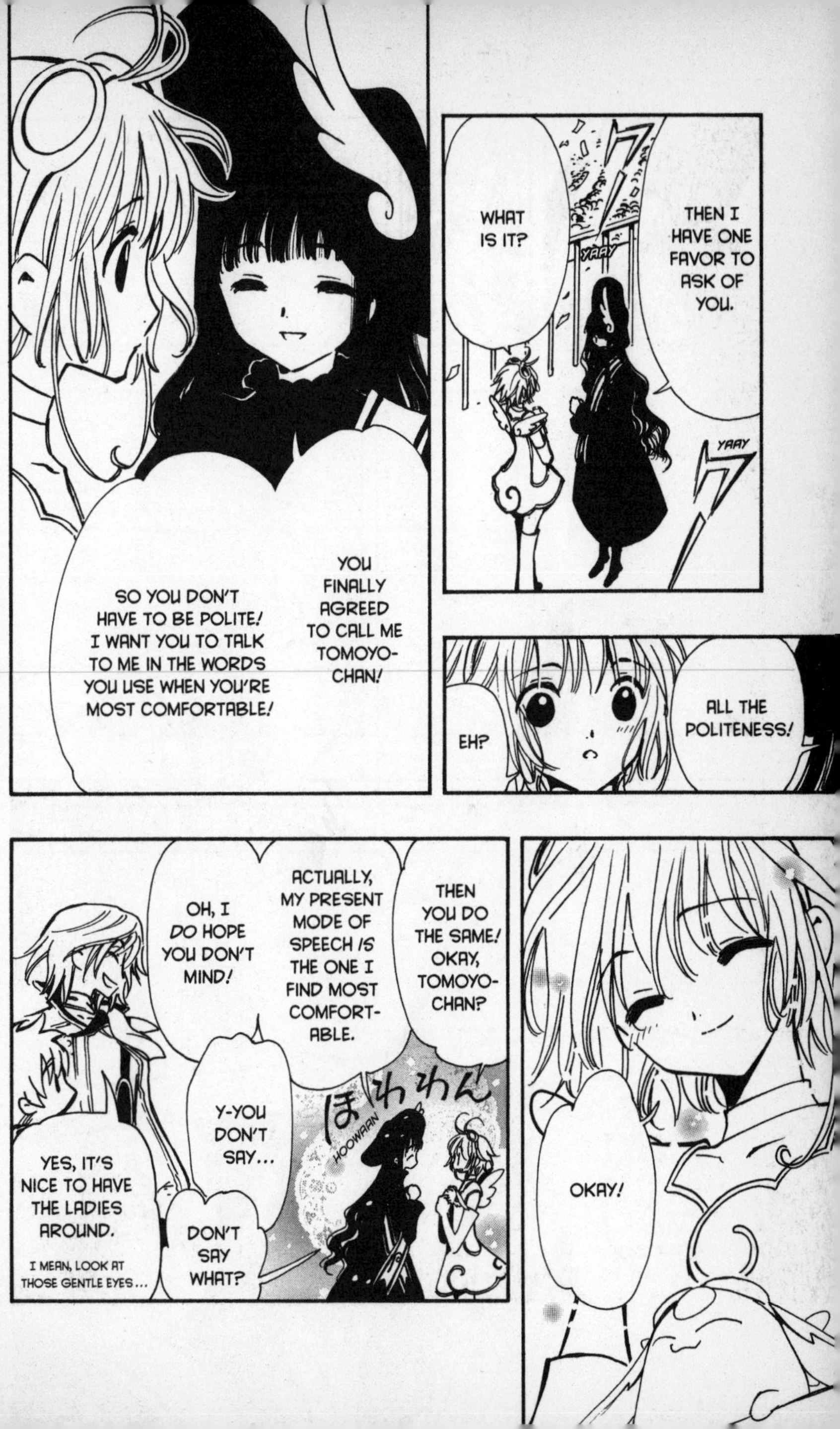
THEN I HAVE ONE FAVOR TO ASK OF YOU.
YAAY
WHAT IS IT?
YAAY
ALL THE POLITENESS!
EH?
YOU FINALLY AGREED TO CALL ME TOMOYO-CHAN!
SO YOU DON'T HAVE TO BE POLITE! I WANT YOU TO TALK TO ME IN THE WORDS YOU USE WHEN YOU'RE MOST COMFORTABLE!
OKAY!
THEN YOU DO THE SAME! OKAY, TOMOYO-CHAN?
ACTUALLY, MY PRESENT MODE OF SPEECH *IS* THE ONE I FIND MOST COMFORT-ABLE.
OH, I *DO* HOPE YOU DON'T MIND!
ほわわん
HOOWAAN
Y-YOU DON'T SAY...
DON'T SAY WHAT?
YES, IT'S NICE TO HAVE THE LADIES AROUND.
I MEAN, LOOK AT THOSE GENTLE EYES...

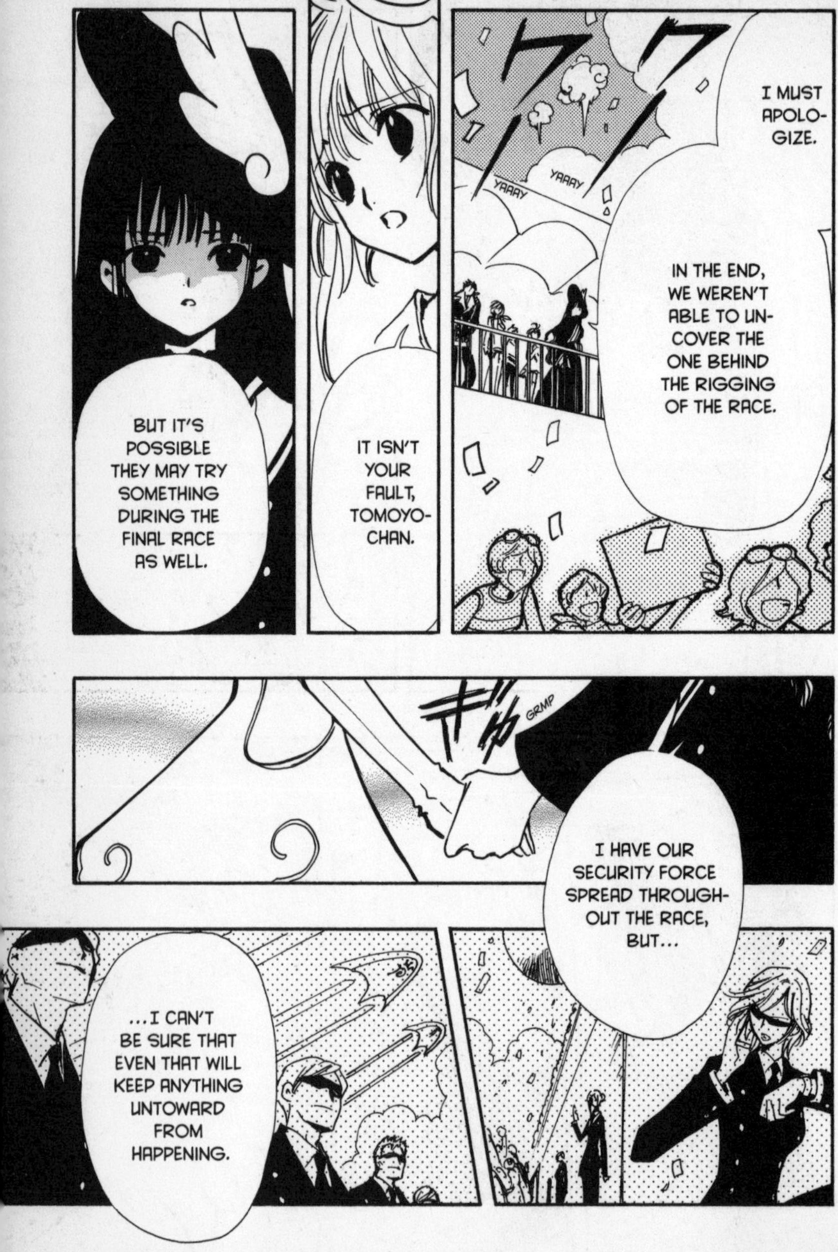
YAAAY
YAAAY
I MUST APOLOGIZE.
IN THE END, WE WEREN'T ABLE TO UNCOVER THE ONE BEHIND THE RIGGING OF THE RACE.
IT ISN'T YOUR FAULT, TOMOYO-CHAN.
BUT IT'S POSSIBLE THEY MAY TRY SOMETHING DURING THE FINAL RACE AS WELL.
GRMP
I HAVE OUR SECURITY FORCE SPREAD THROUGHOUT THE RACE, BUT...
...I CAN'T BE SURE THAT EVEN THAT WILL KEEP ANYTHING UNTOWARD FROM HAPPENING.

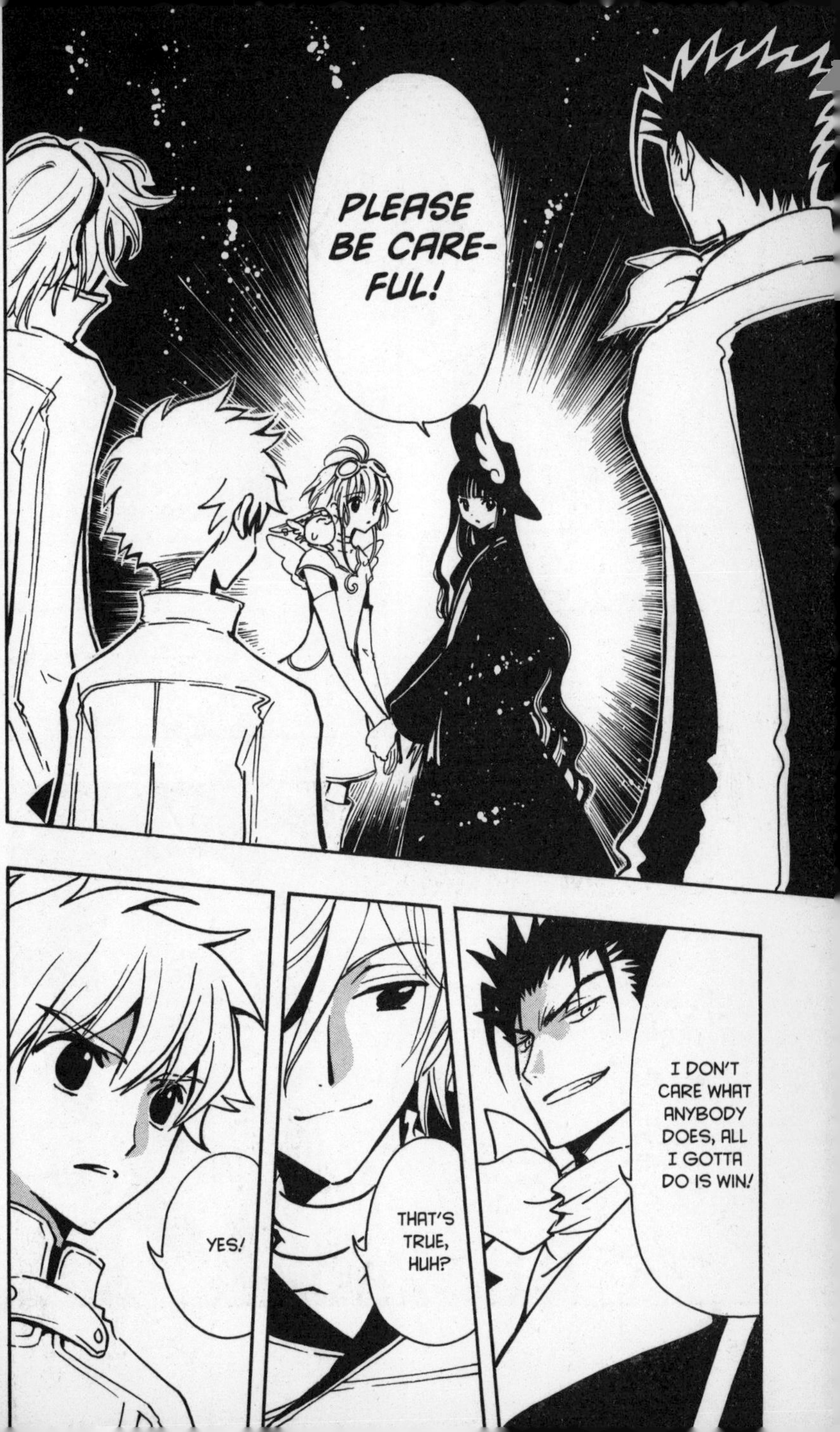
PLEASE BE CARE-FUL!
I DON'T CARE WHAT ANYBODY DOES, ALL I GOTTA DO IS WIN!
THAT'S TRUE, HUH?
YES!

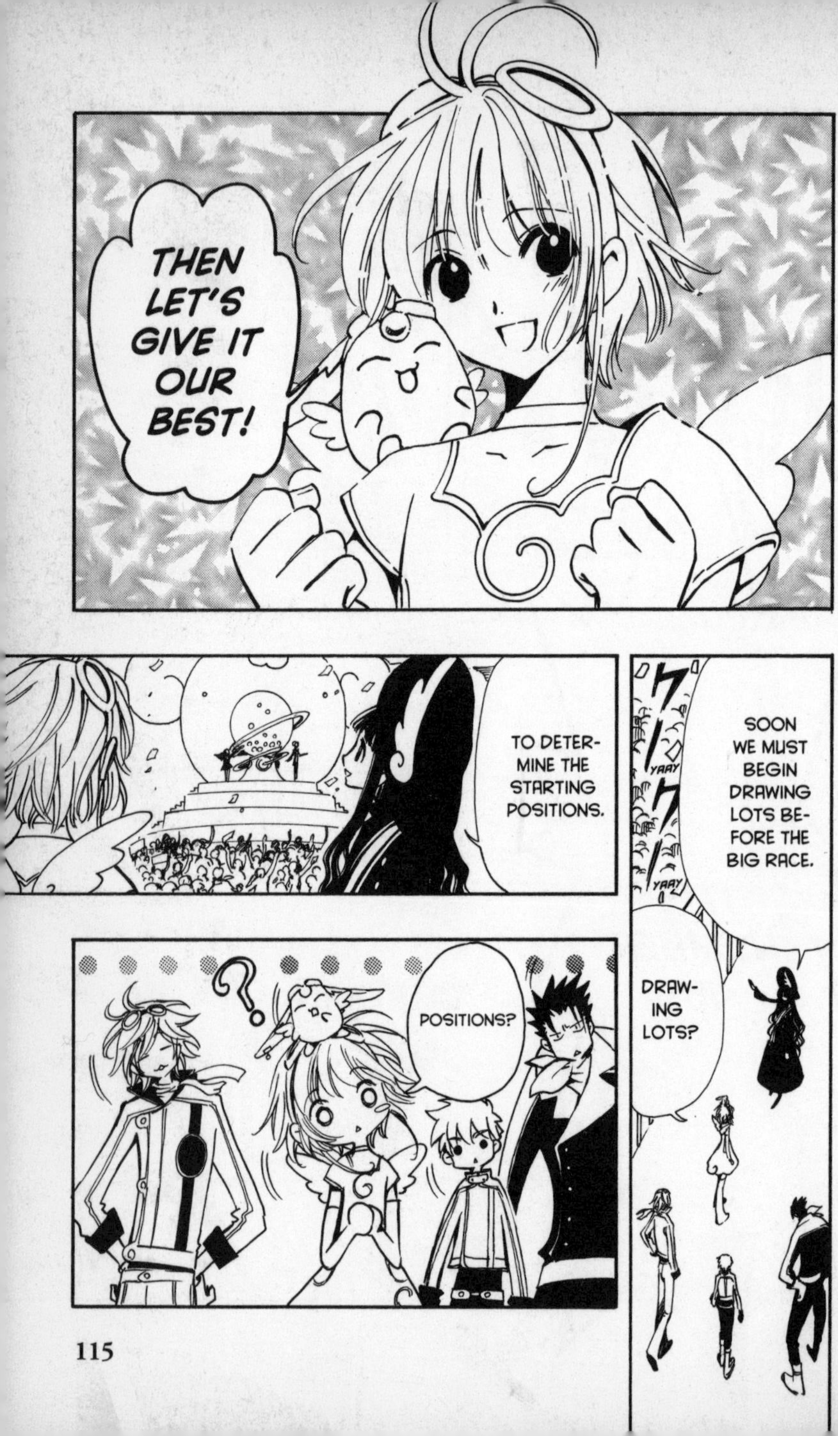
THEN LET'S GIVE IT OUR BEST!
SOON WE MUST BEGIN DRAWING LOTS BEFORE THE BIG RACE.
YAAY
YAAY
DRAWING LOTS?
TO DETERMINE THE STARTING POSITIONS.
POSITIONS?

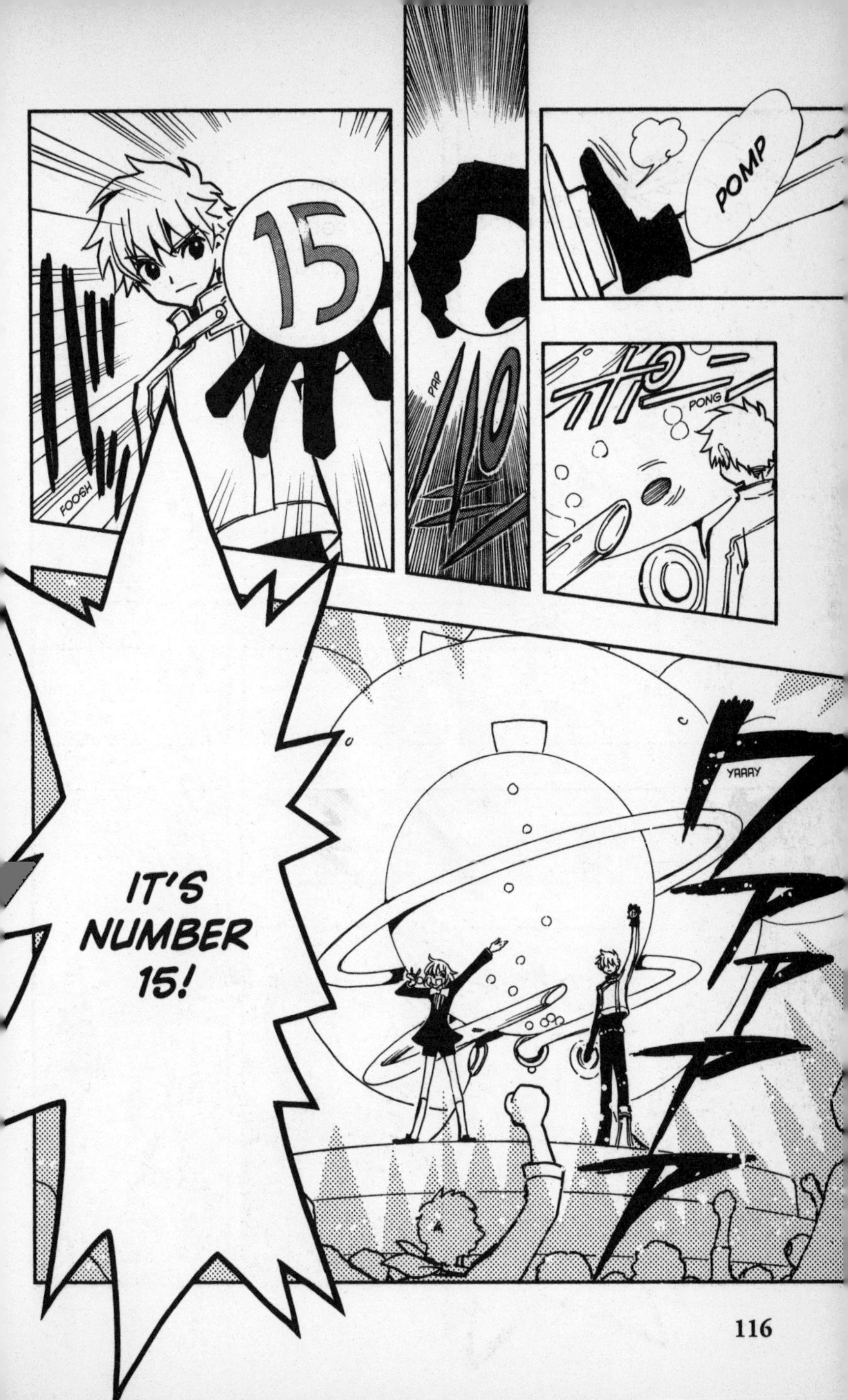
POMP
PONG
PAP
FOOSH
YARRY
IT'S NUMBER 15!

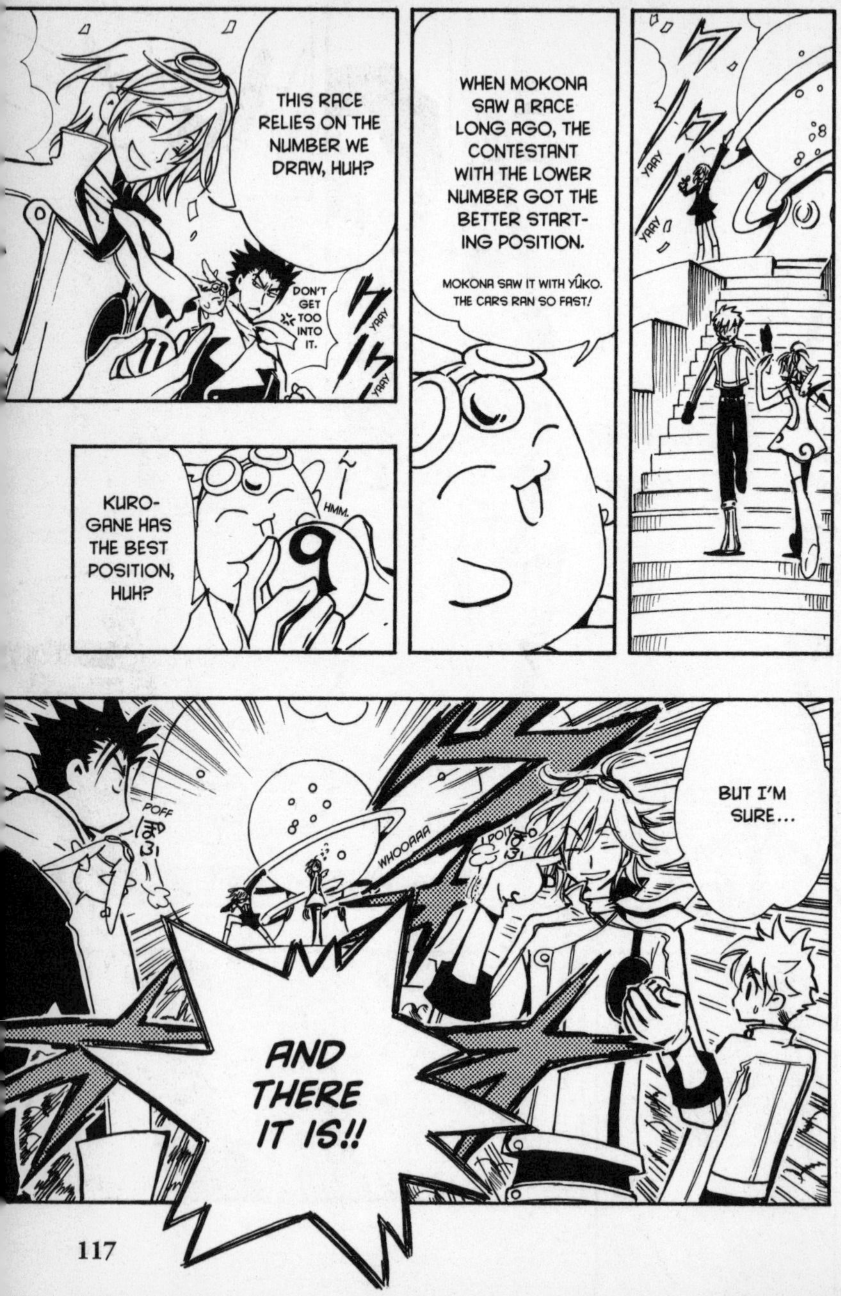

YAAY
YAAY
WHEN MOKONA SAW A RACE LONG AGO, THE CONTESTANT WITH THE LOWER NUMBER GOT THE BETTER STARTING POSITION.
MOKONA SAW IT WITH YÛKO. THE CARS RAN SO FAST!
THIS RACE RELIES ON THE NUMBER WE DRAW, HUH?
YAAY
YAAY
DON'T GET TOO INTO IT.
HMM.
KURO-GANE HAS THE BEST POSITION, HUH?
BUT I'M SURE...
POIT
WHOOAAA
POFF
AND THERE IT IS!!

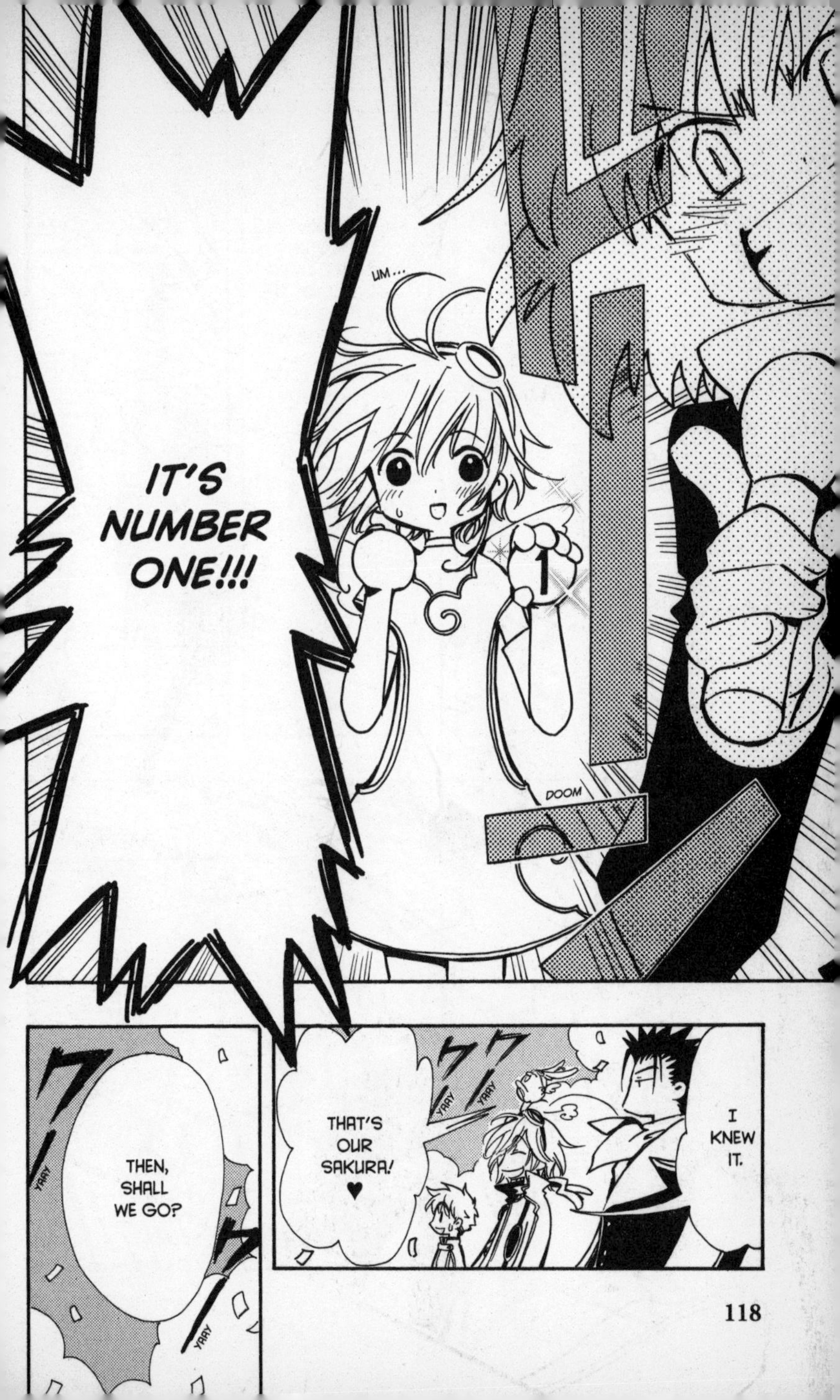
UM...
DOOM
IT'S NUMBER ONE!!!
I KNEW IT.
YAAY
YAAY
THAT'S OUR SAKURA! ♥
YAAY
THEN, SHALL WE GO?
YAAY

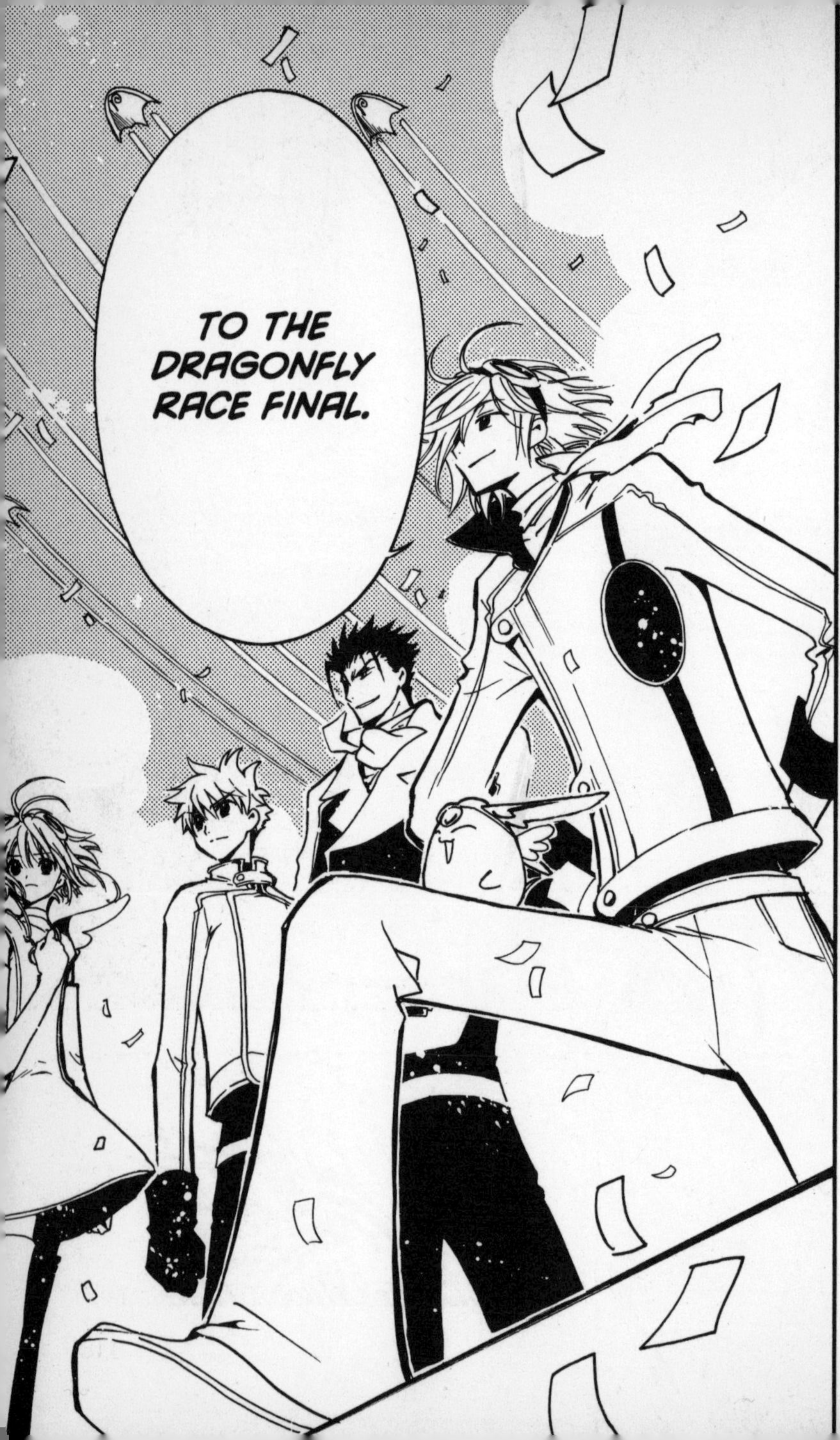
TO THE DRAGONFLY RACE FINAL.

ツバサ

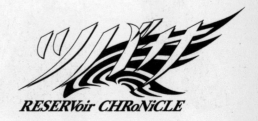

RESERVoir CHRoNiCLE

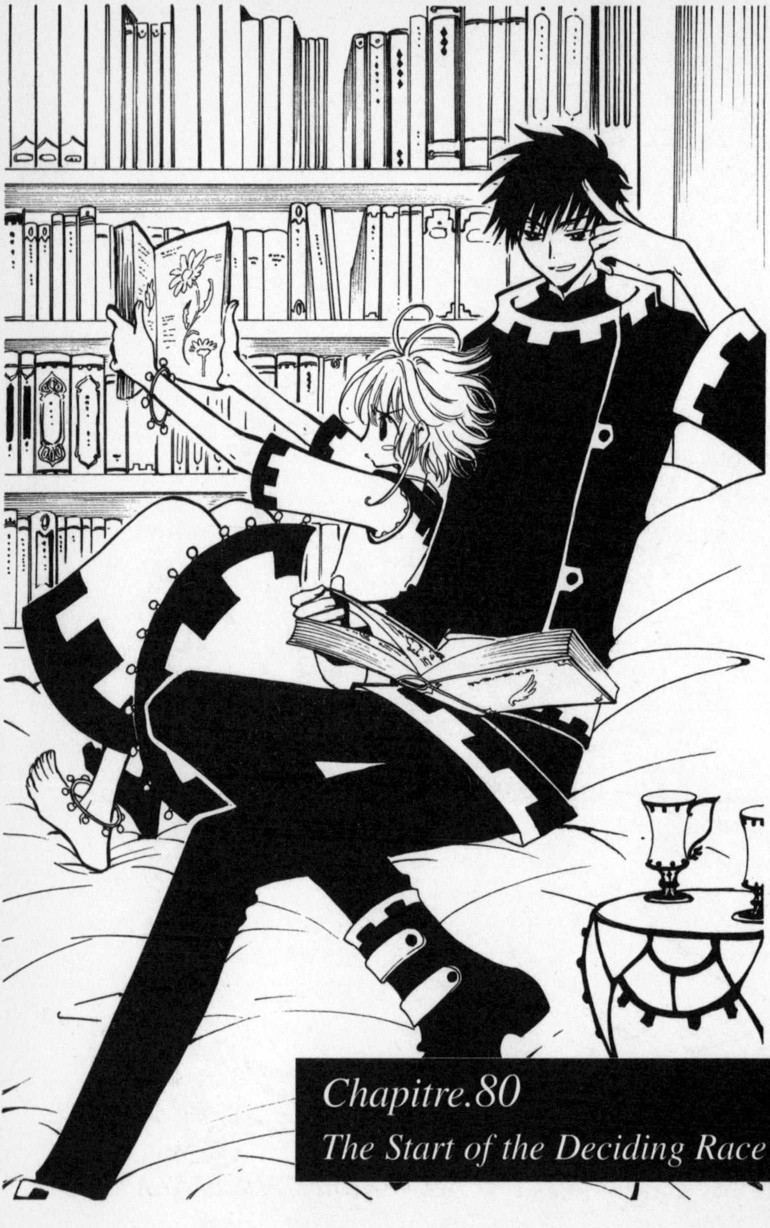
Chapitre.80
The Start of the Deciding Race

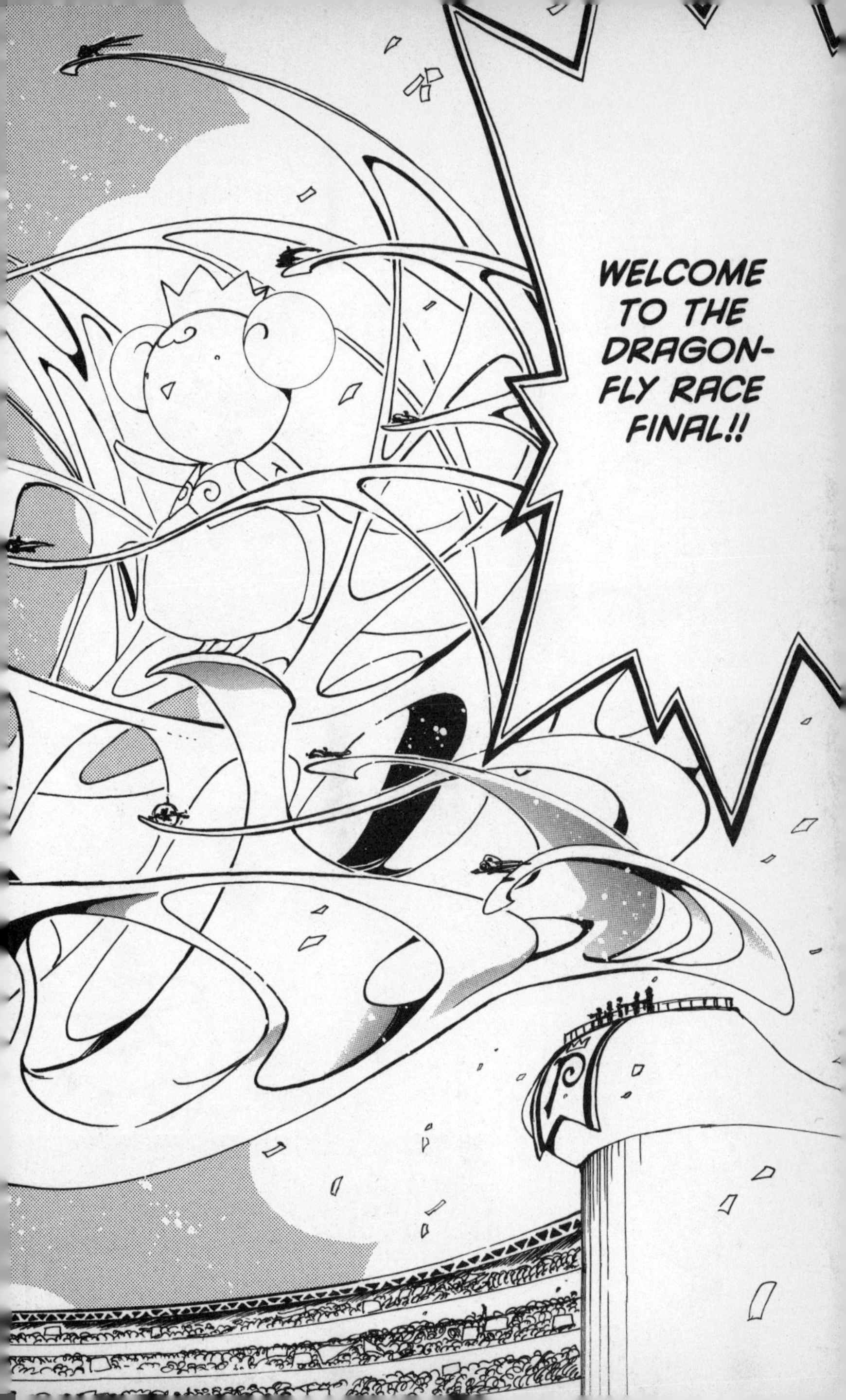
WELCOME TO THE DRAGON-FLY RACE FINAL!!

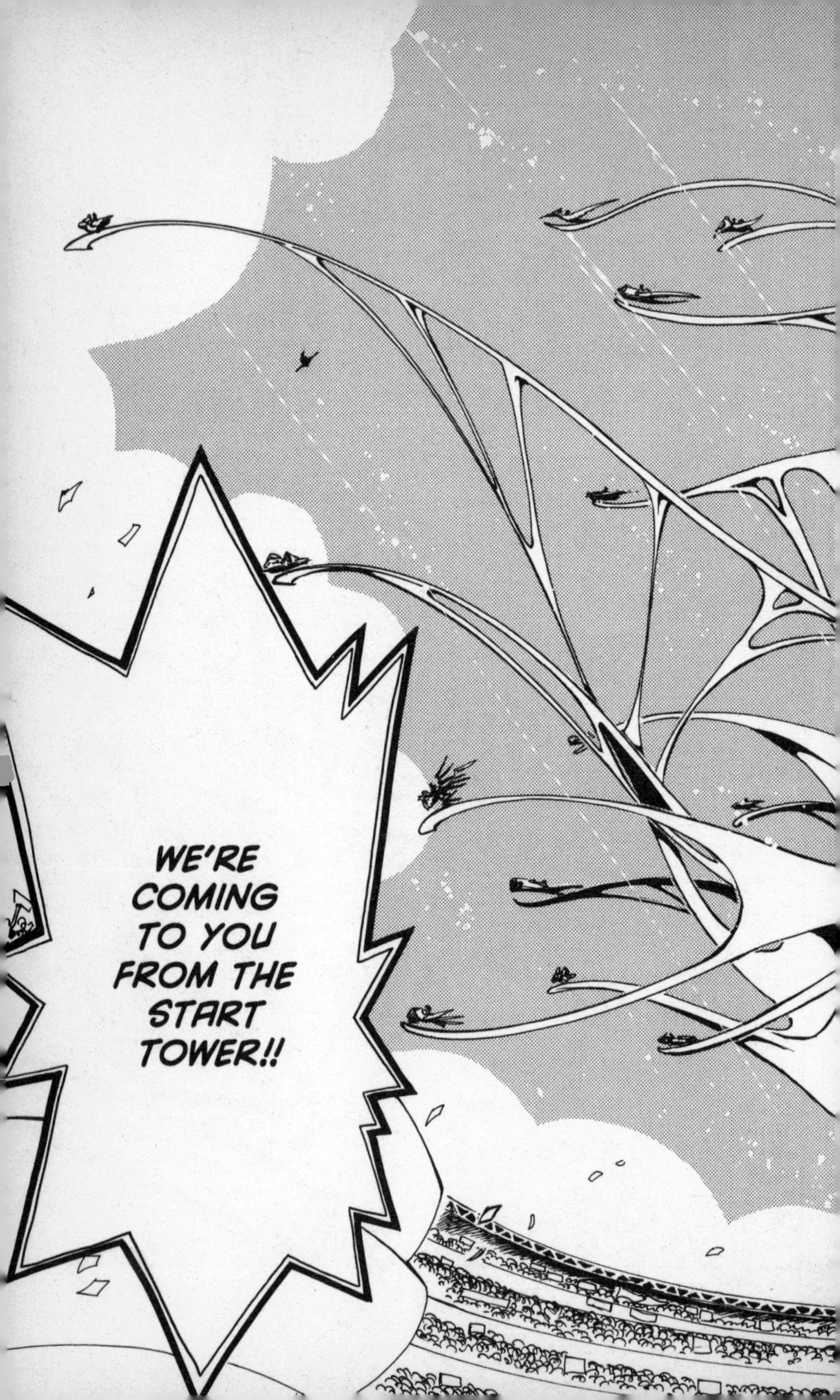
WE'RE COMING TO YOU FROM THE START TOWER!!

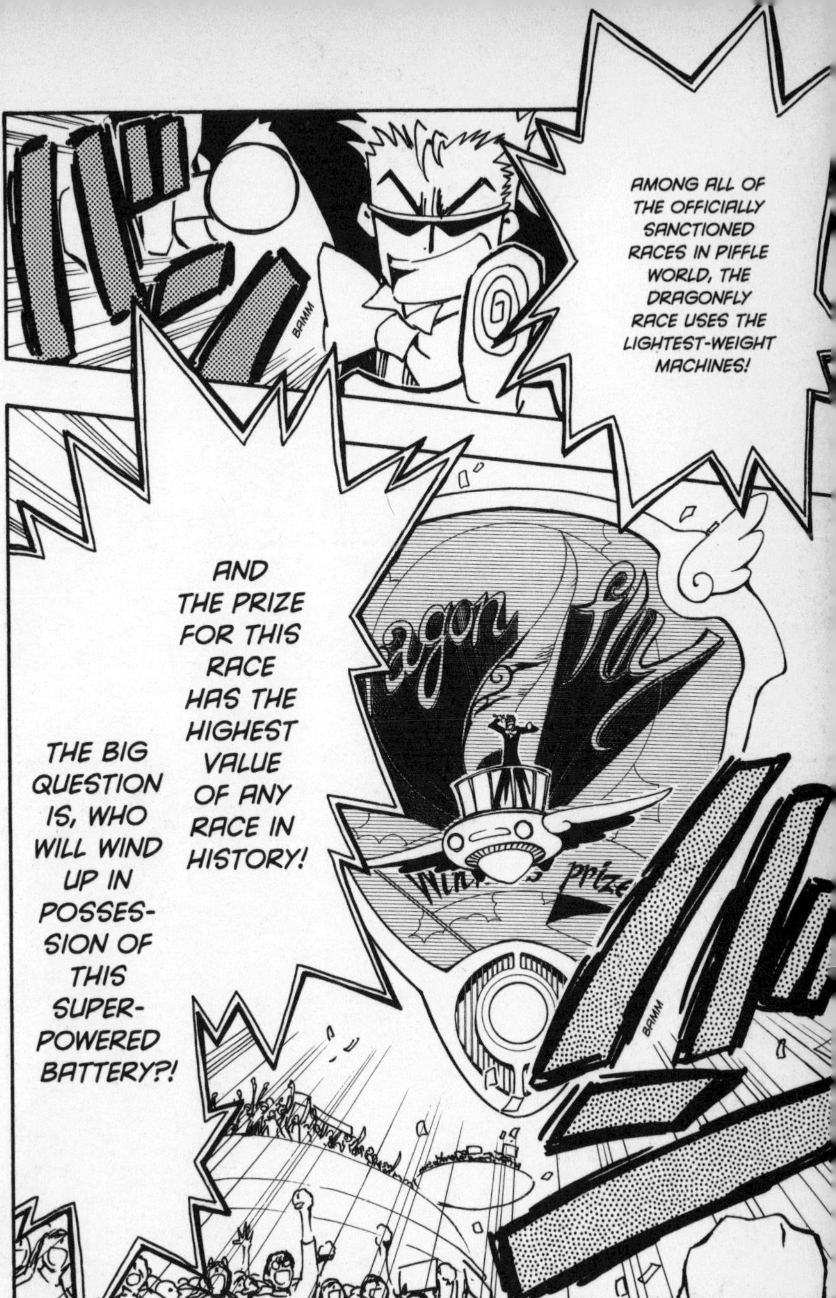
AMONG ALL OF THE OFFICIALLY SANCTIONED RACES IN PIFFLE WORLD, THE DRAGONFLY RACE USES THE LIGHTEST-WEIGHT MACHINES!
BAMM
AND THE PRIZE FOR THIS RACE HAS THE HIGHEST VALUE OF ANY RACE IN HISTORY!
THE BIG QUESTION IS, WHO WILL WIND UP IN POSSES-SION OF THIS SUPER-POWERED BATTERY?!
BAMM

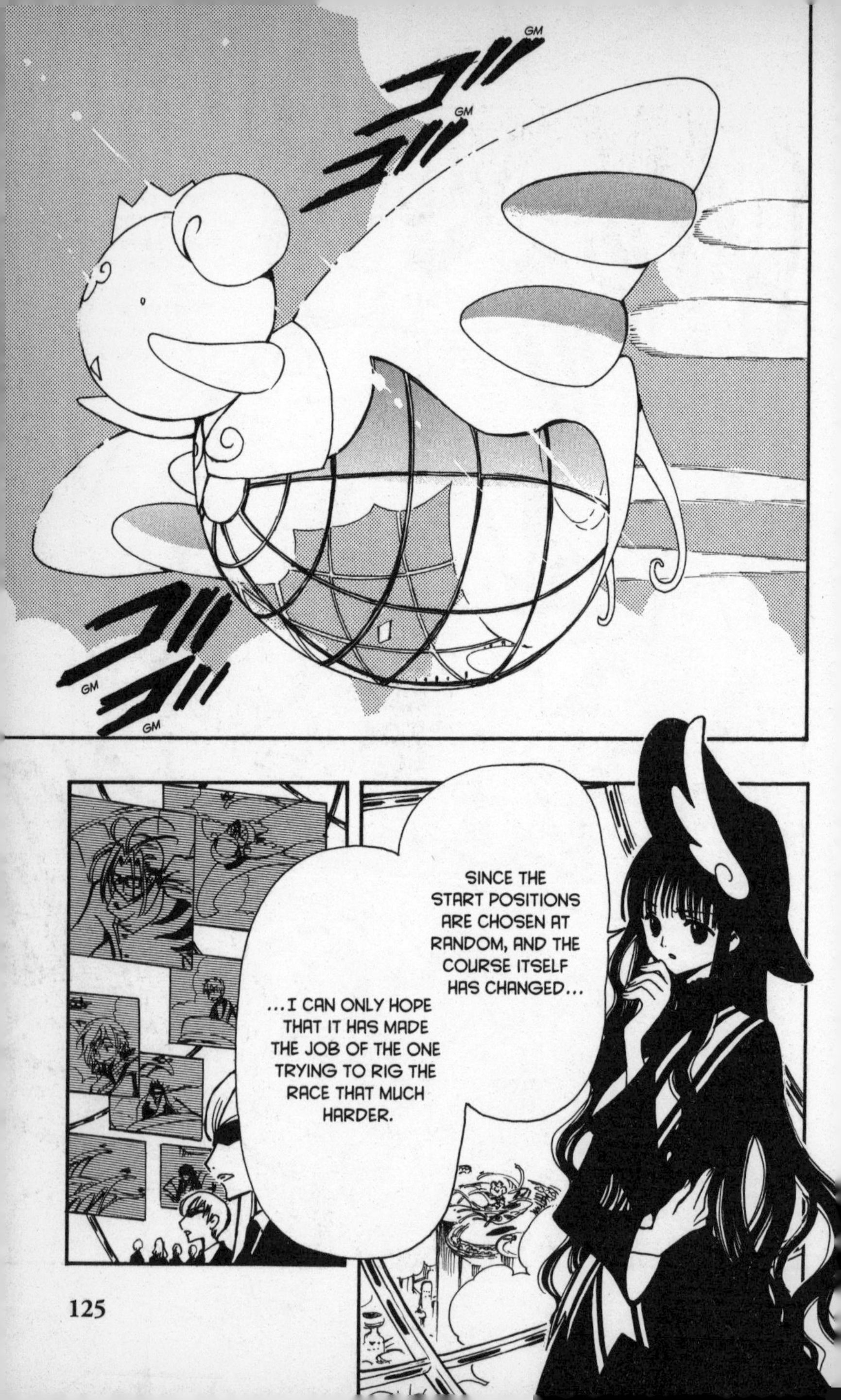
GM
GM
GM
GM
SINCE THE START POSITIONS ARE CHOSEN AT RANDOM, AND THE COURSE ITSELF HAS CHANGED...
...I CAN ONLY HOPE THAT IT HAS MADE THE JOB OF THE ONE TRYING TO RIG THE RACE THAT MUCH HARDER.

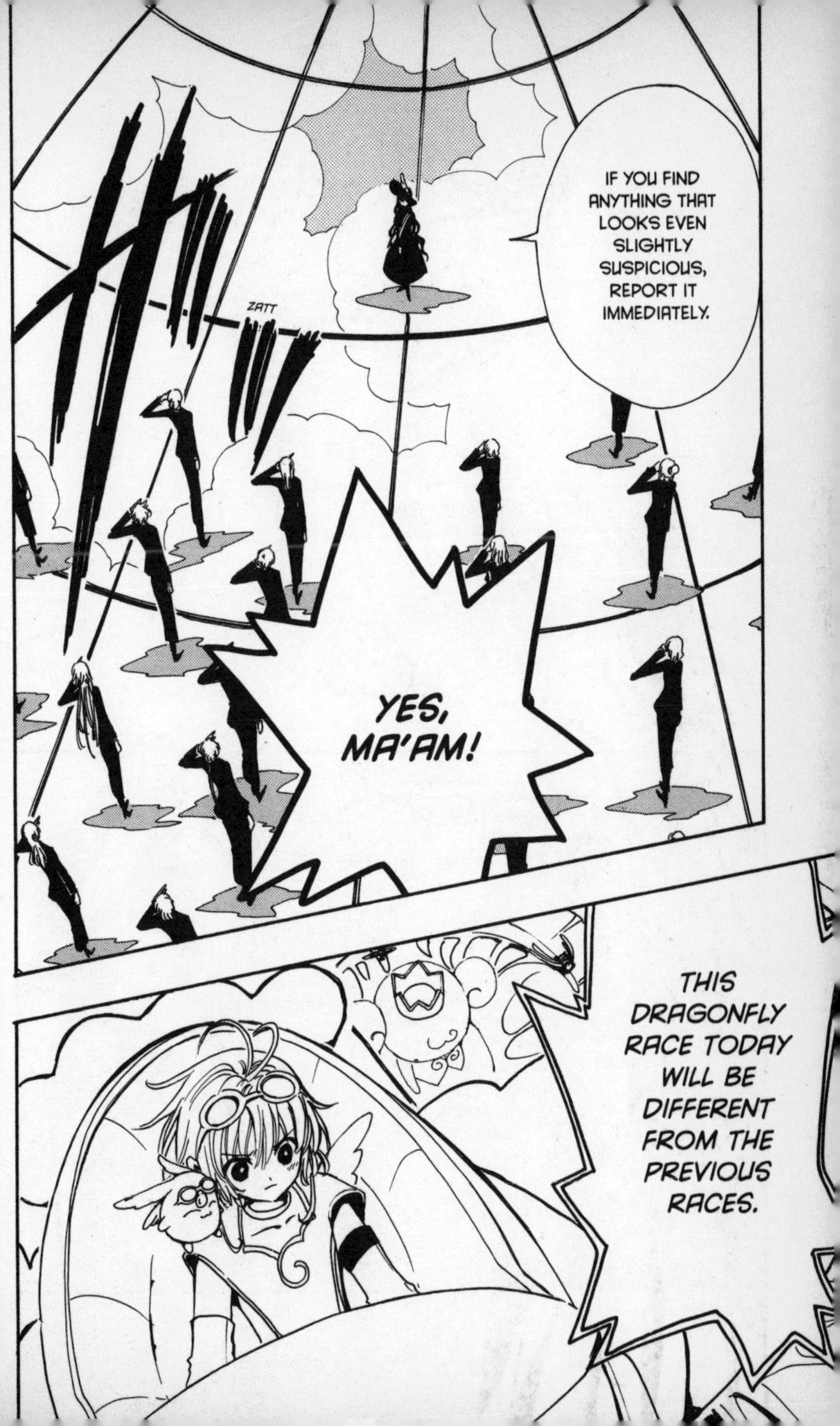
IF YOU FIND ANYTHING THAT LOOKS EVEN SLIGHTLY SUSPICIOUS, REPORT IT IMMEDIATELY.
ZATT
YES, MA'AM!
THIS DRAGONFLY RACE TODAY WILL BE DIFFERENT FROM THE PREVIOUS RACES.

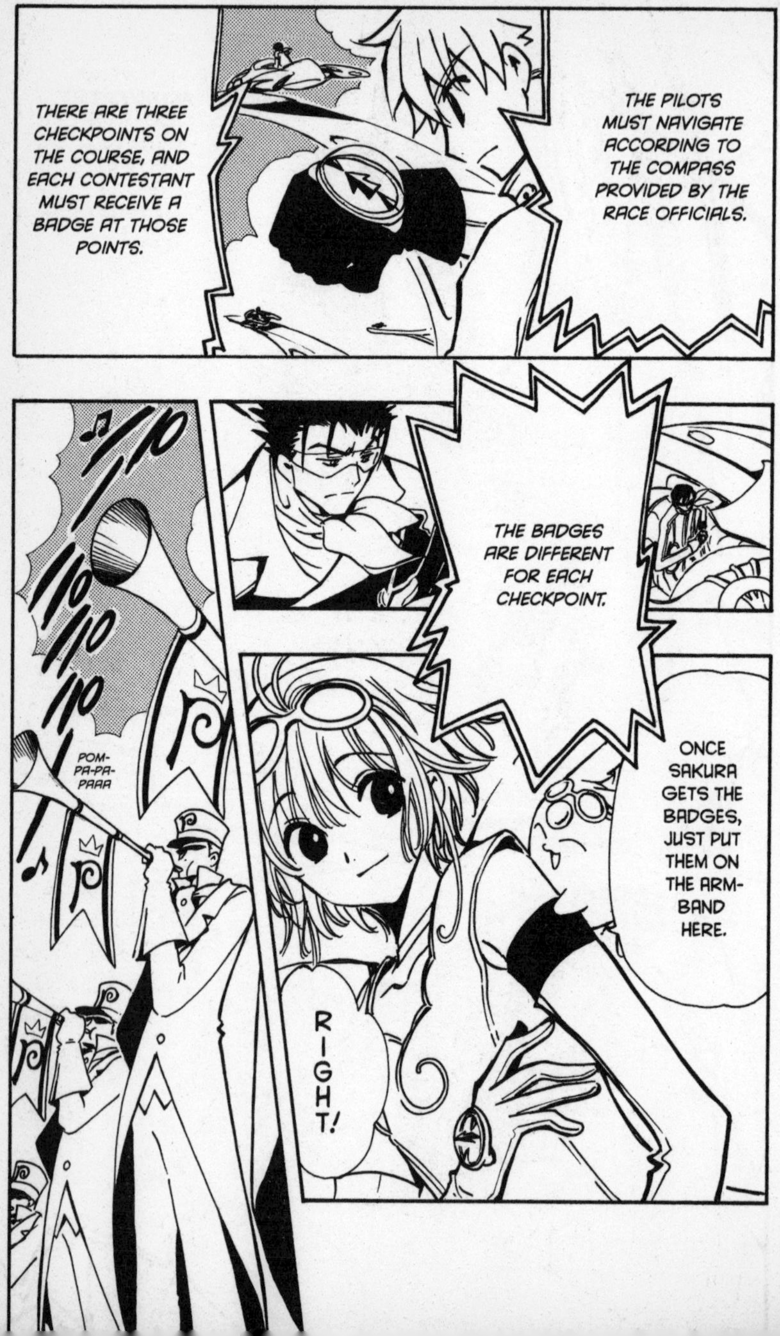
THE PILOTS MUST NAVIGATE ACCORDING TO THE COMPASS PROVIDED BY THE RACE OFFICIALS.
THERE ARE THREE CHECKPOINTS ON THE COURSE, AND EACH CONTESTANT MUST RECEIVE A BADGE AT THOSE POINTS.
THE BADGES ARE DIFFERENT FOR EACH CHECKPOINT.
ONCE SAKURA GETS THE BADGES, JUST PUT THEM ON THE ARM-BAND HERE.
RIGHT!
POM-PA-PA-PAAA

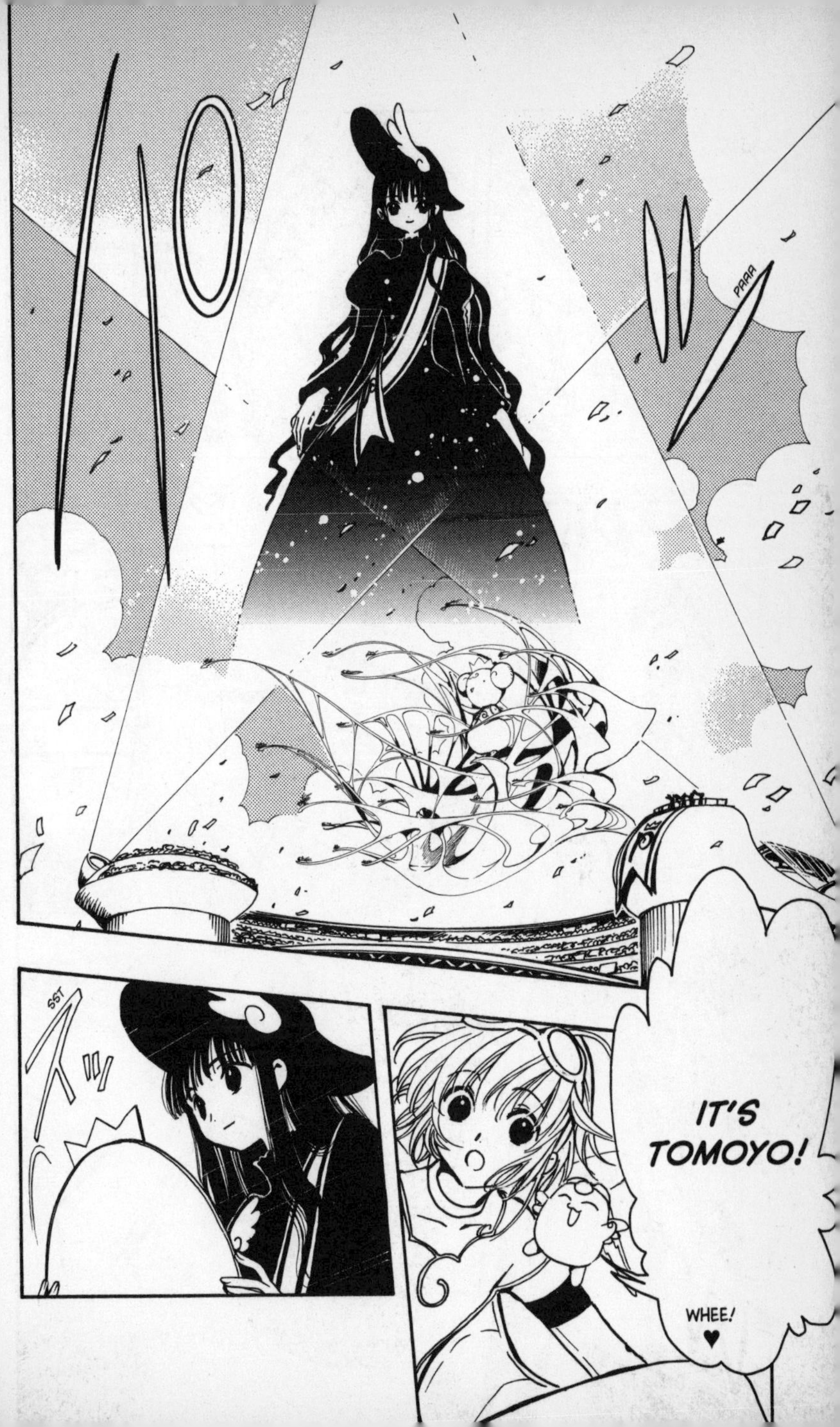
PAAA
IT'S TOMOYO!
WHEE! ♥
SST

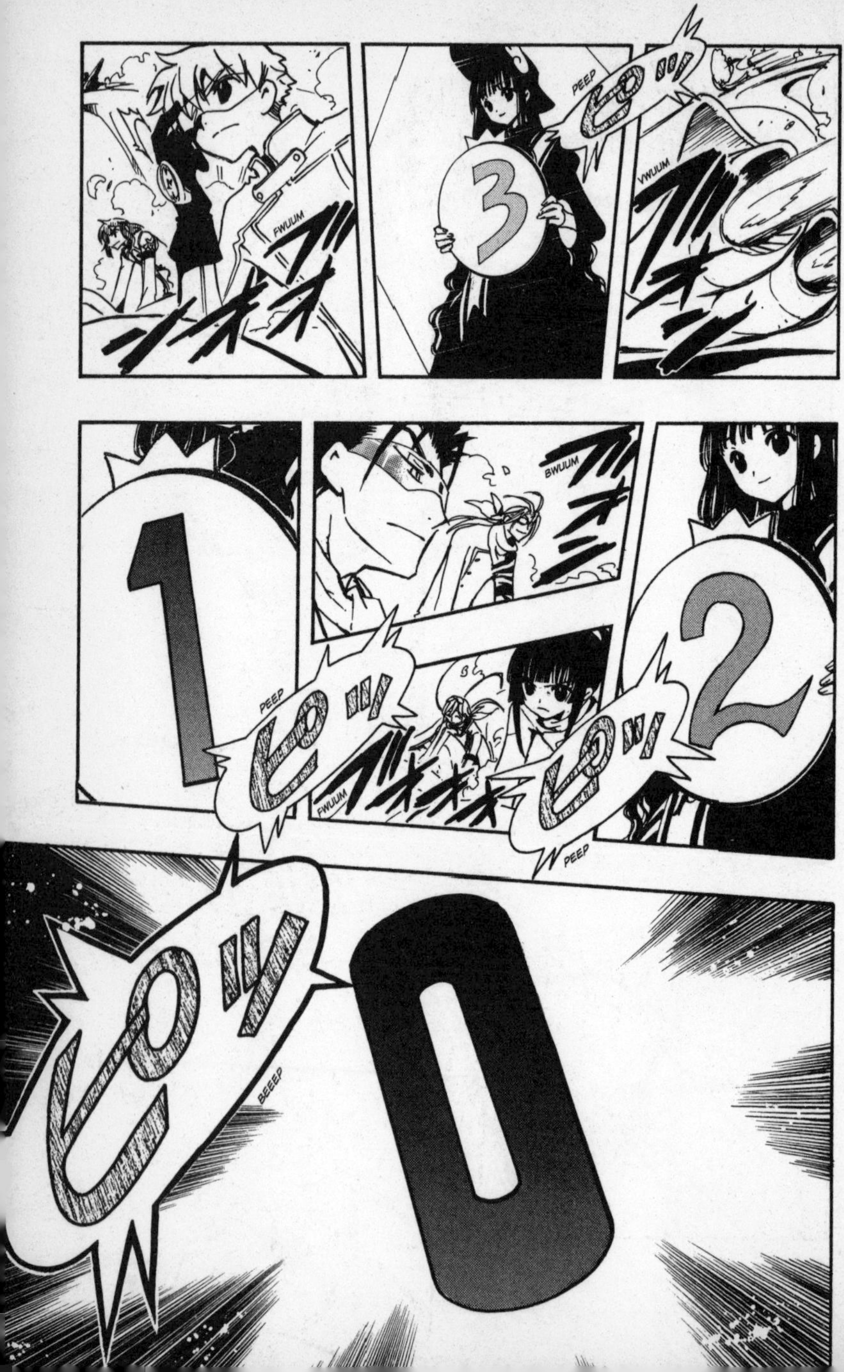
PEEP
VWUUM
3
FWUUM
2
PEEP
BWUUM
FWUUM
1
PEEP
0
BEEEP

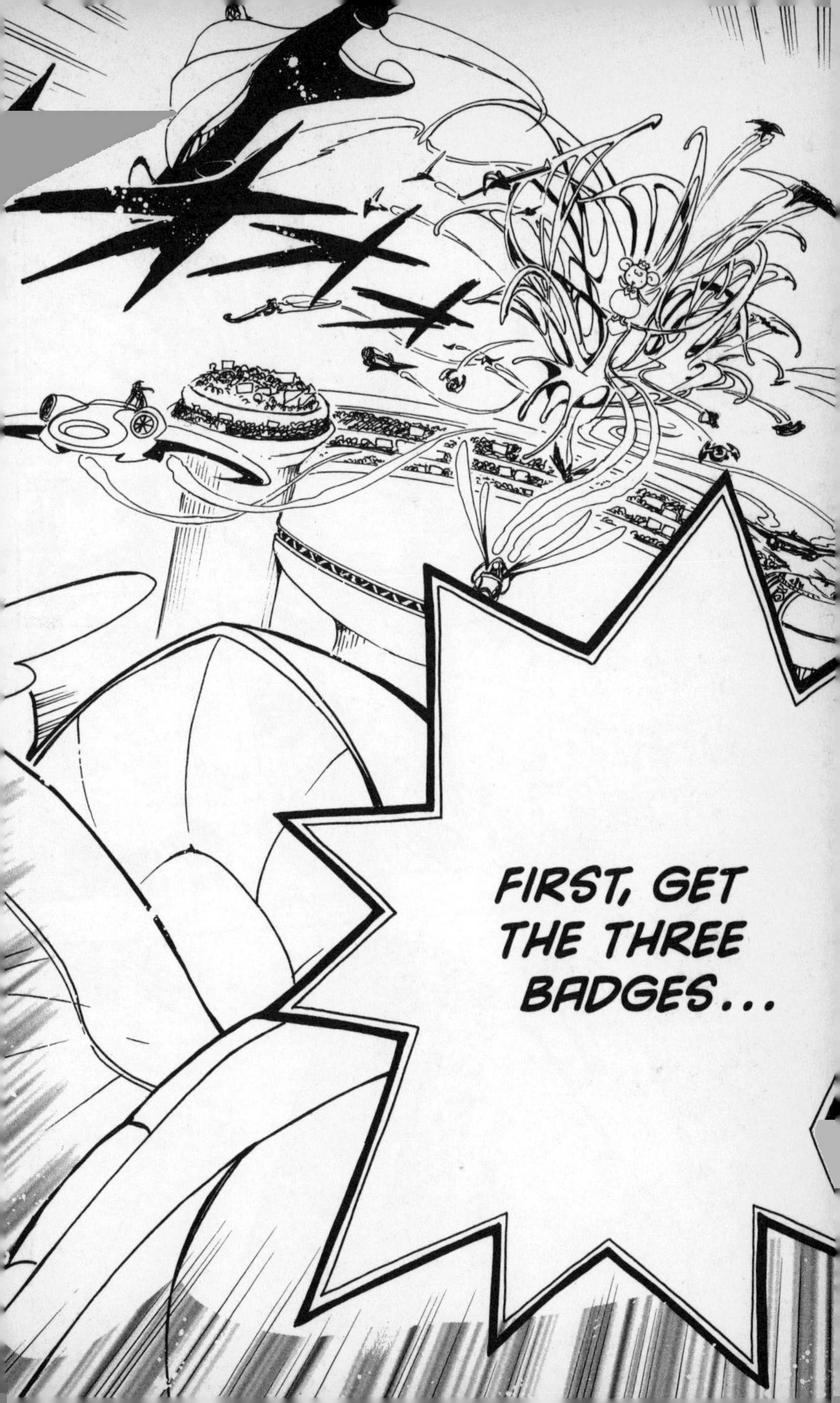
FIRST, GET THE THREE BADGES...

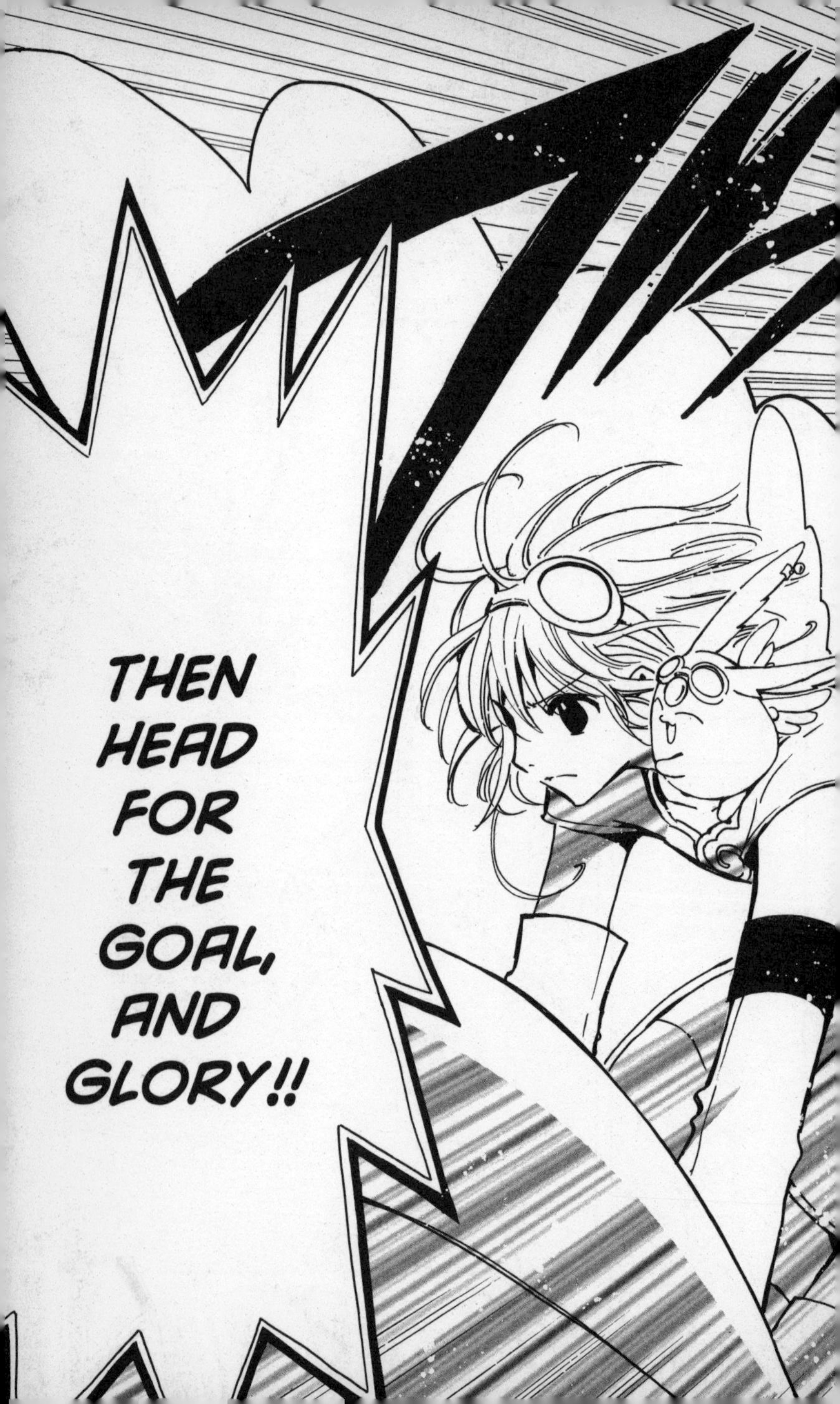
THEN HEAD FOR THE GOAL, AND GLORY!!

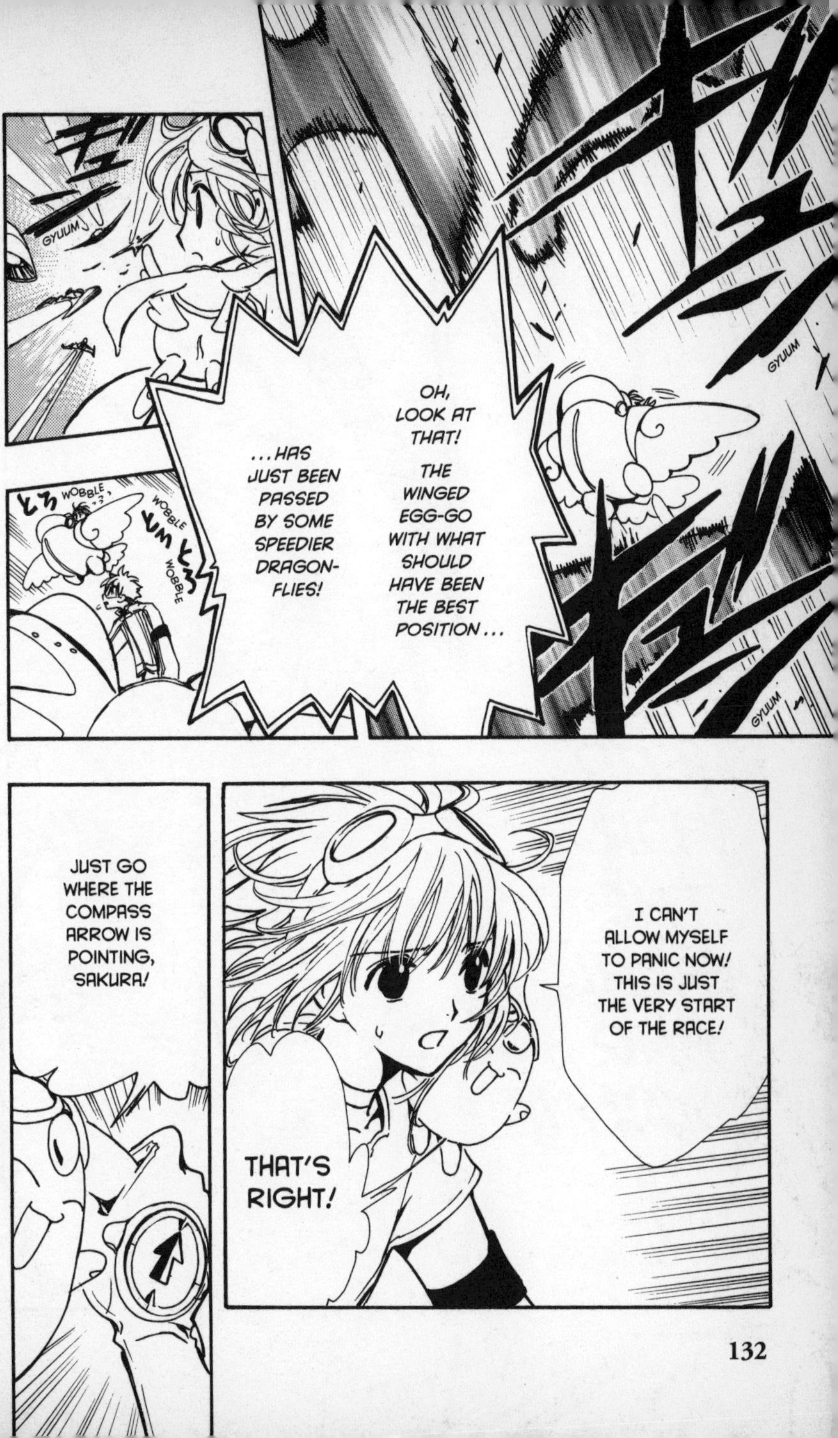
GYUUM
OH, LOOK AT THAT! THE WINGED EGG-GO WITH WHAT SHOULD HAVE BEEN THE BEST POSITION...
...HAS JUST BEEN PASSED BY SOME SPEEDIER DRAGON-FLIES!
GYUUM
GYUUM
WOBBLE
WOBBLE
WOBBLE
I CAN'T ALLOW MYSELF TO PANIC NOW! THIS IS JUST THE VERY START OF THE RACE!
THAT'S RIGHT!
JUST GO WHERE THE COMPASS ARROW IS POINTING, SAKURA!

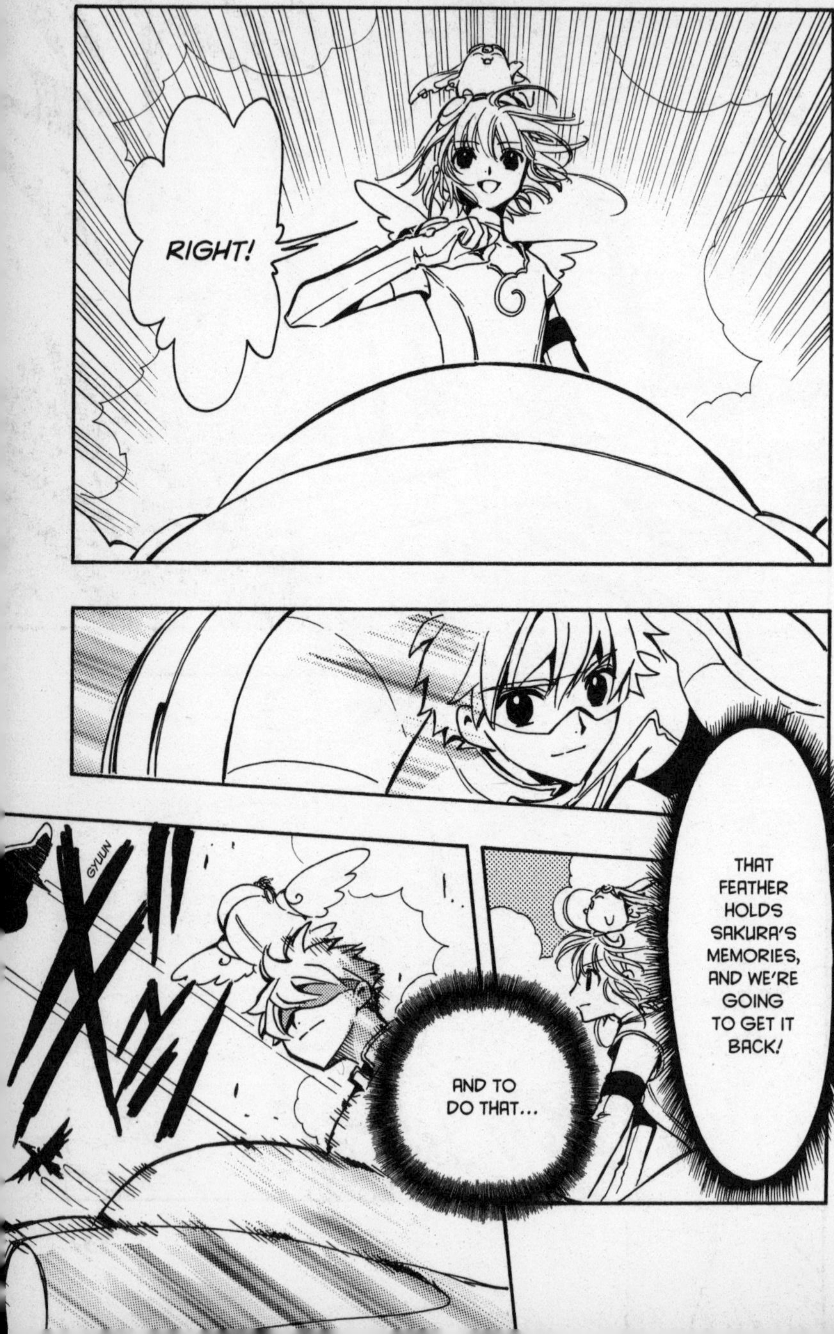
RIGHT!
THAT FEATHER HOLDS SAKURA'S MEMORIES, AND WE'RE GOING TO GET IT BACK!
AND TO DO THAT...
GYUUN

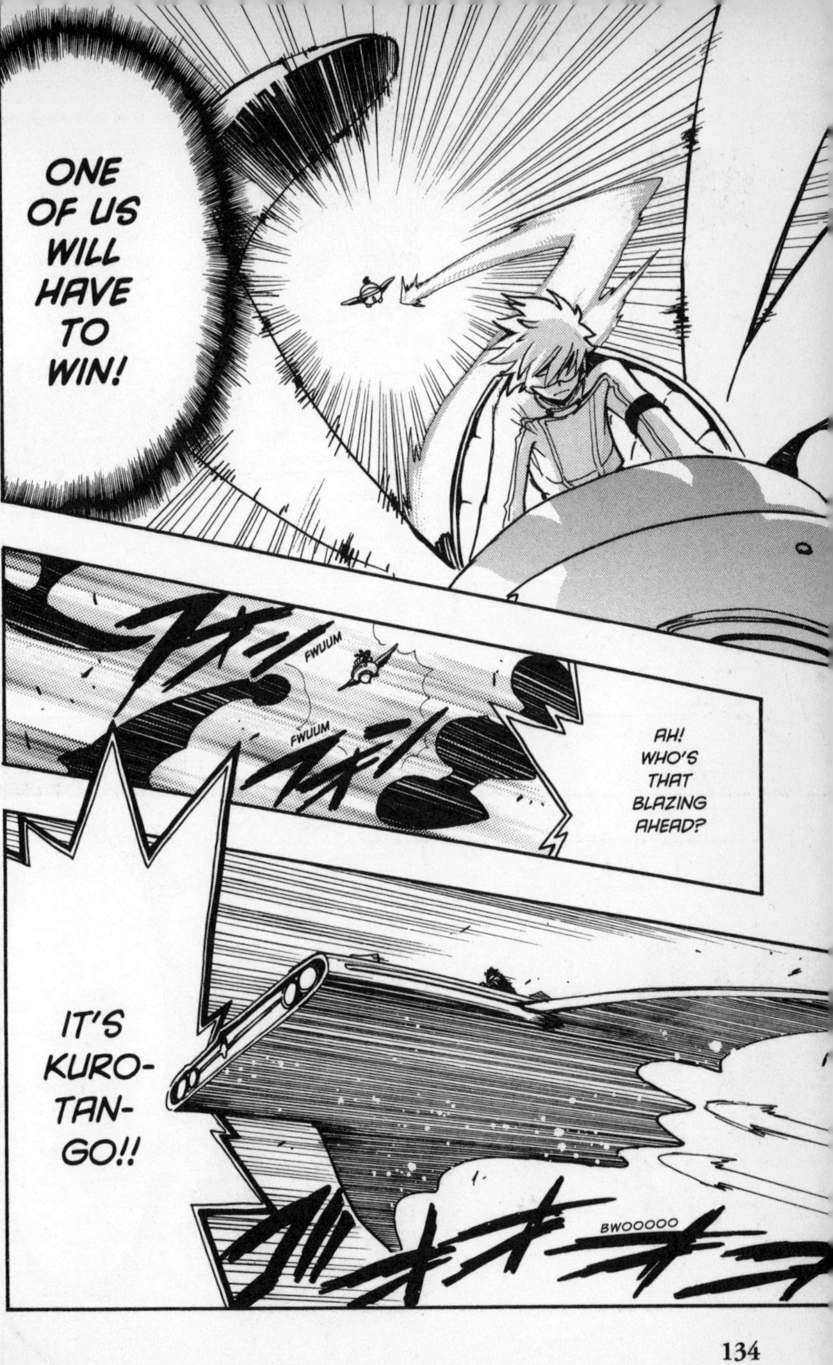
ONE OF US WILL HAVE TO WIN!
AH! WHO'S THAT BLAZING AHEAD?
FWUUM
FWUUM
IT'S KURO-TANGO!!
BWOOOOO

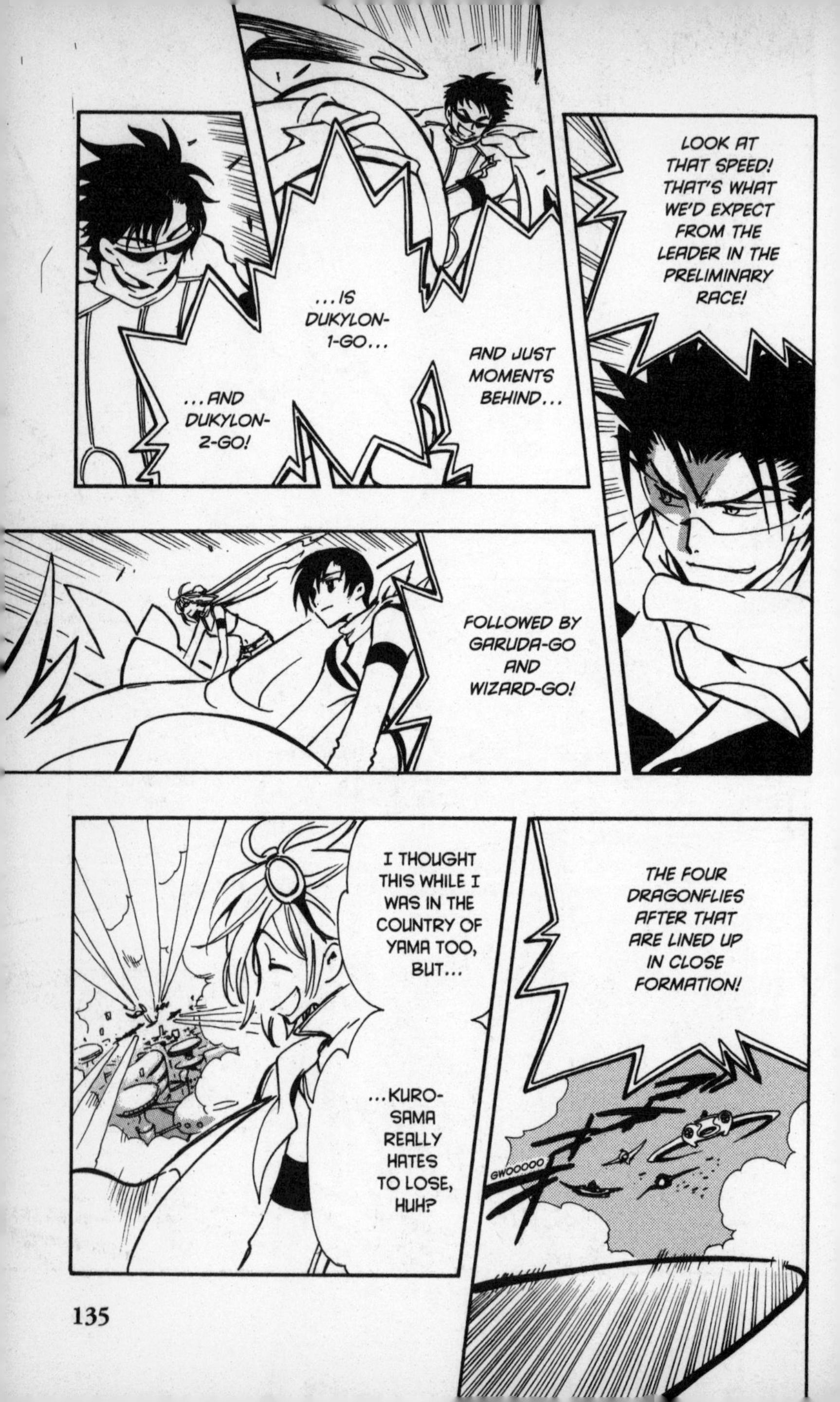
LOOK AT THAT SPEED! THAT'S WHAT WE'D EXPECT FROM THE LEADER IN THE PRELIMINARY RACE!
AND JUST MOMENTS BEHIND...
...IS DUKYLON-1-GO...
...AND DUKYLON-2-GO!
FOLLOWED BY GARUDA-GO AND WIZARD-GO!
THE FOUR DRAGONFLIES AFTER THAT ARE LINED UP IN CLOSE FORMATION!
GWOOOOO
I THOUGHT THIS WHILE I WAS IN THE COUNTRY OF YAMA TOO, BUT...
...KURO-SAMA REALLY HATES TO LOSE, HUH?

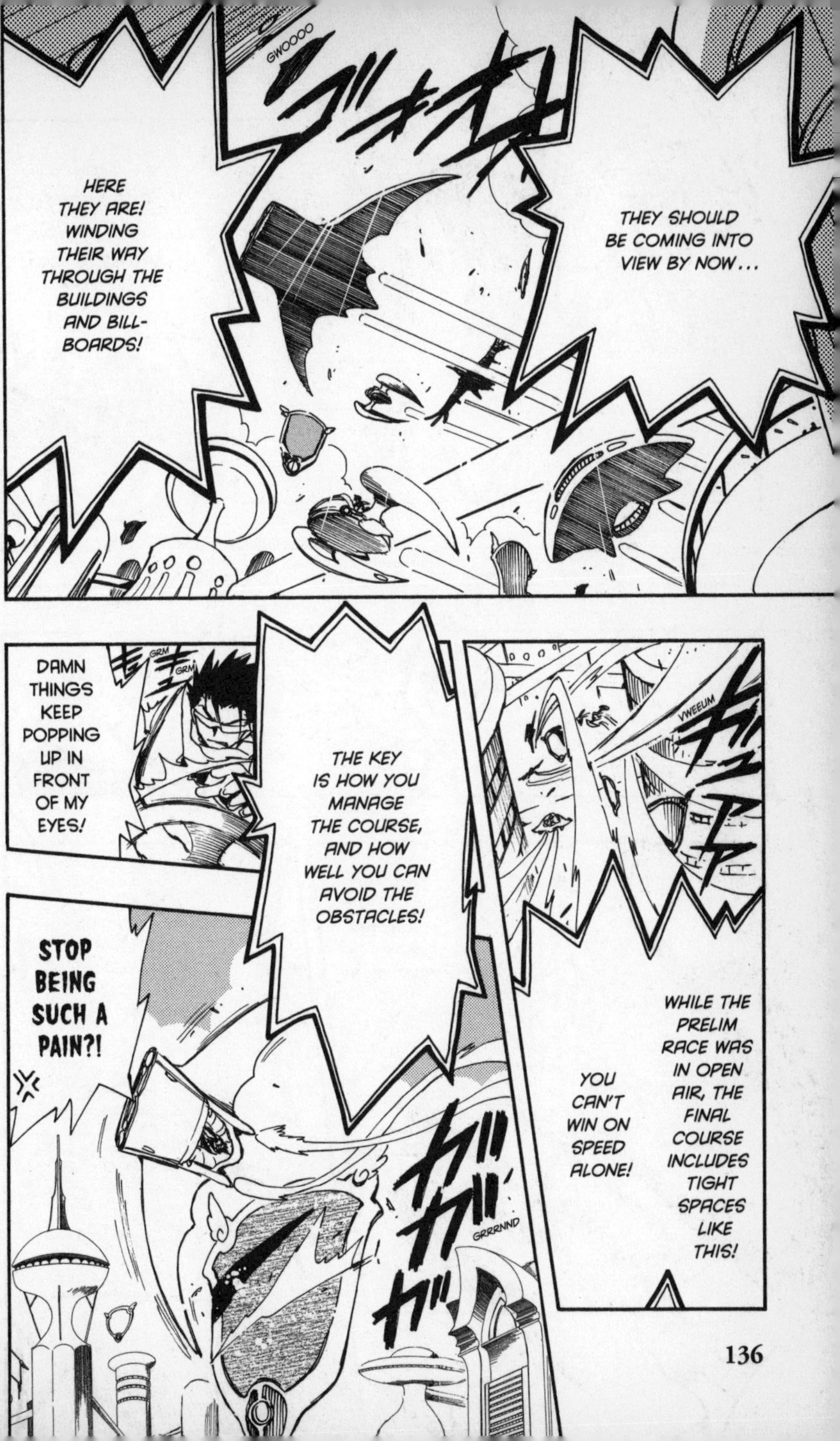
GWOOOO
THEY SHOULD BE COMING INTO VIEW BY NOW...
HERE THEY ARE! WINDING THEIR WAY THROUGH THE BUILDINGS AND BILL-BOARDS!
VWEEUM
WHILE THE PRELIM RACE WAS IN OPEN AIR, THE FINAL COURSE INCLUDES TIGHT SPACES LIKE THIS!
YOU CAN'T WIN ON SPEED ALONE!
THE KEY IS HOW YOU MANAGE THE COURSE, AND HOW WELL YOU CAN AVOID THE OBSTACLES!
GRM
GRM
DAMN THINGS KEEP POPPING UP IN FRONT OF MY EYES!
STOP BEING SUCH A PAIN?!
GRRRNND

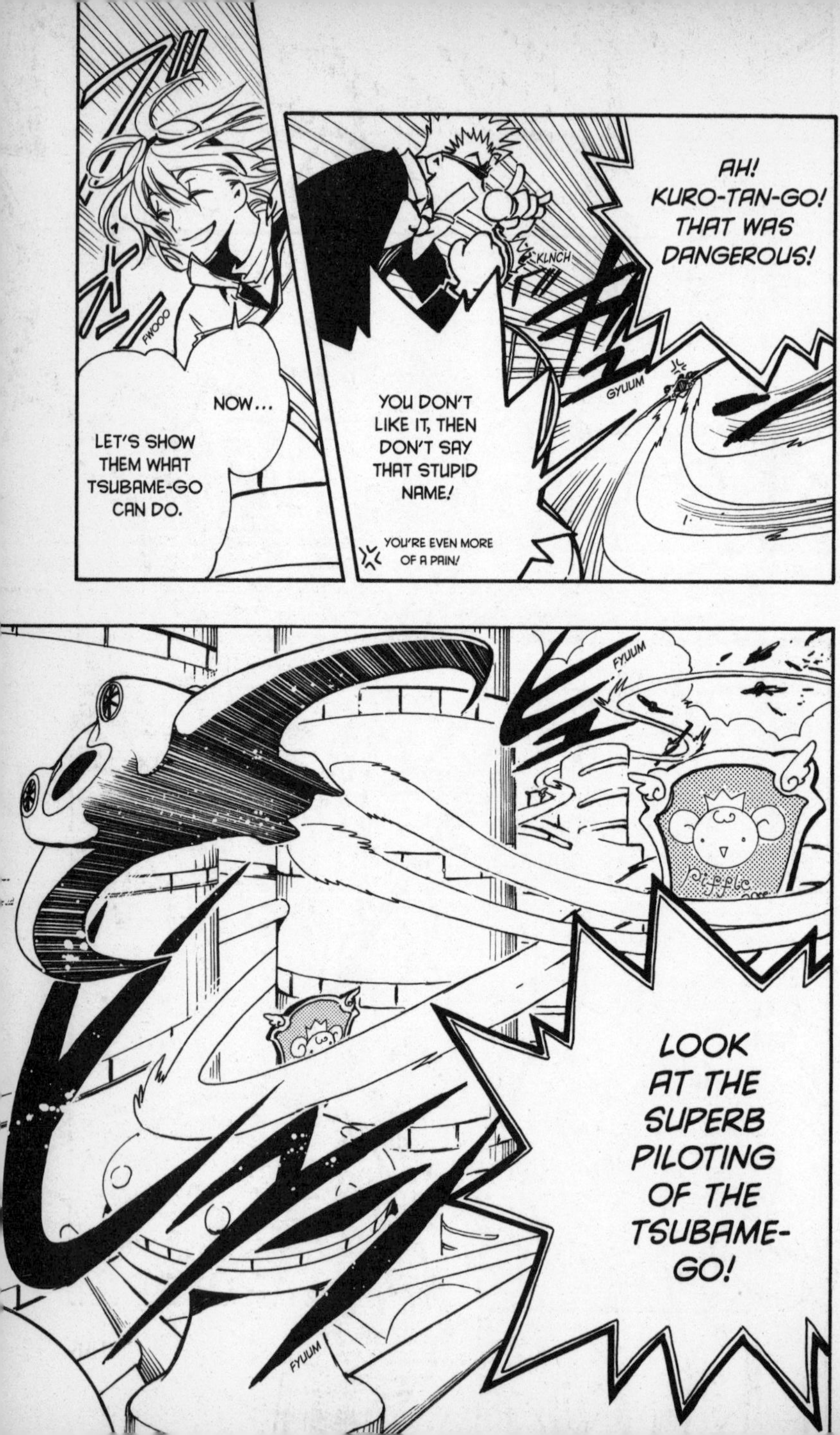
AH! KURO-TAN-GO! THAT WAS DANGEROUS!
KLNCH
GYUUM
YOU DON'T LIKE IT, THEN DON'T SAY THAT STUPID NAME!
YOU'RE EVEN MORE OF A PAIN!
FWOOO
NOW...
LET'S SHOW THEM WHAT TSUBAME-GO CAN DO.
FYUUM
LOOK AT THE SUPERB PILOTING OF THE TSUBAME-GO!
FYUUM

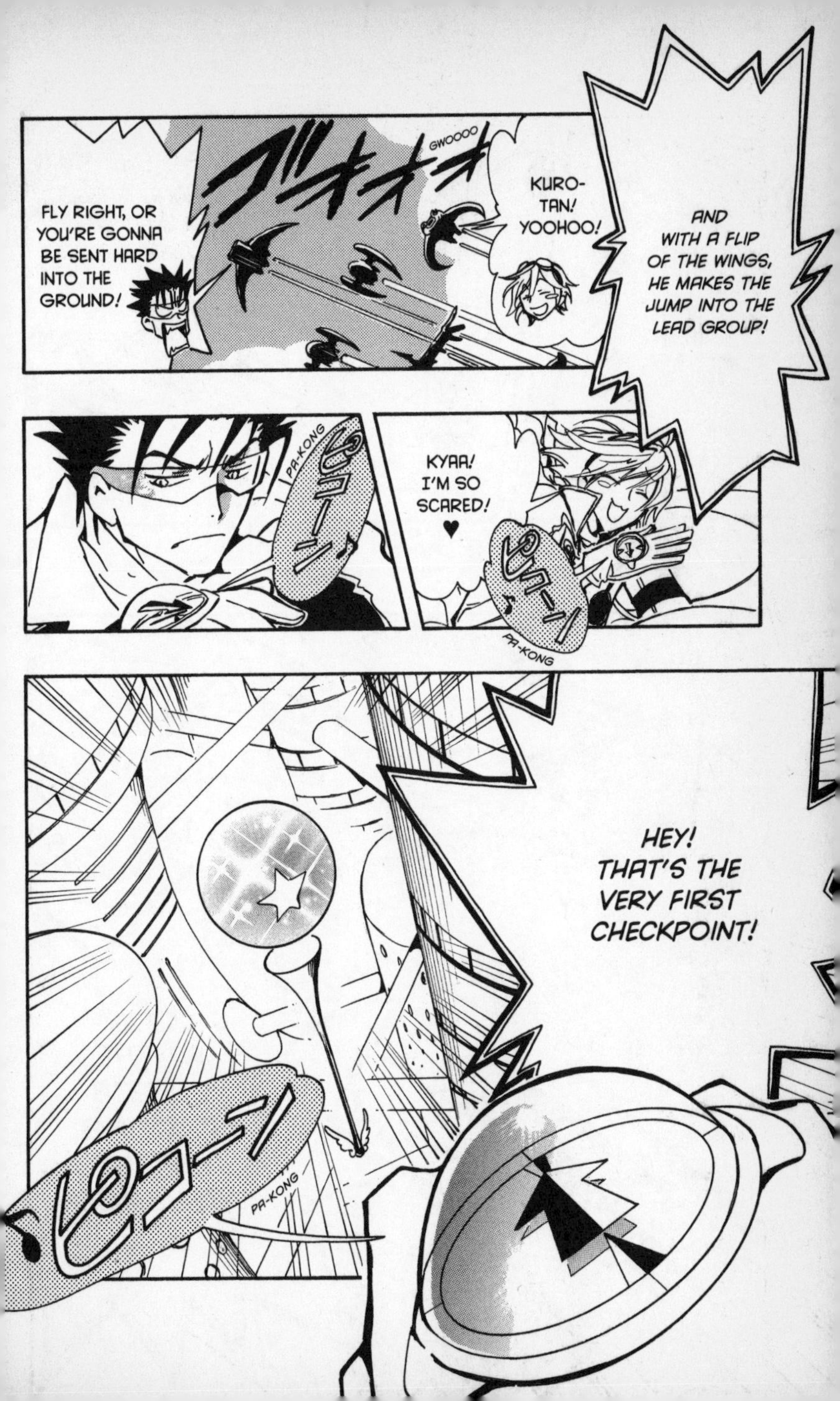
AND WITH A FLIP OF THE WINGS, HE MAKES THE JUMP INTO THE LEAD GROUP!
KURO-TAN! YOOHOO!
GWOOOO
FLY RIGHT, OR YOU'RE GONNA BE SENT HARD INTO THE GROUND!
KYAA! I'M SO SCARED! ♥
PA-KONG
PA-KONG
HEY! THAT'S THE VERY FIRST CHECKPOINT!
PA-KONG

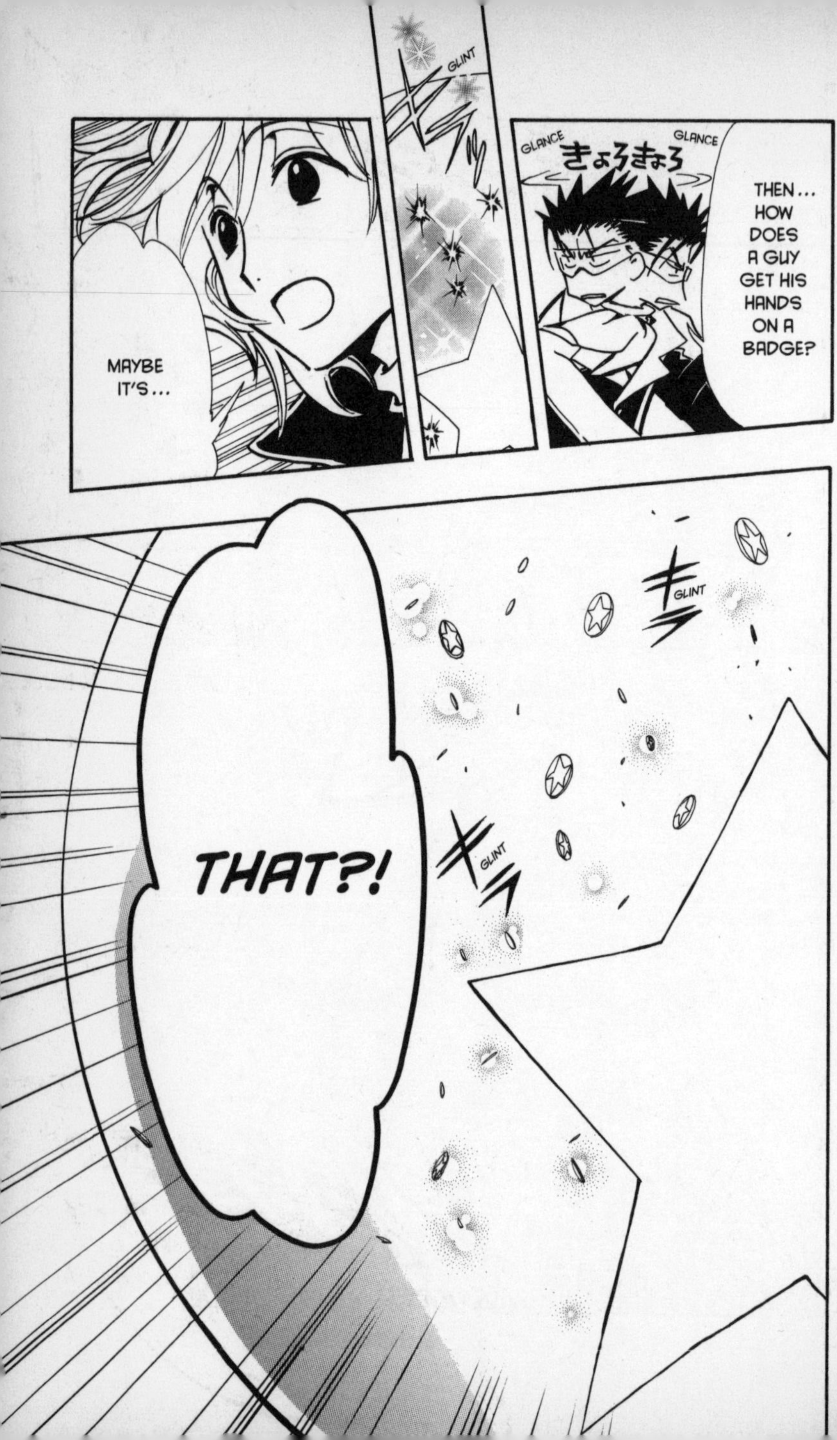
GLANCE
きょろきょろ
GLANCE
THEN... HOW DOES A GUY GET HIS HANDS ON A BADGE?
GLINT
MAYBE IT'S...
GLINT
GLINT
THAT?!

ツバサ

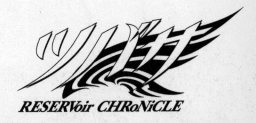

RESERVoir CHRoNiCLE

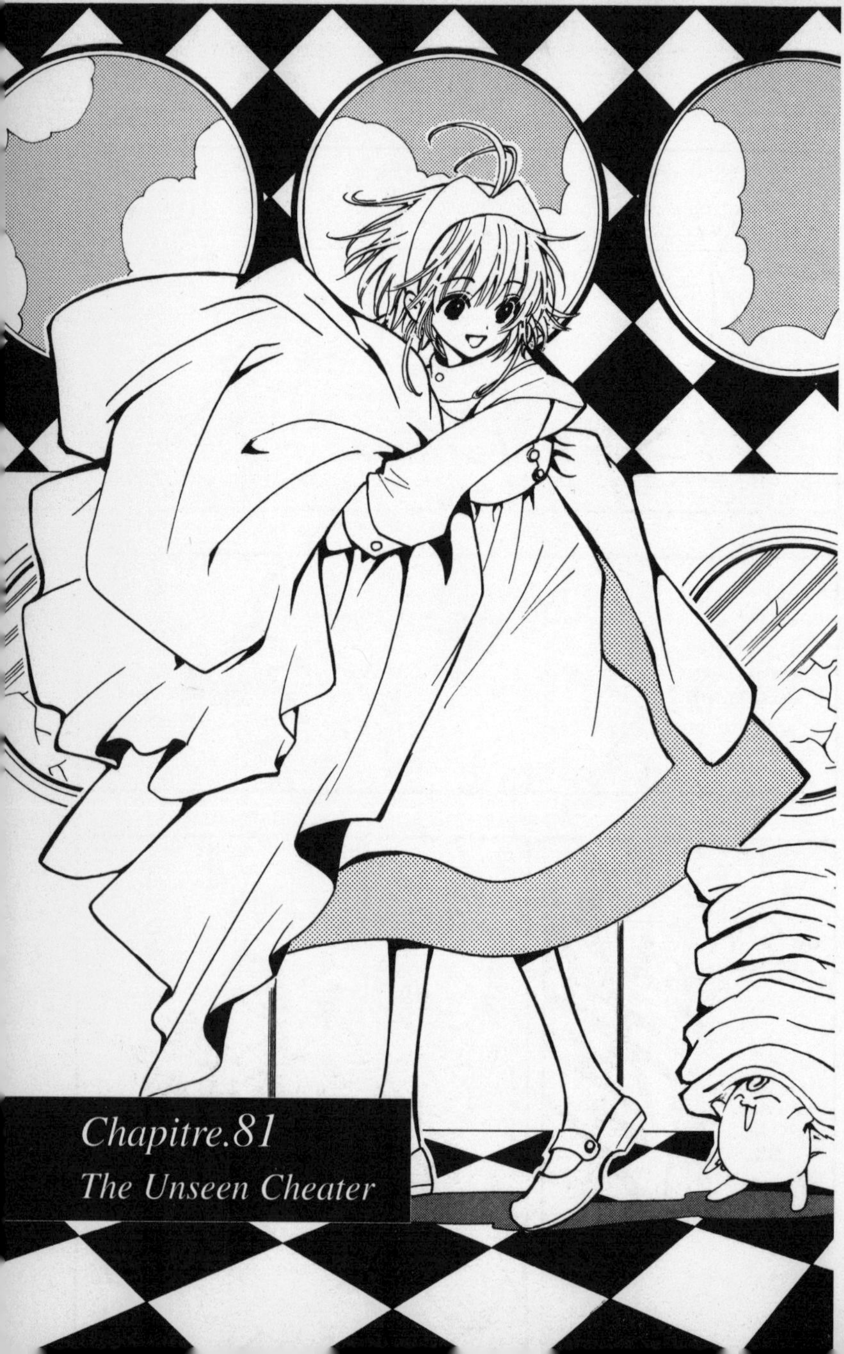

Chapitre.81
The Unseen Cheater

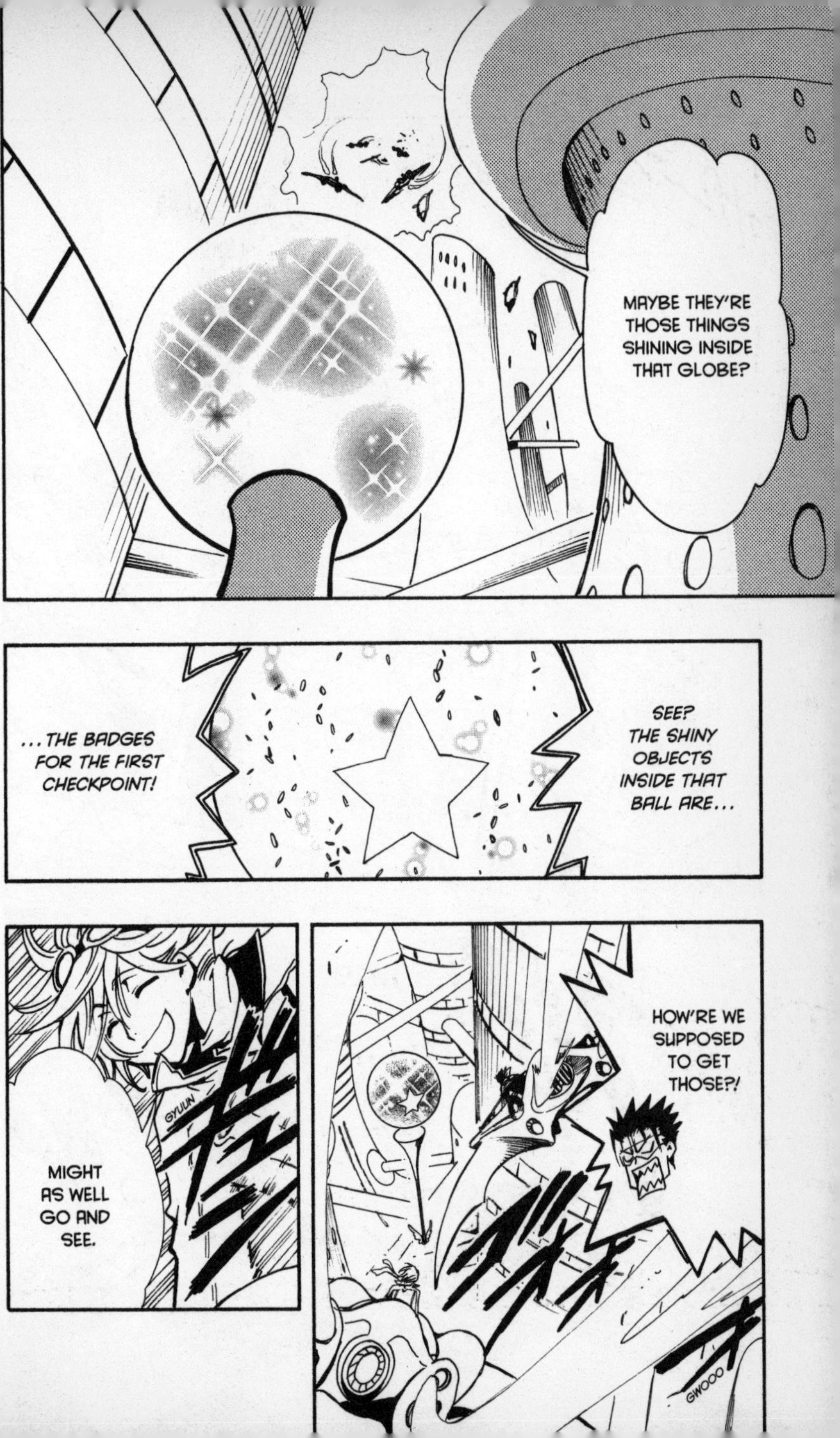
MAYBE THEY'RE THOSE THINGS SHINING INSIDE THAT GLOBE?
SEE? THE SHINY OBJECTS INSIDE THAT BALL ARE...
...THE BADGES FOR THE FIRST CHECKPOINT!
HOW'RE WE SUPPOSED TO GET THOSE?!
GWOOO
GYUUN
MIGHT AS WELL GO AND SEE.

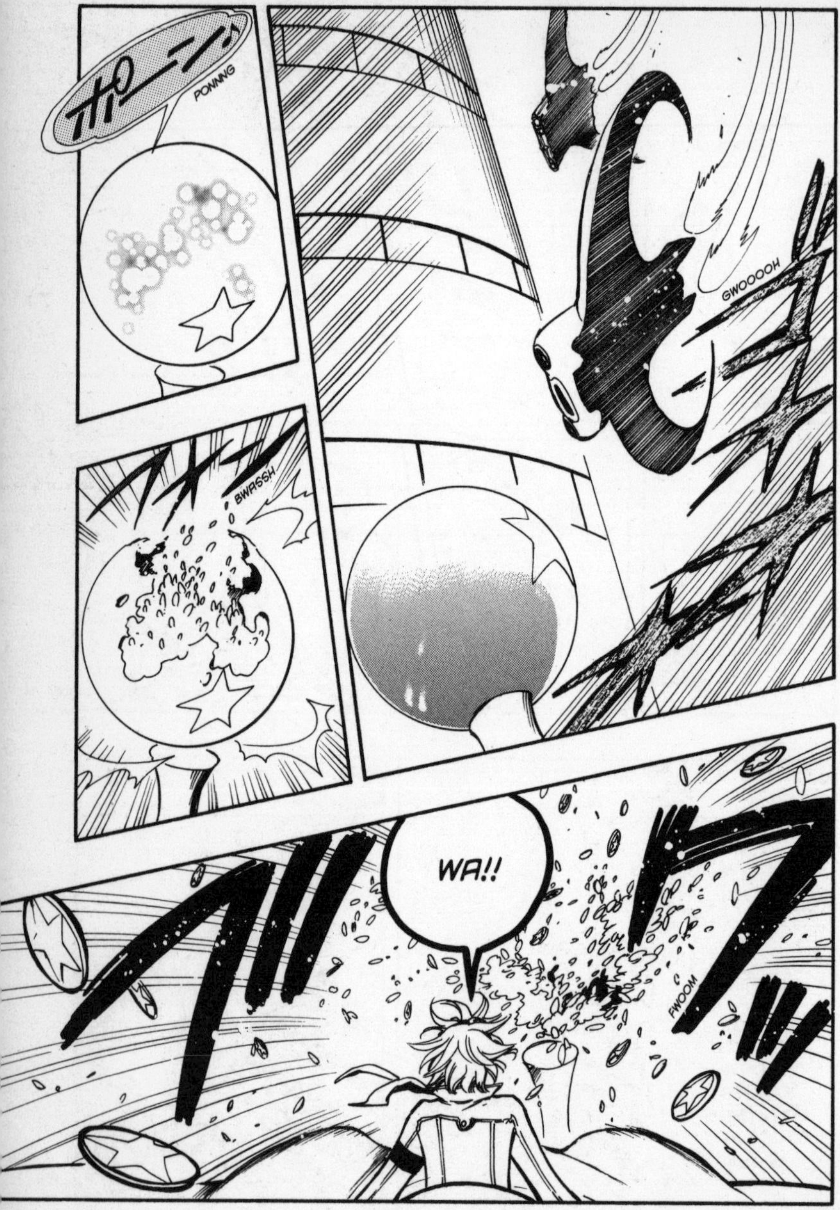
GWOOOOH
PONNNG
BWASSH
WA!!
FWOOM

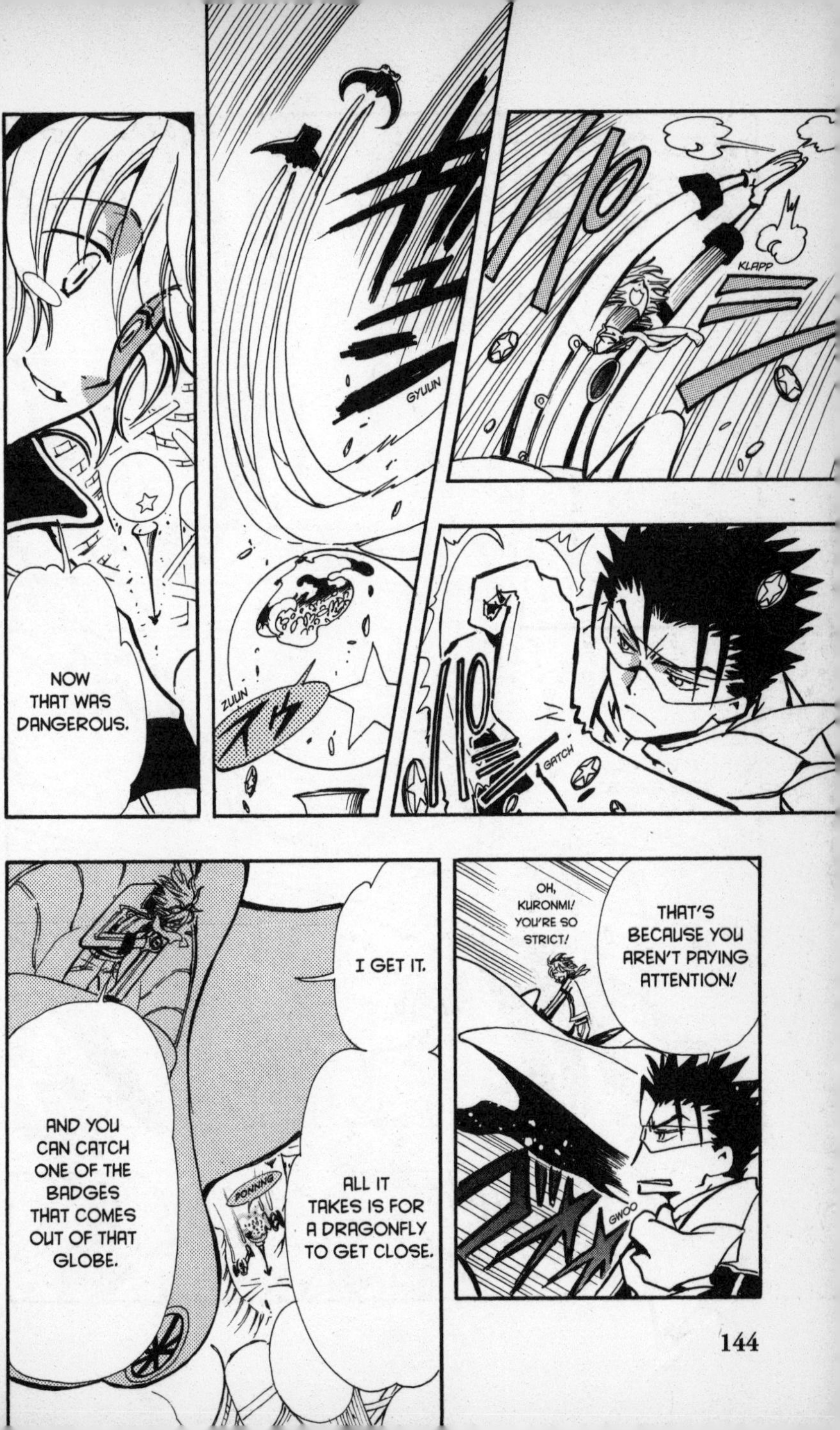

KLAPP
GATCH
GYUUN
ZUUN
NOW THAT WAS DANGEROUS.
OH, KURONMI! YOU'RE SO STRICT!
THAT'S BECAUSE YOU AREN'T PAYING ATTENTION!
GWOO
I GET IT.
ALL IT TAKES IS FOR A DRAGONFLY TO GET CLOSE.
AND YOU CAN CATCH ONE OF THE BADGES THAT COMES OUT OF THAT GLOBE.
PONNNG

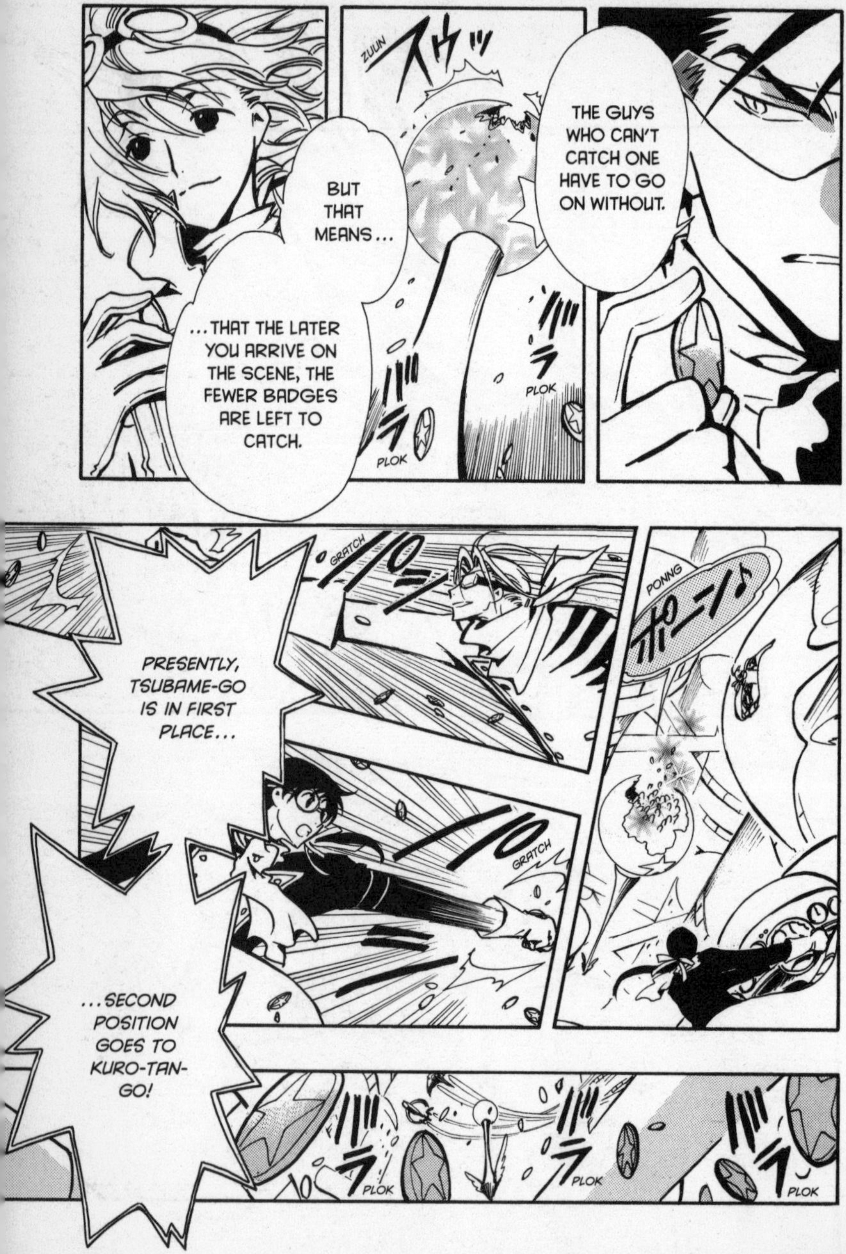
THE GUYS WHO CAN'T CATCH ONE HAVE TO GO ON WITHOUT.
ZUUN
スウッ
BUT THAT MEANS...
PLOK
PLOK
...THAT THE LATER YOU ARRIVE ON THE SCENE, THE FEWER BADGES ARE LEFT TO CATCH.
PONNG
ポーン♪
GRATCH
PRESENTLY, TSUBAME-GO IS IN FIRST PLACE...
GRATCH
...SECOND POSITION GOES TO KURO-TAN-GO!
PLOK
PLOK
PLOK

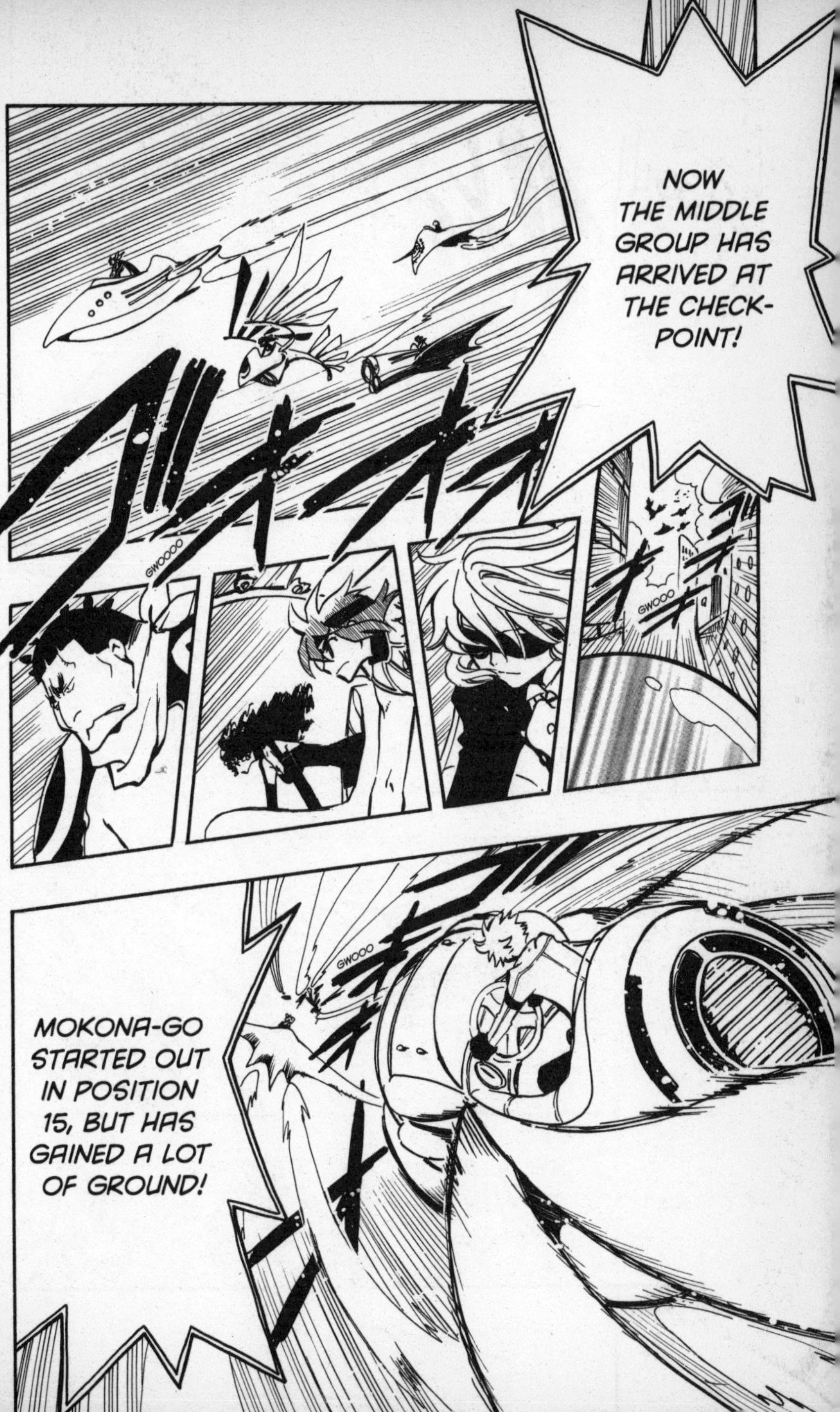
NOW THE MIDDLE GROUP HAS ARRIVED AT THE CHECK-POINT!
GWOOOO
GWOOO
GWOOO
MOKONA-GO STARTED OUT IN POSITION 15, BUT HAS GAINED A LOT OF GROUND!

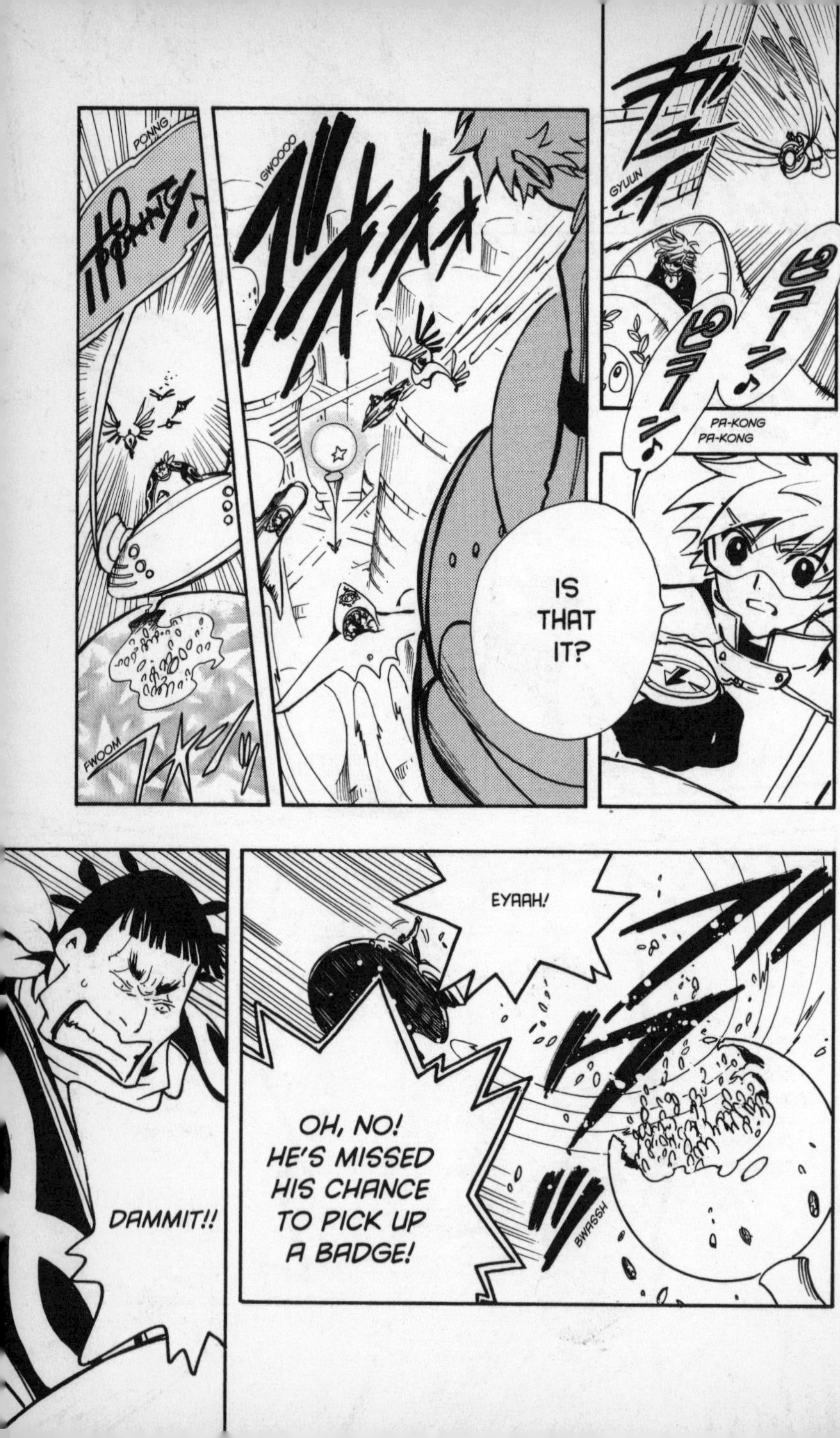
GYUUN
PA-KONG
PA-KONG
IS THAT IT?
GWOOOO
PONNG
FWOOM
EYAAH!
OH, NO! HE'S MISSED HIS CHANCE TO PICK UP A BADGE!
BWASSH
DAMMIT!!

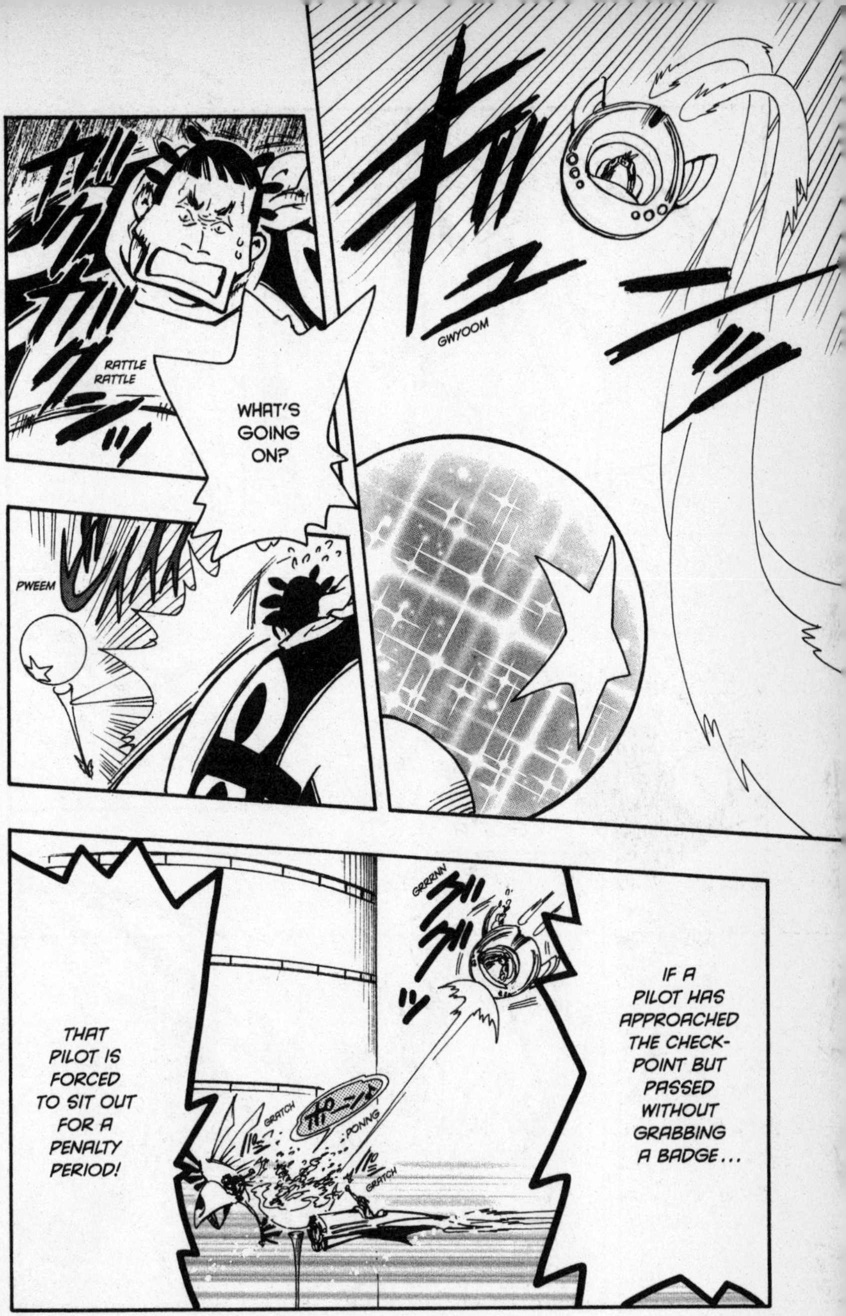
GWYOOM
RATTLE RATTLE
WHAT'S GOING ON?
PWEEM
GRRRNN
IF A PILOT HAS APPROACHED THE CHECK-POINT BUT PASSED WITHOUT GRABBING A BADGE...
THAT PILOT IS FORCED TO SIT OUT FOR A PENALTY PERIOD!
GRATCH
PONNG
GRATCH

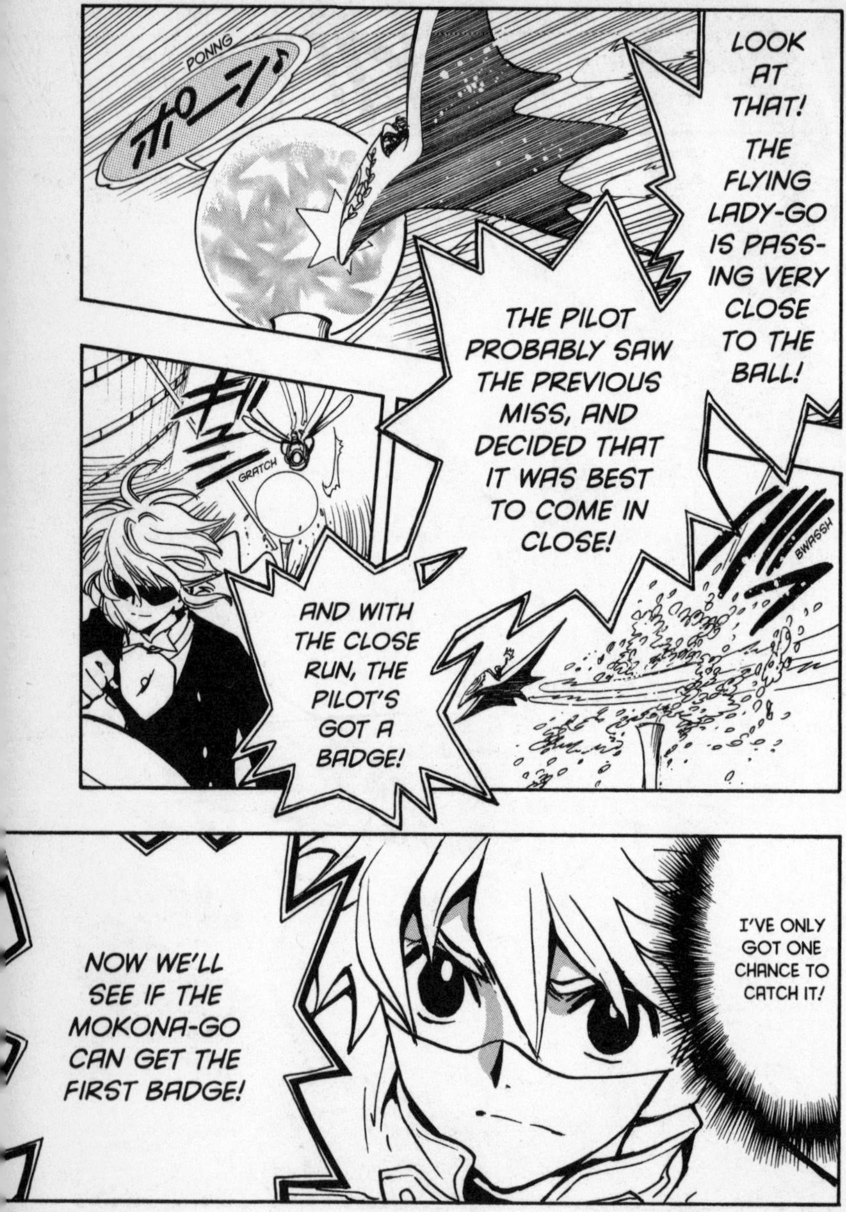
LOOK AT THAT! THE FLYING LADY-GO IS PASSING VERY CLOSE TO THE BALL!
PONNG
THE PILOT PROBABLY SAW THE PREVIOUS MISS, AND DECIDED THAT IT WAS BEST TO COME IN CLOSE!
BWASSH
AND WITH THE CLOSE RUN, THE PILOT'S GOT A BADGE!
GRATCH
I'VE ONLY GOT ONE CHANCE TO CATCH IT!
NOW WE'LL SEE IF THE MOKONA-GO CAN GET THE FIRST BADGE!

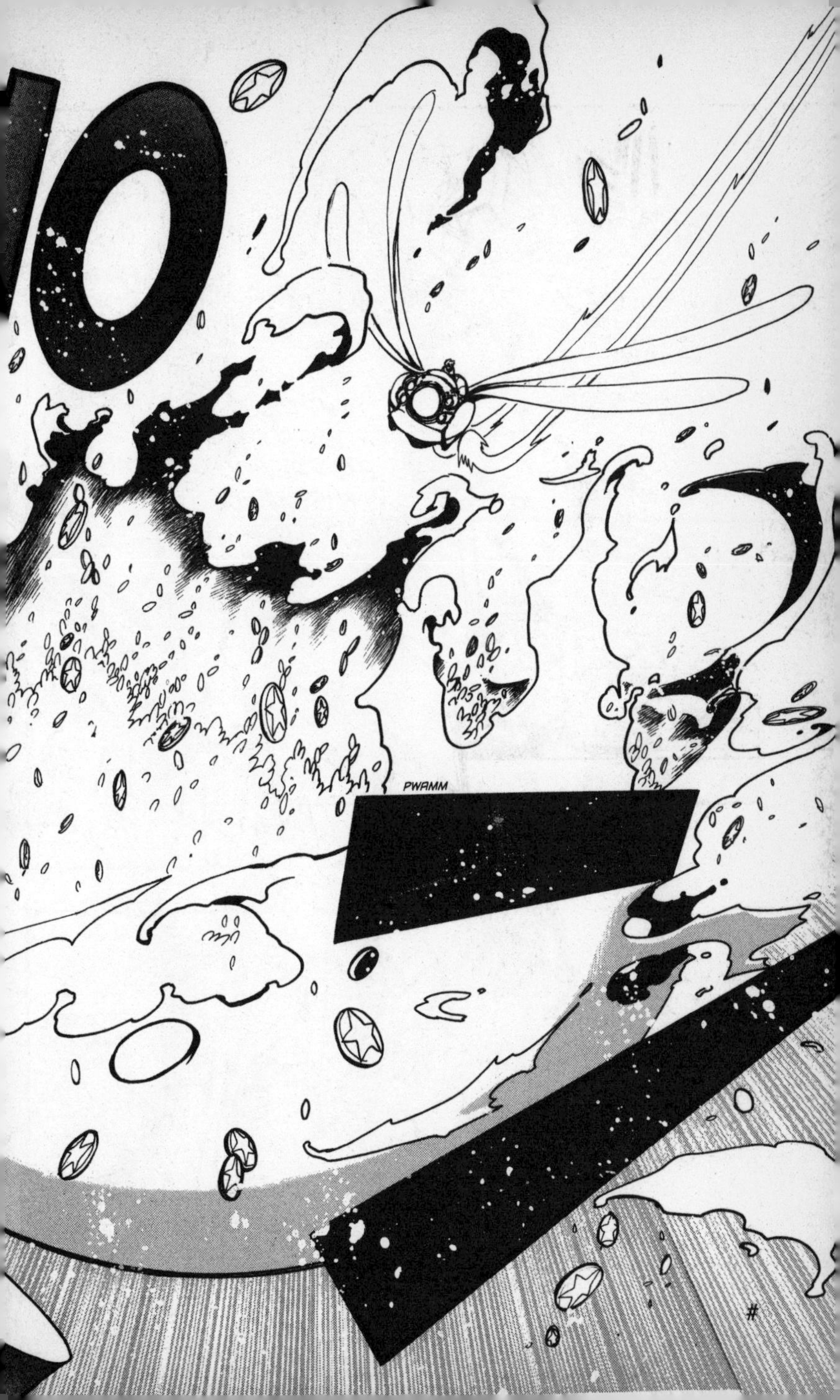
PWAMM

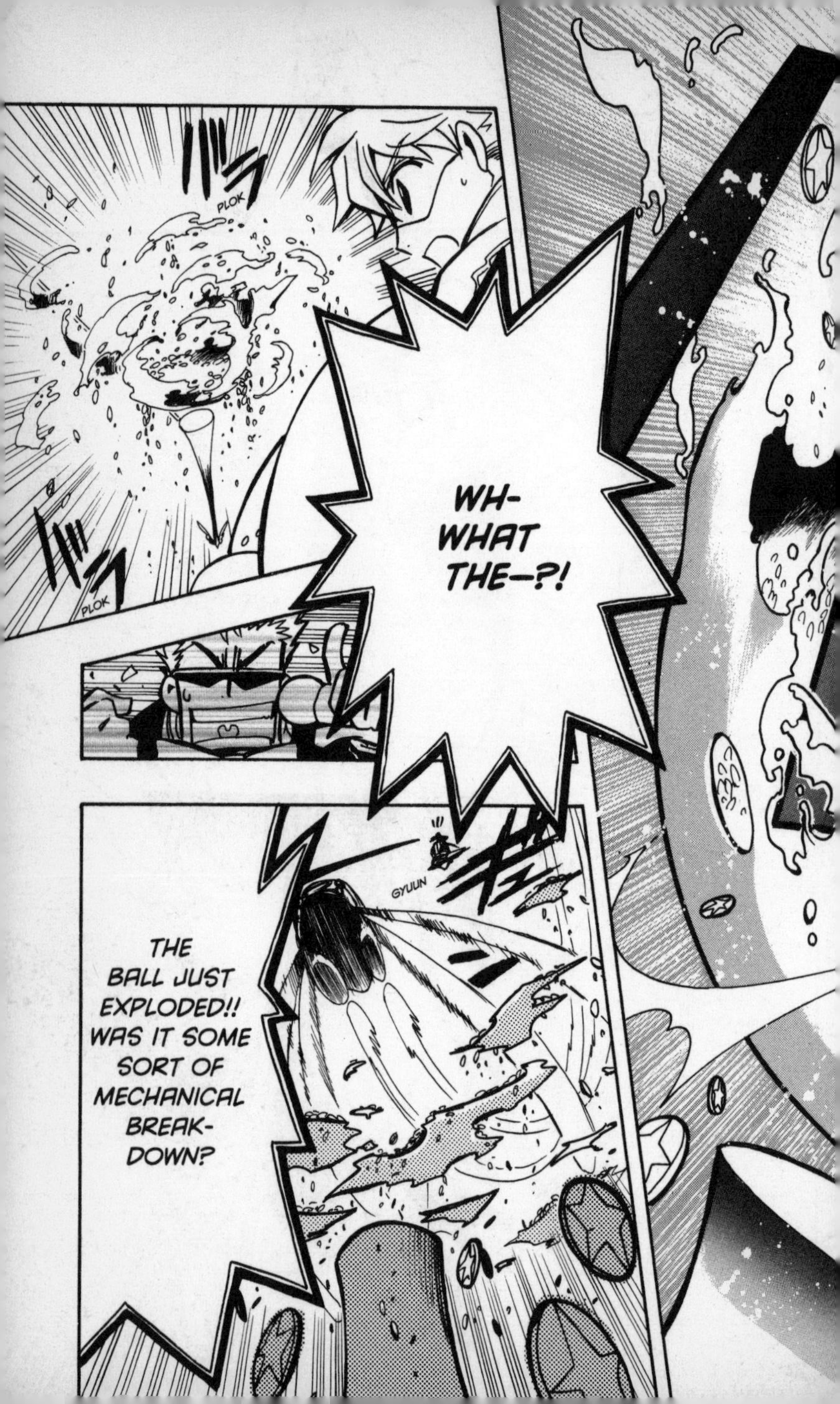
PLOK
PLOK
WH-WHAT THE--?!
GYUUN
THE BALL JUST EXPLODED!! WAS IT SOME SORT OF MECHANICAL BREAK-DOWN?

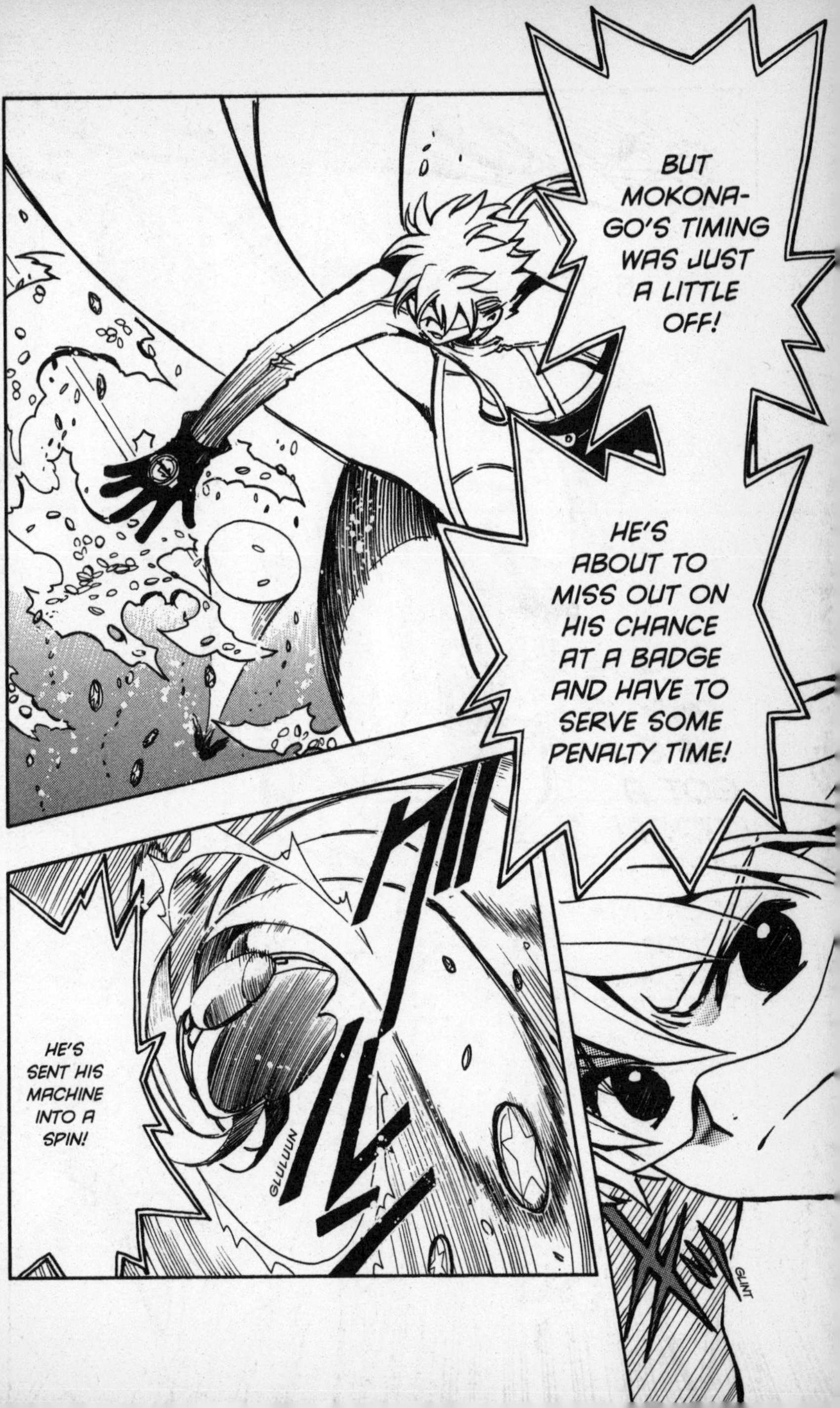
BUT MOKONA-GO'S TIMING WAS JUST A LITTLE OFF!
HE'S ABOUT TO MISS OUT ON HIS CHANCE AT A BADGE AND HAVE TO SERVE SOME PENALTY TIME!
HE'S SENT HIS MACHINE INTO A SPIN!
GLULUUN
GLINT

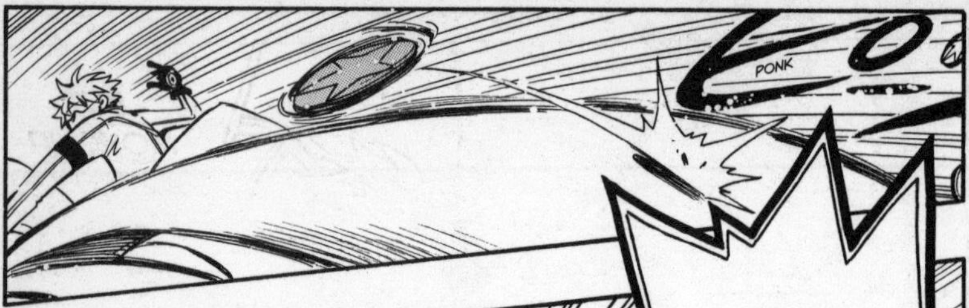
PONK
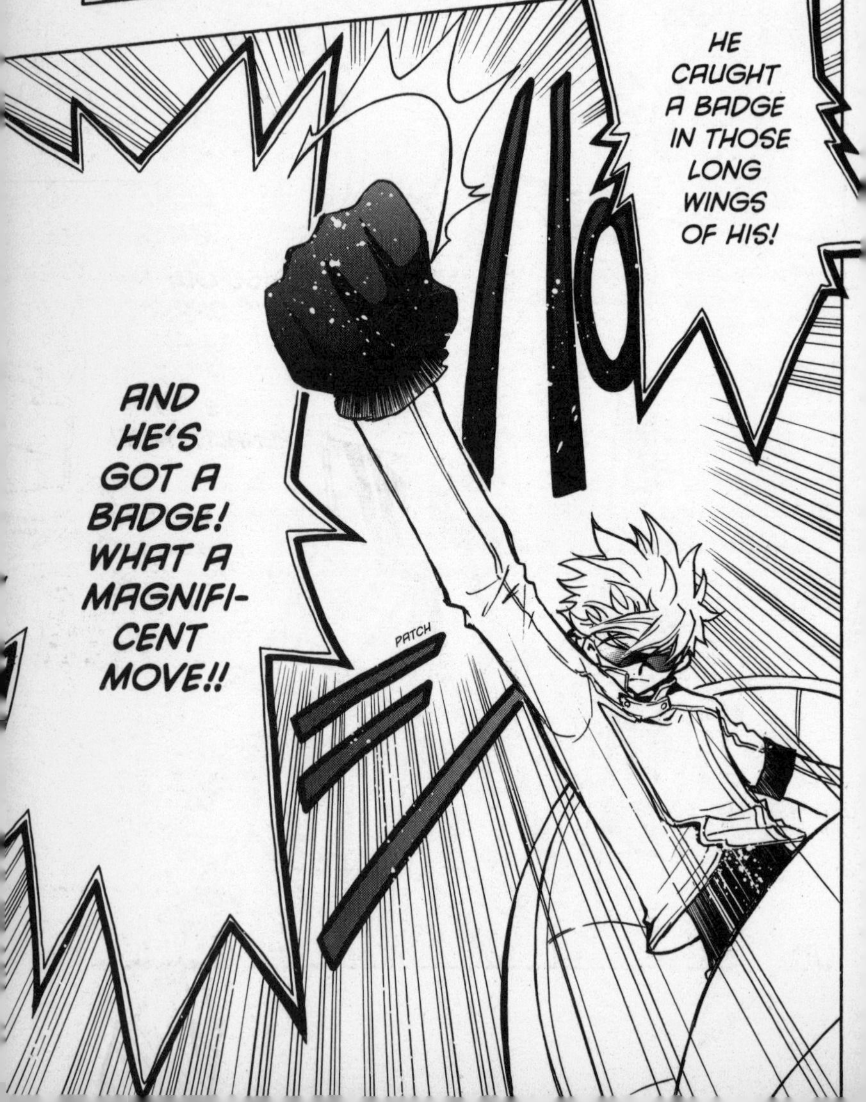
HE CAUGHT A BADGE IN THOSE LONG WINGS OF HIS!
AND HE'S GOT A BADGE! WHAT A MAGNIFI-CENT MOVE!!
PATCH

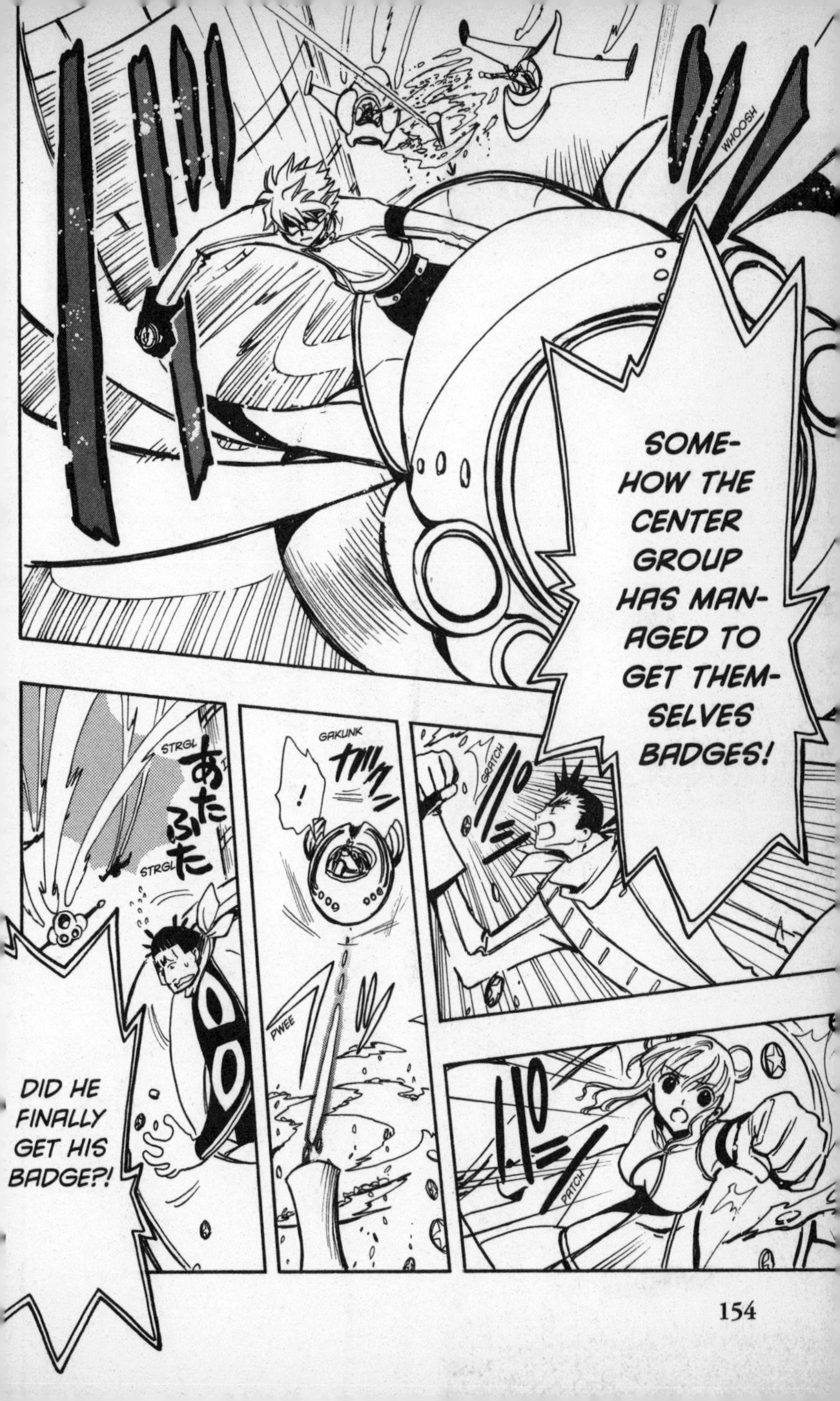
WHOOSH
SOME-
HOW THE
CENTER
GROUP
HAS MAN-
AGED TO
GET THEM-
SELVES
BADGES!
GRATCH
GAKUNK
ガクン
!
PWEE
STRGL
あたふた
STRGL
PATCH
DID HE
FINALLY
GET HIS
BADGE?!

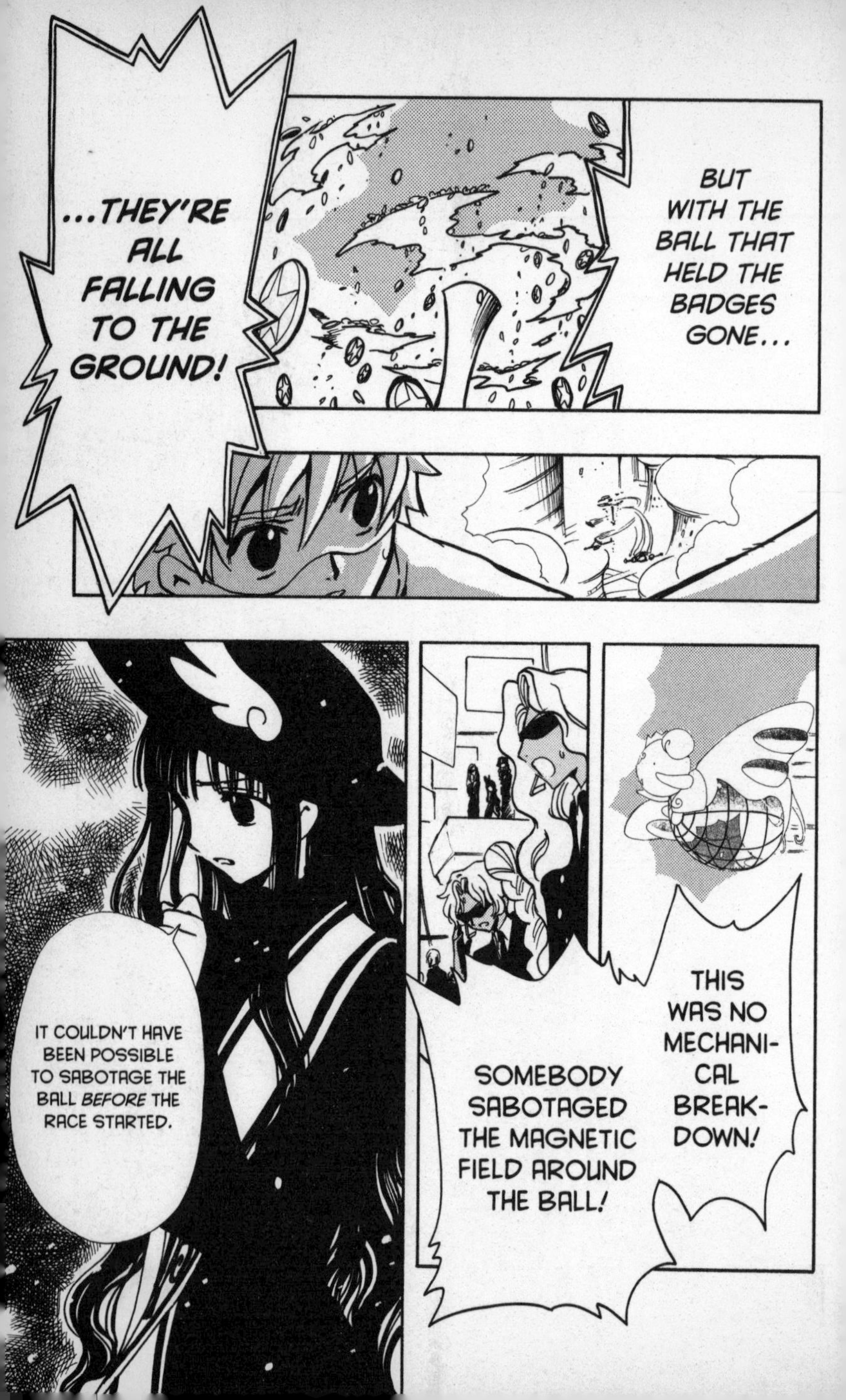
BUT WITH THE BALL THAT HELD THE BADGES GONE...
...THEY'RE ALL FALLING TO THE GROUND!
THIS WAS NO MECHANI-CAL BREAK-DOWN!
SOMEBODY SABOTAGED THE MAGNETIC FIELD AROUND THE BALL!
IT COULDN'T HAVE BEEN POSSIBLE TO SABOTAGE THE BALL *BEFORE* THE RACE STARTED.

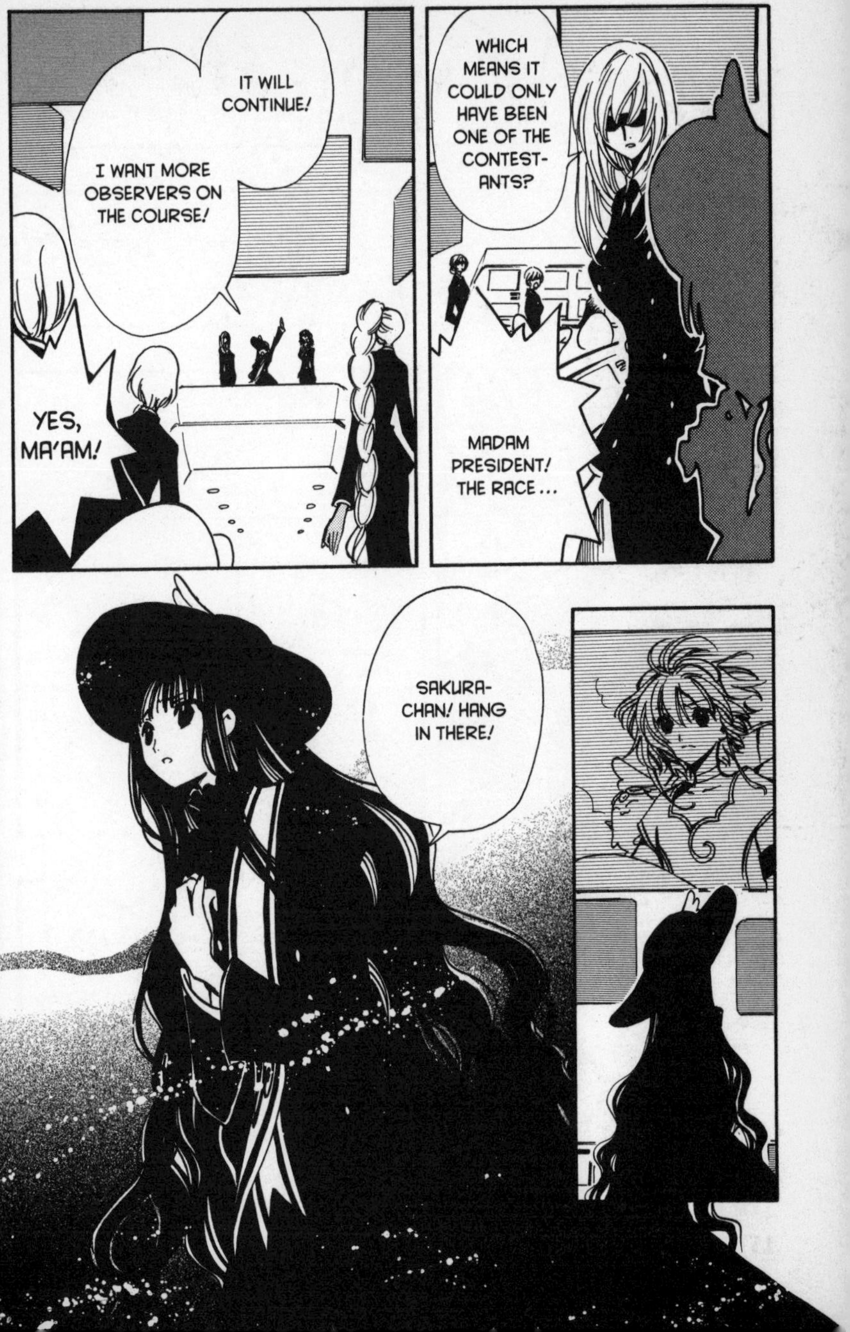
WHICH MEANS IT COULD ONLY HAVE BEEN ONE OF THE CONTEST-ANTS?
MADAM PRESIDENT! THE RACE...
IT WILL CONTINUE!
I WANT MORE OBSERVERS ON THE COURSE!
YES, MA'AM!
SAKURA-CHAN! HANG IN THERE!

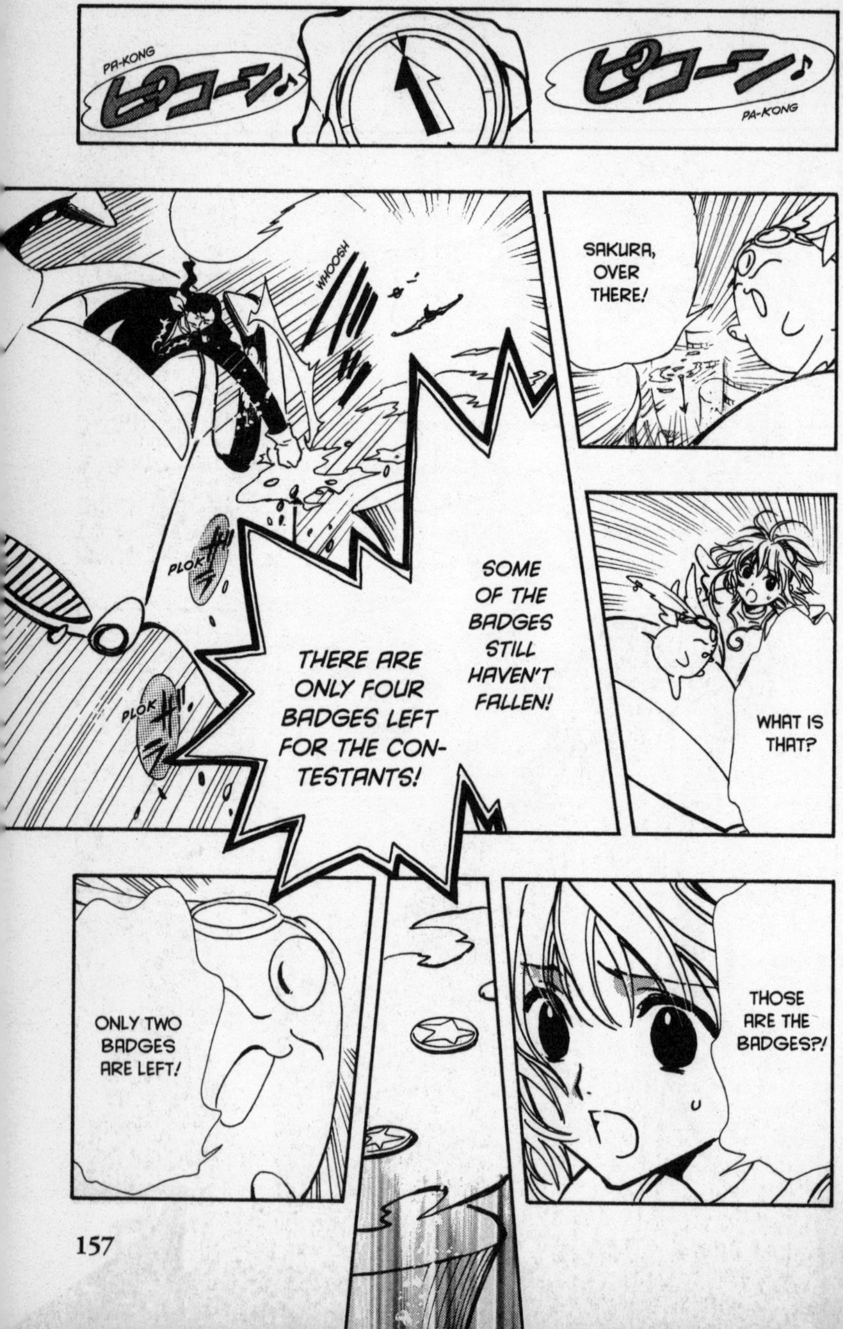
ピコーン♪
PA-KONG
ピコーン♪
PA-KONG
SAKURA, OVER THERE!
WHAT IS THAT?
SOME OF THE BADGES STILL HAVEN'T FALLEN!
THERE ARE ONLY FOUR BADGES LEFT FOR THE CON-TESTANTS!
WHOOSH
PLOK
PLOK
THOSE ARE THE BADGES?!
ONLY TWO BADGES ARE LEFT!

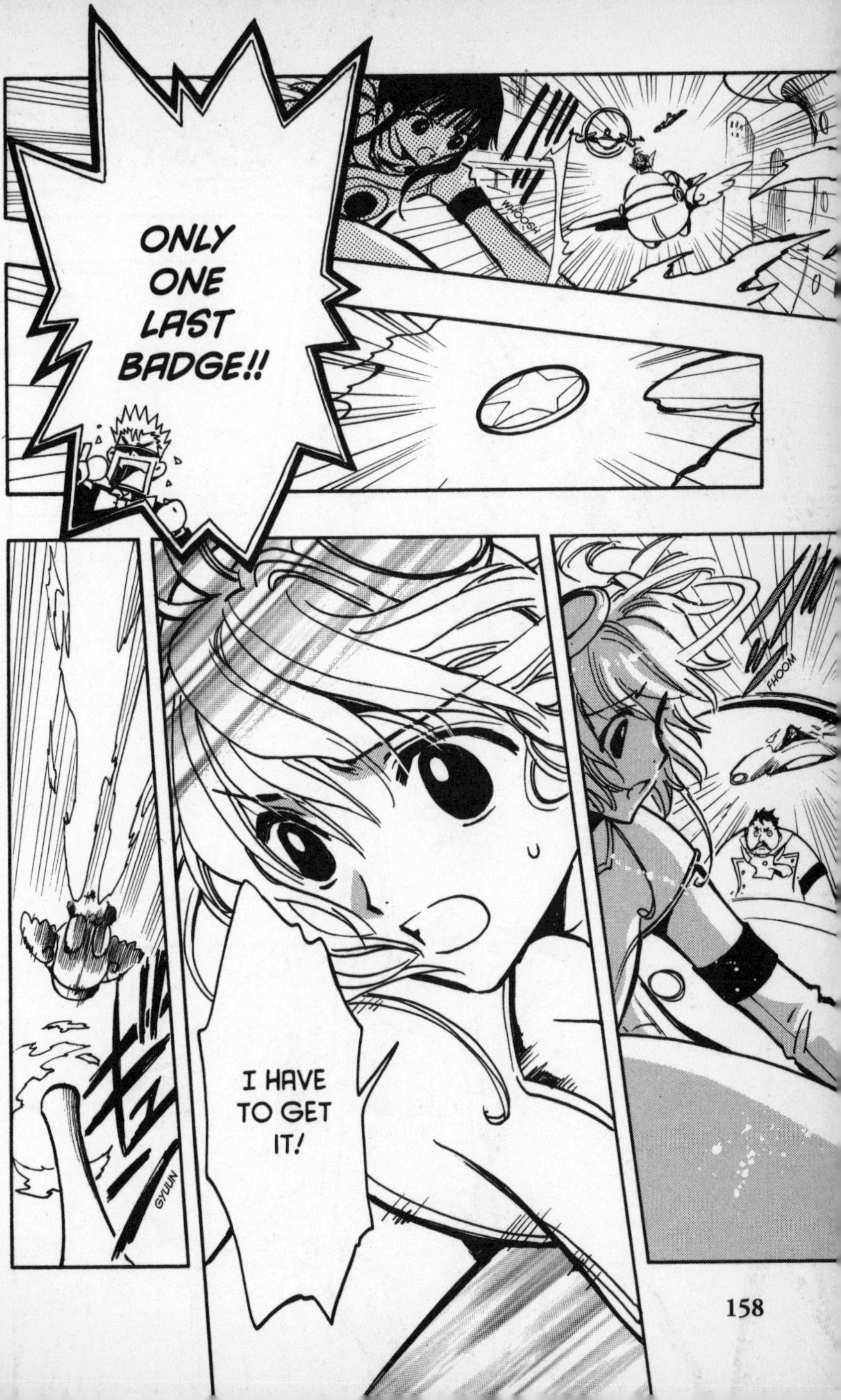
WHOOSH
ONLY ONE LAST BADGE!!
FHOOM
I HAVE TO GET IT!
GYUUN

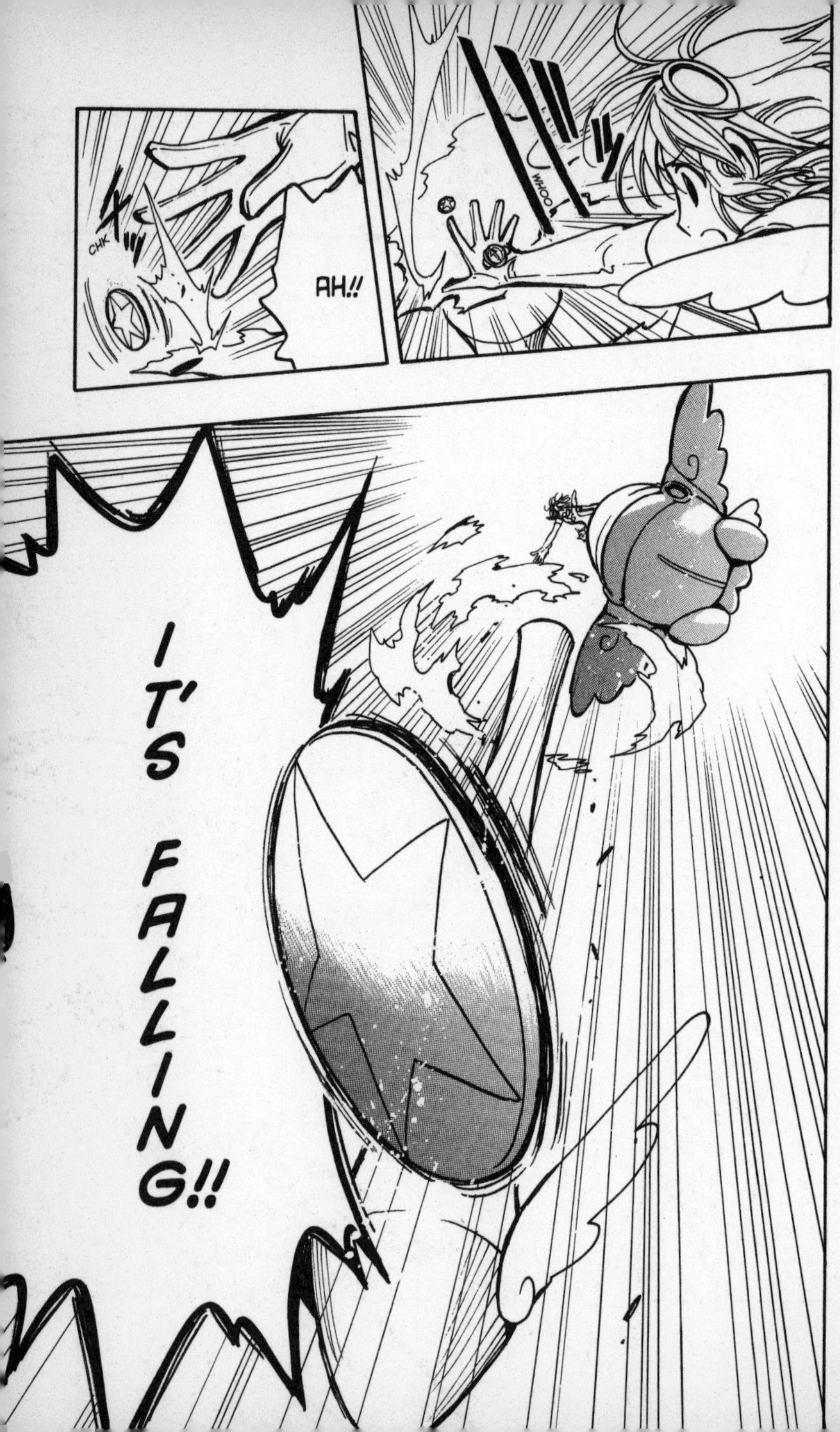
WHOOO
AH!!
CHK
IT'S FALLING!!

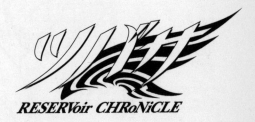

RESERVoir CHRoNiCLE

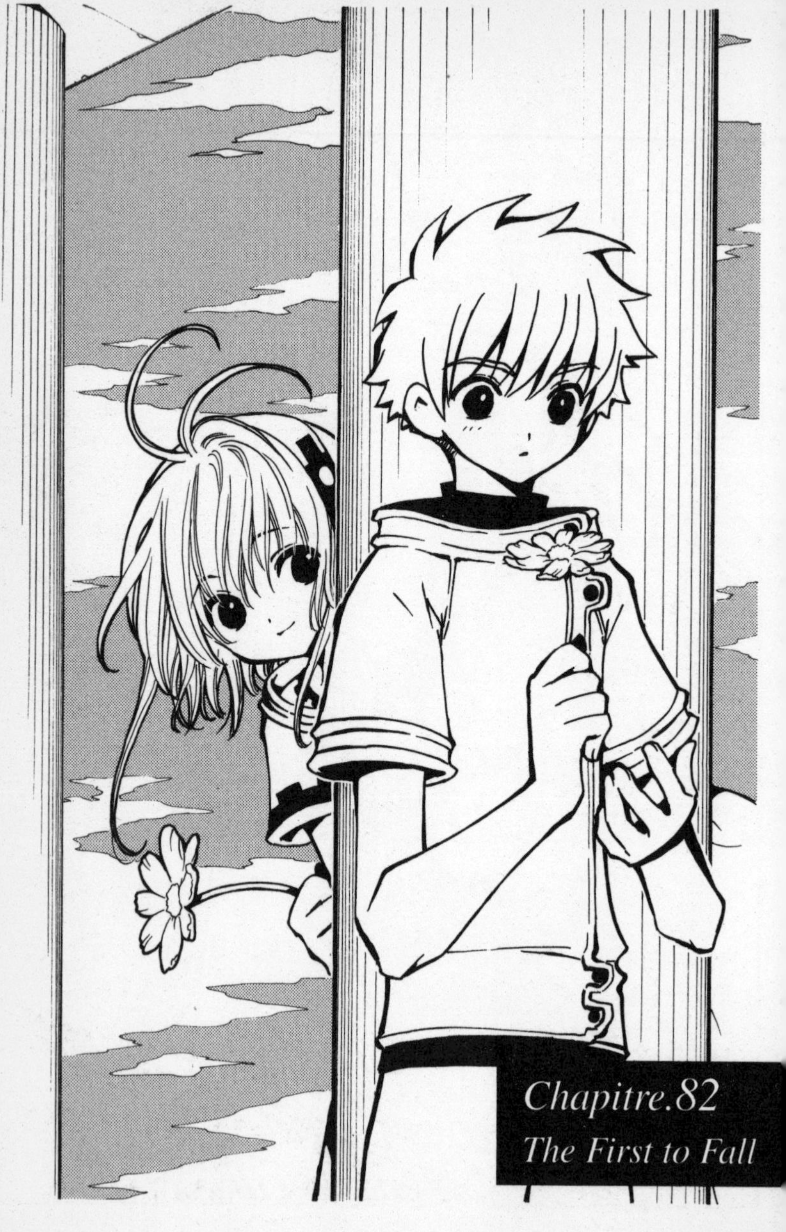
Chapitre.82
The First to Fall

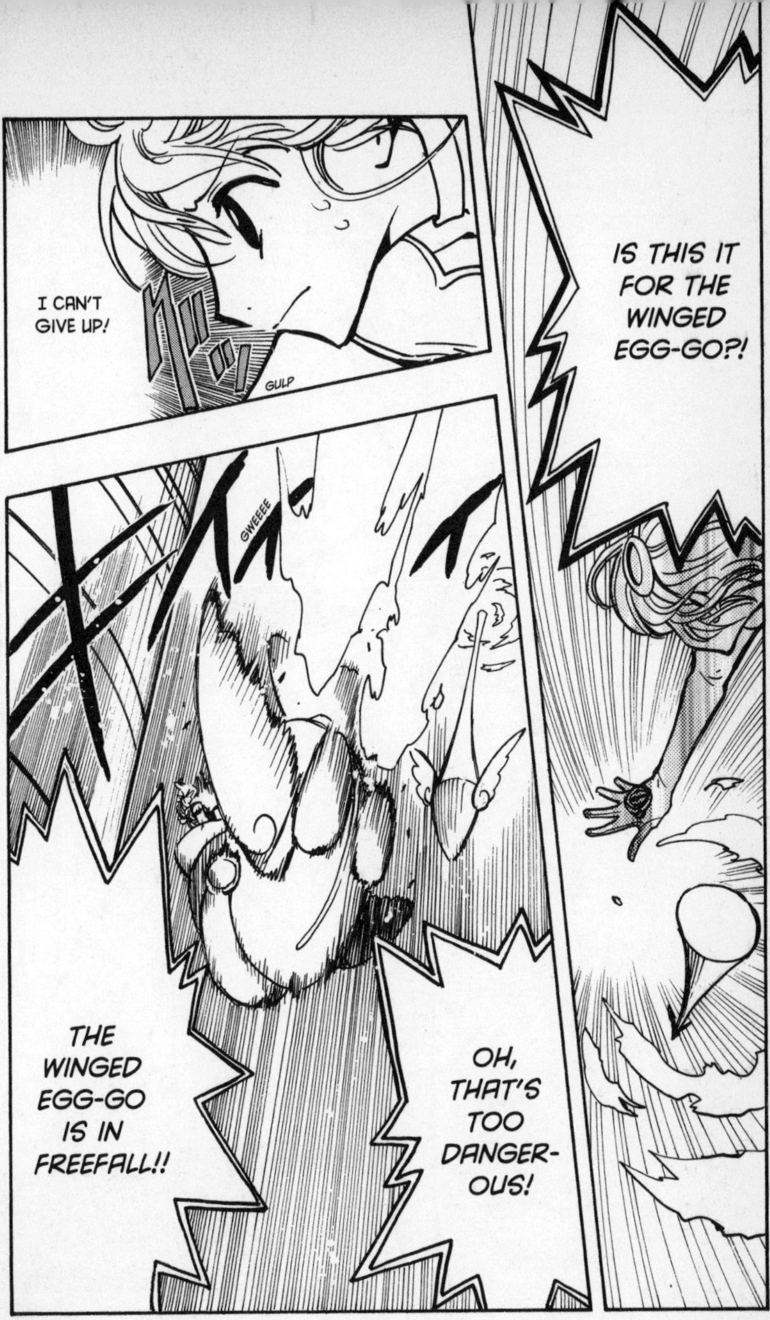
IS THIS IT FOR THE WINGED EGG-GO?!
I CAN'T GIVE UP!
GULP
GWEEEE
OH, THAT'S TOO DANGER-OUS!
THE WINGED EGG-GO IS IN FREEFALL!!

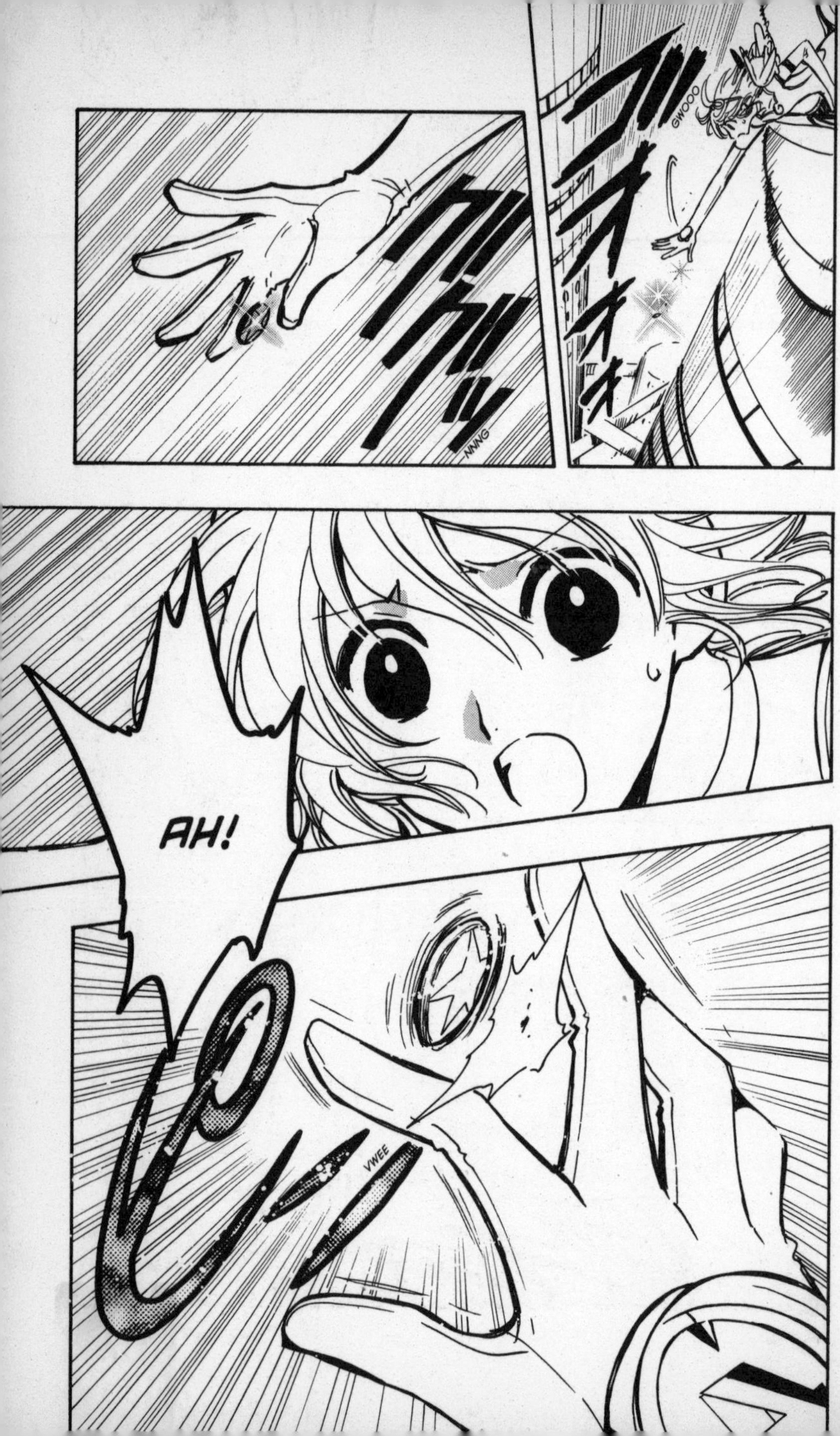
GWOOO
NNNG
AH!
VWEE

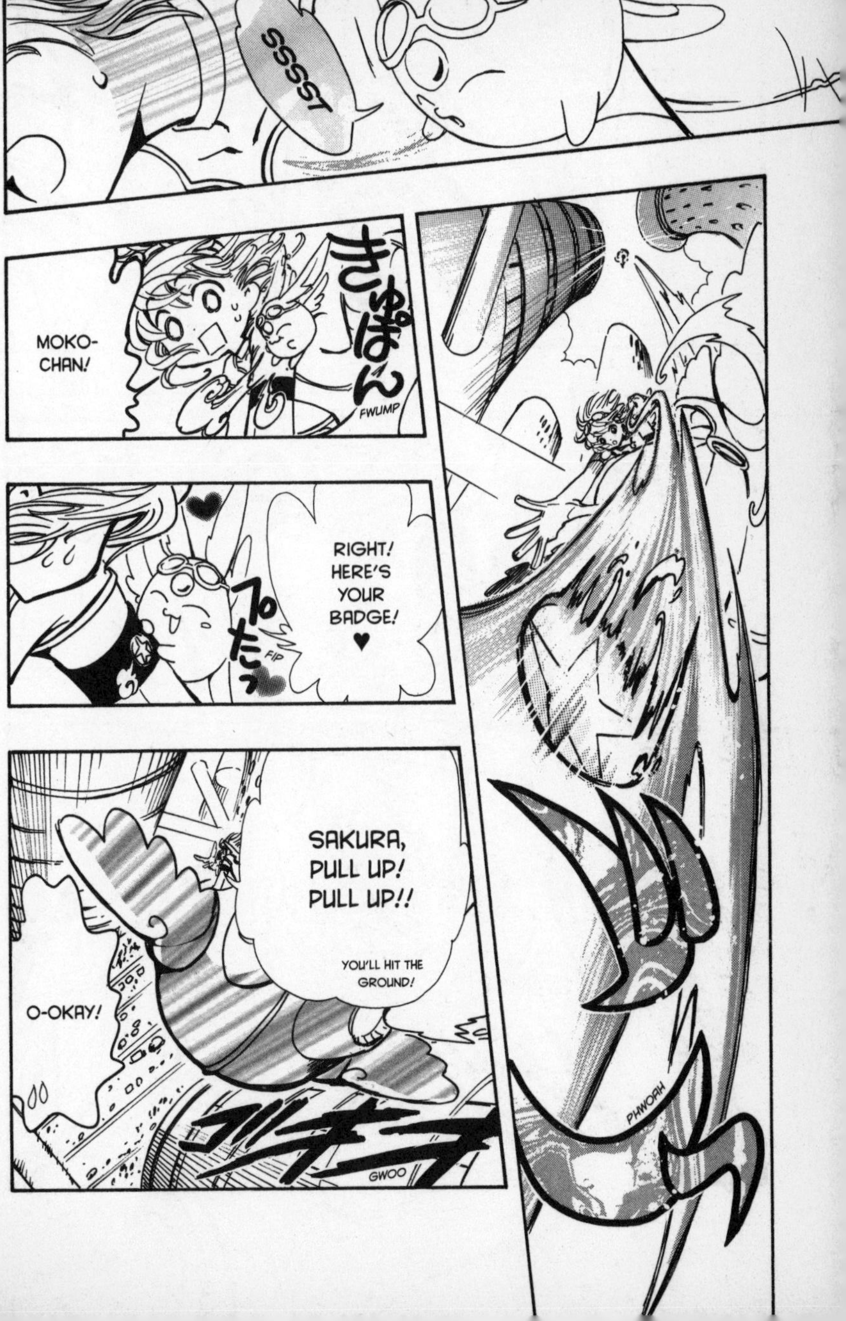
SSSST
PHWOAH
きゅぽん
FWUMP
MOKO-CHAN!
ぺたっ
FIP
RIGHT! HERE'S YOUR BADGE! ♥
SAKURA, PULL UP! PULL UP!!
YOU'LL HIT THE GROUND!
O-OKAY!
GWOO

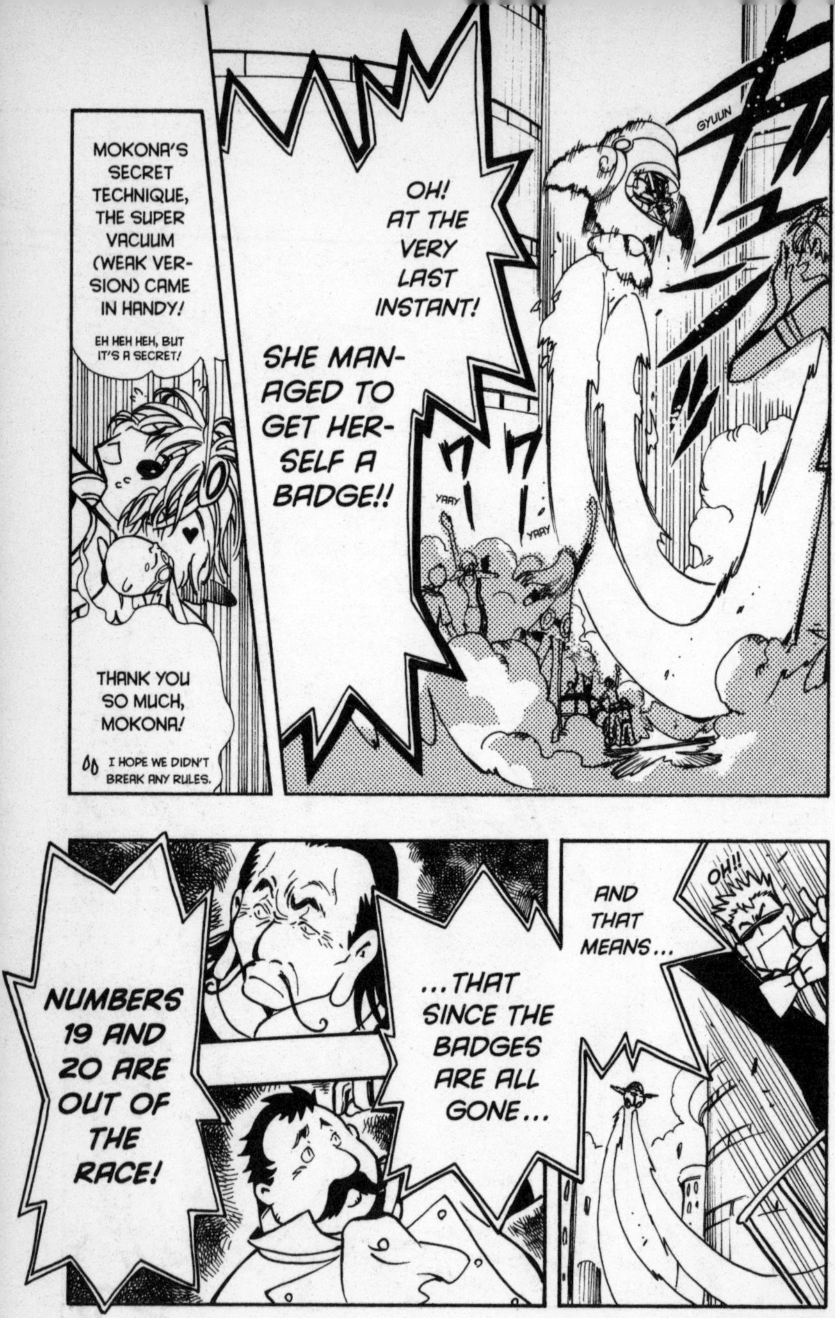
GYUUN
OH! AT THE VERY LAST INSTANT!
SHE MANAGED TO GET HERSELF A BADGE!!
YAAY
YAAY
MOKONA'S SECRET TECHNIQUE, THE SUPER VACUUM (WEAK VERSION) CAME IN HANDY!
EH HEH HEH, BUT IT'S A SECRET!
THANK YOU SO MUCH, MOKONA!
I HOPE WE DIDN'T BREAK ANY RULES.
OH!!
AND THAT MEANS...
...THAT SINCE THE BADGES ARE ALL GONE...
NUMBERS 19 AND 20 ARE OUT OF THE RACE!

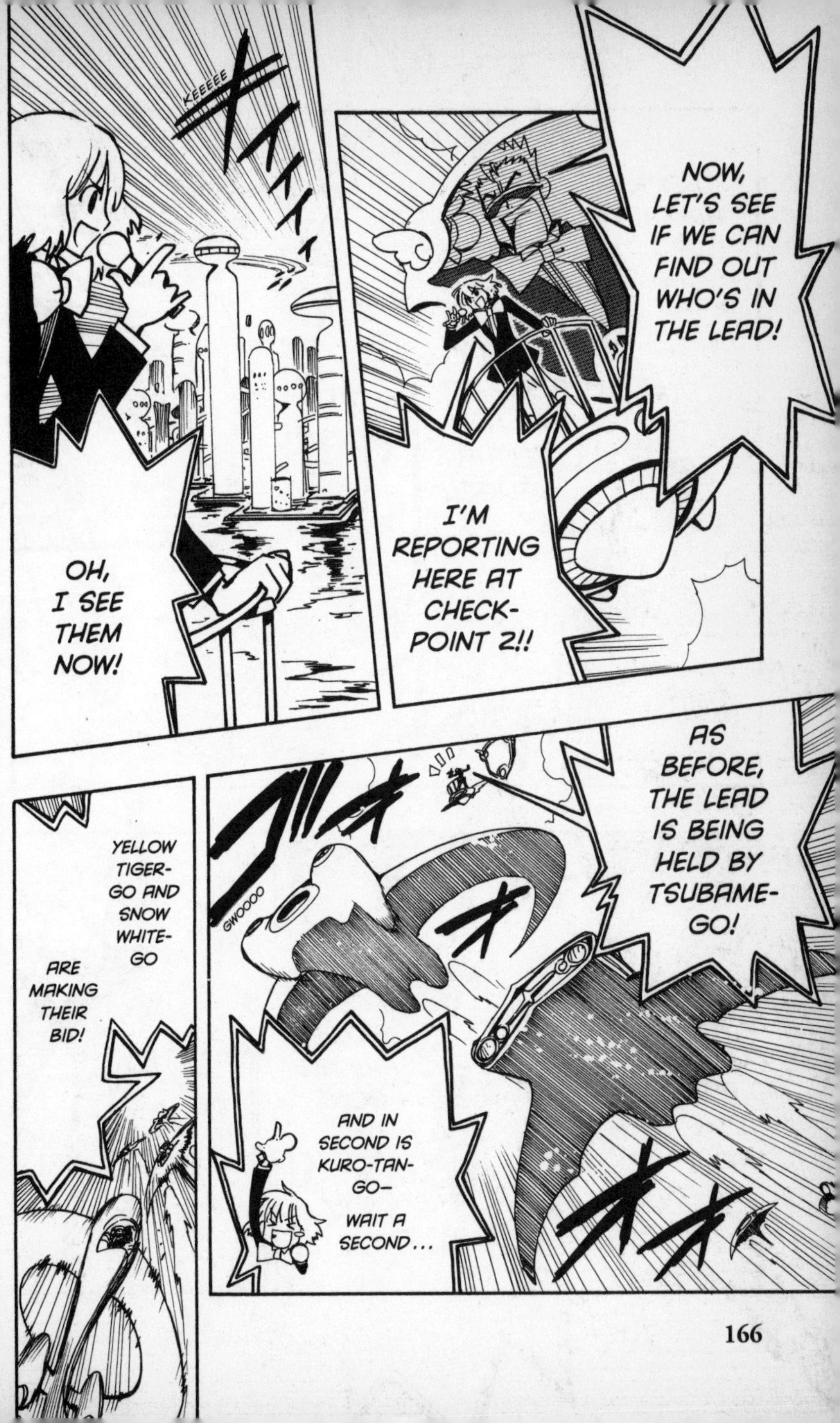
NOW, LET'S SEE IF WE CAN FIND OUT WHO'S IN THE LEAD!
I'M REPORTING HERE AT CHECK-POINT 2!!
KEEEEE
OH, I SEE THEM NOW!
AS BEFORE, THE LEAD IS BEING HELD BY TSUBAME-GO!
GWOOOO
AND IN SECOND IS KURO-TAN-GO—
WAIT A SECOND...
YELLOW TIGER-GO AND SNOW WHITE-GO
ARE MAKING THEIR BID!

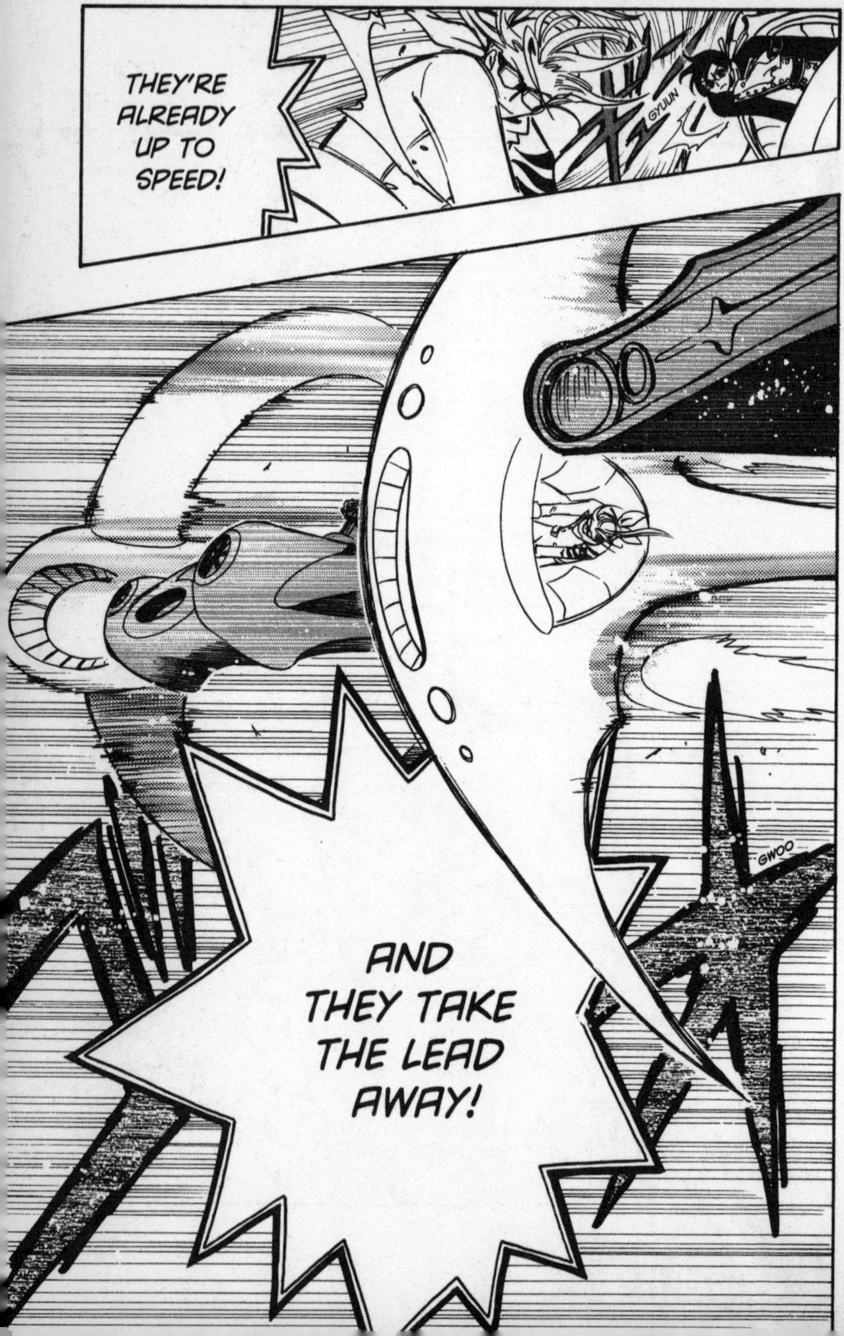
GYUUN
THEY'RE ALREADY UP TO SPEED!
GWOO
AND THEY TAKE THE LEAD AWAY!

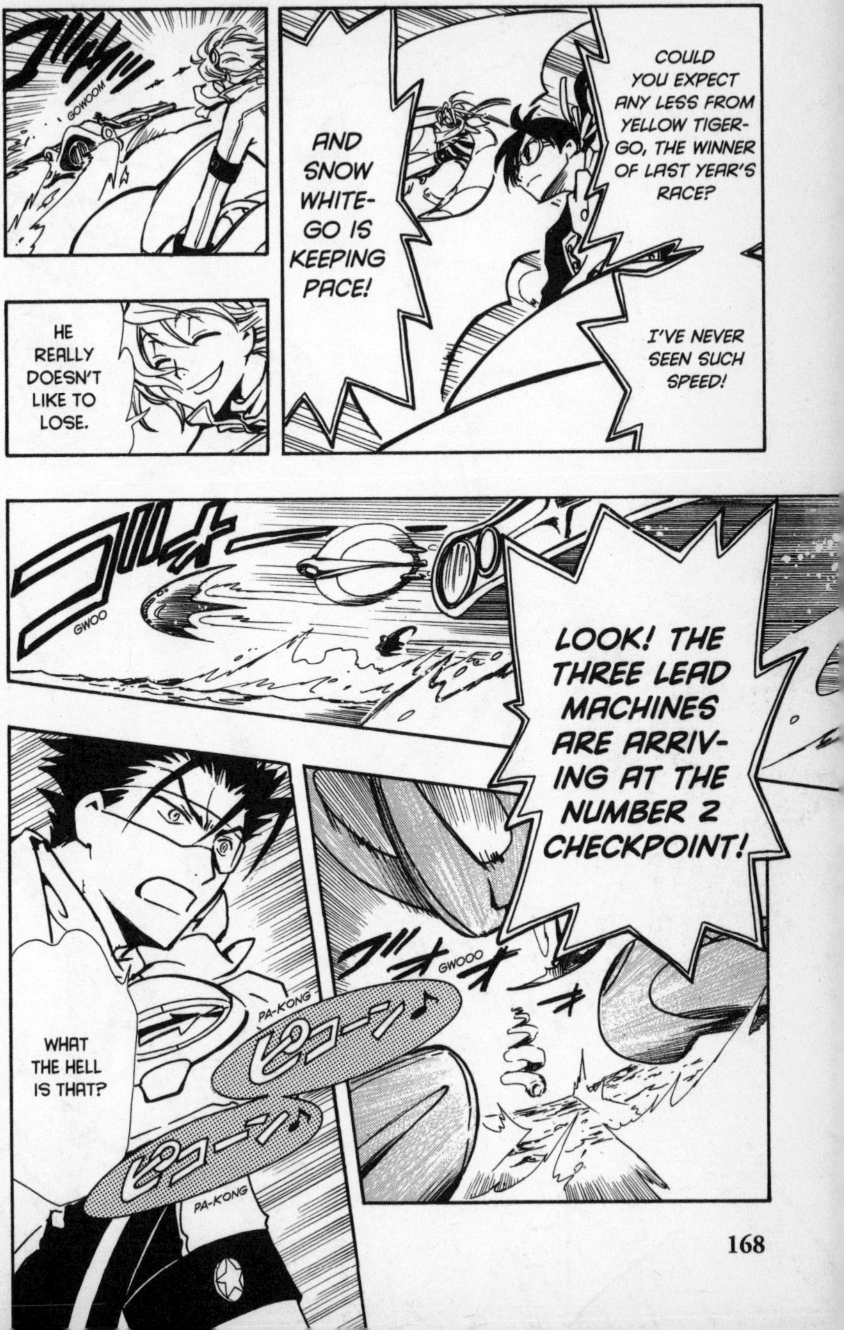
COULD YOU EXPECT ANY LESS FROM YELLOW TIGER-GO, THE WINNER OF LAST YEAR'S RACE?
AND SNOW WHITE-GO IS KEEPING PACE!
I'VE NEVER SEEN SUCH SPEED!
GOWOOM
HE REALLY DOESN'T LIKE TO LOSE.
GWOO
LOOK! THE THREE LEAD MACHINES ARE ARRIVING AT THE NUMBER 2 CHECKPOINT!
GWOOO
PA-KONG
WHAT THE HELL IS THAT?
PA-KONG

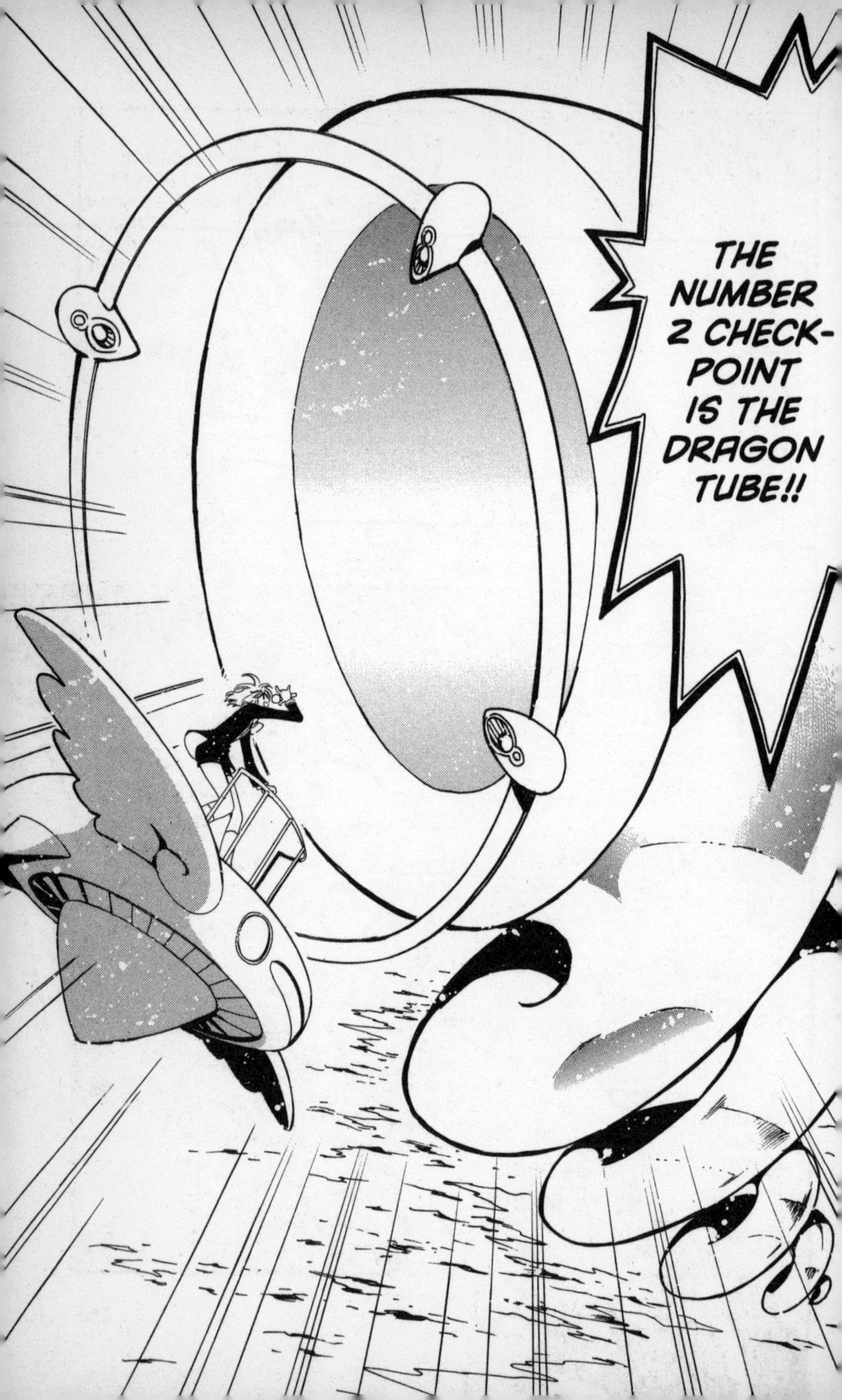
THE NUMBER 2 CHECK-POINT IS THE DRAGON TUBE!!

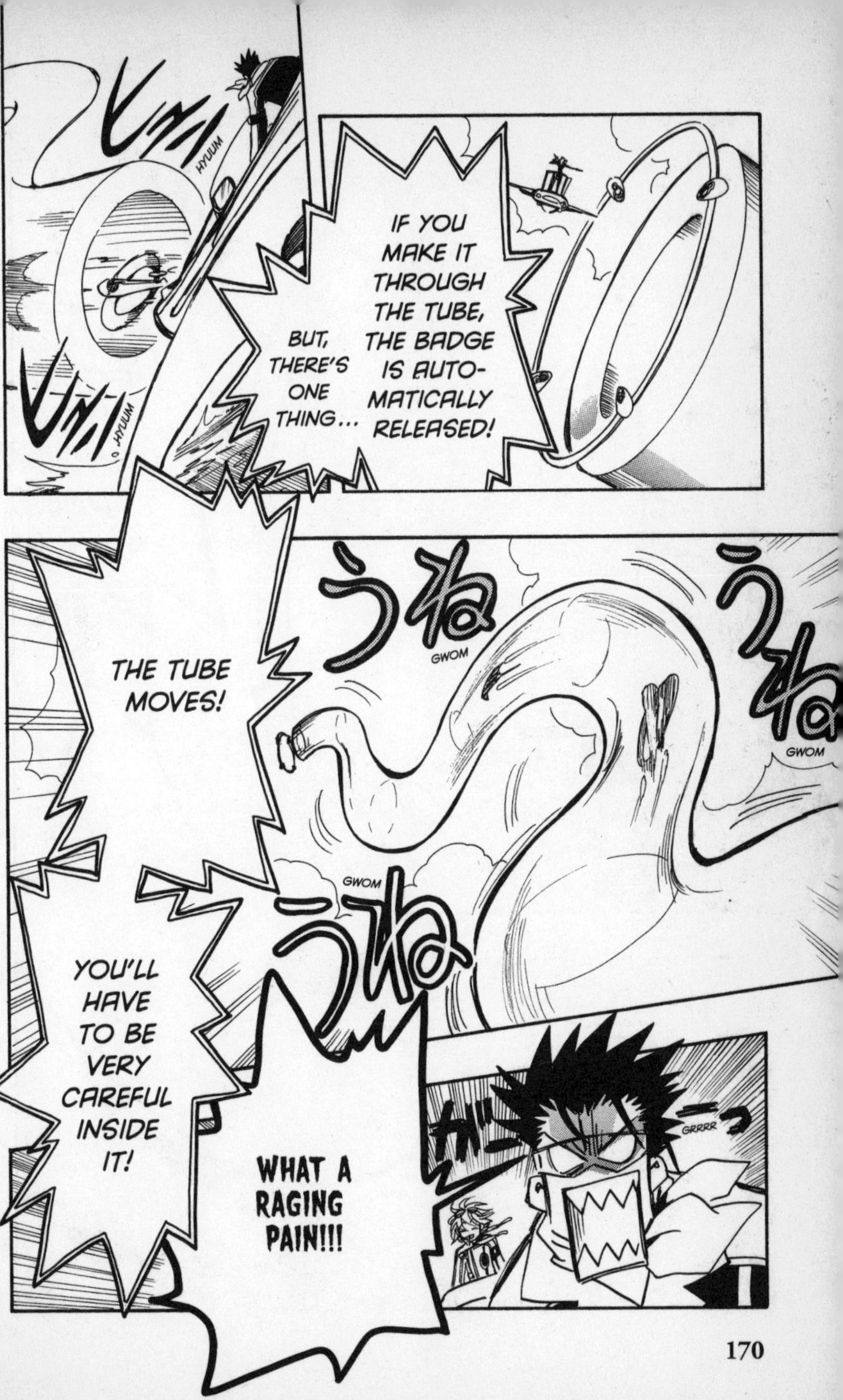
IF YOU MAKE IT THROUGH THE TUBE, THE BADGE IS AUTO-MATICALLY RELEASED!
BUT, THERE'S ONE THING...
HYUUM
HYUUM
うね
GWOM
うね
GWOM
THE TUBE MOVES!
GWOM
うね
YOU'LL HAVE TO BE VERY CAREFUL INSIDE IT!
GRRRR
WHAT A RAGING PAIN!!!

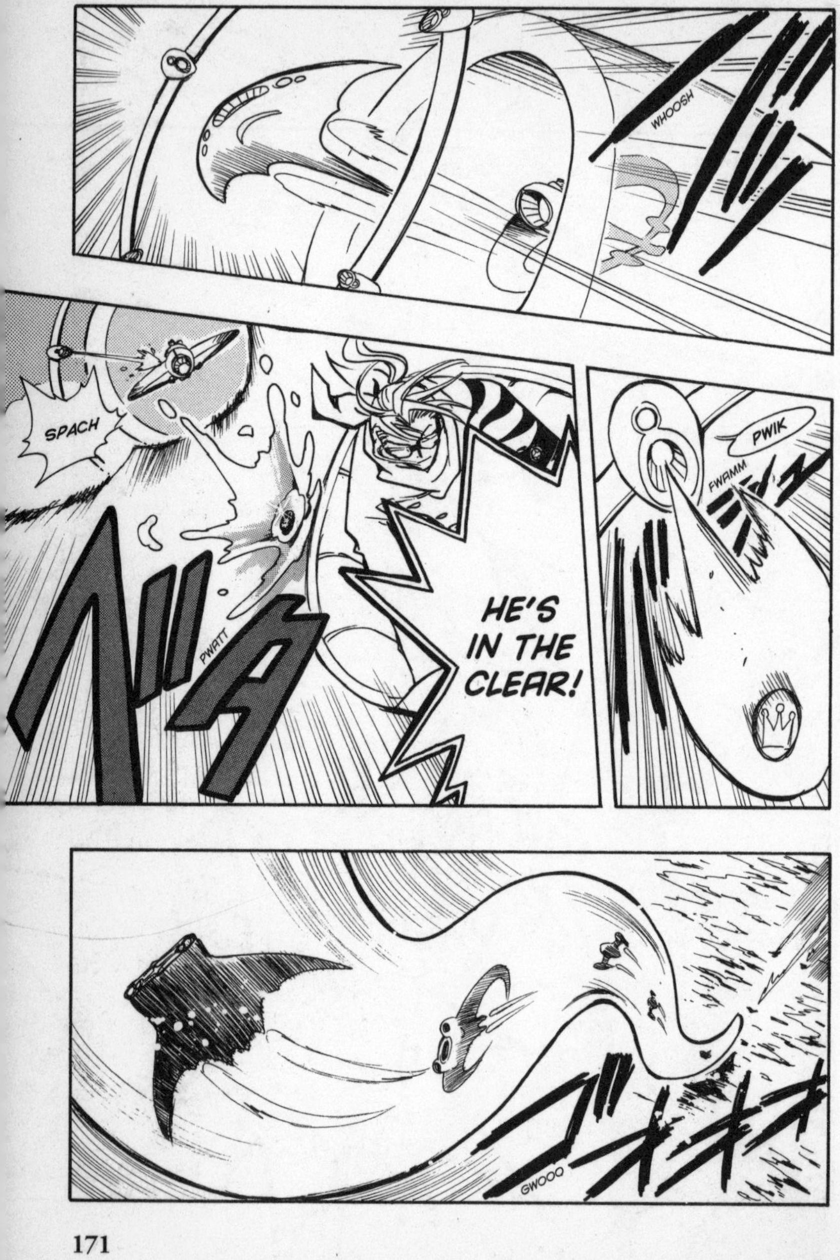
WHOOSH
PWIK
FWAMM
SPACH
HE'S IN THE CLEAR!
PWATT
GWOOO

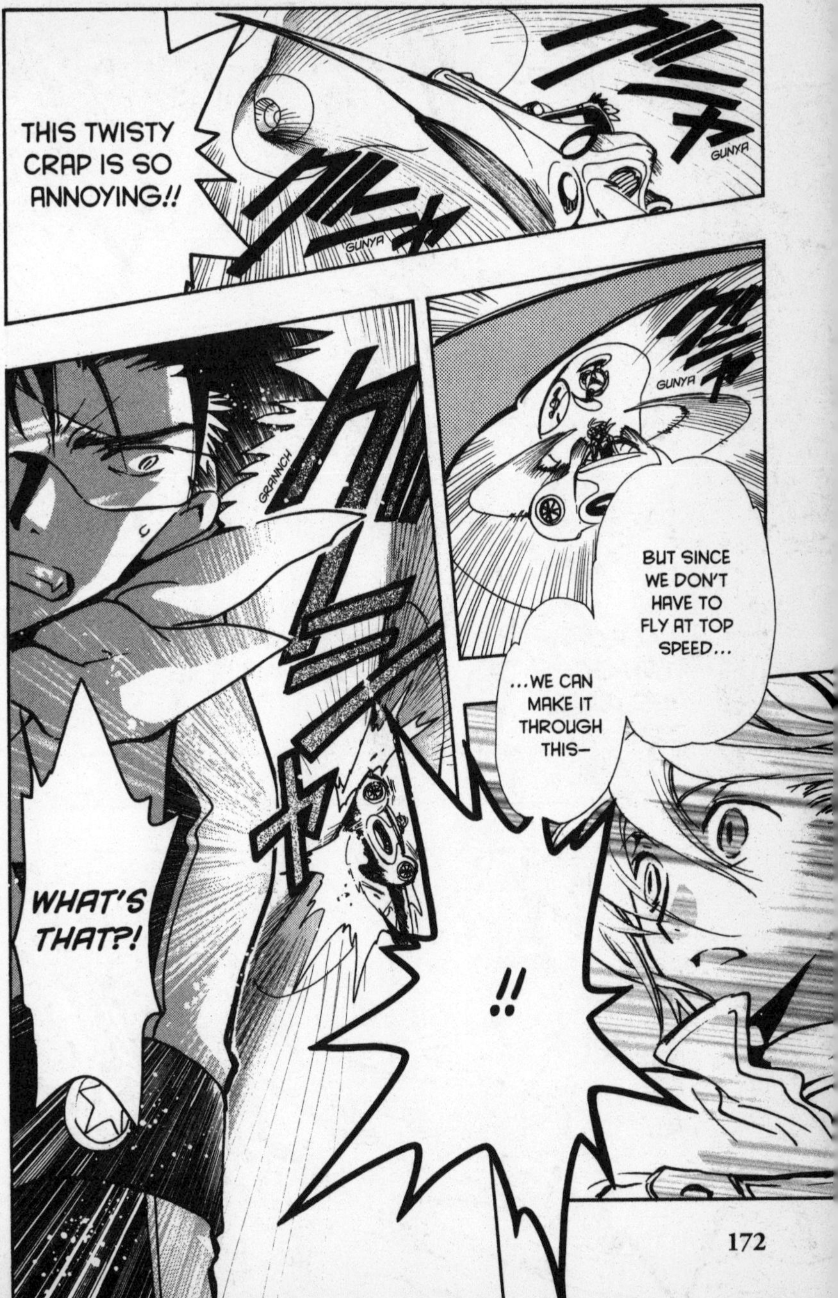
THIS TWISTY CRAP IS SO ANNOYING!!
GUNYA
GUNYA
GUNYA
BUT SINCE WE DON'T HAVE TO FLY AT TOP SPEED...
...WE CAN MAKE IT THROUGH THIS—
!!
GRANNCH
WHAT'S THAT?!

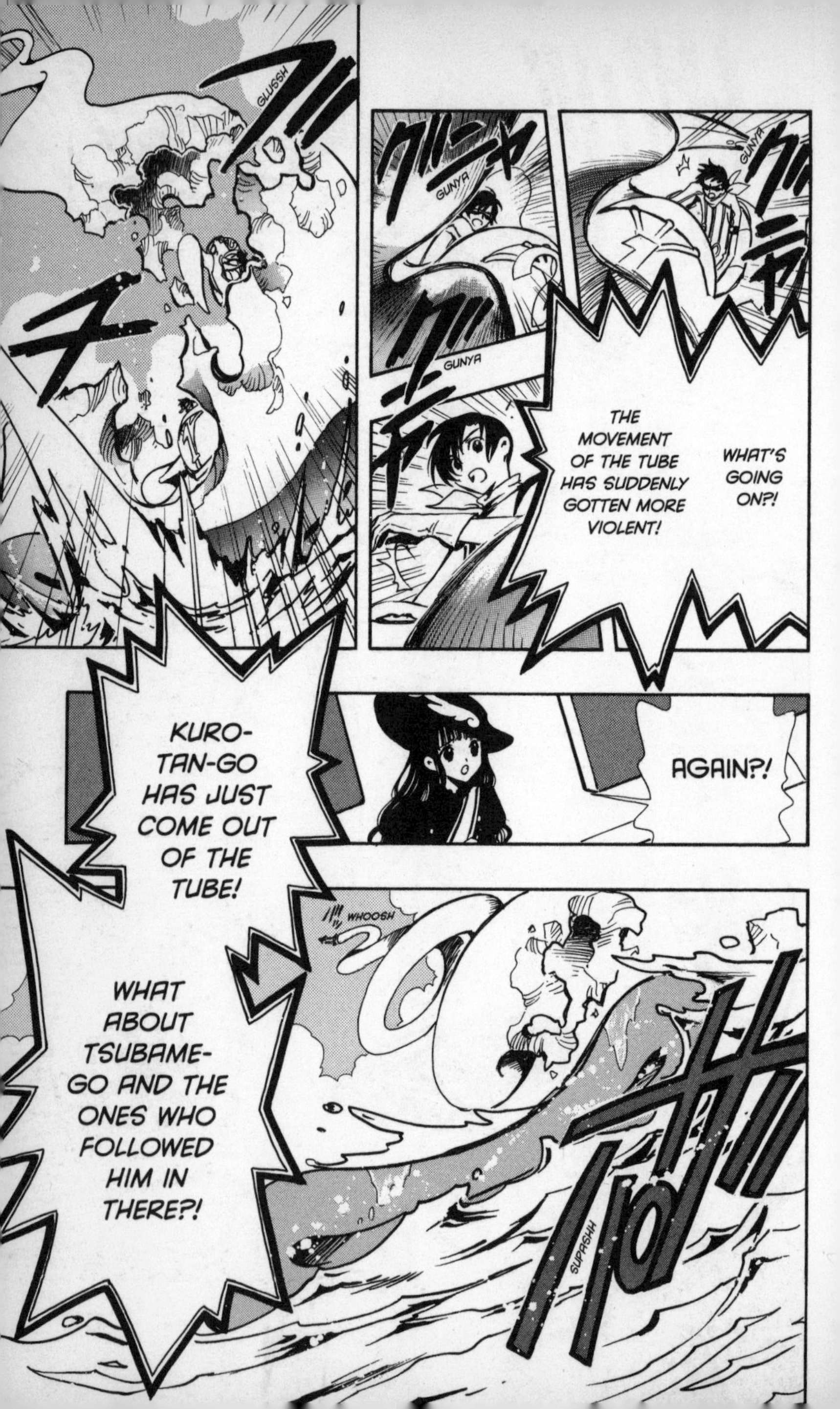
GUNYA
GUNYA
GUNYA
WHAT'S GOING ON?!
THE MOVEMENT OF THE TUBE HAS SUDDENLY GOTTEN MORE VIOLENT!
GLUSSH
AGAIN?!
KURO-TAN-GO HAS JUST COME OUT OF THE TUBE!
WHOOSH
SUPASHH
WHAT ABOUT TSUBAME-GO AND THE ONES WHO FOLLOWED HIM IN THERE?!

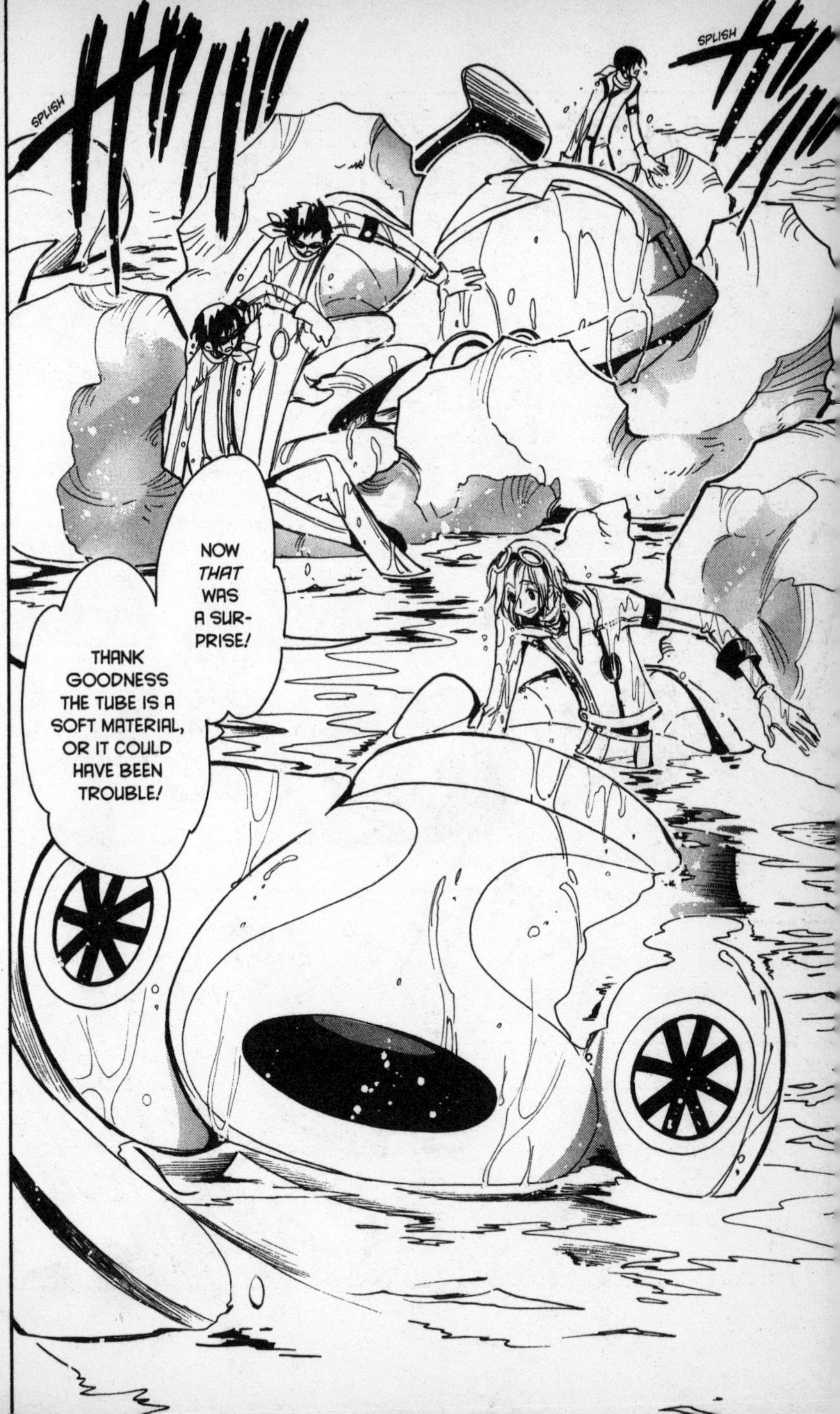
SPLISH
SPLISH
NOW THAT WAS A SUR-PRISE!
THANK GOODNESS THE TUBE IS A SOFT MATERIAL, OR IT COULD HAVE BEEN TROUBLE!

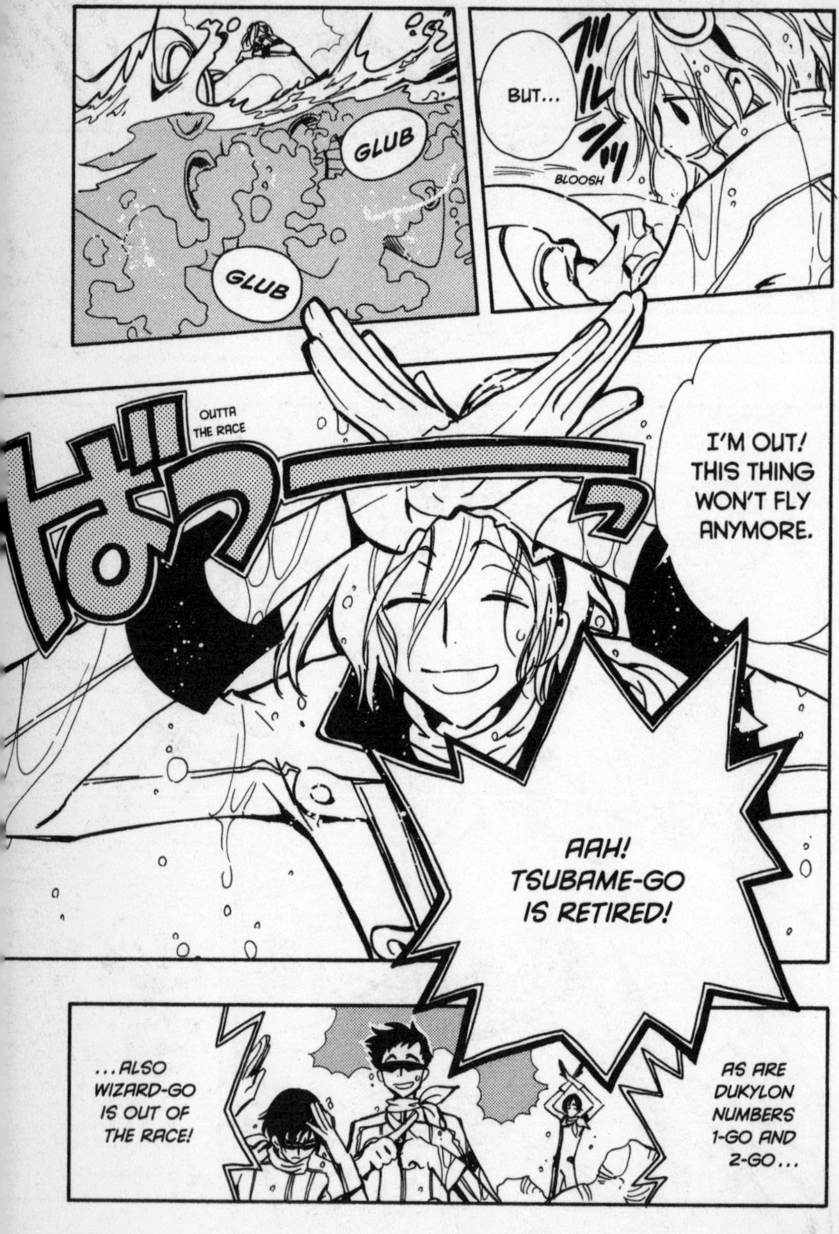
BUT...
BLOOSH
GLUB
GLUB
I'M OUT! THIS THING WON'T FLY ANYMORE.
OUTTA THE RACE
AAH! TSUBAME-GO IS RETIRED!
AS ARE DUKYLON NUMBERS 1-GO AND 2-GO...
...ALSO WIZARD-GO IS OUT OF THE RACE!

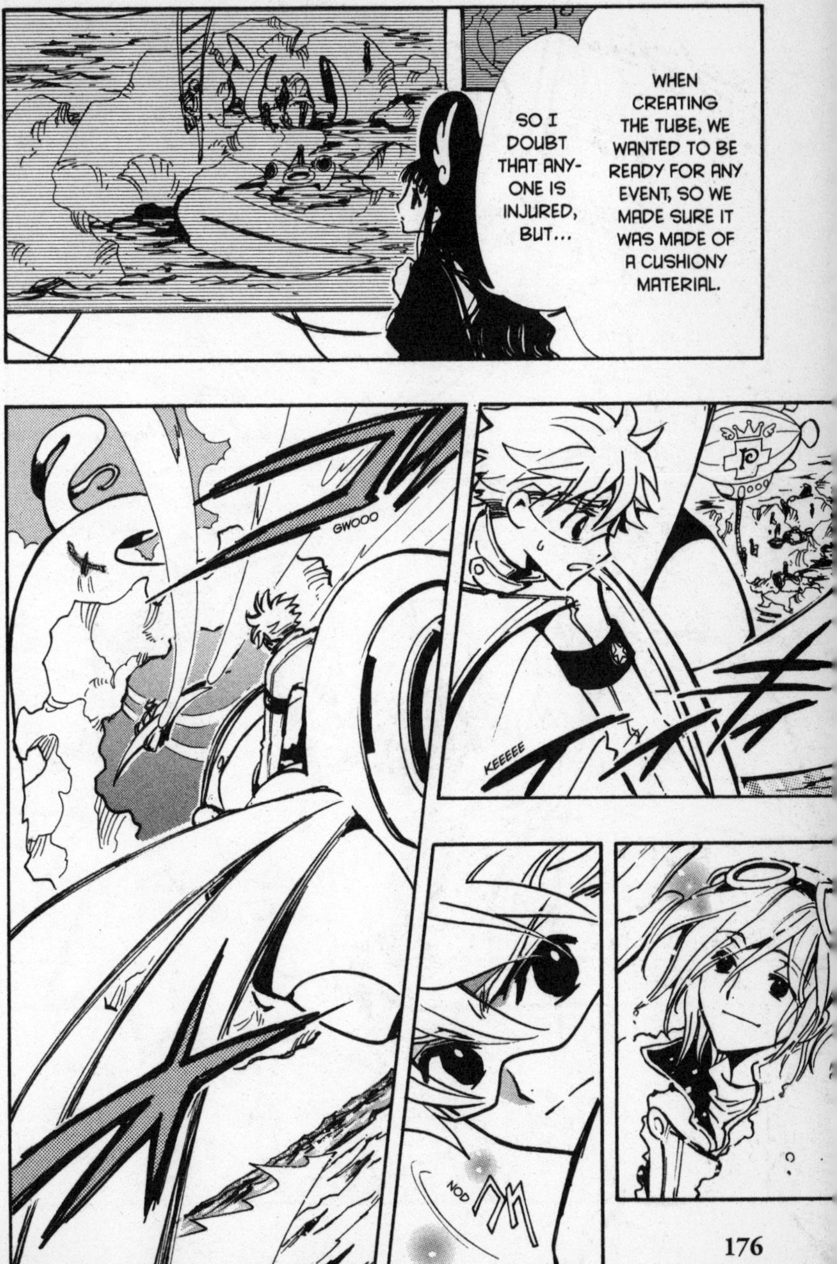
WHEN CREATING THE TUBE, WE WANTED TO BE READY FOR ANY EVENT, SO WE MADE SURE IT WAS MADE OF A CUSHIONY MATERIAL.
SO I DOUBT THAT ANY-ONE IS INJURED, BUT...
KEEEEE
NOD
GWOOO

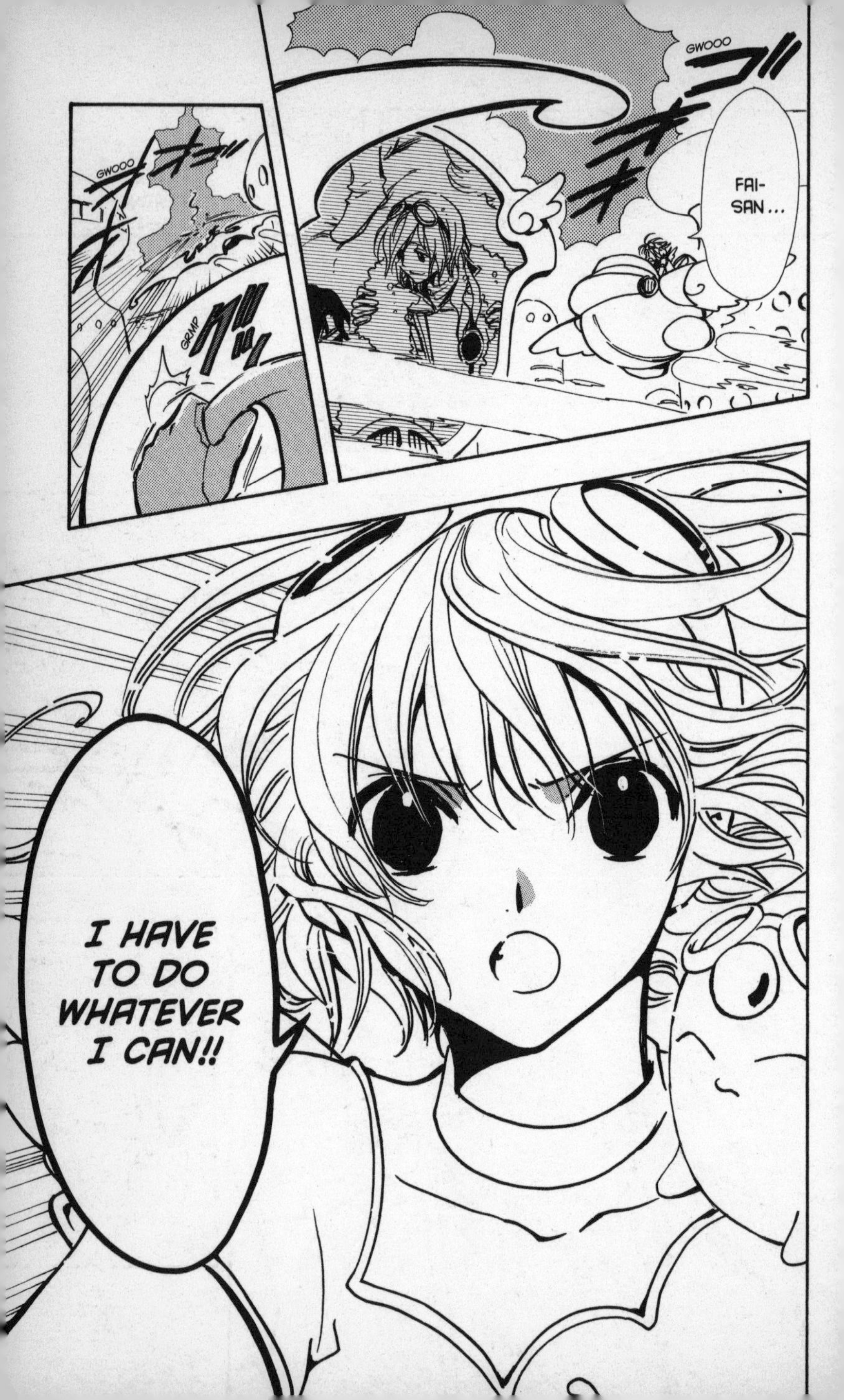
GWOOO
FAI-SAN...
GWOOO
GRMP
I HAVE TO DO WHATEVER I CAN!!

To Be Continued

About the Creators

CLAMP is a group of four women who have become the most popular manga artists in America—Ageha Ohkawa, Mokona, Satsuki Igarashi, and Tsubaki Nekoi. They started out as *doujinshi* (fan comics) creators, but their skill and craft brought them to the attention of publishers very quickly. Their first work from a major publisher was *RG Veda*, but their first mass success was with *Magic Knight Rayearth*. From there, they went on to write many series, including *Cardcaptor Sakura* and *Chobits*, two of the most popular manga in the United States. Like many Japanese manga artists, they prefer to avoid the spotlight, and little is known about them personally.

CLAMP is currently publishing three series in Japan: *Tsubasa* and *xxxHOLiC* with Kodansha and *Gohou Drug* with Kadokawa.

Translation Notes

Japanese is a tricky language for most Westerners, and translation is often more art than science. For your edification and reading pleasure, here are notes on some of the places where we could have gone in a different direction in our translation of the work, or where a Japanese cultural reference is used.

Piffle World

If you're a CLAMP fan, you've probably seen Piffle Princess products scattered throughout the various recent books by CLAMP, the most recent being the White Day gift that Kimihiro Watanuki gives to the Zashiki-Warashi in volume 5 of *xxxHolic*. But the heart and soul of Piffle Princess can be found in the CLAMP tournament manga, *Angelic Layer*. Piffle World looks like it's the ultimate stage in the evolution of the Piffle Princess store and line of products.

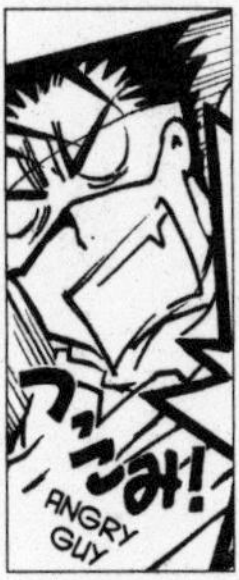
ANGRY GUY

Angry Guy, page 9

The popular type of Japanese comedy team called *manzai* is made up of two types of people, the *boke*, the dumb guy, and the *tsukkomi*, the angry guy. As in the comedy of Laurel and Hardy and the Smothers Brothers, the *boke* makes a dumb remark and in response the *tsukkomi* usually slaps the *boke* over the head and complains about him. In this case, Kurogane is acting like the *tsukkomi*.

Kampai!, page 30

Alternatively spelled *kanpai*, this toast literally means "empty glass," but for all intents and purposes, its English equivalent is "Cheers!"

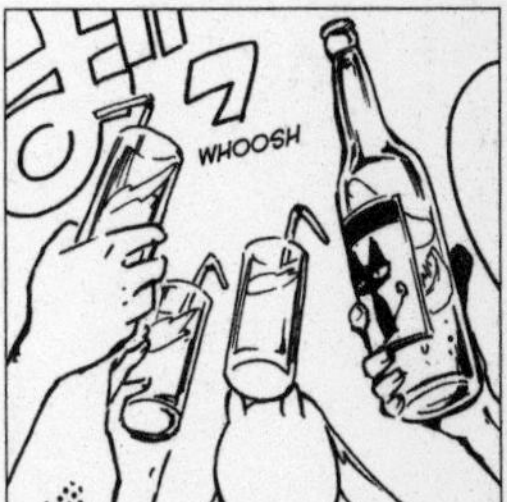
WHOOSH

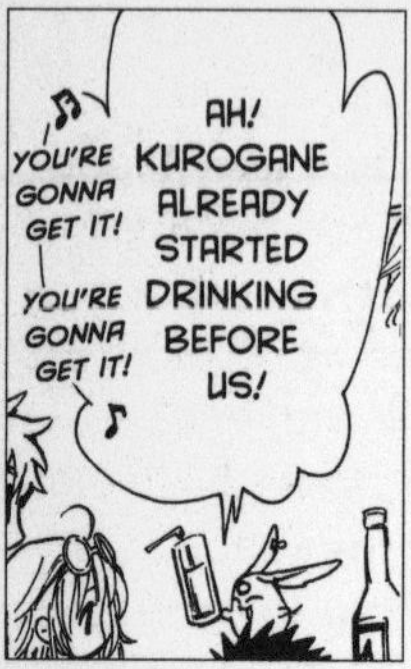
AH! KUROGANE ALREADY STARTED DRINKING BEFORE US!
YOU'RE GONNA GET IT! YOU'RE GONNA GET IT!

You're gonna get it!, page 30

Some Americans might remember hearing a little singsong chant in elementary school when someone happened to go a bit beyond the school rules, and the other children sang out, "You're gonna get it!" The Japanese version, *"Ikenai-nda, ikenai-nda!,"* means exactly the same thing.

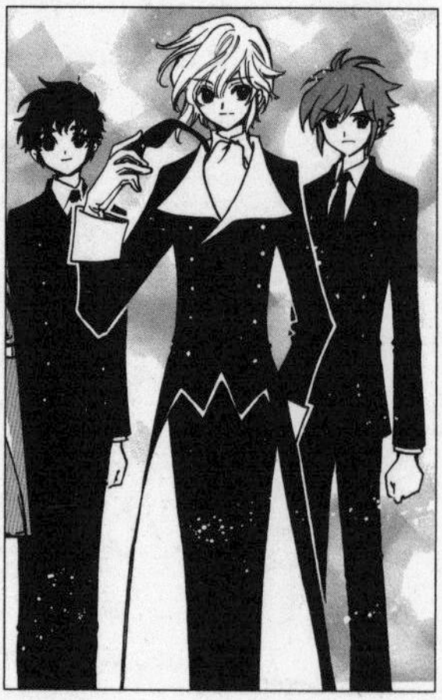

Nokoru, Suô, and Akira, page 60

Although they've appeared in *Tsubasa* before, this is the first time our heroes have met an incarnation of the CLAMP School Detectives. For a bit more information, check the entry for Amen'osa in the translation notes section of *Tsubasa*, volume 4.

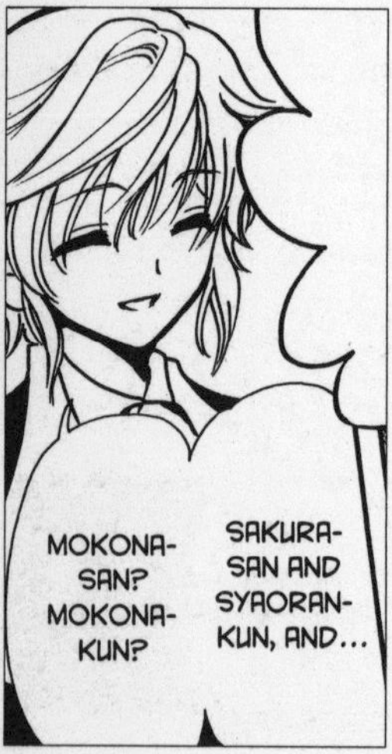
SAKURA-SAN AND SYAORAN-KUN, AND...
MOKONA-SAN? MOKONA-KUN?

***San? Kun?*, page 67**

As you probably already guessed, Nokoru is trying to determine Mokona's gender so that he can add the proper honorific to Mokona's name. (In this case, the polite stranger would address a younger male with *kun* and a younger female with *san.*) But Mokona's ambiguous answer leaves us still guessing whether Mokona has a gender at all.

Grew Up Together, page 68

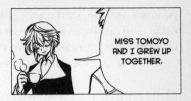

MISS TOMOYO AND I GREW UP TOGETHER.

There is a special relationship between people who have known each other since childhood, especially in Japanese fiction. *Osananajimi*, childhood friends, are considered to have the right to be perfectly frank with one another, and many of the more traditional romance stories have the childhood friends marrying at the end, or at least feature the *osananajimi* as a serious love-interest rival.

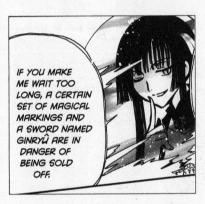

IF YOU MAKE ME WAIT TOO LONG, A CERTAIN SET OF MAGICAL MARKINGS AND A SWORD NAMED GINRYÛ ARE IN DANGER OF BEING SOLD OFF.

Magical Markings and Ginryû, page 91

To learn more about these items and how they came into the possession of the Time-Space Witch, check out pages 97–100 in *Tsubasa*, volume 1.

Politeness, page 112

There are different levels of politeness in the Japanese language that are marked by distinct vocabulary words. For example, doesn't it seem like, in the English version, Kurogane isn't polite, Mokona doesn't bother with being polite but treats everyone as a close friend, Fai is a little polite, and Syaoran and Sakura are very polite? As a translator, I've tried to bring what I know of English-language politeness to my translation of the levels found in the

ALL THE POLITENESS!
EH?

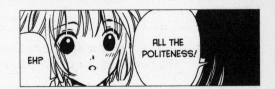

Japanese version. By the way, polite language in Japanese is called *keigo*, and *keigo* can range from the language you use with a person you were just introduced to all the way up to the special words you might use when speaking with the Emperor.

The Country of Yama, page 135

When Sakura, Syaoran, and Mokona were in the Country of Shura with Ashura-ô, Fai and Kurogane were in the Country of Yama with the feather-generated image of Yasha-ô.

Tsubame-go, page 137

Tsubame is the Japanese word for "swallow" (the bird).

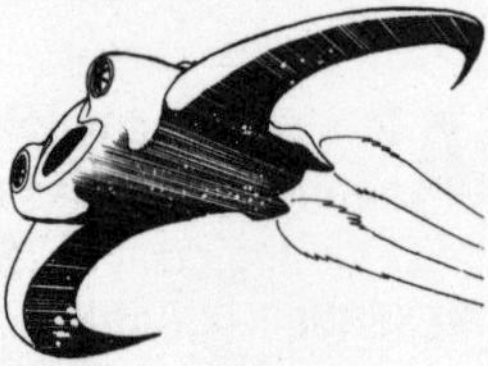

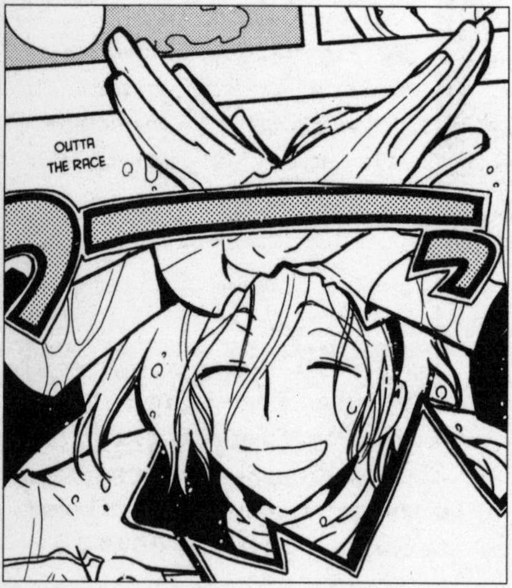
OUTTA THE RACE

Outta the Race, page 175

In Japan, success is marked by an O shape (*maru*), or an X shape (*batsu*) for failure. These can be communicated to people far away by making a large circle over one's head with the fingertips touching for *maru*, or crossing one's forearms to make the *batsu* like Fai does here.

***Tsubasa* Volume 12 will be available in English February 27, 2007. Don't miss it!**

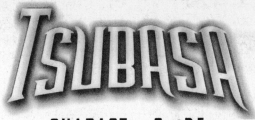

TSUBASA

CHARACTer GuiDE

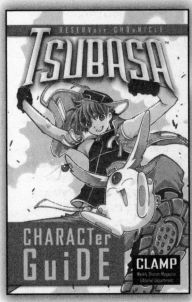

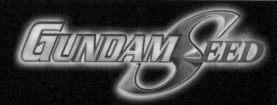

GUNDAM SEED

ART BY MASATSUGU IWASE
ORIGINAL STORY BY HAJIME YATATE
AND YOSHIYUKI TOMINO

In the world of the Cosmic Era, a war is under way between the genetically enhanced humans known as Coordinators and those who remain unmodified, called Naturals. The Natural-dominated Earth Alliance, struggling to catch up with the Coordinators' superior technology, has secretly developed its own Gundam mobile suits at a neutral space colony. But through a twist of fate, a young Coordinator named Kira Yamato becomes the pilot of the Alliance's prototype Strike Gundam, and finds himself forced to fight his own people in order to protect his friends. Featuring all the best elements of the legendary Gundam saga, this thrilling series reimagines the gripping story of men, women, and magnificent fighting machines in epic conflict.

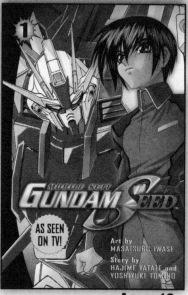

AS SEEN ON TV!

Art by MASATSUGU IWASE
Story by HAJIME YATATE and YOSHIYUKI TOMINO

Ages: 13 +

Special extras in each volume! Read them all!

VISIT WWW.DELREYMANGA.COM TO:
- View release date calendars for upcoming volumes
- Sign up for Del Rey's free manga e-newsletter
- Find out the latest about new Del Rey Manga series

TOMARE!

[STOP!]

You're going the wrong way!

Manga is a completely
different type of reading
experience.

To start at the *beginning*,
go to the *end*!

That's right! Authentic manga is read the traditional Japanese way—from right to left. Exactly the *opposite* of how American books are read. It's easy to follow: Just go to the other end of the book, and read each page—and each panel—from right side to left side, starting at the top right. Now you're experiencing manga as it was meant to be.